A Quality Education for Every Child: Stories from the Lawyers on the Front Lines

A publication of the
Institute for Educational Equity and Opportunity

Edited by
David Long, Esq.
Molly A. Hunter, Esq., Education Justice,
The Education Law Center of New Jersey
Cheryl Hardy, Esq., Assistant Executive Director,
Institute for Educational Equity and Opportunity
Sheilah D. Vance, Esq., Executive Director,
Institute for Educational Equity and Opportunity

Institute for Educational Equity and Opportunity, Washington, DC
2009

A Quality Education for Every Child:
Stories from the Lawyers on the Front Line

Published by
The Institute for Educational Equity and Opportunity
Washington, DC

Library of Congress Control Number [tk]

ISBN: 978-0-615-28729-4

Jacket and interior design by Stephanie Patience

Published in the United States by The Institute for Educational Equity and Opportunity

This book was printed in the United States.

To order additional copies of this book, contact:
The Institute for Educational Equity and Opportunity
1200 G Street, NW, Suite 800
Washington, DC 20005
202-434-8792 (p) 202-434-8707 (f)
info@ifeeo.org

A Quality Education for Every Child: Stories from the Lawyers on the Front Lines

IFEEO

A publication of the
Institute for Educational Equity and Opportunity

Also from
The Institute for Educational Equity and Opportunity

**Education in the 50 States:
A Deskbook of the History of State Constitutions and Laws About Education**

Table of Contents

Acknowledgments vii

Introduction 1

1 School Finance Litigation in Nebraska:
Nebraska Coalition for Educational Equity
and Adequacy v. Heineman
by Elizabeth Eynon-Kokrda and Jill Robb Ackerman 15

2 CFE v. State of New York:
Ensuring A Meaningful High School Education for All Students
by Michael A. Rebell and Joseph P Wayland 33

3 Pennsylvania School Finance Litigation I:
Marrero v. Commonwealth of Pennsylvania
by Michael Churchill 69

4 It's Not Just Philadelphia:
Pennsylvania Association of Rural Schools (PARSS) v.
Thomas J. Ridge
by Thomas B. Schmidtt, III 93

5 Texas School Finance Litigation:
Great Progress and Some Regression
by Albert Kauffman 109

6 The Leandro Case: Leandro v State of North Carolina
by Robert W. Spearman 157

7 Quest for Educational Equity in Massachusetts:
The Case of Hancock v. Driscoll
by Michael Weisman and Rachel Lipton **187**

8 Making the Case for Rural Schools:
Lessons Learned from Finance Litigation in Five States: West Virginia, Arkansas, Tennessee, Alabama, and South Carolina
by Amanda Adler **213**

9 Education in Alaska, The Last Frontier:
An Analysis of Moore v. State
by R. Collin Middleton, Robert J. Sato and Howard Trickey **271**

10 Montoy v. Kansas:
The Fight for Educational Equity and Adequacy for All Kansas Kids in the Home of Brown v. Board of Education
by Alan L. Rupe and W. John Robb **291**

11 Pennsylvania School Finance Litigation II:
Powell v. Ridge
by Michael Churchill **307**

12 New York Civil Liberties Union v. New York:
Reflections on Promises Unfullfilled
by Arthur N. Eisenberg **335**

13 Beyond Educational Adequacy:
Looking Backward and Forward Through the Lens of New Jersey
by Paul L. Tractenberg **357**

14 Mississippi Education Stuck at the Bottom:
A Good Case For A New Frontier In Adequacy Funding Litigation?
by John C. Brittain, Michelle L. Woolley and Michele Keegan **411**

Acknowledgements

The Institute for Educational Equity and Opportunity (IFEEO) would like to thank David Long, Esq., and Molly A. Hunter, Esq., Director, Education Justice, The Education Law Center of New Jersey, for their work as principal editors of "A Quality Education for Every Child: Stories from the Lawyers on the Front Lines."

We also would like to thank Sheilah D. Vance, Esq., IFEEO Executive Director; and Cheryl Hardy, Esq., IFEEO Assistant Executive Director, for their further work in editing and overseeing the production of this book.

Our greatest thanks are extended to the following people who wrote the articles that make this book such a thoughtful, helpful and unique publication:
Alan L. Rupe, Esq., John W. Robb, Esq., Amanda Adler, Esq., Elizabeth Eynon-Korda, Esq., Jill Robb Ackerman, Esq., Paul L. Tractenberg, Esq., Arthur N. Eisenberg, Esq., Robert W. Spearman, Esq., John C. Brittain, Esq., former IFEEO Fellow Michelle L. Woolley, Esq., Michele Keegan, Esq., Michael Churchill, Esq., Albert Kauffman, Esq., Michael Weisman, Esq., Rachel Lipton, Esq., Thomas B. Schmidt, III, Esq., R. Collin Middleton, Esq., Robert J. Sato, Esq., Howard Trickey, Esq., Michael A. Rebell, Esq., and Joseph P. Wayland, Esq.

Introduction

by Michael A. Rebell

In recent years, as the federal courts have decisively retreated from active enforcement of school desegregation[1] and have declared that education is not a "fundamental interest" under the federal constitution,[2] the state courts have become the main judicial forum for advancing concepts of equal educational opportunity. In 1973, the U.S. Supreme Court recognized, but refused to remedy, the severe funding inequities caused by Texas's property-tax-based education finance system.[3] Since then, civil rights advocates have sought relief in the state courts for the funding inequities that have existed in almost every state between schools that serve disadvantaged students and schools that serve their wealthier peers. The response of these courts has been extraordinary. Challenges to the constitutionality of state education finance systems have been brought in 45 of the 50 states, and education finance reform has become the most extensive and dynamic area of state court constitutional involvement in the history of the United States.

Overall, plaintiffs have prevailed in 60 percent of these state court litigations, and, in the more recent subset of "education adequacy" cases decided since 1989, plaintiffs have won 20 of 29 (almost 70%) of the final constitutional decisions.[4] In this area, Justice Brandeis's vision of "a laboratory of the states" developing creative approaches to legal doctrine and social reform[5] has been fulfilled. Indeed, judges and lawyers in New Jersey overwhelmingly voted that state's education adequacy decision "the most important state court decision of the 20th century."[6]

Although many have marveled at plaintiffs' successes in these litigations, few have analyzed how plaintiffs and their attorneys actually managed to achieve this remarkable record during a basically conservative era. This book fills that gap. It documents the litigation history, the doctrinal developments, and the political and educational impact of fiscal equity and educational adequacy litigations in fourteen states, ranging from the urban centers of New York and Pennsylvania to the rural settings of West Virginia and Nebraska.

The attorney-authors of these chapters candidly discuss the extensive background research and consultations with educational experts that is required to develop the educational theories that are presented in these cases,[7] the need to draft flexible complaints that advance plausible alternative legal theories,[8] and the trial strategies that are used to present in convincing fashion the reams of evidence that need to be marshaled.[9] They also reveal some of the interesting tactical maneuvers attorneys use to maximize adversarial advantage, like the Omaha, Nebraska, attorneys' gaining a hometown advantage by suing two state board members who lived their county in order to avoid having to file the case in Lincoln, the state capital, where they thought their claims would be viewed less sympathetically.[10]

All litigation, like all politics, is fundamentally local. Each of these chapters describes the context of the particular case, the emphases and the quirks of the particular state law, and the personalities of the judges, the lawyers, and the policymakers whose decisions influenced the ultimate outcomes. Nevertheless, a number of important cross-cutting strategic themes permeate the volume. The first is the importance of invoking the state's own educational standards in order to develop a strong constitutional definition of an adequate education. In New York, for example,

> ....[P]laintiffs embraced the State's standards. The Regents had recently established higher learning standards, raising the academic bar for all students, and the State's position at trial was that these standards were aspirational. Plaintiffs' position was that, as the public record demonstrated, the Regents' standards had been specifically developed to ensure that students would be prepared for successful civic participation and competitive employments, and, therefore, that these standards were an important barometer of what the minimum acceptable constitutional standards would be.[11]

Such invocation of the state's own standards explains why "the concept of an adequate education emerging from state courts invalidating school finance systems goes well beyond a basic or minimum educational program that was considered the acceptable standard two decades ago."[12] The emphasis on the state's own standards also was used to show the gap between the state's academic expectations and the resources it had committed to achieving those ends, especially for poor and minority students. For example, in New Jersey, the litigation's emphasis on substantive educational content and standards led the court to recognize "that the State might have an obligation 'to spend in excess of the norm in view of the presumed greater needs of [disadvantaged] students.'"[13]

A second theme is the importance of using of cost studies, especially studies that are endorsed by the legislature or state education department, to demonstrate decisively to the court the gap between the resources currently being made available to students in high-needs urban and rural areas and the amounts that are needed to allow students in these schools to meet the state's challenging academic expectations. In Alaska, for example, plaintiffs' experts used three separate methodologies to calculate the cost of an adequate education, and, interestingly, "each of the methods used came out with the same results."[14] In Kansas, plaintiffs' emphasis on a cost study that the state legislature had commissioned but then ignored in its educational funding allocation decisions proved to be a decisive factor in the successful outcome of the case.[15]

The intersection of law and politics throughout the progression of these case studies constitutes a third major cross-cutting theme. These attorney-authors are realists: they acknowledge that at times the positions of their clients will shift because of changing political tides.[16] And they certainly know that the political background of the judges is a factor with which they must reckon: the replacement of six of the seven justices who had issued the original education adequacy decision in Massachusetts with Republican appointees by the time of the follow up compliance ruling a decade later was a reality that the plaintiff attorneys recognized and tried to counter by seeking "to garner bipartisan support . . . outside the courthouse."[17]

Although the composition of the court is a matter that attorneys always consider, the cases also demonstrate that the judges' political background does not invariably predetermine the outcomes in these cases. The strong evidence that plaintiffs have been able to present in these cases has repeatedly overcome the skepticism of conservative jurists. Speaking of both the trial judge and the author of the supreme court's major decision in North Carolina, the dean of the University of North Carolina Law School wrote:

> What I find surprising — and hugely encouraging — about these rulings is that they came from Manning and Orr. These are hardly wide-eyed social engineers or Warren Court enthusiasts. They don't believe in government by judiciary.... They aren't...liberals or bleeding hearts. They aren't ideologues or utopians. They aren't even Democrats. They are, instead, old-fashioned craftsmen who followed where the cases led.[18]

In order to deal with the realities of these high visibility public policy litigations, the authors repeatedly remind us of the importance for plaintiffs of building coalitions of urban and rural districts at the outset of the litigation, of trying to include broad groupings of parents, teachers, school boards, and advocacy groups in the plaintiff class, of making effective use of the media, and of consciously promoting public engagement at every stage of the process. The attorneys for the Omaha Public Schools (OPS) described in detail how they dealt with the political environment in which they knew their case would be developed:

> First, OPS decided it could not bring suit alone for both legal and political reasons. Hence there was a need for parents, students, and other interested individuals in OPS with a stake in funding of schools to come forward and be willing to sue. Likewise, there was a need for other similarly situated school districts to join with OPS....Second, OPS recognized that

> ultimately the Legislature would be called on to deal with the issue and that political as well as social policy and legal considerations would be important there. Therefore, OPS helped put together a coalition of school districts, the Nebraska State Education Association, the Nebraska Association of School Boards, and the Nebraska Department of Education to fund a cost study of education in Nebraska.[19]

The Campaign for Fiscal Equity's strategy in New York went even further. CFE developed a multi-year, statewide public engagement campaign that brought the major statewide education organizations into a dialogic coalition and genuinely utilized public input in the formulation of trial strategies and remedial proposals:

CFE's commitment to public engagement meant that ... critical remedial concepts and legal strategies would be decided not just by lawyers and experts, but also by the broad group of stakeholders who would be drawn into the public engagement process — and that these stakeholders would likely then form a strong core of supporters who could help implement the remedies in the Court should ultimately adopt them.[20]

Most studies of judicial involvement in cases of this type concentrate on analyzing the final decisions of the court and their relation to existing legal doctrines. These chapters provide ample doctrinal analysis, but they also go much further. Many of them reveal important details of the judicial and legislative follow through. For example, we learn that in North Carolina, as a result of the *Leandro* litigation, spending increased by over $2 billion from 2004-2009 and

> [t]he litigation has resulted in creation of a new Disadvantaged Students Supplemental Fund for at-

> risk students, full funding of a separate Low Wealth fund to enhance education opportunities in low wealth counties, institution of a Statewide pre-kindergarten education program for at-risk four year olds, significant reductions of class sizes in early grades, and a variety of other reforms and new programs.[21]

In New Jersey and Arkansas, among other states, sufficient data have now been accumulated to demonstrate that the reforms also resulted in marked improvement in student performance.[22] The case studies also candidly discuss outcomes that plaintiffs did not anticipate and do not relish, like the fact that, in Arkansas, the legislative response to the court order included a massive program of consolidation of rural districts that resulted in the elimination of the prime, named plaintiff school district.[23]

Another unique aspect of this volume is the inclusion of a number of case studies of litigations that were unsuccessful from plaintiffs' point of view. The lessons that the attorney-authors drew from these experiences are instructive. For example, Michael Churchill, lead counsel for the plaintiffs in several unsuccessful cases brought by the City of Philadelphia, candidly concluded that "a case brought on behalf of Philadelphia alone rather than on behalf of a wide cross section of districts was inherently weak."[24]

Win or lose, one point on which virtually all of the authors seemed to agree is that initiation of a funding litigation tends to put the issues of fiscal equity and educational adequacy at the top of the political agenda. Although at times it is difficult to pinpoint precise causal relationships, these cases tend to send shock waves through the political system that almost invariably result in increased spending on education, and a focus on issues of equity and efficiency.

Some critics have recently opined that the courts have begun to step back from their support of constitutional rights in this area,[25] but the pattern of plaintiff victories on the basic constitutional liability issues has remained constant over the past decade. There has been no diminution in the willingness of the state supreme courts to issue strong rulings on students' basic constitutional right to an adequate education. What has changed in recent years is that more cases have reached the remedy stage, and more courts are experiencing difficulty in seeing constitutional compliance through to a successful conclusion.

The adequacy movement has matured, and the courts are now grappling with many of the same implementation and compliance issues that have stymied governors and legislatures for years. The remedial problems faced by the judges in these cases call for thoughtful responses and nuanced solutions, rather than the knee-jerk charges of "judicial activism" that many critics lodge against the courts if their intervention does not immediately cure long-standing educational ills. Many people tend to assume that judicial intervention is a panacea for education reform and for resolving inequities that have plagued a state's school systems for decades. If, several years after a court order has been issued, inequities persist in state funding formulas and/or student test scores have not dramatically risen, they lose faith in the courts' powers or join the chorus of critics of "judicial activism."

As Wisconsin law professor Neil Komesar has insightfully pointed out, however, "All societal decision makers are highly imperfect."[26] Governors, state education departments, legislatures, and the U.S. Congress have been unable to solve the nation's educational problems over the past half century, so why should anyone expect judicial interventions magically to achieve prompt, decisive results? The courts have gotten involved in educational issues in most states in recent years precisely because the consequences of inequity are great, and governors and legislatures have promised much and delivered little. Although raising expectations for both educational excellence and equity, the political branches have maintained highly inadequate and inequitable educational funding systems that block progress on both counts. These failings raise significant issues under state constitutions that judges cannot ignore.

The stakes involved in this endeavor are extremely high, both for the individuals involved and for the nation as a whole. Whereas 30 years ago, a high school dropout earned about 64 percent of the amount earned by a diploma recipient, in 2004 he or she would earn only 37 percent of the graduate's amount.[27] Inadequate education also dramatically raises crime rates and health costs, denies the nation substantial tax revenues, and raises serious questions about the civic competence of the next generation to function productively in a complex democratic society.[28] The stark fact is that over the next 50 years, the students from minority groups who are now disproportionately represented among dropouts and low achievers, will constitute a majority of the nation's public school students. If they are not capable citizens and productive workers, the continued vitality of our democratic culture and America's ability to compete effectively in the global marketplace will be seriously jeopardized.[29]

At this stage, all three branches of our state governments must work in concert to solve the nation's pressing educational problems. Courts on their own cannot solve these immense educational problems. But neither can the legislative or executive branches.

The greatest progress toward school desegregation was achieved in the late 1960s when Congress's enactment of Title VI of the 1964 Civil Rights Act,[30] which authorized the termination of funding to school districts that failed to desegregate their schools, was combined with active enforcement efforts by the federal Office for Civil Rights and by assiduous efforts federal courts throughout the South to implement *Brown*. Similarly, fiscal equity and education adequacy reforms have proved most effective in states like Kentucky, Vermont, and Massachusetts where the legislative and executive branches decided early to cooperate with their state courts in developing effective remedies to cure constitutional inequities in school finance.

To achieve excellence and equity in our public school systems requires a concerted effort by all three branches of government to bring their relative functional strengths to bear on ensuring constitutional compliance and solving the nation's educational ills. Legislatures should make basic educational policy decisions; state education departments and local school district should determine how best to implement educational reforms. What courts can add to the mix is a principled insistence on providing students meaningful educational opportunities, mandates to motivate the political branches to develop appropriate policies and workable implementation mechanisms for achieving this end, and the "staying power" to monitor the enterprise over time to ensure that the legislative and executive branches actually do their jobs. The educational chaos that has accompanied the imposition of substantial budget cuts in many states during the current recession also points to a need for the courts to apply constitutional mandates for educational adequacy not only to the amounts, but also to the stability of educational funding.

Although basic policy making and its implementation are the responsibility of the legislative and executive branches, the courts must ensure that these policies meet constitutional requirements and that they are coherent, adequately funded, and consistently implemented; moreover, the court should maintain jurisdiction and a nonintrusive presence over a reasonable, extended period of time to be sure that the reforms are adequately implemented and that lasting results are achieved.[31]

In many states whose highest courts have held that large numbers of students are being denied their constitutional right to a sound basic education, the courts have terminated their jurisdiction before they had ensured that appropriate remedies were in place and that lasting constitutional compliance had been achieved. Since for practical purposes, remedies control the value of constitutional rights, millions of students in these states continue to be denied the meaningful educational opportunities to which they are entitled. Judges must, of course, be sensitive to separation of powers precepts, but the fact is that if the courts are not committed to completing the job of establishing and sustaining meaningful educational opportunities in education adequacy cases, the other branches are not likely to do so their own.

The state courts have achieved astounding success in putting a spotlight on the huge funding inequities and inadequacies that have plagued this country's public school systems for decades. The chapters in this book chronicle the energy and the ingenuity that plaintiff attorneys throughout the nation have contributed to this effort. The challenge for the courts at this stage is to complete the task they have begun by ensuring that successful remedies that ensure long-lasting constitutional compliance are developed and that they remain in place.

Some of the essays in this book hint at the directions that courts need to take to do so, such as defining constitutional concepts of "efficiency"[32] and holding states responsible for providing "assistance and direction to those schools that are identified as failing to meet the State's constitutional obligation."[33] One hopes that the attorney-authors who wrote these chapters and their colleagues throughout the country will persevere in developing and advocating for remedial theories and mechanisms that can help the state courts finish the critical task of ensuring equal educational opportunity to all of our children. Perhaps a decade from now, IFEEO will be able to issue another volume that can chronicle these further efforts and their accomplishments.

---

1 This retrenchment began with the Supreme Court's ruling in 1974 that extensive patterns of urban segregation could not be remedied by metropolitan area solutions without a finding of intentional segregation by the suburban school districts, Milliken v. Bradley, 418 U.S. 717 (1974). It culminated recently in the Court's invalidation of voluntary desegregation plans adopted by the Seattle and Louisville school districts in Parents Involved in Community Schools v. Seattle School District, 127 S.Ct. 2738 (2007).

2 San Antonio Independent School District v. Rodriguez, 411 U.S. 1 (1973).

3 Ibid.

4 "Equity" cases challenge disparities in the level of educational funding among school districts whereas "adequacy" claims seek opportunities for a basic level of education as guaranteed by specific provisions in state constitutions. For a detailed analysis of these distinctions and a discussion of the history of the state court challenges to state education finance systems, see MICHAEL A. REBELL, COURTS AND KIDS: PURSUING EDUCATIONAL EQUITY THROUGH THE STATE COURTS, (University of Chicago Press, forthcoming, 2009). For up-to-date information on the state court litigations, see National ACCESS Network, http://www.schoolfunding.info.

5 New State Ice Co. v. Liebmann, 285 U.S. 262, 311 (1932).

6 Tractenberg, p. 1. Similar opinions have been expressed in other states. See, e.g. Spearman, p. 2 (The Leandro case in North Carolina has been described as " the most important in modern state history."); Kansas, p. 1 (Supreme Court Chief Justice calls the Montoy case " the most significant case to come before the Court in my [30 year] tenure.")

7 See, e.g.Eisenberg, pp.__; Brittain, et al.

8 See, e.g. Spearman, p. ___

9 See, e.g. Rebell and Wayland p. ___

10 Nebraska, p.___

11 Rebell and Wayland, p. ___

12 Deborah A. Verstegen, Judicial Analysis During the New Wave of School Finance Litigation: The New Adequacy in Education, 24 J. EDUC. FIN. 51, 67 (1998). See also, William H. Clune, The Shift From Equity to Adequacy in School Finance, 8 EDUC. POL'Y 376 (1994) (describing the thrust of the cases as calling for "a high minimum level").

13 Tractenberg, p. ___.

14 Alaska, p. ___.

15 Kansas, p. ___.

16 Powell, p. ___.

17 Weissman, p. ___.

18 Spearman, pp. ___.

19 Nebraska, pp. ___.

20 Rebell and Wayland, p. ___.

21 Spearman, p. ___.

22 Tractenberg, p. ___; Rural, p. ___.

23 Rural study, p. ___.

24 Marrero p. ___.

25 See, e.g. Alfred A. Lindseth, "A Reversal of Fortunes: Why the Courts Have Cooled to Adequacy Lawsuits," EDUCATION WEEK, September 12, 2007.

26 Neil K. Komesar, A Job for the Judges: The Judiciary and the Constitution in a Massive and Complex Society, 86 MICH. L. REV. 657, 698 (1988).

27 Cecilia Elena Rouse, Consequences for the Labor Market, in THE PRICE WE PAY; ECONOMIC AND SOCIAL CONSEQUENCES OF INADEQUATE EDUCATION 99, (Clive R. Belfield and Henry M. Levin ed., 2007).

28 See, generally, THE PRICE WE PAY, supra.

29 See, e.g., Thomas R. Bailey, Implications of Educational Inequality in a Global Workforce, in THE PRICE WE PAY, supra n.24 at 74 (arguing that due to globalization, emerging nations are now competitive with more developed nations); THOMAS L. FRIEDMAN, THE WORLD IS FLAT: A BRIEF HISTORY OF THE TWENTY-FIRST CENTURY (2005) (discussing relationship between education and productivity).

30 42 U.S.C.A § 2000d (2000).

31 In COURTS AND KIDS, supra, n. 3, I propose a detailed "successful remedies" model that defines in detail how such a functional division of labor among the branches could work.

32 Trachtenberg, pp. ___.

33 Alaska, pp. ___.

1 School Finance Litigation in Nebraska *Nebraska Coalition for Educational Equity and Adequacy v. Heineman*

By Elizabeth Eynon-Kokrda and Jill Robb Ackerman

Introduction

On June 30, 2003, three Nebraska school districts, joined soon thereafter by a fourth school district, and several individual plaintiffs filed litigation in state district court in Omaha challenging Nebraska's school funding system. The plaintiffs challenged the funding system under state constitutional provisions requiring: free education in a system of common schools for children between the ages of five and 21; equal protection of the laws; and, due process of law.

The four plaintiff school districts, Omaha Public Schools (OPS), Grand Island Public Schools, Lexington Public Schools, and South Sioux City Community Schools, formed the Nebraska Schools Trust (NST) in order to prosecute the suit and gain public support for the effort. Each of these school districts has high concentrations of racial and ethnic minority students and students eligible for free or reduced price lunches. Individual plaintiffs included the school superintendents of the four plaintiff school districts, several school board members from the districts, interested citizens, and parents and students in two of the four school districts.

The plaintiffs asserted the following basic claims in the original complaint: Nebraska's school funding system does not provide funding from either or both state and local resources to enable the school districts to educate students to the standards set by Nebraska's constitution and laws; the funding system does not provide equal educational opportunities to racial and ethnic minority students, limited English proficiency (LEP) students, disabled students, or students from economically disadvantaged homes; and the funding system is so irrational as to violate the requirements of substantive due process.

In July 2003, the complaint was amended to assert that the school funding system also violated a provision in the Nebraska Constitution's Bill of Rights.The Nebraska Constitution's Bill of Rights requires the legislature to pass suitable laws to encourage schools and the means of instruction because knowledge is essential to good government. In August 2004, approximately a year after the NST complaint was filed, several smaller rural school districts filed a companion case in state district court in Lincoln. The rural school districts raised only state education clause issues, but focused on the inadequacy of state funding for districts with high concentrations of poor and minority students.

In May 2004, the district court dismissed the NST's claims of violation of the bill of rights and education provisions on the ground that these claims were non-justiciable. Likewise, in October 2005, the district court in the rural case reached the same conclusion. The district court in the NST case did however rule that the equal protection and substantive due process claims were issues the court could decide.

The district court's ruling that the NST's equal protection and substantive due process claims were justiciable prevented the plaintiffs in the NST case from immediately appealing the adverse ruling on the Bill of Rights and Education clauses. Conversely, since the rural suit plaintiffs did not claim any violations other than those of the Bill of Rights and education clauses, they immediately appealed to the Nebraska Supreme Court. Unfortunately, the Nebraska Supreme Court affirmed the district court in the rural case terming these "adequacy" claims a "Stygian swamp" into which it refused to enter. *Neb. Coal. for Educ. Equity & Adequacy v. Heineman*, 273 Neb. 531, 731 N.W.2d 164, 183 (Neb. 2007). As a result, the rural case came to an end and the NST case continued toward trial set, after extensive discovery, for September 2008 on the claims of violation of equal protection and substantive due process.

Throughout the extensive discovery process, the litigants continued to work with the legislature to seek legislative changes that could resolve the funding situation. In the 2007 legislative session, certain changes were made to the funding structure which created a common levy, which was a key positive initiative for plaintiffs; however, at the same time, the legislature took specific negative actions in the funding formula which caused plaintiffs to amend their complaint. The amended complaint included only those claims relating to equal protection and substantive due process. In a motion to dismiss challenge, the Court held that plaintiffs had stated a claim of facial equal protection violations based upon the actual statutory language of the 2007 amendments to the funding structure. This decision came during the 2008 legislative session. The 2008 legislative session then ultimately made significant positive changes to the funding structure, which coupled with the common levy gains, resulted in addressing every aspect of plaintiff's complaint with the exception of special education reimbursement. Due to the significant positive changes in the funding structure, plaintiffs voluntarily dismissed their own case, without prejudice, upon the 2008 legislation being signed into law by the Governor of Nebraska.

Status of Education Finance in Nebraska

Prior to the NST Suit

This school finance litigation started because the Board of Education of OPS found itself without the legal authority to raise enough money to continue its current educational programs, purchase needed new textbooks, and provide its teachers a decent raise. This confronting of school finance reality in Nebraska caused OPS to bring suit, but only after careful study of the funding system and an effort to bring other public school interests into a broad coalition to seek legislative change.

Nebraska's school funding system was and remains a system heavily dependent on the local property tax. State revenue provides approximately 35% of the total cost (general fund operations and capital expenditures) of public K-12 education. Consequently, Nebraska ranks at the bottom or very near the bottom of all the states in levels of state funding of K-12 education. [1]

Prior to the 2008 legislative changes, Nebraska's school funding system did not sufficiently recognize or account for the changed circumstances of school districts and education. Nebraska's school funding system had been based on the expenditures school districts made when the system was originally set up in 1990 and revised in 1997. Moreover, up until 2008, the school funding system recognized both growth in the number of LEP students and students in poverty differently than growth in the general student population.

Finally, the funding system placed both spending lids and levy lids on school districts. These spending and levy lids resulted in many cases in authority to spend money the district could not legally levy and/or authority to levy tax money it could not legally spend. These limitations prevented school districts from spending local resources to make up for the inadequate level of state support for public K-12 education and prevented school districts from providing equal educational opportunity to racial and ethnic minority students, LEP students, disabled students, and students in poverty.

Changes to School Funding System Since Filing of NST Suit

The Nebraska Legislature made some changes to the school funding system during the course of the NST suit. In order to understand those changes, some background is necessary. OPS is located partially within and partially without the boundaries of the city of Omaha. Currently, there are four other school districts wholly or partially within the city's boundaries. These other districts have student enrollments that are predominantly white and middle or upper middle income and property tax bases that are generally significantly larger per pupil than in OPS.

The stated legislative policy for Nebraska has been that for cities of 1,000 people or more, the boundaries of the city school district grow with the boundaries of the city. For reasons too complicated to adequately explain here, that policy with respect to Omaha had not been followed since the mid 1950's. OPS became concerned about its growing inability to provide socio-economically integrated education to its students due to decreasing enrollment of middle and upper middle income students and having a property tax base to support the education of increasing numbers of racial and ethnic minority students, students in poverty, LEP students, and disabled students. Therefore, in June 2005, the OPS Board decided to enforce the statutes requiring school district boundaries to enlarge with the city boundaries. This decision resulted in significant public outcry in the suburban school districts affected and in efforts in the legislature to repeal the laws OPS sought to enforce.

The initial end result in the legislature was a bill that divided OPS into three separate racially identifiable school districts, formed a learning community of all the school districts in the two county area that make up the Nebraska portion of the Omaha metro area, and changed school finance provisions to make it more difficult for districts with high concentrations of LEP students and students in poverty to obtain state aid.[2]

The passage of this bill and its signing by the governor resulted in both federal and state court litigation apart from the NST funding suit. The state district court was presented with the issue of whether the then-new law, LB 1024, should be enforced or stayed while a law suit proceeded before it. The state district court ruled that LB 1024 should be stayed.

During this period, Omaha metro area school district leaders and other community leaders started talking in earnest about how to organize schools in the metro area and were able to reach a joint recommendation to the 2007 Nebraska Legislature. As a result, the 2007 legislature passed a bill, LB 641, that put OPS back together, kept school district boundaries where they were before June of 2005, and formed a learning community with a common tax base and impetus to focus on closing the achievement gap between white students and racial and ethnic minority students and between students in poverty and middle and upper middle income students.

Unfortunately, LB 641 retained and even exacerbated the discriminatory school finance features of LB 1024. The most significant such features were the transformation of weightings for

LEP students and students in poverty in the state aid formula into maximum caps for state aid for helping LEP students and students in poverty; the reduction of the poverty cap to 61% of the dollars produced by the former weighting; a separate allowance for lower class size in grades K-8 that either induced educationally unsound concentrations in classrooms of students in poverty or was impossible to take advantage of due to lack of space or qualified teachers; a requirement that school districts must fund at least 17.65% of the cost of programs and services for LEP students and students in poverty from local dollars, with no commensurate requirement for districts without such student populations; and the imposition of draconian financial penalties on school districts for failure to spend on LEP students and students in poverty the dollars school districts reported they would spend in order to obtain state aid, again, without any such commensurate requirements for spending on non-poverty, non-LEP students. Although LB 641 did make strides toward equity in the Omaha area by creating a common property tax levy for schools in the two county area surrounding Omaha, but was flawed in that the legislation, because of the spending lid, made no provision to access potential additional revenue.

Strategic Litigation Decisions

Prior to filing suit several strategic decisions were made.

First, OPS decided it could not bring suit alone for both legal and political reasons. Hence there was a need for parents, students, and other interested individuals in OPS with a stake in funding of schools to come forward and be willing to sue. Likewise, there was a need for other similarly situated school districts to join with OPS. The potential suit concerned issues of principle applicable to multiple other school districts in Nebraska, and it was important to present a united front of such school districts. This legal and quasi political concern led to another strategic consideration.

Second, OPS recognized that ultimately the legislature would be called on to deal with the issue and that political as well as social policy and legal considerations would be important there. Therefore, OPS helped put together a coalition of school districts, the Nebraska State Education Association, the Nebraska Association of School Boards, and the Nebraska Department of Education to fund a cost study of education in Nebraska. That cost study then formed the basis for efforts to obtain relief from the legislature prior to filing suit.

Third, OPS recognized that it was important to give the legislature and the governor the opportunity to appropriately change the school funding system prior to seeking relief in the courts. OPS recognized that lawsuits cause animosity and that this lawsuit would be both controversial and expensive. Taking the matter first to the legislature made good sense both in terms of respecting the legislature's role in governance of schools and in terms of expenditure of public money. OPS also recognized that since the most a court in Nebraska could do was declare the current school funding system unconstitutional, the legislature was the entity responsible for crafting a constitutional funding system in the final analysis anyway. Thus, giving the legislature the opportunity to do the right thing first made good sense for multiple reasons.

Fourth, when the legislature failed for three consecutive years to enact any pertinent school funding reforms, OPS recognized that a coalition of school district plaintiffs was necessary. OPS then formed a trust with three other school districts that also have high concentrations of LEP students and students in poverty to prosecute the suit.

Fifth, OPS and its attorneys recognized that expert witnesses are critical to the success of any school funding suit. As a result, OPS attorneys sought advance assistance from experts in all types of school finance studies. Additionally, OPS sought experts on teacher quality, experts on the history of Nebraska's constitution, experts on reading levels needed to participate in our democracy, experts on student assessment, experts on the causes and cures for school dropouts, experts on programs that work in helping to close the achievement gap, experts on early childhood education, experts on education of LEP students, experts on the education of students in poverty, and experts on school funding formulas. These contacts helped OPS attorneys develop the claims made in the NST complaint and provided a group of potential expert witnesses for OPS. Securing these contacts also helped to assure that the best minds in school finance were working for providing equal educational opportunity rather than against it.

Sixth, decisions had to be made about where and whom to sue. Strategically, OPS felt it would be better to have the case filed in Omaha. This decision could raise venue concerns since Lincoln is Nebraska's capitol city. One way to obviate that concern was to sue defendants who resided in Douglas County, the county in which Omaha is located. Two state board of education members, clearly legitimate defendants in any event, resided in Douglas County. Hence, the decision was made to include them as defendants. A strategic decision was also made to sue only officials who in one way or another were charged by statute with carrying out the school funding laws.

Seventh, decisions had to be made about what claims to bring. Clearly, adequacy lawsuits were having much success at the time these strategic decisions were being made. It was also clear that the level of state support for public K-12 education in Nebraska was abysmally low compared to other states. Therefore, the general adequacy of the level of funding for schools in Nebraska was a claim that would be made despite the rather bare bones nature of Nebraska's education clause. The central concern in each of the plaintiff school districts, however, was the need for additional resources to focus on efforts to improve the educational achievement of racial and ethnic minority students, LEP students, students in poverty, and special education students.

This concern was enhanced by the requirements for disaggregating test score results for these groups and for these groups each meeting state benchmarks under the federal No Child Left Behind Act, 20 U.S.C. §§ 6301-8923 (2002) (NCLB). Even before NCLB became law, the NST districts recognized that it took substantial additional resources to provide numerous students in each of these groups with an equal educational opportunity. This focus caused the inclusion of equal protection claims and to some extent the inclusion of a substantive due process claim.

Subsequent to the filing of suit several additional strategic decisions weremade.

First, the second largest school district in Nebraska, the Lincoln Public Schools (LPS), sought to intervene on the side of the state defendants. A decision had to be made about how to respond to this proposed intervention. A decision was made to vigorously oppose LPS's motion because of the unnecessary complexity and expense LPS's intervention would bring to the lawsuit. This opposition was successful both in the trial court and on appeal. *Douglas County Sch. Dist. 0001 v. Johanns*, 269 Neb.664, 694 N.W. 2d 668 (Neb 2005).

Second, a decision had to be made on whether to continue with efforts for change in the legislature. For the reasons discussed above in strategic decisions prior to litigation, a decision was made to continue to try to seek a resolution in the legislature.

Third, a decision had to be made on how to respond to a motion filed by counsel for the state defendants for Rule 30(b)(6) depositions regarding certain programs and services in each of the school districts. Opposing counsel moved for 30(b)(6) depositions on the programs and services currently in place in the school districts to help struggling students and on what additional programs and services the school districts were asserting they needed to meet these students' needs. A strategic decision was made to prepare a full written explanation of current programs and programs needed rather than simply responding to deposition questions. This choice served to clarify the claims of the NST school districts and to help the testifying school officials in their depositions to address the multiple issues raised in the 30(b)(6) depositions.

Fourth, multiple strategic decisions had to be made on discovery issues concerning both paper and electronic documents. One key piece of wisdom learned from this process is that school districts should install an e-mail system that facilitates retrieval of e-mails and attached documents from back-up storage files. Another is to make certain that electronic documents are securely retained for use in litigation. A third is that the cost of discovery in a document-heavy lawsuit, particularly one claiming a violation of equal protection, is very large indeed. In this case, the State produced approximately 2.25 million pages of paper. From the 2.25 million pages, plaintiff attorneys selected 500,000 pages to store electronically. Plaintiff attorneys copied approximately 1 million pages from the plaintiff school districts and the State into an electronic database. Additionally, millions of e-mails were reviewed during this process. Counsel for the defendants spent over a year reviewing documents from the four plaintiff school districts. They copied 353,850 pages from OPS documents and many thousands of pages from each of the other three plaintiff districts. This does not include copies of the e-mails furnished electronically to defense counsel.

Fifth, decisions must be made on whom to call as fact witnesses. In large school districts with multiple central office officials and multiple building principals, this can be a significant effort. Building principals are generally in the best position to articulate what the problems are for struggling students, how serious these problems are, and what can be done to provide racial and ethnic minority students, LEP students, students in poverty, and special education students an equal educational opportunity. However, building principals are usually far removed from the intricacies of school finance. Therefore, central office administrators are necessary to testify on what the links are between the school finance system and the problems and solutions articulated by the building principals and other school personnel.

Sixth, strategic decisions must be made on how to demonstrate the harm happening to students from the current school funding system. In the era of NCLB, there is a tendency to look only at state specified test results and how the respective groups of students do on those tests. Only studying state specified test results can be a mistake, particularly if the state is using statistics to mask true gaps. No one measure can fully show the problem. Among other factors, the NST districts looked at the following:

1. group performance on norm referenced national achievement tests,
2. graduation rates for racial and ethnic minority students,
3. group performance for the state on the National Assessment of Educational Progress (NAEP),
4. percent of group in top half of graduating class from high school,
5. percent of group enrolled in courses needed for college admission and success such as calculus, chemistry, physics,

6. percent of group obtaining a grade of C or higher in these courses,
7. percent of group enrolled in Advanced Placement (AP) courses,
8. percent of group successfully completing AP courses,
9. percent of group taking the ACT or SAT exam,
10. average ACT or SAT score of group and whether that score is sufficient for admission to the state university, and
11. percent of group reading two or more grade levels below current grade at the transition grades from elementary school to middle school and middle school to high school.

Community Engagement

Contemporaneous with the passage of LB 641, the private sector formed a group called Building Bright Futures (BBF). BBF (which is on the web at buildingbrightfutures.net) recognizes that although it is the responsibility of the legislature to close the achievement gaps between middle and upper middle income students and students in poverty and between white students and racial and ethnic minority students, the community should support the legislature's efforts with financial resources. Accordingly, BBF is focusing private sector money and efforts to supplement the legislature's efforts to close achievement gaps. The group has the support of the publisher of Omaha's daily newspaper, the Mayor of Omaha, area school superintendents, and many other community leaders. BBF has made it clear that private dollars can help to close these gaps, but that the public sector must commit additional resources if the gaps are to be significantly improved. The efforts of BBF helped considerably with obtaining public involvement and understanding of the need to make a concerted effort to provide the financial resources needed to realize equal educational opportunity.

Lessons Learned

Since this litigation remained in the pre-trial stage, there are limited litigation lessons learned from this effort. Several insights have already been shared in the process of discussing strategic issues. Additional initial lessons learned are the following:

First, school finance litigation is not for the faint-hearted. This litigation is highly complex and takes significant commitments of time by attorneys and school officials. School finance litigation also takes a willingness on the part of boards of education to commit significant financial resources to the effort.

Second, state defendants are now aware of strategies with significant chances of success in defeating adequacy lawsuits, particularly given the intransigence of state legislatures in the face of court orders striking down school finance systems on this ground.

Third, the real problem in education finance in the United States is not whether we are committing the necessary resources to educate white middle and upper income students. Rather, the issue that must be faced is whether states are committing the necessary resources to provide equal educational opportunities to students from economically disadvantaged homes, to racial and ethnic minority students, to LEP students, and to special education students.

Fourth, one of the key issues for lawyers for plaintiffs in litigation seeking the funds necessary to provide equal educational opportunity is how to distinguish for the court between guaranteeing equal results and guaranteeing equal opportunity to obtain equal results.

Fifth, the problem of equal educational opportunity is a systemic national problem. State policy decisions, however, can exacerbate this problem, a problem that has particularly egregious manifestations in some states and not in others. Nebraska, for instance, is a state with stark achievement gaps. Nebraska has the largest gap in the country on the 2007 NAEP between white students and African-American students in percent of students proficient in eighth grade math and the second worst such gap for fourth grade math.[iii] Nebraska also has the worst gap on the 2007 NAEP in fourth grade reading between white students and African-American students.[iv]

Sixth, anyone undertaking to represent school districts and/or parents and students as plaintiffs in school finance cases must be committed to continuous, comprehensive study of how education practices interact with student achievement results in a broad array of types of achievement. These attorneys must also study how school district budgeting decisions and state school finance structures relate to those education practices and to student achievement broadly construed. It is the responsibility of plaintiffs' lawyers to translate this study into admissible evidence and cogent presentation and argument, which will persuade a court that equal educational opportunity is an issue the court can deal with, must deal with, and must decide in favor of plaintiffs.

Conclusion

The successes reached in this case arose both through the lessons learned during the discovery phase of the legislation, concerted efforts to work with key legislators to explain the root causes of lack of educational equity, and, uniquely, through the unmistakable error made early in the case by legislators who sought a racially-based split of the OPS district. The ensuing uproar over the legislature's response to OPS integration attempts caused significant public attention to be brought to the real underlying issues of educational inequity and spurred the legislation that not only repaired the OPS split and put in place a metro-wide diversity plan, but also then saw the funding inequities in a new light. While the case did not need to get to trial, the five years of work from the commencement of the filing of suit have demonstrated the importance of a national network of attorneys representing plaintiffs in these cases and likewise the significance for this country's future of assuring that all of our children have a genuinely equal opportunity to meet rigorous state educational standards and to graduate from high school with the skills needed to actively participate in the world economy and in our democracy.

Biographies

Elizabeth Eynon-Kokrda, a partner at Baird Holm LLP practices in the Education and Government section, providing general counsel services covering all the daily issues faced by school administrators and their Boards of Education. She brings an investigative/compliance background as former Special Agent for the Federal Bureau of Investigation (FBI). Ms. Eynon-Kokrda regularly presents to administrators, fellow education lawyers and community members, on a local and national basis. She has served as a member of the adjunct faculty at Creighton University and at the University of Nebraska, Omaha, teaching legal writing and education law. Ms. Eynon-Kokrda is listed in *The Best Lawyers in America 2009* for her work in Education Law.

Jill Robb Ackerman is the chairperson of the Litigation Section of Baird Holm LLP. She represents individual and businesses with respect to complex business litigation in federal and state courts concerning corporate disputes, copyright, trademark and unfair competition, computes and technology and products. Ms. Ackerman is listed in *The Best Lawyers in America 2008*, *America's Leading Lawyers for Business*, *Nebraska Super Lawyers*, and *Benchmark, America's Leading Litigation Firms and Attorneys* for her work in intellectual property litigation and business litigation. In addition to being a member of numerous bar and trial associations, Ms. Ackerman served and Chairperson of the Federal Practice Committee, and has served on the Federal Advisory Committee for the Eighth Circuit. She is a Fellow of the Nebraska Bar Foundation and a charter member of the Robert Spire Inn of Court. She has also taught Trial Advocacy at Creighton University School of Law

---

1 U.S. Census Bureau *Public Education Finances 2005*, Table 5, issued April 2007.
2 LB 1024, 2006 Legislature, http://uniweb.legislature.ne.gov/FloorDocs/99/PDF/Final/LB1024.pdf.
3 *The Nation's Report Card Mathematics 2007*, National Center for Education Statistics, U.S. Department of Education, NCES 2007-494, pp 50, 58.
4 *The Nation's Report Card Reading 2007*, National Center for Education Statistics, U.S. Department of Education, NCES 2007-496, p.54.

2 *CFE v. State Of New York*: Ensuring A Meaningful High School Education For All Students

By Michael A. Rebell and Joseph P. Wayland[1]

Introduction

In 1993, the Campaign for Fiscal Equity ("CFE"), filed a constitutional challenge to New York State's school funding system. The complaint in *Campaign for Fiscal Equity, Inc. v. State of New York* claimed that the State's school finance system under-funded New York City public schools and denied its students their constitutional right to the opportunity for a sound basic education. CFE's membership consisted of most of New York City's education advocacy organizations, parent organizations, and about half of the City's community school boards.

New York's highest court, the Court of Appeals, denied the State's motion to dismiss by distinguishing a prior New York State school funding equity case, allowing the case to proceed to trial.[2] The seven-month trial resulted in a strong victory for the plaintiffs. The trial judge defined the students' right to a "sound basic education" as involving the skills students need to be capable citizens and competitive workers in the global economy, determined that the current educational system was not providing the opportunities for all students to obtain such skills, and held that there was a strong causal link between the state education finance system and these deficiencies.[3] At the same time that it was preparing for this extensive trial, CFE mounted a major, statewide public engagement process to solicit public input on many of the issues that were being presented to the court and to build statewide support for an eventual remedy.

Then Governor George E. Pataki appealed the trial court decision. Although the intermediate appeals court upheld his position that the state constitution guarantees that schools provide the opportunity to learn at an 8th-grade skill level and found that the current funding system sufficiently allowed for this,[4] that ruling was promptly reversed by the Court of Appeals in 2003.[5] The high court, in a landmark 4-1 opinion, rejected the 8th-grade standard, finding that a "high school education is now all but indispensable" to prepare students for employment and civic engagement.[6] It held that the Constitution requires the State to provide all students the opportunity for "a meaningful high school education, one which prepares them to function productively as civic participants…[and] to obtain 'competitive employment.'"[7]

After reviewing the range of remedies ordered by courts in other states, the court issued a tri-partite remedial order which required the State to: a) determine the actual cost of providing a sound basic education; b) reform the current system of school funding and managing schools to ensure that all schools have the resources necessary to provide a sound basic education; and c) ensure a system of accountability to measure whether the reforms actually provide the opportunity for a sound basic education.[8] The order gave the State 13 months, until July 30, 2004 to implement this remedy.[9]

The State's failure to meet that deadline triggered a further round of compliance litigation. The trial court, based on a detailed evidentiary hearing conducted by three special referees, concluded that New York City schools needed an additional $5.63 billion in operating aid and $9.2 billion for facilities to provide their students the constitutional right to the opportunity for a sound basic education.[10] The legislature subsequently adopted a plan to provide the full amount of facilities funding but failed to agree on a plan for providing operating aid. On appeal, the Court of Appeals in 2006 determined that the requisite "constitutional floor" for operating aid was approximately $2 billion, although in concurring and dissenting opinions, 3 of the 6 Justices emphasized that the legislature was not limited to the constitutional minimum and indicated that it should give serious consideration to an approximately $5 billion increase.[11] Subsequently, in 2007, the newly-elected governor, Eliot Spitzer, proposed, and the legislature adopted, a plan that would provide approximately $5.2 billion in increased operating aid for New York City's schools, and an additional $4 billion for schools in the rest of the state, to be phased in over four years, together with a "Contract for Excellence" accountability plan.

Education Finance in New York Before *CFE* and the Court Of Appeals' Initial Ruling

A prior litigation, *Levittown v. Nyquist*, filed in 1978 by a group of property-poor Long Island school districts, and joined by New York City and the other four large urban New York districts, had challenged the constitutionality of New York State's education finance system. Although the trial court had held that the substantial inequities in this system rendered it unconstitutional, the Court of Appeals reversed. In its 1982 decision, the court held that while substantial inequities in funding did exist, the New York Constitution does not require equal funding for education.[12]

The *Levittown* Court indicated that the Legislature should take responsibility for ensuring "fair and equitable educational opportunity."[13] The court's ruling may, in fact, have been influenced by the pendency in the legislature at that time of an extensive set of reforms to the State education finance system that had been recommended by a commission appointed in the wake of the trial court ruling in the case. Shortly after the Court of Appeals dismissed the case, however, the reform proposals were put on the back burner and the inequities in the funding system remained unchanged. By some measures they became even worse over the subsequent decade.

CFE's complaint alleged that students in New York City received approximately $400 per student (or 12%) less in State education aid during the 1992-93 school year than the average of their peers in the rest of the state, even though New York City enrolled at the time approximately 70% of the students in the state from backgrounds of concentrated poverty, over 51% of the state's students with severe disabilities and 81% of the state's pupils with Limited English Proficiency.[14]

After citing these basic disparities and inequities, the complaint emphasized the impact of the reduced resources and the extent to which the deficiencies in the State education finance system deprived students in New York City of an adequate or "sound basic" education. Picking up on a measure of inadequacy that had been mentioned by the Court of Appeals in *Levittown*, the complaint grounded its allegations in comparisons of actual resources available in the New York City schools with the standards promulgated by the Regents and the State Education Department. For example: "[A]verage class sizes in New York City are in excess of those which the Regents and the Commissioner consider adequate to assure that all students have an opportunity to meet the minimum standards."[15] Many students in New York City schools did not have access to required courses, while many students taking science courses did not have access to the required laboratory facilities.[16]

Furthermore, CFE argued, New York City students had inadequate access to instructional materials,[17] computers and other technology,[18] and library services,[19] in the amounts demanded by State regulations. On top of all of that, many students were attending schools that were severely overcrowded and that lacked adequate lighting, heat, ventilation, and sanitation.[20] Educational outcomes were also indicative of inadequacy, as New York City students' record on State examinations and other measures was abysmal. For instance, New York City's failure rate on the Regents Competency Test in mathematics was 43%, compared to 17% for the rest of the state.[21] Only 26% of New York City's average enrollment passed the more demanding Regents comprehensive examination in Mathematics I, compared to 59% for the rest of the state.[22]

Although the *CFE* Complaint included a claim that the current inequities in the State education finance system were even worse that those that had existed a decade earlier, the thrust of plaintiffs' argument in opposition to the motion to dismiss was that the Court of Appeals should distinguish its prior "equity" ruling in the *Levittown* case and allow plaintiffs to proceed to trial to demonstrate that New York City's school children were being denied the opportunity for an adequate or "sound basic education" as guaranteed by Article XI, § 1 of the state constitution. The court essentially accepted this distinction. On the day it issued its 1995 ruling upholding plaintiffs' adequacy claims in *CFE v. State* ("*CFE I*"), the court also dismissed *Reform Educational Inequities Today* (*R.E.F.I.T.*) *v. Cuomo*, a new equity case that had been brought by the same coalition of Long Island school districts that brought the original *Levittown* case.[23]

In ruling for the *CFE* plaintiffs, the Court of Appeals had to reconsider its initial approach to defining the constitutional right to a "sound basic education." Although, as noted above, the *Levittown* ruling had implicitly equated the constitutional requirement with the "minimum statewide standards of educational quality and quantity established by the regents and the Department of Education," on closer examination the court now indicated that some of these standards appeared to exceed a constitutional concept of sound basic education. The court, therefore, charged the trial court with the responsibility for determining what the constitutional concept entails. The court provided the trial judge a "template" of its initial thinking in this regard to guide his assessment of the evidence at trial and the building of a record which the high court could then use to evaluate the constitutional concept in detail when the case returned to the Court of Appeals after the trial court's ruling. The Court of Appeals' "template" said that a "sound basic education" should consist of: "….the basic literacy, calculating, and verbal skills necessary to enable children to eventually function productively as civic participants capable of voting and serving on a jury…."[24](*CFE v. State*, 1995, p. 666).

Once the parameters of the definition were established, the trial court would need to determine two other major issues: were children in New York City being denied the opportunity for a sound basic education, and, if so, was there a causal link between this denial and shortcomings in the State education finance system.[25]

Litigation Strategies

In 1993, Robert Jackson, the president of one of New York City's 32 local community school boards, who also was a parent of three New York City public school students, decided that something had to be done to counter recent drastic cutbacks in State aid to education. He asked Michael A. Rebell, an attorney with a practice specializing in education law, to bring a constitutional challenge to the State's education finance system. Rebell replied that Jackson's perception that the State aid formulas were inequitable and unfair to New York City was correct, but, unfortunately, others had beaten him to the courthouse and this issue had been raised but finally rejected by the state's highest court a decade earlier (i.e., *Levittown v. Nyquist*).

Jackson, however, refused to take "no" for an answer. His adamant stance induced Rebell to further research and consider the issue. Doing so, Rebell sensed that a new trend of judicial support for an "adequacy" approach was emerging in a number of recent court decisions in other parts of the country. He told Jackson that in light of the negative *Levittown* precedent, achieving victory in New York would be a real long shot, but given the stakes, it might be worth the effort. The two of them then discussed the possibilities with a number of interested parents, advocates, and community board leaders and formed the Campaign for Fiscal Equity to bring the suit.

Public Engagement

At their first meeting, Rebell asked CFE's board of directors to adopt an explicit public engagement strategy as an integral part of the litigation effort. They enthusiastically did so. This early commitment to public engagement resulted from concerns about the outcome of the remedial stages in many of the early fiscal equity litigations, as well as other education reform class action litigations. Too often, judicial intervention in cases in which plaintiffs had won dramatic legal victories did not result in effective, lasting solutions to deep-rooted education controversies. After considering this issue at length, Rebell became convinced that long-lasting reform could best be achieved by involving the broad range of diverse stakeholders who are affected by education policy reforms in both the development and the implementation of judicial remedies.

CFE's commitment to public engagement meant that principles for reforming the funding problems raised by the lawsuit would be developed early and would guide the legal strategies during the trial and appeals. It also meant that critical remedial concepts and legal strategies would be decided not just by lawyers and experts, but also by the broad group of stakeholders who would be drawn into the public engagement process—and that these stakeholders would likely then form a strong core of supporters who could help implement the remedies if the Court of Appeals ultimately should adopt them.

Defining a "Sound Basic Education"

The Court of Appeals' issuance of a tentative "template" definition of "sound basic education" in its *CFE I* decision provided CFE an extraordinary opportunity for jump-starting the public engagement campaign to which it was now committed. Although the court probably intended that only the lawyers and expert witnesses would respond to their tentative definition and provide input for its ultimate revisions, CFE decided to expand the dialogue to encompass the broad range of education stakeholders. Thus, the initial issue around which the statewide public engagement forums were organized was how to define a "sound basic education." The realization that their views might help determine the outcome of this major constitutional issue intrigued and excited many of the education advocates, parents, teachers, administrators, school board members and other community members that CFE engaged in this public dialogue.[26]

After three years of active statewide public dialogue, a definition of "sound basic education" emerged that had widespread support throughout the state. This was the definition that CFE's attorneys asked the trial court to adopt when the trial began in the fall of 1999. The proposed definition was formally presented by Tom Sobol, the former State Commissioner of Education, who had agreed to be an expert witness for the plaintiffs; three other plaintiff witnesses also endorsed the definition. Dr. Sobol strongly supported public engagement, and he had personally participated in a number of the forums.

The constitutional definition of a "sound basic education" that the trial court articulated in its 2001 decision contained almost all of the recommendations that had emerged from the public engagement process, including a more explicit emphasis on the development of employment skills than had been apparent in the Court of Appeals' template definition: "[A] sound basic education consists of the foundational skills that students need to become productive citizens capable of civic engagement and sustaining competitive employment."[27] The trial court also expanded the template's original list of four essential resources to the following seven-fold concept: [28]

1. Sufficient numbers of qualified teachers, principals and other personnel.
2. Appropriate class sizes.
3. Adequate and accessible school buildings with sufficient space to ensure appropriate class size and implementation of a sound curriculum.
4. Sufficient and up-to-date books, supplies, libraries, educational technology and laboratories.
5. Suitable curricula, including an expanded platform of

programs to help at-risk students by giving them more "time on task."

6. Adequate resources for students with extraordinary needs.
7. A safe orderly environment.

Ultimately, the Court of Appeals upheld the thrust of the trial court's findings regarding the foundational skills and the essential resources that students need for a sound basic education including the strong emphasis on the development of employment skills that had been stressed by the public engagement participants. In the same ruling, it emphatically rejected the intermediate Appellate Division Court's conclusion that low-level skills would suffice for these purposes.[29] The high court emphasized that a sound basic education means a "meaningful high school education," not eighth or ninth grade level skills.

Building a Statewide Coalition

The other major issue CFE included in its initial public engagement forums was the remedy question: precisely how should the education funding system be reformed? The first item that had to be addressed in this regard was whether the goal of the litigation should be strict dollar equity in spending, which would probably require substantial transfers of funds between rich and poor districts, or caps on spending in the affluent suburbs, or major resource infusions and educational improvements for students in New York City and other high need districts, while "holding harmless" the level of expenditure in the affluent areas. CFE put this question to its core New York City constituents in a series of all-day conferences attended by representatives of approximately 100 education advocacy, parent, and community groups during the first year of public engagement.

These individuals were aware that the per-pupil expenditures for New York City public school students were substantially below the state average and approximately 33% lower than the average expenditures in the neighboring suburbs, even though New York City students often had far greater educational needs.

A strict equalization remedy had great appeal to many New York City parents and educators who resented the fact that thousands more dollars were being spent on the education of suburban students than on their children's education. This view tended to predominate in the early discussions. But as the series of conferences progressed, there was a growing realization that taking money from the rich districts to provide more for the poor would likely spark a heavy political backlash from the suburbs and lead to an upstate/downstate confrontation that could threaten any possibilities for real reform. Based on this strong sentiment, CFE adopted a remedial position that sought to "level up" the resources in New York City and other under-funded districts by expanding the pool of educational resources, rather than seeking a "Robin Hood" remedy that would take from rich districts to give to the poor.

This key strategic decision allowed the public engagement process to broaden into a full statewide dialogue the next year. Seeking to avoid the "upstate/downstate" splits that had stymied past efforts to reform the State's funding formula, CFE worked to build coalitions with residents of urban, rural, and suburban districts throughout the state. This entailed promoting sustained conversations about directions for reform, not only with residents of poor urban and rural areas, who constituted CFE's natural allies, but also with residents of affluent communities whose political support (or at least attenuated opposition) was deemed an essential part of the political equation. By explicitly eschewing a Robin Hood remedy, CFE was able to appeal to the democratic ideals of the residents of affluent districts without threatening their immediate self-interests.

CFE's forums were co-sponsored by many statewide organizations, such as the League of Women Voters, the New York State School Boards Association, the New York State PTA, the teachers' unions, the Urban Leagues of New York State, the New York State Business Council, as well as numerous local education advocacy, business and civic organizations. Not all of these groups supported CFE's positions in the lawsuit, but they all agreed to participate in the public engagement process after it was made clear that the forums would promote candid, wide-ranging discussion of all issues and there would be no pre-conceived outcome for the deliberations.

The fact that diverse constituencies from around the state participated in formulating many of the major positions that were adopted by the trial court meant that when the trial court's decision was issued in 2001 and the final Court of Appeals decision was issued in 2003, they received broad statewide support from education stakeholders and newspapers and other media throughout the state.[30]

This level of statewide support continued even though the Court of Appeals ruling technically applied only to New York City, and not to the rest of the state. Immediately after that 2003 decision was issued, CFE issued press releases announcing that in practice the decision could only be implemented successfully on a statewide basis and that CFE was committed to continuing to press for statewide solutions. The statewide partners accepted those assurances, and another potential upstate/downstate confrontation was avoided.

Trial Strategies

At the same time as it was working with the public to define the meaning of a sound basic education and develop a proposed remedy,

CFE was gathering evidence of the inadequacy of the education system and the causal role that the funding system played. New York City as a plaintiff had been dismissed from the case, leaving the task of developing a record completely to CFE, which had limited resources. At this point, CFE obtained *pro-bono* the services of a team of attorneys from the firm of Simpson Thacher & Bartlett, headed by Joseph Wayland, a litigation partner. The Simpson attorneys took over 100 depositions and formed the core of the trial team. At the peak of the seven-month trial, there were eight Simpson attorneys, three paralegals and two CFE attorneys working on the case.[31]

At the beginning of the discovery process, CFE encountered difficulty gaining access to the information it needed in order to develop its case. This all changed when the court appointed a judicial hearing officer to oversee discovery and make the State respond. It was only then that CFE was able to meet with the Commissioner of Education and other officials at the Education Department. The unique structure of New York's education system ultimately redounded to the benefit of CFE, as the Commissioner and the Department were under the aegis of the Board of Regents, rather than the governor. Thus, these officials were probably more cooperative than had they not been insulated from the governor.

The trial team's strategy focused on several core, interrelated objectives:

1. ***Show a "sustained and systemic" failure in the New York City public school system.*** The plaintiffs' attorneys were concerned that the Court of Appeals would be reluctant to order sweeping reforms if they did not convince the court that the inadequacies in the New York City public school system were not transient, but long-standing and the result of systemic failure that had defied many previous reform efforts. Thus, rather than focusing simply on a

"snapshot" of the system as it existed at some point in time, they tracked resource inadequacies and academic failures over decades.

Through this effort the attorneys also sought to explain to the court the cumulative effect of resource inadequacies. They wanted the court to understand that denying resources to a student over a sustained period of time results in serious educational harm. They sought to show the court what students faced during their 13 or more years in the New York City public school system beginning, for example, with overcrowded kindergarten classes taught by unprepared and unqualified teachers and continuing through high school classes in schools without functioning laboratories or libraries and where the majority of math and science teachers were not certified or had initially failed their subject area teaching exam.

One of the key evidentiary issues plaintiffs faced was how to balance the use of macro-level evidence of system-wide resource inadequacy with the school-specific evidence to emphasize the reality of the actual conditions affecting children in the classroom. For example, on the facilities issue, an extensive, data-intensive study of the condition of the buildings throughout the system was presented together with pictures and testimony concerning the abysmal conditions in a few individual schools. At the time of trial, the New York City school system of 1.1 million students was divided into 32 community school districts; plaintiffs called a representative sample of superintendents from these districts to describe conditions in their districts, using both district-wide data and descriptions of individual schools.

2. ***Show the unique needs of the poor urban school population.*** The State's position was, in essence, that poor academic outcomes arose from the socioeconomic conditions of the New York City public school population rather than the lack of adequate resources. One

of plaintiffs' objectives was to show the court that socioeconomic conditions identified need and did not excuse failure. They introduced extensive data, expert testimony and other evidence to show that the educational impediments pervasive in poor urban neighborhoods could be overcome with additional resources such as smaller class sizes, intensive reading programs, extended school days and school year, professional development and adequate facilities. They identified specific programs with demonstrated success in helping poor urban children achieve academic success.

3. ***Rely on the extensive public record of inadequacy created by the State and other public agents.*** The plaintiff attorneys repeatedly emphasized at every level of the litigation that the proof of inadequacy rested largely on the State's own reports and studies that had catalogued gross resource deficiencies and rampant academic failure for decades. The State Board of Regents, the Department of Education, and numerous legislative committees and commissions, as well as the New York City Board of Education and various independent boards and commissions, had created a massive public record of failure that proved the case beyond any doubt. Plaintiffs' objective was to show that they were not asking the courts to make radical findings but simply to confirm that the record created by the State and other public agents proved that the New York City schools were not providing their students with an opportunity to obtain a constitutionally adequate education.

Plaintiffs also emphasized the long record of the State's recognition of resource inadequacies and academic failure as a means of convincing the courts that judicial action was necessary because the State had tolerated constitutionally inadequate conditions for so long. The attorneys were concerned about the Court of Appeals' historic deference to the governor and the

Legislature in matters of public policy and their objective was to convince the court that no more deference was due in the face of a long-standing constitutional violation.

4. ***Emphasize the State's academic standards.*** In assessing academic outcomes, plaintiffs embraced the State's standards. The Regents had recently established higher learning standards, raising the academic bar for all students, and the State's position at trial was that these standards were aspirational. Plaintiffs' position was that, as the public record demonstrated, the Regents' standards had been specifically developed to ensure that students would be prepared for successful civic participation and competitive employment, and, therefore, these standards were an important barometer of what the minimum acceptable constitutional standards should be.

5. ***Master the facts and data.*** The State built its case around several simplistic, but superficially appealing truisms, including "New York City is already one of the highest spending districts in the country" and "New York City school children do just as well and often better than children in other large urban school districts." The litigation team anticipated and responded to these claims (and the State's implication that the State had therefore met its constitutional obligation) with extensive factual analysis that included, *inter alia*, detailed studies of regional and state-level spending patterns and a school-by-school budget review of the New York City system. They also developed expertise in statistical analysis of the effect of spending on student achievement as well expertise in the analysis of standardized test data. This expertise was used to show that New York City schools simply did not have enough money to fund the educational resources necessary to provide their students with the constitutionally required

opportunity, and that the test scores of New York City students, when properly interpreted, showed that nearly one-third of elementary students were functionally illiterate.

Liability Decision and Remedy

Given the Court of Appeals' directive in *CFE I*, the trial judge, Leland DeGrasse, needed to determine 1) how to define a "sound basic education;" 2) whether New York City public school students were being denied such an education and 3) if students were being denied a sound basic education, whether there was a causal connection between that deprivation and the State education finance system.

Based on the extensive evidence compiled in the record, Justice DeGrasse explicated the Court of Appeals' template definition, which he re-formulated somewhat by emphasizing that a sound basic education "consists of the foundational skills that students need to become productive citizens capable of civic engagement, and sustaining competitive employment."[32]

Although the Court of Appeals had used the term "minimum adequacy" half a dozen times in its *CFE I* decision, Justice DeGrasse's detailed explication of the specific skills that students need to function productively as civic participants, and specifically as voters, jurors and competitive employees, led him to accept plaintiffs' view that effective citizens and competent workers in the 21st century need skills that are at least at the level of a competent high school graduate, and not at the minimal 6th to 8th grade level math skills and 8th to 9th grade reading skills that had been proposed as the constitutional minimum by the defendants. Although his decision clearly was informed by the detailed analysis of the Regents' Learning Standards provided at trial,

Justice De Grasse held that these standards, *per se*, can not be considered equivalent to the constitutional definition because "this approach would essentially define the ambit of a constitutional right by whatever a state agency says it is."[33]

Justice DeGrasse explained his reasons for rejecting the State's minimalist position as follows:

> Productive citizenship means more than just being *qualified* to vote or serve as a juror, but to do so capably and knowledgeably. It connotes civic engagement. An engaged, capable voter needs the intellectual tools to evaluate complex issues, such as campaign finance reform, tax policy, and global warming, to name only a few.
>
> ...[J]urors may be called on to decide complex matters that require the verbal, reasoning, math, science, and socialization skills that should be imparted in public schools. Jurors today must determine questions of fact concerning DNA evidence, statistical analyses, and convoluted financial fraud, to name only three topics.[34]

On the employment issue, Justice DeGrasse concluded that there was an implied economic aspect to "productive citizenship."[35] He reasoned that in order to educate productive citizens, the State had to implement a system that balanced the economic needs of society with the economic needs of graduates. Thus, the system had to educate students so they could satisfy New York's demand for labor, but it also had to prepare graduates to "move beyond" work that did not pay a living wage.[36]

After defining the key constitutional concept, Justice DeGrasse also concluded that New York City's public school students were not receiving an adequate education, based on the lengthy list of educational inputs and outcomes unearthed in the trial: "The majority of the City's public school students leave high school unprepared for more than low-paying work, unprepared for college, and unprepared for the duties placed upon them by a democratic society. The schools have broken a covenant with students, and with society."[37]

The first input evaluated was teaching quality. The evidence showed that 14% of New York City's teachers were uncertified, a finding that was not surprising in light of the fact that New York City teachers' failure rates on certification examinations was significantly higher than those of teachers in the rest of the state. For instance, the first-time failure rate on the Liberal Arts and Science Test was 31.1% for New York City teachers, as compared to 4.7% for teachers in the rest of the state. Underlying the disparity in teaching quality was the salary differential between New York City and neighboring districts, and the court's specific finding that New York City teachers earned approximately 20% to 36% less than teachers in the surrounding suburbs.[38]

Other inputs that Justice DeGrasse cited as evidence contributing to a finding of inadequacy were overcrowding, lack of functioning laboratories, a dearth of quality library books, and a lack of instructional technology. Overcrowding was a problem because of its impact on class size, and class size had been shown to have an effect on student performance.[39]

As for outcomes, the Judge considered evidence of New York City students' performance on standardized tests, as well as graduation rates, to be indicative of inadequacy. Justice DeGrasse had this to say about graduation rates:

> [I]n recent years approximately 30% of ninth graders in New York City public schools did not receive a high school diploma of any kind by the time they reached 21 years of age. Roughly ten percent of ninth graders obtained a GED-a certificate that is conferred upon a demonstration of marginal skills. Approximately 48% ultimately received a local diploma-which measures the skills expected of sixth to ninth graders, not those of high school graduates. The remaining 12% or so obtained a diploma that actually demonstrates that they have received a sound basic education. This evidence depicts a public school system that is foundering.[40]

Having concluded that the education being provided to New York City students was inadequate, Justice DeGrasse also held that there was "a causal link between funding and educational opportunity."[41] He then held that the education funding system was in fact the cause of inadequacy, mainly because funding was not linked to student need. Indeed, although the funding mechanism included an elaborate assortment of formulas, these formulas were, in fact, manipulated to serve political ends and they did not direct funding to where it was needed most:

> It is well known that the formulas are annually "worked backwards" until the politically negotiated "share" for the City schools is hit in the calculations. In this context, the data feeding into the school aid formulas for New York City is really of no practical consequence whatsoever-the City will get the negotiated share of aid regardless of what data they report...annual increases in State education aid are

> allocated pursuant to an agreement struck by the Governor and the leaders of the State Assembly and the State Senate as part of the overall annual budget negotiations.…This phenomenon is commonly referred to as "three men in a room." For New York City, the inevitable result of "three men in a room" was a 38.86% share of any increase in education funding, regardless of need or the operation of any particular formula.[42]

Justice DeGrasse rejected the State's attempt to place the blame for the funding system's inadequacies on the City. After noting that the City's ability to contribute to education funding is hampered by its higher costs for other municipal services, he held that constitutional responsibility for education funding rests with the state legislature and that the legislature has the constitutional responsibility to ensure that appropriate levels of funding are available in the schools, whether it provides such funds on its own or takes steps to ensure that they are provided by New York City and other localities.[43]

After a reversal by the Appellate Division on appeal,[44] the case returned to the Court of Appeals, which reversed once more, largely reinstating the trial court's ruling in favor of CFE.[45] In terms of the meaning of a sound basic education, the court resoundingly rejected the Appellate Division's conclusion that an eighth-grade education was sufficient: "More is required. While a sound basic education need only prepare students to compete for jobs that enable them to support themselves, the record establishes that for this purpose a high school level education is now all but indispensable."[46]

The Court of Appeals' consideration of educational inputs and outcomes led it to reach the same conclusion as Justice DeGrasse. While conceding that some of New York City's schools were providing an adequate education, the court concluded that, on the whole, educational inputs were inadequate: "[T]ens of thousands of students are placed in overcrowded classrooms, taught by unqualified teachers, and provided with inadequate facilities and equipment. The number of children in these straits is large enough to represent a systemic failure."[47]

In considering the "outputs" of the system, the court first articulated a presumption that dropouts could not be considered to have received an adequate education.[48] Next it rejected the Appellate Division's reliance on tests geared to 6th to 8th grade math levels and 8th to 9th grade reading as a measure of adequacy, noting that these tests "measure a level of proficiency far below a sound basic education…."[49] The court agreed with the trial court's determination that CFE had proven that the funding system caused the education system's failure to deliver a sound basic education. In reaching this conclusion, the court specifically rejected the State's argument, which had been accepted by the Appellate Division, that the education system was not responsible for students' lack of success, because the failing students came from disadvantaged backgrounds:

> While it may be that a dollar spent on improving "dysfunctional homes" would go further than one spent on a decent education, we have no constitutional mandate to weigh these alternatives. And, again, we cannot accept the premise that children come to the New York City schools ineducable, unfit to learn.[50]

The court also rebuffed the State's reliance on the fact that New York's per-student expenditures were substantially higher than the national average expenditure, holding that, as with norm-referenced scores on national examinations, the key concern is compliance with

New York State's constitutional requirements and not with national norms that are based on other factors.[51]

The court's consideration of remedial issues was extensive. It made clear that it had reviewed remedies ordered by other state courts throughout the country and concluded that offering "detailed remedial directions" tends to avoid extensive follow-up litigation.[52] The court rejected Justice DeGrasse's call for a mandatory state-wide remedy (although a majority of the Judges indicated that the legislature would be wise to treat the issue on a state-wise basis) because the evidence in the case was limited to the specifics of the New York City system and courts "must fashion their directives based on the proof before them."[53] The Court of Appeals then directed the State to:

> ....ascertain the actual cost of providing a sound basic education in New York City. Reforms to the current system of financing school funding and managing schools should address the shortcomings of the current system by ensuring, as a part of that process, that every school in New York City would have the resources necessary for providing the opportunity for a sound basic education. Finally, the new scheme should ensure a system of accountability to measure whether the reforms actually provide the opportunity for a sound basic education.[54]

The State's failure to comply with the Court of Appeals' July 30, 2004 deadline for implementing this remedy led to further compliance litigation that culminated with a final ruling on the compliance issues by the Court of Appeals in November 2006, in "*CFE III*." The core issue was the calculation of "actual cost of providing a sound basic education." Cost studies had been undertaken by a commission appointed by the governor, the State Education Department, and consultants retained by the plaintiffs. The trial court, based on a detailed analysis of these cost studies by a panel of three expert referees it had appointed, determined that a figure close to the number proposed by plaintiffs' experts, i.e., approximately $5.6 billion in extra operating aid, to be phased in over a four year period, was the appropriate "actual cost."[55]

Emphasizing the importance of deferring to the legislature, the majority of the court of Appeals held that approximately $2 billion was an appropriate "constitutional" minimum for complying with its directives.[56] This ruling, however, ignored the critical fact that, as Chief Judge Kaye pointed out in her dissent,[57] the whole reason the compliance controversy arose and the trial court felt that it had to set a cost figure was that the governor and the legislature had not been able to come to an agreement on any cost figure or any remedy. Although Governor Pataki had proposed the $2 billion amount, the legislature could not agree on that figure or any other. (In fact, the Assembly passed a bill that would have provided New York City over $6 billion in additional operating aid.)58

Although the Court of Appeals' majority established approximately $2 billion as the "constitutional minimum," in concurring and dissenting opinions, three of the six Judges emphasized that the legislature was not limited to this minimal amount, and that the legislature should give serious consideration to a $5 billion increase.[59] This is precisely what the legislature did. In 2007, the newly-elected governor, Eliot Spitzer, proposed, and the legislature adopted, a reform plan that established a new needs-based foundation formula approach. Including promised increases in local aid by New York City, the City's school children were promised approximately $5.2 billion in increased annual operating aid, to be phased in over four years;

students in the rest of the state were to receive an additional $4 billion phased in over the same time period.

As part of its CFE package, the legislature also adopted a "Contracts for Excellence" accountability mechanism. These contracts require New York City and 55 other districts around the state that are receiving large increases to specify plans for spending their foundation funding increases in specified priority areas, i.e., class size reduction, programs that increase student time on task, teacher and principal quality initiatives, middle school and high school restructuring, and full-day kindergarten or pre-kindergarten. Up to 15% of the funds can be used for "experimental programs" approved by the commissioner of education.[60] The law also requires these programs to predominately benefit students with the greatest educational needs; beginning with the 2008-09 academic year, the contracts must be developed through a public process, including at least one public hearing.

Lessons Learned

Despite its lengthy duration, we believe that the *CFE* litigation was a success on four major dimensions: 1) the establishment of a strong constitutional standard; 2) substantial increases in educational funding; 3) creation of a highly effective public engagement process; and 4) the significance of the remedial directives issued by the Court of Appeals, even though the court's failure to insist on thorough-going compliance with these directives somewhat undermined their precedential impact.

Strong Constitutional Standard

Although some had predicted that the definition of "sound basic education" that would ultimately emerge from the *CFE* case would ensure only minimal benefits to New York State's schoolchildren, the actual constitutional standard guarantees a high level of educational opportunity. Two factors were important here. First was the court's articulation of a template standard that emphasized the skills students would need to function productively as civic participants capable of voting and serving on a jury. This, of course, is a common sense definition, shared, in substantial part, by numerous educational researchers and about a dozen other state courts. But by directing the trial court to develop a factual record on this definitional issue, the Court of Appeals set in motion a judicial process that maximized the likelihood that a high standard would ultimately emerge.

Any objective analyst who closely considers the skills that a student will actually need to be a capable voter in a modern democracy or an effective juror is likely to conclude, as did Justice DeGrasse, that high-end cognitive skills are required to properly carry out these responsibilities. The State's prime defense was that citizens don't have to actually understand the language in ballot initiatives about which they are voting because surveys show that most voters make up their minds, based on media recommendations, before they enter the voting booth. It is hard to imagine that any judge could accept the proposition that voters in a democratic society need not be capable of reading and understanding the issues about which they are voting.

Similarly, once the State articulated the position the Constitution requires that students in the 21st century only receive 6th to 9^{h} grade level math and reading skills (and once the Appellate Division held that the Constitution only guaranteed work skills at a level that would keep an individual off the welfare rolls), it was almost inevitable that the State's highest court would need to definitively reject this position and clarify that students are entitled to a "meaningful high school" education. On its face, middle school level skills simply are not sufficient to render students capable voters and jurors and competitive workers in the 21st century.

The clear lesson here for other litigators is that they need to structure their claims and their arguments to encourage the court to specifically define the meaning of the State Constitution's education article language in light of the universally acknowledged purposes of public education, i.e., preparing students for citizenship and employment. Once such an analysis is undertaken, it will become extremely difficult for any judge to straightforwardly declare that the State can allow its citizens to be civically illiterate or that students can be expected to compete for jobs without the high level cognitive skills needed for 80% of the jobs now available in our economy.

Increased Educational Funding

By any measure, the amount of funding this litigation has brought to the school children of New York City — and New York State — is enormous. Although lawyers in the *CFE III* arguments forcefully argued about the differences between the $2 billion minimal constitutional level sought by the governor and the $5.6 billion figure espoused by the plaintiffs and endorsed by the trial court, even the lower amount, the minimum finally ordered by the court majority, constitutes the largest education operating aid increase ever ordered by a state court. Equally significant was the fact that during the long pendency of the case, annual funding increases substantially exceeded historical levels. The facts revealed at trial, which were constantly discussed in the print and broadcast media as the case progressed through its lengthy appeals and compliance stages, changed the political dynamic in the state regarding education funding. Noteworthy in this regard is that after the intermediate appellate court endorsed plaintiffs' position that $9.2 billion in additional capital funding was needed for New York City, a plan providing for this full amount was adopted by the legislature, and the capital funding issue largely disappeared from the ensuing appeals.

Public Engagement

CFE's decision early on to engage in a serious and thorough-going public engagement process clearly brought massive dividends during the legislative deliberations that led to the ultimate reform package. Strong statewide coalitions were forged which outlasted a recalcitrant governor and resulted in a final outcome that was in line with the plaintiff's full funding proposals, even though the Court of Appeals had ordered a much lower minimum constitutional figure. The formula reforms and the Contract for Excellence accountability system that were adopted also were substantially in accord with plaintiffs' positions. Public engagement was crucial, not only for building the statewide political coalitions, but also for bolstering the media effort that built broad public support for the reform issues and heavily influenced the politicians' perspectives. Public engagement educated the media throughout the state about the issues in the case and stimulated and sustained their interest. Local newspapers and television stations usually featured CFE forums whenever they came to town, and the issues raised in the forums often motivated editorial writers and talk show hosts to follow up and urge the Governor and the legislature to reform the educational funding system.

The public engagement process also had importance beyond the forging of a winning political coalition: public engagement sessions were occasions for seriously analyzing issues and developing positions.

CFE's consideration of public input was not mere "window dressing." The core of the definition of a sound basic education that the court ultimately adopted, the major strategic decision to include the employment issues, and the key remedial commitment to avoiding a confrontational "Robin Hood" approach were all developed through the public engagement process. Plaintiffs' formula reform, capital funding and accountability proposals also were forged at statewide meetings of the 50 organizations constituting the "Sound Basic Education Task Force" that CFE had convened for this purpose. And although the court opinions did not explicitly refer to the public engagement process, it seems likely that strong public support for the CFE remedy — and public outrage at the idea that students in the 21st century were entitled to be educated only to 6th to 9th grade level skills — had a significant impact on the judges.

The Well-Conceived Remedy

The Court of Appeals labored long and hard over the remedy that it issued in *CFE II.* The court devoted about 75% of its questions during the lengthy 2 ½-hour oral argument to the remedy issues, and many of these questions carefully probed the substance and the outcomes of the remedies issued by other state courts throughout the country. The *CFE II* decision set forth in great detail the court's reasoning on the remedial issues and its "effort to learn from our national experience."[61] The court made clear that in adopting specific remedial directives, it saw itself as adopting a middle ground between those state courts that deferred fully to the legislative and executive branches and other courts that attempted to micro-manage the reform process.

The court's simple, yet profound, tripartite remedial order well captures the essence of the core reforms that plaintiffs seek in an education adequacy litigation: a fair analytic focus on the resources and funding needed to provide an adequate education, reform of the State education finance system that will make certain that all schools actually receive the requisite funding, and an accountability scheme that will ensure that the funding is used effectively and results in substantial improvements in student achievement. These guidelines clearly delineated what needed to be done, but left the executive and legislative branches maximum discretion to devise the specific policies that would accomplish these ends.

When, despite the convening of a gubernatorial commission and a special session of the legislature, the executive and legislative branches were unable to agree on a remedial plan that would comply with the court's order, the trial court properly took responsibility for determining itself the cost of a sound basic education. The Court of Appeals was wrong to defer to the governor, in what essentially was a dispute between him and the legislative branch. Since the two other branches were unable to come to agreement on an appropriate figure, it was necessary and proper for the judicial branch to ultimately resolve the issue.

An insight into what may have been at the heart of the court's core concerns in *CFE III* is provided by the concurring opinion of Judge Rosenblatt, a Pataki appointee who sided with the plaintiffs in *CFE II*, but provided the crucial deciding vote to uphold the low constitutional minimum amount in *CFE III*. Rosenblatt seemed to agree with the plaintiffs and the dissenters that a figure in the $5 billion range was more appropriate than Governor Pataki's $2 billion figure. He was, however, leery of involving the court in a constitutional confrontation with the governor and/or the legislature. Instead, he seemed to be sending a strong message to the new governor and the legislature about how they should ultimately resolve the issues in the case:

> Judging by...the...heartening indications that Governor-elect Spitzer will continue in a direction higher than the minimum, there is every indication that the amounts dedicated will be well above the constitutional floor. When it comes to educating its children, New York State will not likely content itself with the minimum. Indeed, after this suit was initiated the State provided for an additional $9 billion investment in capital improvements for the City's schools. How much more it can and should spend, however, is a matter for the political branches, which will be free to avail themselves of the valuable work performed by the distinguished panel of referees.[62]

During the 2007 session of the legislature, Governor Spitzer and the legislature seemed to heed Justice Rosenblatt's words, and they enacted a $5.2 billion operating aid plan and a funding reform and innovative accountability scheme. Spitzer's successor, Governor David Paterson, kept the state's commitment by supporting virtually full funding Year 2 of the four year phase in — will continue to accept this non-binding advice and adhere fully to the plan as adopted in 2007 remains to be seen.

Biographies

Michael A. Rebell is Executive Director of the Campaign for Educational Equity and Professor of Law and Educational Practice at Teachers College at Columbia University. Previously, Mr. Rebell co-founded and served as Executive Director and Counsel of the Campaign for Fiscal Equity, and was co-counsel for plaintiffs in *CFE* *v. State*. Rebell has also taught at Yale Law School and Harvard Law School, and he has litigated numerous class-action lawsuits, including the landmark New York State case, *Jose P. v. Mills*. He has written three books (*Moving Every Child Along: From NCLB Hype to Meaningful Educational Opportunity*, *Equity and Education* and *Education Policymaking and the Courts*) and several dozen articles on a wide range of education issues, including educational equity, education finance, testing, the rights of disabled students and theories of institutional reform litigation. Mr. Rebell is a graduate of Harvard College and Yale Law School.

Joseph F. Wayland is a Partner in the Litigation Department of the law firm of Simpson Thacher & Bartlett LLP, where he specializes in complex business litigation, including antitrust matters. Mr. Wayland served as lead counsel for the Simpson team in *CFE v. State of New York*. Mr. Wayland served for nearly a decade as the Chairman of Simpson Thacher's Pro Bono Committee. He is active in many education matters and serves as a member of the Boards of Trustees for two charter schools serving poor communities in Brooklyn, as well as a member of the Board of Trustees of the Allen-Stevenson School and as a member of the National Council of Washington University's College of Arts and Sciences. Mr. Wayland is a former Coro Leadership New York fellow and the recipient of the John Dewey Award of the United Federation of Teachers and the New York State Bar Association President's Pro Bono Service Award. Prior to joining Simpson Thacher in 1988, Mr. Wayland served as a Captain in the Air Force for four years and was selected for the Honors Program of the Air Force General Counsel. Mr. Wayland is a graduate of Washington University and Columbia University Law School, and received his LL.M. in International and Comparative Law from Georgetown University.

1 Adam Waite, a second year law student at NYU School of Law, provided valuable research assistance for this chapter.

2 Campaign for Fiscal Equity, Inc. v. State (*CFE I*), 655 N.E.2d 661 (N.Y. 1995).

3 Campaign for Fiscal Equity v. State, 719 N.Y.S.2d 475 (Sup. Ct. 2001).

4 Campaign for Fiscal Equity, Inc. v. State, 744 N.Y.S.2d 130 (App. Div. 2002).

5 Campaign for Fiscal Equity, Inc. v. State (*CFE II*), 801 N.E.2d 326 (N.Y. 2003).

6 *Id.* at 331.

7 *Id.* at 331-32.

8 *Id.* at 348.

9 *Id.* at 349.

10 Campaign for Fiscal Equity v. State, No. 0111070/1070, 2005 WL 5643844 (N.Y. Sup. Ct. Feb. 14, 2005).

11 Campaign for Fiscal Equity v. State (*CFE III*), 861 N.E.2d 50 (N.Y. 2006).

12 Bd. of Educ., Levittown Union Free Sch. Dist. v. Nyquist, 439 N.E.2d 359 (N.Y. 1982).

13 *Id.* at 370 n.9.

14 Amended Complaint ¶¶ 34, 36.

15 *Id.* at ¶ 49.

16 *Id.* at ¶ 52.

17 *Id.* at ¶ 54.

18 *Id.* at ¶ 56.

19 *Id.* at ¶ 60.

20 *Id.* at ¶ 61.

21 *Id.* at ¶ 65.

22 *Id.* at ¶ 66.

23 655 N.E.2d 647 (N.Y. 1995). The Court also dismissed a parallel suit that had been brought by the City of New York and the New York City Board of Education, City of New York v. State, 655 N.E.2d 649 (N.Y. 1995). Although the complaint in this case also emphasized an adequacy claim, the Court determined that the City and the Board of Education, being "creatures" of the State, lacked the legal capacity to sue their "creator."

24 *CFE I* at 666. The Court of Appeals also held that children were entitled to certain "educational essentials:"

> The State must assure that some essentials are provided. Children are entitled to minimally adequate physical facilities and classrooms which provide enough light, space, heat, and air to permit children to learn. Children should have access to minimally adequate instrumentalities of learning such as desks, chairs, pencils, and reasonably current textbooks. Children are also entitled to minimally

adequate teaching of reasonably up-to-date basic curricula such as reading, writing, mathematics, science, and social studies, by sufficient personnel adequately trained to teach those subject areas.

Id.

25 *Id.* at 667.

26 A detailed discussion of CFE's public engagement process is set forth in Michael A. Rebell, "Adequacy Litigations: A New Path to Equity?" in Janice Petrovich and Amy Stuart Wells, Bringing Equity Back: Research for a New Era in American Educational Policy 291 (2005).

27 Campaign for Fiscal Equity v. State, 719 N.Y.S.2d 475 (Sup. Ct. 2001).

28 *Id.* at 550.

29 *CFE II*, 801 N.E.2d 326 (N.Y. 2003).

30 *See, e.g.*, *Judge Orders Reform: Victory for School Equity*, SYRACUSE POST-STANDARD, Jan. 11, 2001, at A8; *Changing School Funding Won't Solve Whole Problem*, BINGHAMTON PRESS AND SUN-BULL., Jan. 11, 2001, at 6; *Fix the School-Aid Formula*, WESTCHESTER J. NEWS, July 14, 2003, at 6b; *Schools Here May Gain from N.Y. City Ruling*, BUFFALO NEWS, June 27, 2003, at C1, C4.

31 For its part, the State retained the services of Sutherland Asbill & Brennan, an Atlanta firm known for defending Southern school districts in school desegregation cases. The value of the services provided pro-bono by Simpson, Thacher & Bartlett can be gauged by the fact that the State of New York paid the Sutherland firm approximately $13 million for its trial work, while the Simpson attorneys worked not only on the lengthy trial, but also on the extensive pre-trial depositions and through all of the extensive trial appeals and compliance proceedings.

32 719 N.Y.S.2d at 487.

33 *Id.* at 484.

34 *Id.* at 485.

35 *Id.*

36 *Id.* at 486.

37 *Id.* at 520.

38 *Id.* at 498.

39 *Id.* at 501-15.

40 *Id.* at 516.

41 *Id.* at 525.

42 *Id.* at 533-34.

43 *Id.* at 535-40.

44 Campaign for Fiscal Equity, Inc. v. State, 744 N.Y.S.2d 130 (App. Div. 2002).

45 *CFE II*, 801 N.E.2d 326 (N.Y. 2003).

46 *Id.* at 331.

47 *Id.* at 336.

48 *Id.* at 337.

49 *Id.* at 340.

50 *Id.* at 341.

51 *Id.* at 342.

52 *Id.* at 349.

53 *Id.* at 347.

54 *Id.* at 348.

55 Campaign for Fiscal Equity v. State, No. 0111070/1070, 2005 WL 5643844 (N.Y. Sup. Ct. Feb. 14, 2005).

56 *CFE III* at 59.

57 *Id.* at 62 (Kaye, C.J., dissenting).

58 The Appellate Division had modified the trial court's ruling to say that the Legislature could adopt a figure between $4.7 and 5.63 billion, based on the fact that the Governor's proposal to the legislature had said that $1.93 billion was the constitutional minimum, but as a matter of policy the Governor recommended a $4.7 billion plan. (As indicated above, no plan reflecting any of these amounts had been adopted by the legislature by the deadline date.)

59 *CFE III* (Rosenblatt, J., concurring); *id.* (Kaye, C.J., concurring in part and dissenting in part (Judge Ciparick joined Chief Judge Kaye's opinion.)).

60 N.Y. Education Law § 211-d.

61 *CFE II* at 349.

62 *CFE III* at 61.

3 Pennsylvania School Finance Litigation I: Marrero v. Commonwealth of Pennsylvania

By Michael Churchill

Introduction

Marrero was an unsuccessful declaratory judgment/injunctive relief action in state court to enforce the Pennsylvania state constitutional clause requiring the legislature to provide a "thorough and efficient system of public education." The complaint alleged that the state did not provide adequate funding to the Philadelphia School District and therefore the District was unable to provide an adequate education to its students. Rather than examine the merits of these allegations, the state courts dismissed the suit on the grounds that this Constitutional mandate was not justiciable.

The suit was filed in February, 1997 by the Philadelphia School District, the City of Philadelphia, two organizations representing minority students and their parents (ASPIRA, an Hispanic educational organization, and the NAACP Philadelphia Branch) and four families with Philadelphia public school students. Defendants were the

Governor, Secretary of Education, the Department of Education, and the State Board of Education (the Administrative Respondents), and the legislative leaders of the state Senate and House of Representatives (the "Legislative Respondents"). The Administrative respondents and Legislative respondents retained separate counsel. Each group filed preliminary objections requesting the case be dismissed, based on broad and diverse procedural and substantive grounds, and the petitioners responded over the course of the summer.

The case was heard by a panel of six Commonwealth Court judges on September 10, 1997. Six months later, in March 1998, the Court upheld the preliminary objections by a 5 to 1 vote and dismissed the case on the grounds that the Constitutional clause was not justiciable and could not be enforced against the legislature. Judge Pellegrini dissented, simply stating that it was a duty of the judiciary to ensure that the constitution was complied with and, consequently, the case was justiciable.[1]

The Pennsylvania Supreme Court agreed to review the case and in July, after the first round of briefs was filed, it accepted the petition of the Pennsylvania Association of Rural and Small Schools ("PARSS") to consolidate the appeal in its case, which also challenged the state funding system as violating the "thorough and efficient system" constitutional clause. The *PARSS* case had gone to trial in the Commonwealth Court before *Marrero* was filed, but was still awaiting decision by Judge Pellegrini when the full Court entered the decision dismissing *Marrero*. While the *Marrero* appeal was pending in the Supreme Court, Judge Pellegrini issued the trial court decision in *PARSS*, finding on the merits that plaintiffs had failed to prove a violation of the Constitutional mandate because there was no evidence that the education in any plaintiff district was inadequate, despite the wide disparity in funding that he found that they had available. He then held procedurally that he was constrained by the opinion in *Marrero* to hold that there was no cause of action.[2]

The *Marrero* case was taken by the Supreme Court without oral argument in December 1998, and then on October 1, 1999, it upheld the dismissal with four justices joining in the opinion and three justices concurring.[3] The opinion extensively quoted the Commonwealth Court decision and then in total concluded:

> The foregoing summary of the rationale of Commonwealth Court discloses no error, but rather a conscientious adherence to precedent which forecloses the relief sought by appellants. The judgment of Commonwealth Court will be affirmed.[4]

On that same day, the Supreme Court issued a one line order affirming the Commonwealth Court judgment on behalf of the state in the *PARSS* case, without any opinion.[5]

Context is Everything

Because so many of the issues raised by the case — such as the relationship between courts and legislature, whether state or local authorities must raise taxes for schools, and how to determine whether the education of thousands of students is adequate — were not unique to this case but had ramifications to a series of relationships throughout the Commonwealth, its outcome was greatly influenced by the legal and political context in which it was brought.

Twenty years earlier, in 1976, the Philadelphia School District brought a similar case against the state, called *Danson v. Casey*,[6] for failure to sufficiently fund the District so that it could provide "a normal program of educational services" to its students, in violation of the Education Clause of the state constitution. At that time, however,

Philadelphia was the 5th highest spending district in current expenditures and 7th highest in total expenditures (out of 505) in the state. There was no allegation of any deficiency in state funding except for Philadelphia. The Pennsylvania Supreme Court three years later dismissed the lawsuit on the grounds that there was no pleading that the education offered by the District was "inadequate" or did not meet "minimum" standards, and no allegation there were " gross disparities in total and per child expenditures throughout the state."[7] Given those pleading deficiencies, the court held, there could be no violation of the constitutional mandate because that provision afforded great discretion to the General Assembly to determine the content of a normal or proper education.

By the mid 1990s the factual situation was starkly different: Philadelphia had been falling further and further behind. Its spending was below average. On state test scores begun in the late 1980s, Philadelphia's were consistently in the lowest five districts in the state. The drop-out rate was nearly 50 percent of its students. Moreover, the General Assembly had changed the method of allocating state funding. Until 1990, the General Assembly had allocated funds to districts pursuant to a formula which accounted for the wealth of districts, even though it had often failed to sufficiently fund the formula. Abandoning any consistent formula, the legislature decided district funding beginning in 1991 on an ad hoc basis each year based on the prior year funding and on political decisions. As a consequence, although Philadelphia added 20,000 new students from 1989 to 1999, equivalent in size to the third largest district in the state, it received no extra funding based on that growth. State funding to Philadelphia after 1992 did not keep up with inflation and, by 1996-7, it was $60 million less in real dollars than it had been in 1992.

The District's experienced Financial Director, Irv Davis, calculated that by dropping the funding formula used until 1991 to allocate funds, the School District was receiving $99 million less in state funding for 1996-97 than it would have under the formula, and it had lost a total of $315 million since the change. In 1991, Philadelphia had the resources to spend $6,876 per student, or $689 less than the average per student spending of the districts in the other four counties of metropolitan Philadelphia.

By 1997 the disparity more than doubled to where Philadelphia's gap with suburban students had risen to $1,522 per student. That gap badly understated the problem because a much higher proportion of Philadelphia's students came from families in deep poverty who did not provide the same level of support that suburban children received, and a much higher proportion of students were English language learners or in special education. As a consequence, the District needed more than just parity in per student funding, although that was all that was being sought in the suit.

That need for additional resources was demonstrated through the use of state wide tests, allowing comparisons across school districts. Year in and year out, Philadelphia's test scores were in the five lowest scoring districts, with more than two-thirds of its students not reaching acceptable levels on the state-wide tests. Class size in Philadelphia averaged 30 in elementary school, well above the normal suburban levels. By the mid-1990's, Philadelphia was no longer the pay leader in the area. The district was paying less than neighboring districts and finding it increasingly difficult to attract new teachers or to retain experienced ones. Philadelphia also was faced with enormous numbers of old schools which had deferred maintenance until they reached the point of requiring significant capital improvements which the district could not afford. Leaders in the School District and in the City did not see how they could keep Philadelphia a competitive destination for families and businesses if they could not obtain the funds necessary to reinvigorate the declining system.

In 1991, the Pennsylvania Association of Rural and Small Schools ("PARSS"), representing approximately 150 districts (one-third of the state districts), brought suit in Commonwealth Court against the state alleging violation of the Education Clause and the Equal Protection Clause of the State Constitution because of the very disparities which had not been alleged in *Danson*. Although the Philadelphia School District had been invited to join the case by the plaintiffs when first brought, it had declined to do so, and the Court had closed intervention to new parties. By the beginning of 1997, plaintiffs and their experts had presented extensive evidence of the statewide inequity and inadequacy of funding to Judge Pellegrini and were presenting final briefs.

In 1995, the Pennsylvania Supreme Court unequivocally declared that public education in the state was a fundamental right in *School Dist. of Wilkinsburg v. Wilkinsburg Education Ass'n.*[8] Based on that right, it declared that a state statute which prohibited contracting out teaching at a school might violate the "thorough and efficient" constitutional clause in circumstances where students were failing to receive a quality education. As a consequence, it reversed a preliminary injunction obtained by the teachers based on a facial violation of the statute without a trial and returned it for hearing on whether the statute violated the state constitution in the light of the education Wilkinsburg provided.

The *Marrero* case was also a direct outgrowth of the failure to obtain additional funding for the Philadelphia School District under a different set of legal theories in the Philadelphia School Desegregation litigation. At the beginning of 1995, community educational advocates, represented by the Public Interest Law Center of Philadelphia, had succeeded in having a Commonwealth Court judge (Doris Smith-Ribner) declare that the School District of Philadelphia was continuing to be in violation of the state Human Relations Act by failing to give an equal education to its minority students. Following appointment of an independent team of educators to assess the district's programs, the court had issued a decree directing implementation of a remedial program. Because the Philadelphia School District, uniquely in the state, had no taxing authority and was dependent for its revenues upon the City and Commonwealth, both the advocates (who had intervened on the side of the Human Relations Commission) and the School District (the initial defendant who now embraced the remedial program), requested the court to join the Commonwealth and City as parties to determine if additional funding was necessary to implement that remedial program.

In November 1995 the court did so, stating that compliance by the General Assembly with the mandate of the State Education Clause presented a justiciable question. The state hired outside counsel that vigorously opposed the joinder and then, after Judge Smith-Ribner joined it, vigorously opposed the claim that the District needed any additional funds, bringing in teams of auditors and outside experts in a major assault upon the District's operations. During the 19 day trial, held in the summer of 1996, the State sought from the Supreme Court an order removing jurisdiction from the Commonwealth Court and immediate review of the joinder.

That July the Court, in an extraordinary order, directed the Commonwealth Court to promptly conclude the trial and issue its opinion on the merits so that the Supreme Court could review the entire matter. Judge Smith then found that the District needed additional funds (in the amount of $45.1 million in the first year) to comply with her earlier decree. She also found that there was insufficient evidence to prove that the City was required to provide more funding, and that therefore the state was responsible for providing the additional amount. [9]

Four other states (Ohio, New Jersey, West Virginia and Maryland) have the identical "thorough and efficient" clause in their constitutions, all having borrowed Ohio's formulation. By 1997, all four had found the clause justiciable, and three out of the four had found that their state system of funding violated that provision. Only in Maryland had the court found the range of disparities and the level of funding complied with the constitution. The successful adequacy funding litigation in neighboring New Jersey in particular spurred the educational community toward a lawsuit.

The final piece of context was the long running interaction between the State Supreme Court and the General Assembly over funding of the state court system. Historically the state trial courts were funded by the counties in which they were located. In 1988 the Supreme Court held that changes in the state Constitution in 1968 unified the courts into a single system requiring the state to pay for the cost of the entire system. Despite this declaration the legislature had refused for ten years (until shortly after the decision dismissing the *Marrero* litigation) to even begin to provide the funding. Many observers believed the Court was seeking ways to propitiate the Legislature in order to obtain this funding and further their control of the consolidated system, and therefore, was reluctant to confront the legislature.

Strategy

The *Marrero* litigation was a response to its context: 1) the deteriorating finances of the District, 2) the looming failure of the effort to get better funding for the District from the Desegregation litigation described above, and 3) the political weakness of Philadelphia in the state capital. In 1997 a Republican governor was beginning his third year in office. Governor Ridge had spent his first two years trying to get vouchers for public school students which could be used at religious schools and had enacted an unprecedented budget which contained no increase in state appropriations for public schools. Political leaders at City Hall and in the District turned to litigation because they had been completely unsuccessful in obtaining any relief from the onerous problems facing the District which arose from conditions controlled by Harrisburg.

In evaluating the wisdom of challenging the state in litigation, the governmental leaders were very conscious of the status of the pending *PARSS* suit which appeared to have established a very solid evidentiary record concerning the disparities in funding throughout the state and the difficulties the poor districts were facing in providing an adequate education. The *Wilkinsburg* decision also created some hope that the Court was sensitive to the plight of students not receiving an adequate education. In light of this, Philadelphia leaders were afraid that a favorable decision in *PARSS* would result in negotiations where they would not have a seat at the table.

There was a counter-indication to a court-based strategy arising from the Supreme Court's clear hostility to Judge Smith-Ribner's handling of the Desegregation case and the willingness to let that appeal languish. But some of that was dismissed as personal hostility to Judge Smith-Ribner who had garnered wide favorable publicity for her handling of the Desegregation case and, at the beginning of 1997, it was not yet apparent how long the court would let the case go without any decision. Moreover, the plaintiffs and their attorneys believed that the strength of the factual unfairness of the current system was so overwhelming it would drive the courts to provide some relief in some form.

At work in developing the strategy was a new alliance forged in the joinder phase of the Desegregation case which had brought the Intervenor community groups and their lawyers working together with the School District and their lawyers versus the Commonwealth. In part, that was due to the commonality of interest where both groups wanted increased funding from the state; in part if arose out of pre-existing relations between the recently installed Superintendent David Hornbeck and the Intervenors and between Board President Rotan Lee and the Intervenors. Lee, for example, had begun his work at the School District as a consultant in affirmative action to the Acting General Counsel, Michael Churchill, who was now lead attorney for the Intervenors, while Hornbeck had relationships going back to the mid 1960s with the Philadelphia advocacy community and the Law Center attorneys.

In the assault upon the School District launched by the Commonwealth's attorneys in the Desegregation case, the lawyers for the District and for the community organizations came to work together in assembling evidence and examining witnesses. A working relationship also developed with the City's attorneys who, although they opposed the motion to hold the City responsible for increased funding needed by the District, were anxious to help establish the state's liability as a way of lifting any pressure on the City to make its tax base more available to the District. City Solicitor Joseph Dworetzky, for example, provided key help in cross examining state witnesses.

Clearly jaw boning was not working with Governor Ridge, who regarded every call for more funding as an unfriendly assault. The

Law Center and its allies had spent time beginning in 1995 developing a Close the Gap Coalition in the Philadelphia area to publicize the difference between what the City had to spend per student and its neighboring districts. Members included city wide organizations like Philadelphia Citizens for Children and Youth, Parents Union, Philadelphia Student Union, the NAACP, ASPIRA, the Home and School Council and many neighborhood organizations like EPOC (Eastern Pennsylvania Organizing Committee). In 1998 this was expanded to include a state-wide effort, meeting with the Pennsylvania Council of Churches, the Pennsylvania League of Women Voters, and the AFL-CIO.

While these organizations were willing to be supportive and distribute information concerning funding inequities, they were not able or willing to invest significant resources to mount a major campaign to get legislators to adopt a new funding system, and none had significant business contacts. Attempts to interest Philadelphia businesses in spear heading funding increases had died when the Governor had told them they had to choose between business tax cuts (which he delivered) and increased school funding. The PARSS organizing effort appeared to have played itself out, with almost all of its talent devoted to keeping its lawsuit going.

For the community groups, therefore, it did not appear there was an alternative to litigation: they did not have the political ability to change state wide policies, and civic engagement and communication strategies emphasizing the need for increased funding would be the same whether in support of the litigation or of legislative change.[10]

The litigation strategy assumed that a majority of legislators were willing to adequately fund state schools but were afraid of the voter backlash from raising taxes. If a court directed increased funding but left it to the legislators to devise how, proponents thought the legislators could claim to be off the hook and would do "what was right." The continual public disparagement of the litigation by Governor and legislative leaders reveals that this under-estimated the loss of control or threat those respondents thought they faced from a court ruling.

The litigation also underestimated the impact that a Philadelphia-based suit would have on taking the focus off the *PARSS* suit, which had a constituency which the majority of legislators were more supportive of. Once Philadelphia filed its suit legislators could denounce changing funding as helping Philadelphia without having to deal with the fact that scuttling Philadelphia would also sink the claims of the rural and small districts.

The litigation strategy also assumed that there would be a fair fight in the state courts. While there was some recognition that the legal claims could have difficulties because some courts had been reluctant to interpose themselves into the thicket of determining just what was the minimum necessary to assure "adequate" educational services, the recent successes of such litigation in other states and the strong declaration in *Wilkinsburg* led sponsors of the litigation to believe their biggest problem was the normal partisan polarization, with judges caught up in a Democratic Philadelphia versus a Republican Governor.

To counter that, the School District engaged a prominent Republican, former Supreme Court Justice Bruce Kauffman of the Dilworth office to be their counsel along with Patricia A. Brannan, a partner in the Washington firm of Hogan & Hartson, with whom Superintendent Hornbeck had been affiliated. Brannan was an expert in federal school desegregation law and knowledgeable about school funding matters. Whether Kauffman's presence would have made a difference is unknowable because he was nominated to the federal bench before the case was submitted to the court, but in any event the near unanimity of the decision suggests that normal party politics was not the problem Plaintiffs had to deal with.

What was not considered was the inexperience and evident reluctance of Pennsylvania courts to be involved with on-going institutional litigation requiring monitoring or supervision by the courts, much less any reluctance they might have in confronting the legislature which controlled the courts' purse strings. Unlike some other states, Pennsylvania did not have a history of state courts supervising reform of prisons, mental institutions or welfare and health care delivery systems. There was not a tradition of judicial activism.

According to the state's briefs, the lesson Pennsylvania should take from the long running New Jersey school litigation was that it was a quagmire with no positive results. And the 25 year old Philadelphia School Desegregation case, according to the state's lawyers, demonstrated that reform litigation would keep coming back without final resolution. The argument made by the state's lawyers, that enforcing the constitution would invade the powers of the legislature to determine what was an adequate education, was conflated with fears that the judiciary would be involved in a long struggle to obtain compliance. Finally, and impossible to assess, was the possible reluctance of the Court to confront the very legislature it was trying to persuade to assist it by providing state funding for the unified court system.[11]

Court Briefings and Decisions

The Complaint and briefing on behalf of the City, School District and community petitioners in both Commonwealth Court and Supreme Court was done jointly on a group basis with Patricia

Brannan taking the lead coordinating role. Sheryl Auerbach and Lynn Rauch from the Dilworth firm also represented the District; Richard Feder with the help of Sarah Ricks represented the City; and Michael Churchill, along with Thomas K. Gilhool, from the Public Interest Law Center represented the individual and community plaintiffs.[12] Much of the data in the Complaint concerning the District's funding shortfall set forth above came from information obtained by the Law Center in the Desegregation litigation and then from District staff. There was little disagreement in the process although joint drafting was time consuming.

The March 1998 Commonwealth Court opinion granted the preliminary objections filed by the Respondents and dismissed the case on the grounds that whether there was enough funding was a political decision, that there was not a sufficiently clear standard by which to judge its sufficiency, and therefore, whether the legislature was complying with the constitution was not justiciable, and the constitutional clause mandate was unenforceable.

As a first step, the opinion notes the adoption by Pennsylvania of the federal *Baker v. Carr*[13] standard for determining when a court should not exercise its normal judicial power to determine whether a legislature or executive has violated a constitutional duty. The relevant strand was "a lack of judicially manageable standards for resolving it; or the impossibility of deciding without an initial policy determination of a kind clearly for nonjudicial discretion."[14]

The Court next set forth a long recitation of what it describes as "a comprehensive legislative scheme governing the operation and administration of public education" established by the legislature.

The third step consists of long selective quotes from the *Danson* case from 1979, in which the *Danson* court noted that the appellants there claimed the constitution "guaranteed them a constitutionally mandated minimum level of educational services, provided to the children of all other districts."[15] The quotes from *Danson* then set up, in opposition to a positive mandate of the education clause, the need for future legislative flexibility by citing a case from the 1930s which had justified changes in tenure provisions in the face of the depression:

> "...all matters, whether they be contracts bearing upon education, or legislative determinations of school policy or the scope of educational activity, everything directly related to the maintenance of a 'thorough and efficient system of public schools,' must at all times be subject to future legislative control. One legislature cannot bind the hands of a subsequent one; otherwise we will not have a thorough and efficient system of public schools." [16]

The *Marrero* court continues with what can only be described as a colossal non-sequitur from the *Danson* opinion:

> It would be no less contrary to the "essence" of the Constitutional provision for this Court to bind future Legislatures and school boards to a present judicial view of a constitutionally required "normal" program of educational services.[17]

The opinion goes on quoting the *Danson* court to cast the problem as a Philadelphia problem only:

> "appellants by this litigation seek to shift the burden of supplying those revenues from local sources to the Commonwealth. This Court, however, may not abrogate or intrude upon the lawfully enacted scheme

> by which public education is funded, not only in Philadelphia, but throughout the Commonwealth."[18]

The final step of the opinion was to say this is the same:

> "In short, as the Supreme Court was unable to judicially define what constitutes a "normal program of educational services" in *Danson*, this court is likewise unable to judicially define what constitutes an "adequate" education or what funds are "adequate" to support such a program. These are matters which are exclusively within the purview of the General Assembly's powers, and they are not subject to intervention by the judicial branch of our government."[19]

The opinion dismisses in a footnote Petitioners' briefs which devoted pages to discussing the exceptions which *Danson* had explicitly created with the cursory line: "We find petitioners' claims in this regard to be unpersuasive."[20]

A concurring opinion by President Judge Colins stated that if the facts alleged were true, the remedy would be to restructure the Philadelphia School District under the statutory provisions dealing with financially distressed districts.[21]

In the Supreme Court, the Appellants jointly attacked the analysis of the Commonwealth Court and a number of groups filed supporting briefs. The attorneys in the *PARSS* case, at that time still pending undecided in front of Judge Pellegrini, filed an amicus brief on their clients' behalf to ensure the Court understood that the case would determine the outcome of claims by many more districts than just Philadelphia and to demonstrate that there had been a manageable judicial standard consistent with *Danson* applied in the *PARSS* case.

They also noted that the problem of disparate funding had been observed and complained about for a long time in Pennsylvania and was a systemic problem which needed to be addressed.

Another amicus brief, written by University of Pennsylvania Law School scholar Seth Kreimer, was filed on behalf of himself, the Dean of the University of Pittsburgh Law School and a professor from Temple and Rutgers law schools to bring to the court's attention a thorough understanding of what other states had done with similar litigation. A brief by the American Civil Liberties Union, Parents Union for Public Schools, Citizens Committee on Public Education in Philadelphia, Philadelphia Citizens for Children and Youth, and Education Law Center–Pa. presented the importance of adequate funding to accomplishing the constitutional goal of adequate and successful education. The Education Law Center filed an additional amicus brief directed solely to the experience of litigation in New Jersey involving the identical educational clause.

Three Democratic Senators filed an amicus at the time the reply briefs were filed, to make the point that the brief of the Republican legislative leaders did not represent the views of all legislators and to present cases in other areas involving separation of powers issues where the Court had not found a "political question."

At the stage of the final reply brief in the Supreme Court, the Public Interest Law Center filed a separate brief on behalf of the parents and educational advocates, written in large part by Thomas Gilhool. It began with a concise analysis of the sections of *Danson* not quoted by the Commonwealth Court. It then argued that the *Wilkinsburg* and *PARSS* cases demonstrated that the *Danson* standard was workable by showing that the evidence in those cases was consistent with the standard of gross funding disparities and gross educational failure. *PARSS*, it noted, had found that there was a greater disparity in per child spending in Pennsylvania than in all but five states. The brief then presented a history showing a long succession of cases enforcing the Constitutional clause on education, showing that it did constitute a "mandate" which had been enforced in areas apart from school funding, in contrast to the Commonwealth Court assertion that courts had not treated it as enforceable. Finally, the brief contained an extensive analysis of the 1873 Constitutional Convention which enacted the "thorough and efficient" clause, which had rejected four times proposals to grant the legislature power to appropriate "such amounts as they shall deem proper," and where speakers declared they intended a "positive mandate which no legislature can ignore."

As noted before, the state Supreme Court opinion issued October 1, 1999 for four of the justices merely adopts the Commonwealth Court opinion and the other three justices do not state why they affirmed.

As a matter of statutory interpretation, it is interesting that there is no reference in either the Commonwealth Court or the Supreme Court to the decisions of any of the other four states which have an identical constitutional clause nor to any of the other state court opinions enforcing state constitutional claims. *Danson*, 20 years earlier, had at least distinguished those cases by saying there was evidence in all of them of gross disparities in spending, which Philadelphia had not shown at that time. With abundant evidence of those gross disparities now in the Complaint and in the *PARSS* record, the courts chose simply not to attempt any response.

Another curiosity of the decisions is that there is no citation to *Wilkinsburg*, handed down just four years earlier. In that decision, not only had the Supreme Court found a "fundamental right to education" but it had articulated the criteria to determine when it was not being provided: poor performance on standardized tests. *Wilkinsburg* had told the lower court how to tell when there was a failure to provide an adequate education in conformity with the constitutional requirement. But in *Marrero* it was ignored and treated as if it didn't exist.

Finally, and most curious of all at the Supreme Court level, there was no attempt to deal with the fact that Judge Pellegrini had just administered a trial of the same issue in the *PARSS* case and had utilized a "judicially manageable standard" which he concluded entitled the respondent state to a judgment in its favor. Although this fact, which occurred after the Commonwealth Court decision in *Marrero*, was brought to the Supreme Court's attention, it received no mention in that opinion and the court proceeded on the grounds that it was self evident that there was no way to determine whether a district was failing to provide an adequate education, despite *PARSS* and *Wilkinsburg*.

Lessons Learned

The chief lesson that all of the persons involved with *Marrero* initially concluded that they learned was that politically-oriented courts make bad law. There is no reason at this point to doubt that observation or its relevance, even though there was no difference along party lines in the result. The long delay by the Supreme Court in issuing an opinion which merely recited the lower court and stated it was affirmed, also seems to display a remarkable lack of respect for the public.

But there are other lessons to learn also. One was that a case brought on behalf of Philadelphia alone rather than on behalf of a wide cross section of districts was inherently weak The constitutional clause calls for a thorough and efficient "system" of public education and in *Marrero*, as in *Danson*, only one district was contesting the fairness of a statute with statewide applicability. Although the factual pattern was much stronger than in *Danson*, and the statewide unfairness and disparities were liberally demonstrated in the complaint (none of which were recited or referred to in the summary of the complaint contained in the opinions), nevertheless *Marrero* was still a case on behalf of one district — Philadelphia.[22]

It is not surprising that the Court chose to issue its opinion holding challenges to the state funding system not justiciable in the less politically popular Philadelphia case, *Marrero*, rather than in the state wide challenge, *PARRS*, which it decided the same day with a per curiam order affirming the lower court decision. While joining with other districts would probably not have changed the judicial result, it might have broadened the political reaction to the decision.

To the extent there was any substance to the Pennsylvania courts' view that there is no "judicially manageable standard" to determine an "adequate" education, the situation has been drastically changing with the adoption of "standards based" education. As the name implies, it is based on clearly articulated performance standards. Although Pennsylvania had adopted statewide performance testing before the case was brought in 1997, it had not adopted any performance standards as to how much achievement was expected from districts or their students.[23] Pennsylvania required districts to have students complete so many hours of courses before giving them a degree, but there was no statewide requirement of a level of individual achievement. That was left to local determination.

Today, however, the state has adopted performance levels in certain subjects that districts are expected to meet. Whether a court will accept them as constituting a "judicially manageable standard" of an adequate education is an open question but it would appear to be a logically required conclusion. In any analysis of whether to bring a new suit and what the result would be now, this significant change in the context of the litigation would need to be taken into account when trying to determine if *Marrero* is still good law.

The final lesson is that good facts and great need are not sufficient to drive courts to decide for clients when resolution involves wide issues of power or where there are ramifications for the courts because of the need for continuing supervision of the remedy. Isolating the consequences of litigation is difficult in cases seeking to address broad social issues like under-funding of schools, nor is it easy to protect the court from on-going involvement in monitoring and supervising compliance. But resolving those issues to the satisfaction of the court or convincing the court that the benefit is worth the difficulties may be as important as any case analysis that the lawyer makes.

Biographies

The author, **Michael Churchill**, was lead attorney for the community groups in both the Philadelphia Desegregation litigation and then in the *Marrero* case. He was Co-Chief Counsel at the Public Interest Law Center of Philadelphia, where he had practiced since 1976, except for 1984, when he served as Acting General Counsel for the Philadelphia School District. A 1965 cum laude graduate of Harvard Law School, he had clerked for Chief Judge Lumbard in the Second Circuit and became a partner in a Philadelphia law firm before joining the Law Center. His colleague, Thomas K. Gilhool, who participated in conceptualizing the suit and in drafting the Law Center's independent reply brief in the Supreme Court, had been the Commonwealth Secretary of Education in 1986-89. Mr. Gilhool graduated from Yale Law School in 1964 where he was an editor of the Law Journal, had practiced with a Philadelphia firm and as Consumer Advocate at Philadelphia Community Legal Services, and then was Associate Professor at the University of Southern California Law School before returning to Philadelphia to head the Law Center in 1975. Mr. Gilhool's work on behalf of persons with disabilities has included the landmark cases of *PARC v. Commonwealth of Pennsylvania*[24] and *Halderman v. Pennhurst Center*[25].

Patricia A. Brannan, a partner at Hogan & Harston in Washington represented the Philadelphia School District. She is a 1979 cum laude graduate of Harvard Law School and clerked for Judge Ferren of the District of Columbia Court of Appeals. Ms. Brannan has handled a large range of education litigation around the country. Sheryl Auerbach, a partner at Dilworth Paxson in Philadelphia, also represented the District and handled oral argument in the Commonwealth Court on behalf of the District. Ms. Auerbach is a 1976 cum laude graduate of the University of Pennsylvania Law School. She was assisted by Lynn R. Rauch, a 1988 graduate of the University of Pennsylvania Law School.

Richard Feder, Chief Deputy City Solicitor for the City of Philadelphia, is a 1987 summa cum laude graduate of the University of Pennsylvania Law School and clerked for Judge Becker on the Third Circuit Court of Appeals. Mr. Feder is in charge of all appellate advocacy for the City.

---

1 *Marrero v. Commonwealth*, 709 A.2d 956, 967 (Pa. Commw. Ct. 1998).

2 *Pa. Ass'n of Rural & Small Schs v. Ridge* 737 A.2d 246 (Pa. Commw. Ct. 1999).

3 *Marrero v. Commonwealth of Pennsylvania*, 739 A.2d 110 (Pa. 1999).

4 *Id* at 144.

5 The three concurring justices did not state how they differed with the Commonwealth Court opinion or why they affirmed. Id at 114.

6 *Pa. Ass'n of Rural & Small Schs v. Ridge* 737 A.2d 246 (PA. 1999).

7 *Danson v. Casey*, 382 A.2d 1238 (Pa. Commw. Ct. 1978).

8 *Id* at 365.

9 *School Dist. of Wilkinsburg v. Wilkinsburg Education Ass'n*, 542 Pa. 335, 667 A.2d 5 (1995).

10 Although the Supreme Court in July 1996 deprived the Commonwealth Court of jurisdiction acting on an emergency petition for review, it then did not schedule argument until 18 months later. It finally issued its opinion in May 1999, well after *Marrero* had been decided in the Commonwealth Court and argued in the Supreme Court, although before the Supreme Court's decision in *Marrero* in October 1999. The Desegregation opinion, (*PHRC v. School District of Philadelphia*, 557 Pa. 126, 732 A.2d 578 (1999)) reversed an earlier opinion of the Supreme Court in the case and held that the Commonwealth Court did not have authority to join new parties or permit new remedies such as increased funding in a Human Relations Act enforcement proceeding. It avoided any discussion of the merits and stated it need not address the lower court's conclusion that the Education Clause was judicially enforceable.

11 A strategy not considered was whether Philadelphia had bargaining power from its control of the District which could be traded for increased funding for Philadelphia. John Street, eight years later, was able to utilize that strategy because of Republican legislators' interest in patronage. In 1997 community leaders did not suggest changes in political control of the District, as they did not see this as beneficial for students but as a way for interests which should be subordinate to student interests getting a controlling voice.

12 Even where there is no conscious intention to reduce litigants' rights in order to gain legislators' agreement to start funding court unification (which funding, after having been held up ten years, began shortly after the decision in *Marrero*), a reluctance to antagonize the legislature can weaken a court's willingness to stand up on issues of great public importance.

13 The School District paid the outside law firms representing it. The Public Interest Law Center of Philadelphia, as a tax exempt public interest law firm does not receive payments from its clients. It received partial foundation funding for all of its school funding advocacy, including litigation, only in 1995, 1997 and 1999, paying for its salaries and expenses with its general funds.

14 *Baker v. Carr*, 369 U.S. 186 (1962).

15 *Marrero*, 709 A.2d, at 960.

16 *Id* at 963.

17 *Id* at 963.

18 *Id* at 964.

19 *Id* at 965.

20 *Id* at 965.

21 *Id* at 965.

22 *Id* at 966, 967.

23 Judge Colins' concurrence suggesting the appropriate remedy would be restructuring the school district under provisions dealing with financially distressed districts, would not have been possible if the case had been brought as a class action or on behalf of multiple districts (like the *PARSS* case) complaining of the pattern of state under-funding. Id at 966, 967.

24 In the *Powell* case the Legislative Defendants filed a brief asserting Pennsylvania did not even require districts to provide a high school education.

25 *Pennsylvania Association for Retarded Children v. Commonwealth of Pennsylvania*, 334 F. Supp. 1257 (E.D. Pa. 1971); 343 F. Supp. 279 (E.D. Pa. 1972).

26 *Halderman v. Pennhurst*, 446 F. Supp. 1295 (E.D. Pa. 1977).

4 It's Not Just Philadelphia: Pennsylvania Association of Rural and Small Schools (PARSS) v. Ridge

by Thomas B. Schmidtt, III

Introduction

Prior to being elected in 1995, Pennsylvania Governor Thomas Ridge noted that "[t]he evidence is clear that wide disparities exist in our state between the wealthiest and poorest [school] districts."[1] In 1989, the Pennsylvania Association of Rural and Small Schools (PARSS), et al., filed a petition seeking to have Pennsylvania's system for funding public education declared unconstitutional. PARSS is a non-profit Pennsylvania corporation representing over one hundred rural and small school districts in Pennsylvania. Its purpose is to "conduct research, formulate plans, advise governmental bodies and agencies and the general public, and prosecute litigation regarding the rights and interests of rural and small public school districts in Pennsylvania and of the students served by those school districts."[2] PARSS filed their petition in conjunction with eight individual Pennsylvania students and over two hundred Pennsylvania school districts, including members and non-members of PARSS. The

Petitioners argued for a declaratory injunction asserting the unconstitutionality of the state's current education funding scheme as violating the "Education Clause"[3] and the "Equal Protection" provisions of the Pennsylvania Constitution. The Education Clause requires the Commonwealth to provide educational opportunity to its children and vests the General Assembly with the power to "provide for the maintenance and support of a thorough and efficient system of public education to serve the needs of the Commonwealth."[4] The Pennsylvania State Constitution, however, does not have an equal protection clause. Instead, it contains rights equivalent to those guaranteed by the federal Equal Protection Clause to the Fourteenth Amendment.[5]

At the center of Petitioner's Complaint, they claimed that the "thorough and efficient system of public education" requirement of the Education Clause was being violated by the Commonwealth. Petitioners argued that the violation was a direct result of a disparity between the amount of funding and money spent on education between the state's 501 school districts. Petitioners claimed that this disparity correspondingly resulted in the existing discrepancy in the quantity and quality of the education that students received across the state. In essence, the Petitioners maintained that Pennsylvania's system of public education was neither thorough nor efficient, nor had it made equal educational opportunities available to all children; rather, Petitioners claimed that a child's opportunity for a quality education in Pennsylvania was almost entirely dependent upon where the student lived.

PARSS did not contend that poorer, or less affluent school districts did not, or could not, provide their students with an adequate education. However, PARSS did argue that a better education could be correlated to affluent Pennsylvania school districts to which additional states funds were made available based upon the higher tax base in those locations.

Additionally, Petitioners contended that the Pennsylvania funding scheme violated the "Equal Protection" provisions of the Pennsylvania Constitution by infringing on the rights of students' living in less affluent districts. PARSS argued that education should be a fundamental right, subject to strict scrutiny in determining whether the public education funding scheme violated students' equal protection rights to receive comparable educations. PARSS asserted that regardless of whether education is found to be fundamental, students' rights were still being infringed because there was no rational basis why their access to education should be based on the wealth of the district in which he or she resides.

Under the Pennsylvania Constitution, Petitioners argued that the existing public education funding scheme was unconstitutional and that a new scheme should be implemented in accordance with the Education and Equal Protection provisions so as to enable all public Pennsylvania school districts to uniformly fund each district's education curriculums. More specifically, Petitioners sought equitable relief in the form of an injunction declaring the current education funding system unconstitutional and directing the Respondents to respond accordingly and refer the matter to the Pennsylvania Legislature.

In their Complaint, Petitioners named Thomas J. Ridge and Eugene W. Hickok as Respondents for the Commonwealth. The Honorable Thomas J. Ridge, Governor of the Commonwealth, was named in PARSS' petition based on his vested power to approve the appropriation of state funds, including monies appropriated by the General Assembly for the support of public schools. The Honorable Eugene W. Hickok was named in his official capacity as the

Commonwealth's Secretary of Education in consideration of his duty to administer Pennsylvania laws with regard to the establishment, maintenance, and conduct of the public schools. Respondents asserted that under the Pennsylvania Constitution's Education Clause, determining what is a "thorough and efficient" education funding system is non-justiciable, as it is an issue exclusively for the General Assembly to regulate.

Respondents challenged that even if the issue was justiciable, the existing system was constitutional because every Pennsylvania student received an "adequate" education, and according to the Commonwealth, neither the Education Clause nor the Equal Protection provisions required more. They maintained that the Pennsylvania Constitution did not require that the disbursement of educational funds be uniform because such a requirement would raise local tax issues and would impair local control over district spending and educational choices. Respondents argued that, contrary to the assertions made by the Petitioners, the amount of money that a public school district spent on funding its educational programs and curriculum was neither correlated nor directly related in any way to the education students' received or to the students' successes or accomplishments.

PARSS' constitutional claim that the current Pennsylvania educational funding scheme was causing a disparity in the quality of students' education between more or less affluent districts led to a protracted period of discovery and substantial efforts to settle the matter, to no avail. A settlement could not be reached and in January of 1997, the parties began a four week trial. The trial presented both sides with the opportunity offer exhibits and testimony regarding the means by which public education was funded in Pennsylvania, the disparity in available state funds, and if and how that disparity affected the more or less affluent districts across the state. Following the submission of extensive proposed findings of facts, conclusions of law, and briefs in support of each party's respective positions, the Superior Court of Pennsylvania concluded that their decision did not depend on factual findings.

The Court decided that the issue of the funding scheme's constitutionality actually turned on the meaning of the language of the Education Clause and Equal Protection provisions found within the Pennsylvania Constitution. The Court stated that in order to reach a ruling on the constitutionality of the existing funding scheme, it would first have to interpret those Constitutional provisions. However, the Court went on to state that interpreting the provisions was, in fact, grounded in a greater overarching issue: whether review of the constitutionality of the education funding system was even justiciable.

The PARSS Court relied on the 1998 case, *Yesenia Marrero v. Commonwealth of Pennsylvania* in its consideration of its power to review the constitutionality of the current Pennsylvania education funding scheme.[6] In *Marrero*, the Philadelphia City and School District claimed that the local tax base could not provide sufficient proceeds to enable students within the Philadelphia School District to receive an adequate education. Consequently, the *Marrero* court had to determine what constituted an adequate education and whether the state funds available for supporting public education were adequate. The court held that these issues were political and within the exclusive purview of the General Assembly. In following the reasoning of the *Marrero* court, the court in the *PARSS* case determined that the Petitioners were effectively making the same argument as the plaintiffs in *Marrero*. Finding Petitioners' claim to be political in nature, the *PARSS* court correspondingly found the case to be non-justiciable; the action was thereafter dismissed and a verdict was rendered in favor of the Commonwealth."[7]

The Status of Education and Education Finance Before the Litigation

Historically, education has always been a matter of significance within Pennsylvania. William Penn's original colonial charter gave the governor and the Provincial Council the power to create and oversee the Commonwealth's public education. In 1776, this approach was acknowledged by the state's Provincial Constitution which gave the legislature the duty of supporting public schools. The first rural and small schools resulted from the decisions of local families to construct a school, hire a teacher, and provide financial support for the new district. The idea of "financial aid" would have included the donation of food, wood, labor, or land. At the time, urban locales were developing a two-tiered system of education; middle class children were either apprenticed or sent to inexpensive private schools, while the higher class and wealthy students had access to select boarding schools, private schools, or tutors.

Eventually, reformers sought to implement a common school system under which the state controlled the local school districts and was charged with providing free elementary schooling and professional training to every child. In 1834, the Free School Act established a general system of schooling and endeavored to ensure that all students, rich and poor, were educated alike. This Act created the first appropriation of Commonwealth funds to schools.

In 1857, the Pennsylvania Legislature passed an Act intended to unify educational agencies. It created the Department of Education and assigned to it the duty to administer all laws pertaining to public education. This Act laid the foundation for much of Pennsylvania's later educational growth The Pennsylvania Department of Education has been charged with providing advise and information to district officers and citizens, managing public schools to make certain that they are uniform and efficient, prescribing minimum courses of study, condemning unfit school buildings, and validating permanent teaching certificates from other states. Under the Public School Code,[8] school districts have broad responsibilities including operating educational programs and adopting changes intended to accelerate the progress of public education.

In addition, the Legislature is accountable for the funding scheme of basic public education in Pennsylvania, including its design and implementation. The first system of funding public education was created by the General Assembly and was codified in the Public School Code of 1949.[9] Since then, the Legislature has developed numerous mechanisms and formulas to calculate each school district's share of state aid and distribute those funds accordingly to the school districts for expenses related to implementing educational and related programs. These mechanisms have generally been reviewed and amended on an annual basis to meet the ever-changing needs and demands of the education system in Pennsylvania and fiscal requirements of the Commonwealth.

In 1983, Pennsylvania utilized a specific formula for funding education and dispersing aid to schools. The Equalized Subsidy for Basic Education (ESBE) formula took into consideration an aid ratio which was indicative of each school district's relative wealth and was based on each districts market value and the personal income of each district's residence. The formula factored a fixed dollar amount into its calculations, the Factor for Educational Expense, representing the amount of funding per student. It also considered the "average weighted daily membership," or a measurement of each districts enrollment. This method sought to award a greater proportion of state education funding to districts reporting the least local wealth in relation to the number of students.

In the fiscal year 1993-94, the Pennsylvania General Assembly replaced ESBE with the "foundation" approach. In doing so, the General Assembly intended to lessen the disparity of educational spending between school districts. It was designed to ensure that the majority of new education money went to the poorest districts in the state. Under the foundation approach, each district was required to expend a certain amount of its funding and resources on each student. Districts that were unable to meet the requirements received additional funding from the state.

In 1994, Governor Thomas Ridge stated in his Ridge Education Plan that the Commonwealth's role was to provide all children with access to a quality education. He explained that such a quality education was one that would provide children with the skills and knowledge to be productive, self-sustaining citizens. Governor Ridge acknowledged that despite the state's commitment to funding education, Pennsylvania children were still being denied educational opportunities and significant disparities continued to exist between the poorest and wealthiest school districts. According to Governor Ridge, "[t]he future of Pennsylvania depends on the quality of educational opportunities we offer all of Pennsylvania's students, regardless of where they live."[10]

Initiating the Litigation

In its efforts to create and maintain a "thorough and efficient" system of education under the Pennsylvania Constitution, the General Assembly provided for 501 Boards of Educations, one for each

Pennsylvania school district, and bestowed upon each the responsibility of making available adequate public education. Each school board imposes taxes within their respective districts to finance public education, and, in addition to these taxes, the state subsidies were provided to each district. However, the Petitioners in PARSS did not challenge the amount of funding or resources being directed toward education; it contested the Generally Assembly's disbursement of those funds and resources. The Petitioners' case centered on their request that the court adjudicate the current funding scheme unconstitutional, not that the court itself modify the scheme or implement a new one.

The Petitioners' decision to seek a declaratory injunction from the Court as opposed to a legal remedy, stems, in part, from prior unsuccessful Pennsylvania actions concerning the issue of inequities in education funding, specifically, the 1978 case, *Danson v. Casey*.[11] The *Danson* case effectively generated the groundwork for the PARSS litigation and significantly influenced the Petitioners' legal strategy and tactical approach. It was one of, if not the, first Pennsylvania case to address the issue of funding public education and challenge the then-current funding scheme. In *Danson*, the Philadelphia School District, on behalf of the Philadelphia students, sued the Commonwealth and challenged the constitutionality of the education funding system. The plaintiffs alleged that Philadelphia's school children were being denied a "normal program of educational services"[12] and that this violated both the Pennsylvania Constitution's prohibition against special laws[13] and the Education Clause.[14]

The Pennsylvania Supreme Court held that the *Danson* plaintiffs had "failed to state a justiciable cause of action."[15] In rejecting their claims, the Court highlighted the crucial distinction between those claims and constitutional challenges presented to courts in other states that had considered evidence of systemic, gross disparities in educational expenditures. The Pennsylvania Supreme Court thereby identified claims that were identical to those made by PARSS, and substantiated with extensive and unrebutted evidence; those claims were justiciable.

The Pennsylvania Constitution specifically requires the General Assembly to support and maintain a "thorough and efficient" system of education within the Commonwealth. Courts across the country have found that education funding systems are not thorough and efficient when they result in "some school districts having significantly less money than other districts, causing gross disparities in total and per child expenditures throughout the state."[16] In the PARSS case, the evidence of such gross disparities was overwhelming, and therefore, the PARSS Petitioners' strategy was to first argue for the justiciability of their claims.

Over the course of the PARSS litigation, another objective of the Petitioners was to persuade impoverished urban schools to join PARSS and the efforts of the rural and small schools to achieve equal state funding. It was the urban and rural school districts that did not have the tax base necessary to support the money required to balance the education funding in Pennsylvania. It is noteworthy that rural and urban districts were not the only ones to recognize import of a district's tax base and the negative impact that inequitable state aid was having on education.

The Association of School Districts in Support of Excellence and Equity was an Intervenor in the PARSS Litigation representing affluent suburban school districts. It supported PARSS' position that the existing Pennsylvania education funding scheme was unconstitutional. The Association asserted that the Pennsylvania Education Clause required a funding scheme under which all public school districts would be supplied with the means to equally fund "the common branches of education."[17] Petitioners also invited students to be individually named as petitioners in the suit. This was a preemptive device to ensure that the Petitioner-schools would not be challenged on grounds that they lacked standing.

Having achieved this alliance between school districts across the Commonwealth, the Petitioners directed their attention to the theory of their complaint. The most significant distinction between the above-mentioned *Danson* case and PARSS were the cases' theories. In *Danson*, the plaintiffs approached the issue of constitutionality from the position of the inadequacy of the educational funding scheme. The plaintiffs argued that the scheme was resulting in disparate and inadequate educations between and among districts.

The Court, however, found this argument to be vague, and accordingly, the PARSS Petitioners settled on a purely equitable argument which concentrated on the "thorough and efficient" requirement of the Education Clause. Under this approach, it is the states' responsibility to provide an equitable financial support to each district and for each student. However, as the rural and disadvantaged urban districts were acutely aware, a district's tax base significantly influenced the nature of this financial support and consequently even if it the current scheme gave the appearance of being equitable, the result was an even greater disparity in state financial support between districts.

Throughout litigation, PARSS Petitioners considered the importance of relief. Petitioners attempted to achieve a declaratory judgment finding the current education scheme unconstitutional. Anticipating that the Court might reason that their argument was non-justiciable, Petitioners did not ask the court to resolve the issue of inequitable funding. Alternatively, the Petitioners requested that the issue be left to the discretion of the General Assembly. The Petitioners contended that should the court determine the funding scheme to be unconstitutional, it was the responsibility of the state legislature to address the ultimate resolution of the inequities in the system.

Liability Decision and Remedy

The PARSS court, like the *Danson* court, held the matter to be non-justiciable, despite of the convincing case offered by the Petitioners and the equitable remedy that they proposed. Nevertheless, the case brought considerable attention to the case, the issues, and the parties. The case was publicized in all mediums that covered the case's progress and the issues, bringing widespread exposure. This exposure affected the resultant legislative proceedings and the relationships and allegiances that have developed between the state's administration and its educational entities. Since the litigation, within the legislature, proposed improvements and incremental amendments to the funding system have been made. Investigation, inquiries, and studies have been prepared to continue examining and analyzing the current system and the effects it is having on students and their educations across the state.

The Pennsylvania Legislature's administration is also working with the school districts, students, and parents to review the state's budget and its dispersal to contemplate potential reforms. While proposals for modification are underway, the Legislature has not adopted a formal new funding scheme. The connections, feedback, and attention that came as a result of the PARSS litigation and the case's coverage created a sense of satisfaction among the Petitioners. Although the PARSS case was ultimately dismissed, the repercussions of the case were generally positive.

Lessons Learned

The trial judge in PARSS would have held the claims justiciable, but would have denied relief because he believed the Petitioners had not demonstrated that any students were receiving inadequate education. Unfortunately, his memorandum opinion is unpublished. His putative holding regarding proof of inadequacy is belied by this many findings of fact, and it may be the product of a desire to downplay the consequences of the Court's decision that all challenges to public school funding are nonjusticiable. But, his conclusion that inadequacy was not demonstrated teaches that, however strong the evidence of funding disparities, evidence of the consequences of the disparities must be presented in overwhelming detail.

The second principal lesson learned was that the litigation served as a rallying point for advocates, as a catalyst for reform efforts in the legislature, and as a salutary threat to those law makers who were not reform-minded. Many advances toward funding reform in Pennsylvania have been made since the PARSS complaint was filed and the case was tried, and one can say with confidence that the history may have been different without them.

Biographies

Lead counsel, **Thomas B. Schmidt, III**, is of counsel in the Harrisburg office of Pepper Hamilton LLP and the attorney in charge of that office. Mr. Schmidt's litigation practice includes complex commercial disputes, administrative agency matters, professional liability claims, construction claims, product liability claims, and insurance coverage and "bad faith" claims. His appellate practice includes frequent appearances in Pennsylvania's Supreme, Superior and Commonwealth Courts. Mr. Schmidt serves regularly as a court-appointed mediator and has been honored for his service in that capacity by the U.S. District Court for the Middle District of Pennsylvania.

A graduate of Dickinson School of Law in 1974, Mr. Schmidt has maintained a substantial pro bono practice, highlights of which include the subject of this article *PARSS* and as a member of the plaintiffs' trial team in *Kitzmiller vs. Dover Area School District*, the successful challenge to teaching "Intelligent Design" in public schools. In 2008, Mr. Schmidt received Pepper Hamilton's William R. Klaus Pro Bono Award. He is an adjunct instructor of advocacy of the Dickinson School of Law. He has been active in a variety of community organizations and currently serves on the boards of Harristown Development Corportion, Harrisburg Hotel Corporation Education Law Center, The Harrisburg Academy and MidPenn Legal Services.

Co-counselors, **Donna L. Fisher, Esq.** and **Brian P. Downey, Esq.**, assisted Mr. Schmidt in preparing and litigating the PARSS case. Ms. Fisher graduated with highest distinction from the Pennsylvania State University in 1980 and she graduated *magna cum laude* from the Dickinson School of Law in 1983. Ms. Fisher is a partner in the Health Effects Practice Group of Litigation and Dispute Resolution Department of Pepper Hamilton LLP in Harrisburg, Pennsylvania. Her practice concentrates on product liability, and commercial and construction litigation and she is a member of the Pennsylvania Bar Association's Political Action Committee and the Central Pennsylvania Association of Female Executives. Mr. Downey received his Bachelor's Degree in 1987 from Dartmouth College and his J.D. in 1990 from Dickinson School of

Law. He, too, is a partner in the Harrisburg office of Pepper Hamilton LLP and his practice areas include commercial disputes, product liability claims, employment discrimination claims and environmental matters. Additionally, Mr. Downey has been involved in lobbying efforts and a variety of administrative proceedings within the Pennsylvania government, has tried cases in both federal and state courts, and is experienced in the field of Alternative Dispute Resolution.

---

1 Governor Thomas Ridge, "The Ridge Education Plan" (1994).

2 *PARSS v. Thomas J. Ridge & Eugene W. Hickok*, Memorandum Opinion, No. 11 M.D. 1991, Fn. 1 (Pa. Cmwlth. 1998).

3 Pa. Const., Article III, § 14.

4 Pa. Const., Article III, § 14.

5 Article I, § 1; Article I, § 26; Article III, § 32. *PARSS v. Thomas J. Ridge & Eugene W. Hickok*, Memorandum Opinion, No. 11 M.D. 1991, Fn. 7 (Pa. Cmwlth. 1998).

6 709 A.2d 956 (Pa. Cmwlth. 1998).

7 *PARSS v. Thomas J. Ridge & Eugene W. Hickok*, Memorandum Opinion, No. 11 M.D. 1991, page 109 (Pa. Cmwlth. 1998).

8 24 P.S. §§ 2-211 (2007)

9 Public School Code of March 10, 1949, P.L. 30, *as amended*, 24 P.S. §§ 1-101 – 27-2702.

10 Governor Thomas Ridge, "The Ridge Education Plan" (1994).

11 *Danson v. Casey*, 33 Pa. Commw. 614, 382 A.2d 1238 (1978), *aff'd*, 484 Pa. 415, 399 A.2d 360 (1979).

12 *Danson*, 484 Pa. at 424, 399 A.2d at 365.

13 Pa. Const., Article III, § 32.

14 Pa. Const., Article III, § 14.

15 *Danson*, 484 Pa. at 420, 399 A.2d at 363.

16 *Danson*, 484 Pa. at 424 n. 10, 399 A.2d at 365 n. 10.

17 *See*, *PARSS v. Thomas J. Ridge & Eugene W. Hickok*, Memorandum Opinion, No. 11 M.D. 1991, page 5-6 (Pa. Cmwlth. 1998).

5 Texas School Finance Litigation: Great Progress and Some Regression

By Albert Kauffman[1]

Introduction

Efforts to improve the Texas school finance system have been successful in achieving both a significantly more equitable distribution of resources to districts around the state and some higher level of funding to all but the very wealthiest districts. Community groups, advocacy groups, research centers, attorneys, legislators and judges have combined to create this progress. These groups have worked with each other and at times against each other, and the progress has been uneven in pace and degree. Unfortunately, much of the progress made will be increasingly jeopardized by the reversal of direction in the Texas Supreme Court's jurisprudence on the issue, as well as the limits of the present Texas revenue system.

After briefly summarizing the earlier Texas federal court case on school finance, *Rodriguez*, this chapter describes the Texas state litigation on school finance between 1984 and 2007[2] — from the perspective of one of the participants in that struggle.[3] This chapter focuses on the efforts and interrelationships among a broad range of players in this struggle, from the drafters of the Texas Constitution's education provisions[4] to the legislators who responded in 2006[5] to the most recent Texas school finance decision in 2005 (*Edgewood VI*). This chapter also focuses on the first Texas Supreme Court decision in 1989, *Edgewood I*, and the court's latest decision in 2005, while relying heavily on some of the excellent scholarship on the Texas school finance system[6] and details from some of the court decisions.

While the history of the Texas school finance struggle has been thoroughly described elsewhere,[7] some historical trends are especially relevant to this chapter. The following facts and developments place this chapter in perspective:

1. Texas has been and is a low spending state on education, in general, and public education, in particular. Texas spent even less on its low-income and minority children than on other children.
2. From its beginning as a state, Texas segregated its African-American students by law and its Mexican-American population by use of a set of discriminatory practices and procedures.
3. Texas school districts developed almost organically around small communities with almost 4,000 school districts at one time and now about 1,000 school districts. Large urban areas are split into a crazy quilt of school districts not coterminous with past or present city boundaries.
4. As a historically rural state, school districts were central to community development and pride.
5. Until the 1970's, the Mexican-American population of the state was heavily concentrated along the Texas-Mexico border and in the San Antonio area.

6. Texas is now a majority minority state and is projected to be majority Latino by 2040. Approximately 60 % of Texas public school students are Hispanic- or African-American, and virtually all of the growth in public school enrollment is either minority and/or English language learner.
7. During the last 30 years, Texas has undergone an incredible change in political party orientation from a state with virtually all Democratic office holders to a state with all state wide positions and a majority of the House and Senate in Republican hands. Between the first supreme court decision on school finance in 1989 and the last in 2005, the Texas Supreme Court, which is elected in state wide partisan elections, changed from a 6-3 Democratic majority to a 9-0 Republican court.

The Rodriguez U.S. Supreme Court Case

The United States Supreme Court's decision in *San Antonio Independent School District v. Rodriguez*, 411 U.S. 1 (1973) was the sad culmination of the first effort by Texas advocates for school finance equity, which sought protection and support from the federal courts.[8] This case began with a resounding success before three Texas federal judges.[9] This decision was reversed by the Supreme Court in a lengthy and emotional 5-4 decision, which determined that education is not a "fundamental right" and poverty is not a "suspect category" under the U.S. Constitution. The Court did, however, note that the Texas school funding system of 1973 would not meet the standard of "compelling interest" (the standard the State would have had to meet if a fundamental right or suspect category had been found), and that "the need is apparent for reform in tax systems which may well have relied too long and too heavily on the local property tax."[10] The Court also noted that fundamental rights would be implicated by a school finance system that "fails to provide each child with an opportunity to acquire the basic minimal skills necessary for the enjoyment of the rights of speech and of full participation in the political process."[11]

The *Rodriguez* case emanated from a student action in the Edgewood School District, a 90% Mexican-American and very low-income school district in San Antonio, Texas. A student walkout from Edgewood in 1968 brought national attention to some of the conditions in the school district. Those conditions were the manifestation of decades of neglect, insensitivity, and downright arrogance by Texas leaders and officials.[12] A group of parents of Edgewood students, including the named plaintiff Demetrio Rodriquez,[13] worked with organizer Willie Velasquez[14] to approach Arthur Gochman, an attorney in San Antonio to take the issue to court. Such Texas legal luminaries as Justice Rose Spector,[15] Mark Yudof,[16] Frank Herrera[17] and Warren Weir[18] worked on the lawsuit.

In retrospect, one can criticize the record in the *Rodriguez* litigation as focusing too much on the school districts in Bexar County Texas — specifically the low-wealth Edgewood district and the neighboring wealthy Alamo Heights district — and not analyzing the effect of the Texas school finance system on all Texas school districts. Indeed, these weaknesses in the record were extensively exploited in the majority opinion in *Rodriguez.*[19] Yet, many commentators argue that the opinion was based much more on the fear of additional litigation and inclination of the Burger court to retreat from the aggressive protection of personal and civil rights under the Warren court. In any event, the soaring hopes of the students and parents in Texas low-wealth districts — and the advocates, organizers, attorneys and legislators supporting them — were grounded with a thud. *Rodriguez* did cause Texas to go one step forward in school finance. The egregious disparities revealed in the *Rodriquez* case embarrassed Texas enough to spur action that led to slight improvements in the level of funding and the equity of the State's school finance system.[20]

A few years after the *Rodriquez* decision, an extensive set of perceptive analyses by the Intercultural Development and Research Associates (IDRA),[21] and several state study groups led by Dr. Richard Hooker,[22] described the continued gross and debilitating disparities in the Texas school finance system. For example, the IDRA studies revealed gross disparities in property values among Texas school districts, a ratio of 700 to 1 in the property value per student among districts. Furthermore, the effects of these gross disparities were exacerbated by arbitrary and inconsistent property evaluation procedures and use of offsets and hold harmless clauses. IDRA also developed a well-structured public information campaign on the disparities and weaknesses in the Texas system in the late 1970's and early 1980's.

In 1983, the new Texas Governor, Mark White, appointed the SCOPE committee, chaired by Texas billionaire and later Presidential candidate Ross Perot. The SCOPE committee, with verbal and financial support from Perot, issued a comprehensive set of recommendations for changes in school governance, teaching, discipline, and school finance.[23] The committee's report and recommendations became H.B. 72, which passed in a special legislative session in 1984, one month after the filing of the *Edgewood* lawsuit. Most commentators consider H.B. 72 to have been a modest step toward equity and adequacy. But H.B. 72 did not deal with the fundamental cause of the disparities among district abilities to raise educational funds – vastly unequal taxable wealth.

Edgewood I Development, Discovery, Trial and Appeals in State Court

Texas School Finance System Attacked in *Edgewood I*

The Texas school finance system before the changes caused by the *Edgewood* cases was elegantly described by the Texas Supreme Court in its *Edgewood I* decision:

> There are glaring disparities in the abilities of the various school districts to raise revenues from property taxes because taxable property wealth varies greatly from district to district. The wealthiest district has over $14,000,000 of property wealth per student, while the poorest has approximately $20,000; this disparity reflects a 700 to 1 ratio. The 300,000 students in the lowest-wealth schools have less than 3% of the state's property wealth to support their education while the 300,000 students in the highest-wealth schools have over 25% of the state's property wealth; thus the 300,000 students in the wealthiest districts have more than eight times the property value to support their education as the 300,000 students in the poorest districts. The average property wealth in the 100 wealthiest districts is more than twenty times greater than the average property wealth in the 100 poorest districts. Edgewood I.S.D. has $38,854 in property wealth per student; Alamo Heights I.S.D., in the same county, has $570,109 in property wealth per student.
>
> However, the Foundation School Program does not cover even the cost of meeting the state-mandated

minimum requirements. Most importantly, there are no Foundation School Program allotments for school facilities or for debt service. The basic allotment and the transportation allotment understate actual costs, and the career ladder salary supplement for teachers is underfunded. For these reasons and more, almost all school districts spend additional local funds. Low-wealth districts use a significantly greater proportion of their local funds to pay the debt service on construction bonds while high-wealth districts are able to use their funds to pay for a wide array of enrichment programs.

Because of the disparities in district property wealth, spending per student varies widely, ranging from $2,112 to $19,333. Under the existing system, an average of $2,000 more per year is spent on each of the 150,000 students in the wealthiest districts than is spent on the 150,000 students in the poorest districts.

The lower expenditures in the property-poor districts are not the result of lack of tax effort. Generally, the property-rich districts can tax low and spend high while the property-poor districts must tax high merely to spend low. In 1985-86, local tax rates ranged from $.09 to $1.55 per $100 valuation. The 100 poorest districts had an average tax rate of 74.5 cents and spent an average of $2,978 per student. The 100 wealthiest districts had an average tax rate of 47 cents and spent an average of $7,233 per student. In Dallas County, Highland Park I.S.D. taxed at 35.16 cents and spent $4,836 per student while Wilmer-Hutchins

> I.S.D. taxed at $1.05 and spent $3,513 per student. In Harris County, Deer Park I.S.D. taxed at 64.37 cents and spent $4,846 per student while its neighbor North Forest I.S.D. taxed at $1.05 and yet spent only $3,182 per student. A person owning an $80,000 home with no homestead exemption would pay $1,206 in taxes in the east Texas low-wealth district of Leveretts Chapel, but would pay only $59 in the west Texas high-wealth district of Iraan-Sheffield. Many districts have become tax havens. The existing funding system permits "budget balanced districts" which, at minimal tax rates, can still spend above the statewide average; if forced to tax at just average tax rates, these districts would generate additional revenues of more than $200,000,000 annually for public education.[24]

Development and Discovery

The lawsuit began from a series of discussions in 1983 among IDRA, MALDEF,[25] the Edgewood School District and several other advocacy and community groups. MALDEF attorney Norma Cantu[26] did the original legal work on the proposed case, and Albert Cortez[27] of IDRA and Craig Foster of the Equity Center[28] were major technical advisers on the development of the lawsuit. Jimmy Vasquez, the superintendent of the Edgewood school district, helped to organize the school districts supporting the case. Mr. Vasquez also became the real spokesperson and the conscience for the effort. The META project[29] attorneys Roger Rice,[30] Peter Roos[31] and Camilo Perez also actively worked on the development of the case, especially the effects of the system on educational quality.[32] Between March 1984 and May 2002, as a MALDEF attorney, I led the case for the Plaintiffs. MALDEF filed the case on May 23, 1984, before the two special sessions of the Texas legislature in summer 1984 that produced HB 72.

The case was filed in Austin, the Texas capital, but the home of a wealthy school district. Several experienced attorneys recommended the case be filed in a venue with a concentration of low-wealth districts, such as Eagle Pass, Brownsville or Edinburg,[33] all along the Texas-Mexico border in areas of 85% or more Mexican-American students. In order to avoid a protracted venue battle and to avoid any implication of undue "forum shopping," MALDEF filed the case in Austin, where the case remains after 25 years.

The case was originally constructed as a classic "equity" case based on the models developed in California's *Serrano*[34] litigation and in *Rodriguez*. However, the case was also based on an understanding of the very gross disparities, in both finances and program quality, among Texas districts and an understanding of the insidious negative effects of the system on districts with Mexican-American majorities and on the Mexican-American community as a whole. Students of the Texas courts and Texas politics concluded that the courts were much more likely to deal positively with a challenge to the distribution of presently allocated funds than with a claim that appeared to demand significant tax increases and central control of local educational decisions.[35]

The original petition included claims under the Texas Constitution's education clause, Tex. Const. Art. VII §1,[36] equal rights clause, Tex.Const. Art. 1 §3,[37] and equality clause, Tex. Const. Art. 1, §3a.[38] The petition clearly eschewed any reference to the United States Constitution, and was both in intent and effect soundly based on the Texas Constitution. The original plaintiffs included 25families of children in low-wealth districts and seven low-wealth districts[39] themselves. The petition described the wildly varying property wealth, revenue generating ability, tax rates, and actual revenue of the Texas school districts.

Based on a thorough understanding of Texas history and Texas education history, in particular, attorneys for plaintiffs included in the petition claims of discrimination against Mexican-Americans. Specifically, there was, and is, a significant concentration of Mexican-Americans in the lowest wealth districts.[40] In addition, in the minds of most Texans and Texas leaders at the time, the problem of poor districts was a problem of well-known Mexican-American districts like Edgewood, Laredo, Brownsville and the El Paso County districts, i.e., a problem of San Antonio and the Texas-Mexican border. A series of studies by the United States Commission on Civil Rights and IDRA supported these allegations.[41]

Though the attorneys in the case litigated all three issues, i.e., equal rights for students, the inefficiency of the system, and discrimination against Mexican-Americans, the focus in the litigation was on the equal rights claims for students in low-wealth districts and the inefficiency of the system. Nevertheless the inclusion of the Mexican-American claims, and the role of MALDEF[42] as the attorneys for the plaintiffs, did dissuade some districts from joining the ranks of plaintiffs.[43]

After the passage of HB 72 in 1984, discovery in the *Edgewood* case proceeded slowly and no immediate effort was made to bring the case to trial. This slow pace was partially due to the desire for a reasonable delay to analyze the effects of HB 72 on the school finance system, and, in April 1985, the petition was amended to respond to the changes in HB 72. In mid-1986, many other school districts, under the general leadership of the Equity Center, decided to join forces to intervene in the lawsuit, bring in their own attorneys, and pursue the lawsuit without including the discrimination allegation. The plaintiff-intervenors, known as the *Alvarado* intervenors, were represented by two extremely able and experienced attorneys, David Richards[44] and Richard Gray[45].

Trial and State District Court Ruling

The first *Edgewood* trial, in January through April 1987, became the focus of school finance equity activities in Texas. There were three groups of parties in the litigation, generally called the State, the poor districts and the rich districts. In general terms, the poor districts argued that the system was blatantly inequitable both for students in low-wealth districts and for low-wealth districts themselves; and the system discriminated against poor children and Mexican-American children. The wealthy districts argued that the issue was non-justiciable, but that if it was justiciable, the Texas state interests in local control and control of state finances should defeat the claim. Wealthy districts also argued the classic "money doesn't matter" theory. One group of wealthy districts proposed that the "efficiency" clause of the Texas Constitution Art. VII means "low cost or inexpensive," not "productive of results."

The State argued that the case was basically about tax and monetary policy, and those are issues best left to the legislature. According to the State's argument, the Texas Constitution's other education and tax sections create a set of legal barriers to any interpretation of the Education and Equal Rights clauses that would support a judgment for low-wealth districts. Specifically they argued that the Texas Constitution's provision on school district creation and ad valorem tax,[46] Texas Constitution Art. VII §3, give constitutional status to school districts and constitutional protection to the ad valorem taxes generated in school districts. In *Edgewood I* the State argued that the interpretation of the Art. VII §1 standards was non justiciable; but the State did not return to that argument until *Edgewood VI* seventeen years later.

Plaintiffs introduced a compelling case of the disparities among districts in tax wealth, revenue, tax rates and the effects of the finance system on low-wealth districts. The state and wealthy districts introduced evidence on the difficulty — even impossibility —of devising a remedy without violating other constitutional provisions or requiring new expenditures of many billions of new dollars for the state to compensate for the wealth disparities.

The district court found for plaintiffs and plaintiff-intervenors on all of their claims except the claim of discrimination against Mexican-Americans. The judgment and findings of fact and conclusions of law well document the debilitating and insidious inequalities in the Texas system.[47] Based on the Texas Constitution, District Judge Harley Clark declared education to be a fundamental interest and wealth in the context of school finance to be a suspect category. The district court also held that Texas had not shown any compelling interests to support the system, the State had not shown a rational basis for the system, and the school finance system was not efficient.

The part of the judgment that seemed most frightening to the State and wealthy districts was the conclusion that the school finance system was illegal:

> …because it fails to insure that each school district in this state has the *same* ability as every other district to obtain, by state legislative appropriation or by local taxation, or both, funds for educational expenditures, including facilities and equipment, such that each student, by and though his or her school district, would have the *same* opportunity to educational funds

as every other student in the state, limited only by discretion given local districts to set local tax rates. …[48] [emphasis added]

In the language of school finance cases, the judgment granted perfect tax equity based on a weighted student model.

From the perspective of low-wealth districts, and the students and taxpayers within them, it was one of the greatest days in Texas history. The wealthy school districts and their advocates girded themselves for a long fight against the decision.

Court of Appeals and Supreme Court Decisions

The trial court decision was immediately appealed to the intermediate Court of Appeals in Texas and was reversed in a split decision.[49] The Court of Appeals adopted the reasoning of the U.S. Supreme Court in the *Rodriquez* decision[50] on the equal rights issues, e.g. that education is not a fundamental right and poverty is not a suspect classification. On the issue of the responsibilities of the State under the Texas Constitution's education clause,[51] the court found that the school finance system was "authorized" by Tex. Const. Art. VII §3[52] and that an interpretation of the efficiency clause of Art VII §1 was a political question not suitable for judicial review.[53]

In *Edgewood Independent School District v. Kirby*,[54] the Texas Supreme Court unanimously held that the Texas school finance system was unconstitutional under the Texas Constitution's efficiency clause, Tex. Const. art VII §1.[55] The *Edgewood* court decided the case on the efficiency clause, though it asserted its authority to interpret several other terms in art. VII §1, specifically the terms "suitable,"[56] "essential,"[57] and "general diffusion of knowledge."[58] *Edgewood I* was an "efficiency" case. The judgment was based only on the equity theory.[59] Though later Texas Supreme Court school finance opinions have interpreted other provisions of art. VII, §1, art. VII §3 and art VIII §1-e, almost all of the original supreme court opinion and the holding itself were about efficiency and equal educational opportunity.

The supreme court affirmed the district court on the efficiency issue and determined that it "need not consider petitioners' [plaintiffs low-wealth school districts and families in those districts] other constitutional arguments."[60] In other words, the court decided not to decide the equal rights issues on which the district court had found for plaintiffs, i.e., education as a fundamental right, poverty as a suspect classification, and the lack of a compelling interest, or even a rational basis, in the existing system.[61] However, the court clearly noted the link between the "efficiency" clause and "equal rights." After citing with approval several statements of the Texas legislature noting the link between efficiency and equal educational opportunity,[62] the court held that "[n]ot only the legislature, but also this court has previously recognized the implicit link that the Texas Constitution establishes between efficiency and equality."[63]

Edgewood I gave an operational definition of efficiency:

> There must be a direct and close correlation between a district's tax effort and the educational resources available to it; in other words, districts must have substantially equal access to similar revenues per pupil at similar levels of tax effort. Children who live in poor districts and children who live in rich districts must be afforded a substantially equal opportunity to have access to educational funds.[64]

The *Edgewood* court also rejected the State's argument that a holding of unconstitutionality would destroy the local control in the system, because "[a]n efficient system will actually allow for more local control, not less."[65] In another stinging reply to the defendants' "money doesn't matter" theory, the court held that "[t]he amount of money spent on a student's education has a real and meaningful impact on the educational opportunity offered that student."[66]

The *Edgewood I* court did retreat from the district court's judgment in at least two ways. The district court held that the State must have a school finance system in which all school districts have the *same* ability to raise revenues and all students have the *same* opportunity to educational funds. The supreme court substituted the more flexible *substantially* equal access and *substantially* equal opportunity.

Apparently to assuage the fears of wealthy school districts, the court noted that an efficient system does not "mean that local communities would be precluded from supplementing an efficient system established by the legislature; however any local enrichment must derive solely from local tax effort."[67] This ambiguous clarification presaged the opinion in *Edgewood IIa* specifically allowing unequalized enrichment,[68] i.e., that above some level of taxation districts can tax and keep all the funds generated without any supplementation from the State. At these levels of taxation, the vast differences in tax wealth decried by the *Edgewood I* court allow disparities in revenues of 100 to 1 or more in generated funds. Limiting the amount of taxes that can be generated without supplementation (often called guaranteed yield or power equalizing) has always been a goal of advocates for low-wealth districts.

Texas Legislature's Response to *Edgewood I*

Soon after the *Edgewood I* opinion, several groups advocated for school finance systems that they argued would meet the supreme court's requirements. This section focuses on the plans recommended by the low-wealth districts – the *Edgewood* plaintiffs and the *Alvarado* plaintiff-intervenors.

Based on previous theoretical work and computer modeling by IDRA, Dr. Jose Cardenas and Dr. Albert Cortez of IDRA and I, a MALDEF attorney, designed and promoted the Uribe-Luna plan, named for its Senate sponsor Senator Hector Uribe (D-Cameron)[69] and House sponsor Representative Gregory Luna (D-Bexar).[70] The Uribe-Luna plan consolidated the tax bases of each county's school districts, taxed that property at a set rate, distributed that money to districts within the county on an equal weighted student basis and then allowed additional equalized funding above the county equalized level. In other words, all the tax revenues generated in a county up to tax rates of $ .80[71] would be combined in that county and distributed to each district on a per weighted student basis. The plan would have replaced the 700-1 disparities in wealth per pupil among Texas's more than 1000 school districts to a much smaller ratio of about 10 to 1 between the richest and poorest of Texas's 254 counties.

In the Uribe-Luna plan, school districts could supplement the funds from the county with additional equalized funds based on tax rates above $ .80. The Uribe-Luna plan still included some disequalization caused by the disparities among counties; but the plan was almost completely equitable and also "recaptured" hundreds of millions of dollars of revenue from wealthy districts that had historically been protected from equal taxation. The plan was the first plan recommended to the Texas legislature that included recapture, i.e., requiring very wealthy districts to share some part of their tax revenue with the State or other school districts.[72]

Craig Foster of the Equity Center and the plaintiff intervenors recommended a 95-95 plan designed to guarantee to the districts with 95% of the students the revenue available to the district at the 95th percentile of wealth per weighted student. In other words, the legislature would be committed to design and fund a system that would allow at least 95 % of students to attend school within districts that, by a combination of state and local funds would have access to the same revenue available to one of the wealthiest school districts in the state. In effect the 95-95 plan became the base for the first school finance system designed to respond to *Edgewood I*, known as Senate Bill 1,[73] and the Uribe-Luna bill became the basis for the school finance system developed in 1993, the CED plan, after the Supreme court held that Senate Bill 1 was unconstitutional.

Edgewood II

Court Proceedings and DecisionsAfter several unsuccessful special sessions of the Texas Legislature in early 1990, the district court appointed three masters to draw up, but not disseminate, an alternative school finance plan that could be implemented with existing state funds should the legislature fail to develop a plan.[74] The threat of a court injunction of state funding and implementation of the masters' plan finally led the Texas Legislature to pass Senate Bill 1 in June 1990. Plaintiffs and plaintiff intervenors immediately asked the district court to declare Senate Bill 1 unconstitutionally inefficient.

After a two-week trial, Judge Scott McCown,[75] a new judge hearing the case, held Senate Bill 1 unconstitutional. For the reasons listed below, the state supreme court again unanimously found the system to violate the efficiency clause of the Texas Constitution.

In *Edgewood II*, the Texas Supreme Court pointed out the basic weaknesses of Senate Bill 1, as follows:

> Even if the approach of Senate Bill 1 produces a more equitable utilization of state educational dollars, it

does not remedy the major causes of the wide opportunity gaps between rich and poor districts. It does not change the boundaries of any of the current 1052 school districts, the wealthiest of which continues to draw funds from a tax base roughly 450 times greater per weighted pupil than the poorest district. It does not change the basic funding allocation, with approximately half of all education funds coming from local property taxes rather than state revenue. And it makes no attempt to equalize access to funds among all districts. By limiting the funding formula to districts in which 95% of the students attend school, the Legislature excluded 132 districts which educate approximately 170,000 students and harbor about 15% of the property wealth in the state. A third of our students attend school in the poorest districts which also have about 15% of the property wealth in the state. Consequently, after Senate Bill 1, the 170,000 students in the wealthiest districts are still supported by local revenues drawn from the same tax base as the 1,000,000 students in the poorest districts.

These factors compel the conclusion as a matter of law that the State has made an unconstitutionally inefficient use of its resources. The fundamental flaw of Senate Bill 1 lies not in any particular provisions but in its overall failure to restructure the system. Most property owners must bear a heavier tax burden to provide a less expensive education for students in their districts, while property owners in a few districts

> bear a much lighter burden to provide more funds for their students. Thus, Senate Bill 1 fails to provide "a direct and close correlation between a district's tax effort and the educational resources available to it [quoting *Edgewood I*]." [76]

In *Edgewood II*, the court took the additional step of commenting on "available avenues toward greater efficiency."[77] In other words, the supreme court was recommending remedies much more fundamental than anything tried before in Texas school finance. The court took the brave step of recommending school district consolidation (often described as "the third rail" or the "c" of Texas school finance) or tax base consolidation.[78] The recommendation of tax base consolidation was especially provocative. After the Uribe-Luna plan was introduced at the district court hearing on Senate Bill 1, the district court expressed reservations about the plan's constitutionality in light of an old, but venerated Texas Supreme Court opinion, *Love v. City of Dallas*.[79] The supreme court dismissed the trial court's "Love" problem with a clear support for tax base consolidation:

> We disagree with the district court's observation that this option "appears to run afoul of certain constitutional provisions related to taxation.
>
> . . .
>
> Article VII of the Constitution accords the Legislature broad discretion to create school districts and define their taxing authority. The Constitution does not present a barrier to the general concept of tax base consolidation, and nothing in Love prevents creation of school districts along county or other lines for the purpose of collecting tax revenue and

> distributing it to other school districts within their boundaries. While consolidating tax bases may not alone assure substantially equal access to similar revenues, the district court erred in concluding that it is constitutionally prohibited.[80]

After the *Edgewood II* opinion, supporters of school finance equity in general, and advocates of a recapture systems in particular, were very optimistic. The optimism was further enhanced by the change in governor from a very strong anti tax governor to one that most Texans felt would be more amenable to additional taxes or more comprehensive school finance reform.

The plaintiff-intervenor school districts then filed a motion for rehearing to ask the supreme court to overrule the *Love*[81] case and specifically approve of state-wide recapture.[82] The court denied the rehearing; but, in effect, five of its nine judges wrote a significant new opinion. The opinion denying rehearing resurrected the *Love* case and the relevance of Tex. Const. Art VII §3 and Art VIII §1-e to the consideration of school finance remedies. This "Opinion On Motion for Rehearing"[83] (generally known as *Edgewood IIa*) was the first opinion to split the supreme court into factions and set the stage for the many future challenges by wealthy districts and defenses by the State against school finance equity.

In *Edgewood IIa* the supreme court changed its fairly ambiguous position in *Edgewood I* about the power of local school districts to raise unequalized funds from their widely varying school tax bases. The opinion held that the Texas Constitution clearly recognizes the distinction between state and local taxes and that the ability of school districts to tax at levels above the state system is constitutionally required by Art. VII §3. The five justices concluded:

> These constitutional provisions mandate that local tax revenue is not subject to state-wide recapture. …
>
> This conclusion highlights the basic constitutional distinction between the State's primary obligation and the local districts' secondary contributions. The current system remains unconstitutional not because *any* unequalized local supplementation is employed, but because the State relies so heavily on unequalized local funding in attempting to discharge its duty to "make suitable provision for the support and maintenance of an efficient system of public free schools." Tex. Const. Art. VII, §1. Once the Legislature provides an efficient system in compliance with article VII, section 1, it may, so long as efficiency is maintained, authorize local school districts to supplement their educational resources if local property owners approve an additional local property tax."[85] (emphasis in original)

Legislative Response to Edgewood II — the CED System

The *Edgewood II* opinion forced the legislature to consider long-term structural changes to the system. Though the *Edgewood IIa* rehearing opinion slowed down the momentum, the legislature was on the road to designing some system which both more efficiently and equitably used the resources of the State.

In *Edgewood II*, the supreme court set an April 1, 1991 deadline for the legislature to either pass a constitutional system or face an injunction of school funding.[85] Indeed, the supreme court specifically told the district court not to extend this time deadline.[86] Under this judicial pressure, in 1991, the legislature developed County Education Districts (CED) in Senate Bill 351, closely modeling the Uribe-Luna structure of consolidating county tax bases. Indeed, S.B. 351 went a step further than the Uribe-Luna plan. S.B. 351 created 188 CED's including 31 multi-county districts in areas where the wealth per pupil of individual counties was so great that the State would not be able to equalize the low-wealth counties up to the level of the wealthy county.[87] This was the first time that the Texas Legislature had passed a plan that would actually require school districts to "share" their tax revenues, and, as might be expected, the reaction of wealthy districts and their many allies was swift and severe, and led right back to the courthouse.

Edgewood III 1991-1992

At this stage in the litigation the wealthy defendant-intervenor districts, led by Carrollton Farmers Branch and Highland Park, changed from defenders of the state system to the challengers, and plaintiff and plaintiff-intervenors, the *Edgewood* and *Alvarado* parties, joined the State to defend the system. As did the legislature, the district court read the *Edgewood II* opinion to be strongly in support of tax base consolidation and upheld S.B. 351.[88] Indeed, the supreme court had found that "the district court had erred in concluding that it [tax base consolidation] is constitutionally prohibited."[89]

Embracing the arguments that had been raised by the state and wealthy districts and rejected in *Edgewood I* and *Edgewood II*,[90] the supreme court in *Edgewood III* declared the school finance system unconstitutional under provisions requiring voter approval of school district taxes[91] and prohibiting state wide ad valorem taxes.[92]

The *Edgewood III* court first summarized the history of the Texas school finance struggle[93] and the details of the S.B. 351[94] system.[95] The court described the parts of the school finance system that had remained the same as the system found unconstitutional in *Edgewood I* and *Edgewood II* and the changes made by SB 351. Specifically the opinion summarized the "dramatic"[96] changes "in the manner in which local funds are contributed to the system"[97] as follows:

> The State has moved from encouraging school districts to contribute local tax revenue, to conditioning state funds on such contribution, to mandating a specified contribution. This has reduced the geographical disparities in the availability of revenue for education. It has accomplished this, however, by requiring the taxpayers in one school district, without a vote of approval, to fund the schools in other districts over which they have no control.

The court described a continuum of state involvement in local tax matters: from state authorization of a tax with authorization "to levy it entirely up to local authorities, to be approved by the voters if necessary,"[98] which would be a local tax, "[t]o the other extreme, if the State mandates the levy of a tax at a set rate and prescribes the distribution of the proceeds"[99] which would be "a state tax, irrespective of whether the State acts in its own behalf or through an intermediary."[100] This summary and the general analysis of the court in *Edgewood III* became the structure that the state used to design its next school finance system in 1993 — the first, and to this writing, only system that was upheld by the Texas Supreme Court.[101]

The *Edgewood III* court also relied on article VII §3, criticized in the opinion as "a constitutional wilderness,…a rather patched up and overly cobbled enactment," and "an example of how not to write a constitution,"[102] as support for the proposition that "before CED's may levy the statutory tax, it must be approved by the voters in the CED."[103] Replying to a stinging dissent[104] by Justices Doggett[105] and Mauzy[106] the majority in *Edgewood III* defended its opinion and the opinion's consistency with *Edgewood I* and *Edgewood II*. The court specifically rebuffed the allegation in the dissent that the legislature had been mislead by the supreme court's *Edgewood II* opinion to believe that tax base consolidation would be approved, by quoting testimony of the state's attorney and others before the various committees considering S.B. 351.[107]

Justice Cornyn's[108] concurring and dissenting opinion in *Edgewood III* presaged his majority opinion in Edgewood IV and the court's transformation of *Edgewood* from an equity case to an adequacy case.[109] Justice Cornyn wrote that:

> An efficient school system cannot be achieved through simple control of the inputs to the system (and certainly not through control of funding alone); the outputs of the system must be monitored and measured against a standard and the inputs must then be adjusted to correct any deficiencies.[110]

In his opinion in *Edgewood III*, Justice Cornyn also challenged the unanimous holding in *Edgewood I* that "[t]he amount of money spent on a student's education has a real and meaningful impact on the educational opportunity offered to that student."[111] Cornyn quoted adverse social science literature and in effect cross- examined the unanimous opinion of his own court by quoting the same sort of evidence that was rejected in *Edgewood I* and *Edgewood II*.[112] Justice Cornyn did cite with apparent support the work of other state supreme courts that have sought to define the level of education required by their respective state constitutions, e.g. *Rose v. Council for Better Educ.*, 790 S.W. 2d. 186 (Ky. 1989), and then determine the compliance of the system with the constitutional standard. This is the adequacy test, but it was a minor issue in *Edgewood I* and *Edgewood II.* We will consider later in this chapter the *Edgewood VI*[113] decision that did define the constitutional requirement and determined that the Texas system met that standard.

Justice Doggett's dissent[114] detailed that the issues decided in *Edgewood III* to declare S.B. 351 unconstitutional had already been presented to the court in *Edgewood I*[115] and again presented and decided in *Edgewood II.*[116] In each case, the supreme court had found the Art. VIII §1-e and Art. VII §3 not to invalidate a school finance system based on the consolidation of tax bases. Justice Doggett went on to describe Justice Cornyn's opinion as "revisionism" of the court's *Edgewood I* opinion.[117]

Edgewood IV

Development of the Present Texas System of School Finance, 1993-1995

After a year of consideration of a wide variety of proposals to design a school finance system that would meet the standards of *Edgewood I, II and III,*[118] the legislature passed a proposed constitutional amendment that would have allowed state-wide recapture of property taxes. The proposal was soundly defeated by the voters on May 1, 1993.

To meet the court's deadline of June 1, 1993, the legislature then rapidly passed Senate Bill 7[119], which continued the allowance of recapture of local ad valorem funds through a system of five alternatives available to school districts. In order to reduce the district's wealth to a limit of $280,000 per weighted student, a wealthy district could:

(1) consolidate with another district;

(2) detach territory;

(3) purchase average daily attendance credit;

(4) contract for the education of nonresident students; or

(5) consolidate its tax base with another district.

Tex. Educ. Code §36.003.[120]

Both the CED system and the Senate Bill 7 "five option" system had at least these four characteristics that increased the equity and the efficiency of the systems:

1. Recapture of tax revenues from extremely wealthy school districts (those with taxable values per weighted student above the level set in the statute) neutralized the advantages that allowed extremely wealthy districts to raise and spend much more than other districts (and of course use those extra funds to hire and retain the best teachers and implement the best enrichment programs).
2. The addition of the recaptured funds of from $400,000,000 to $ 1,200,000,000 per year [121](an increase of approximately 5% revenue in the system) allowed the State to raise the poorer and middle-wealth districts to a higher revenue level.
3. The tax cap of $1.50[122] for maintenance and operations (M & O) prevented the wealthiest districts from raising "unequalized" funds that, even after recapture, would allow an advantage of 30-1 in revenues per penny of tax.
4. The system was based completely on weighted student funding, i.e., districts were guaranteed certain revenue per weighted student, taking into consideration the extra costs of students with special educational needs or districts with special costs.

However, both systems had at least these inequitable

characteristics:

1. The level at which recapture occurred built in advantages for the wealthiest districts, i.e., the recapture regime did not recapture all the revenue necessary to bring the wealthiest districts down to the level that the State could guarantee. Indeed, SB 7 had an admitted gap of $600 per weighted student on top of a system guaranteeing up to $4,000 per weighted student.
2. The system did not guarantee any tax rate above $1.50, which was available to districts for interest and sinking fund tax rates (I & S) for facilities up to $.50 above the $1.50 basic tax rate. This could allow an additional gap of up to $1,500 per weighted student.

Court Proceedings and Decisions

Unlike the systems addressed in *Edgewood I, II, and III*, Senate Bill 7 was attacked by a variety of groups alleging a wider variety of claims:

1. Low-wealth districts alleged that the system was still inefficient and failed to meet the Edgewood I standard of "substantially equal access to similar revenues per pupil at similar levels of tax effort."[123] Low-wealth districts specifically objected to the failure of the system to fund facilities.
2. Wealthy districts and some others alleged that the State had abdicated its responsibility to make suitable provision for the schools by relying too heavily on local tax revenues to fund the system and that the system with the "five options" still violated the prohibition of a state wide ad valorem tax. They also continued their arguments that the statute created a state-wide ad valorem tax.
3. Several new groups of intervening districts argued that S.B. 7 violated other Texas constitutional prohibitions of grants or

lending of public money, delegation of powers to the commissioner of education, judicial review, impairment of contracts, local or special laws, and even violations of the federal Voting Rights Act.

4. A new group of plaintiff-intervenors argued that the Texas Constitution guarantees a voucher system requiring the state to allow parents to use state education funds to pay for the private or public school of their choice.

Judge McCown upheld SB 7 against all challenges; however he upheld the low-wealth districts' claim that the failure to fund facilities continued to violate the *Edgewood I* standards. The evidence that at $2.00 tax rates, wealthy districts would have up to $1,500 per weighted student revenue more than poor districts at the same tax rate apparently convinced him that the facilities part of the system remained inefficient.

In 1995, for the first and only time to date, the Texas Supreme Court found a school finance system to meet constitutional standards. Eight of the nine justices held that the system met the Texas Constitution's efficiency standard. Five of the justices held that the recapture provisions did not violate the prohibitions of state wide ad valorem taxes.

However, the court in effect re-wrote the *Edgewood I* standard[123] for determining compliance with Art. VII §1. The majority also issued a warning about future tax increases that would approach the tax cap and make the system a prohibited state ad valorem tax; that comment set the stage for the *Edgewood VI* decision holding the tax cap provision to violate the Art VIII §1-e prohibition of state ad valorem taxes. Eight justices of the supreme court signed on the Cornyn opinion in *Edgewood IV* that significantly weakened[125] the *Edgewood I* standard from:

(1) "There must be a direct and close correlation between a district's tax effort and the educational resources available to it; in other words, districts must have substantially equal access to similar revenues per pupil at similar levels of tax effort. Children who live in poor districts and children who live in rich districts must be afforded a substantially equal opportunity to have access to educational funds," *Edgewood I* at 397, to

(2) "districts must have substantially equal access to funding up to the legislatively defined level that achieves the constitutional mandate of a general diffusion of knowledge" and "the Legislature equates the provision of a 'general diffusion of knowledge' with the provision of an accredited education. The accountability regime set forth in Chapter 35, we conclude, meets the Legislature's constitutional obligation to provide for a general diffusion of knowledge statewide." *Edgewood IV* at 730.

This change in the test weakened the *Edgewood I* decision in at least two ways. First, the test no longer applied to the whole system, but only to the part of the system that the legislature decides meets accreditation standards. This was the argument that the State had made in *Edgewood I* that was unanimously rejected by the supreme court in 1989. Second, the test forces the *Edgewood* case to become an "adequacy" case, i.e., a successful challenge to the system must prove that the legislature's definition of the system does not meet the constitutional test of "general diffusion," or show that districts to do not have substantially equal access to the lower level system guaranteed by the State.

The *Edgewood IV* court rejected the wealthy districts' claim that SB 7's options combined with the tax caps created a state wide ad valorem tax.[126] This was based on the court's determination that the restrictions in SB 7 "do not at this time approach the level of control exercised in Senate Bill 351, which set uniform tax rates and prescribed the distribution of all tax proceeds."[127] The *Edgewood IV* court did issue a warning about the future constitutionality of the tax cap:

> However, if the cost of providing for a general diffusion of knowledge continues to rise, as it surely will, the minimum rate at which a district must tax will also rise. Eventually, some districts may be forced to tax at the maximum allowable rate just to provide a general diffusion of knowledge. If a cap on tax rates were to become in effect a floor as well as a ceiling, the conclusion that the Legislature had set a statewide ad valorem tax would appear to be unavoidable because the districts would then have lost all meaningful discretion in setting the tax rate.[128]

The court also rejected the low-wealth districts' claims[129] that, even if the funding of programs was efficient, the facilities portion of the system, not equalized by the State, was in itself inefficient. Relying on its holding that the system must be considered as a whole and that the low-wealth districts had not provided a sufficient record of lack of access to facilities, the court found that "under the present record, plaintiffs have not yet proved that the State has breached its duty to efficiently provide for a general diffusion of knowledge simply because Senate Bill 7 does not include a separate facilities component."[130] Justice Rose Spector dissented and argued that the system was still not efficient. She also strongly criticized the new standard applied in the decision and its lack of foundation in the history of the case or in the facts or briefing before the court. Claims that the Texas Constitution guarantees a "voucher system" were not justiciable because the parties asserting those claims were asking the court to prescribe the structure of the state's public school system.

So, S.B. 7 met all the constitutional tests. However, to their credit, the supreme ourt noted the significant structural and funding problems that remained in the system and concluded: "Our judgment in this case should not be interpreted as a signal that the school finance crisis in Texas has ended."[131]

The five justice majority that upheld SB 7 appeared to be a compromise between those judges still very concerned about the equity of the system and those with continued concerns about the "recapture" provisions. The compromise allowed the majority to uphold the system, and, in effect, get the supreme court out of the school finance morass for several years.

Edgewood V

Though the *Edgewood IV* opinion did not uphold low-wealth districts' claims that the facilities funding system violated the Texas Constitution, the Legislature did in 1997 and 1999 set up new funding programs for facilities. However, after four rounds of litigation and the design and review of four separate systems of school finance in 6 years (1989 to 1995), the parties and the legislature took a break from making significant changes to the system or challenging other parts of it.

Changes in Texas school finance that led to the challenge

The consistency of the system after S.B. 7 allowed school districts to focus on capital improvements and basic education. Unfortunately, after *Edgewood IV*, the State did not significantly increase its contribution to the school finance system and the "state share" of the system slowly decreased. Six years after *Edgewood IV*, four wealthy school districts filed a separate lawsuit alleging that the tax cap of S.B. 7 had become a state ad valorem tax as the supreme court had predicted might occur.[132] The low-wealth districts saw this challenge as an effort to reverse the recapture provisions and allow wealthy districts to "run away" from the rest of the system by increasing taxes above the state guaranteed level. So, low-wealth districts intervened in the case to defend the tax cap and recapture provisions, and to attack the remaining inefficiency and inadequacy of the system.

The district court dismissed the wealthy districts' claims on the pleadings, and the Texas Court of Appeals affirmed the dismissal.[133] The supreme court reversed the lower courts, holding that the plaintiff wealthy school districts could go to trial to prove their allegations.[134] Specifically, the court held that plaintiffs had the right to prove that the districts were "forced to tax at maximum rates either to meet accreditation standards or to provide a general diffusion of knowledge."[135] Further, a "single district states a claim under art VIII §1-e if it alleges that it is constrained by the State to tax at a particular rate."[136]

So, in 2003 the Texas Supreme Court set the standards for the next round of school finance in Texas — a classic adequacy case.

Edgewood VI

Return to Court and Trial Court Decision

School districts with one half of all the students in Texas (approximately 2 million of the 4.3 million students) participated in the trial court in *Edgewood VI*.[137] They were organized into three groups of districts. The most populous districts in the state and a wide range of other districts joined the original four wealthy districts

(West-Orange Cove Consolidated Independent School District) to assert that the tax cap violated the prohibition against state-wide ad valorem taxes, Art. VIII §1-e, and added a claim that the system was not adequate and cannot achieve a "general diffusion of knowledge" as required by Art. VII §1. The *Edgewood* intervenors and *Alvarado* intervenors joined in the adequacy case, but added the claim that the system still did not meet the efficiency standard of Art. VII §1, the original violation found in *Edgewood I*.

The parties created an incredibly detailed and well-documented record in the case in a five-week trial. Based on the excellent record and pleadings of the parties, the district court wrote the most thorough description of the positive and negative aspects of the school finance system of any of the cases.[138] The district court held the Texas school finance system unconstitutional as a violation of both the adequacy required by Art. VII §1 and the prohibition of state ad valorem taxes, under Art. VIII § 1-e. The district specifically held the facilities and weighting systems for bilingual and compensatory education to violate the adequacy provisions.

The district court also held that the system violated the "efficiency" provision of Art. VII §1,[139] because the systems failed to provide an efficient system for facilities funding. However, the district court rejected the claims of the *Edgewood* and *Alvarado* intervenors that the basic funding system (the maintenance and operations part) remained inefficient. All the parties appealed and the case went back to the supreme court, which had outlined the contours of the case in 2003.

Supreme Court Decision

In *Edgewood VI*,[140] the Texas Supreme Court upheld its right to review the Texas school finance system and school districts' rights to challenge the system, i.e., the adherence of the system to Texas constitutional standards is justiciable and school districts have standing to challenge the system. However, the *Edgewood VI* opinion further weakened the constitutional tests for school finance that had been developed in *Edgewood IV* and *V*; and indeed, as described earlier in this chapter, the *Edgewood IV* and *V* tests themselves are weakened versions of the test developed in *Edgewood I* and *II*.

After rejecting the State's proposed standard of review of Art VII §1 challenges as "rational basis" ("That provision [Art. VII § 1] does not allow the Legislature to structure a public school system that is inadequate, inefficient, or unsuitable, regardless of whether it has a rational basis or even a compelling reason for doing so."[141]),the supreme court adopted an arbitrariness standard of review. "If the Legislature's choices are informed by guiding rules and principles properly related to public education-that is, if the choices are not arbitrary-then the system does not violate the constitutional provision."[142] Then, the court summarized its new standard as follows:

> Whether the statutory provisions creating the public school system are arbitrary and therefore unconstitutional is a question of law. To the extent that this determination rests on factual matters that are in dispute, we must, of course, rely entirely on the district court's findings. But in deciding ultimately the constitutional issues, those findings have a limited role.[143]

This test not only sets a very high standard for supporting a claim of unconstitutionality of a school finance system, it also deemphasizes the fact finding powers of a trial court and places the final decision on "arbitrariness" in the hands of the supreme court.

From the perspective of the low-wealth districts, the court added insult to injury when it then weakened the application of the legislature's standards for its education system (previously equated by the court with its definition of "a general diffusion of knowledge," the language of the education clause.) After quoting with apparent approval the Texas law on the goals of education[144] (which includes such vague terms as "access to" and "meaningful opportunity to acquire") the court added this further limitation:

> We agree, with one caveat. The public education system need not operate perfectly; it is adequate if districts are *reasonably* able to provide their students the access and opportunity the district court described.[145] (emphasis in original)

This fuzzy definition was apparently necessary to uphold the Texas education finance system. Districts with passing rates of 54% on the Texas reading tests and 42% on the Texas math tests were considered acceptable,[146] and the State has set low standards based on vague definitions for other parts of its accountability system such as drop out rates.[147]

After a short but accurate summary of the evidence on the incredible struggles and demands on Texas school districts, the court weighed these hardships against the increase in standardized test scores in Texas and Texas's improvement relative to other states in NAEP scores. Pulling together its new fuzzy tests, the supreme court concluded:

> "Having carefully reviewed the evidence and the district court's findings, we cannot conclude that the Legislature has acted arbitrarily in structuring and funding the public education system so that school

> districts are not reasonably able to afford all students the access to education and the educational opportunity to accomplish a general diffusion of knowledge."[148]

As might be expected, the State's school finance system passed the test set out by the court, and the system was found to be efficient, suitable, and adequate.[149]

System Violates State Ad Valorem Tax Prohibition

However, the Court did find one violation of the constitution. The supreme court held that the $1.50 tax cap, which had a disproportionately negative effect on wealthy districts, violated the prohibition of a state wide ad valorem tax, Art. VIII §1-e. At this point in the opinion, the court looked with great sensitivity on the challenges of districts:

> struggling to maintain accreditation with increasing standards, a demographically diverse and changing student population, and fewer qualified teachers, while cutting budgets even further. The district court found that due to inadequate funding: 52.8% of the newly hired teachers in 2002 were not certified, up from 14.1% in 1996; more teachers were being required to teach outside their areas of expertise; and attrition and turnover were growing. The court cited the higher costs of educating economically disadvantaged students and students with limited English proficiency, noting that 90% of the growth in the student population has come from low-income families. And as set out in more detail above, the district court noted the increased curriculum, testing,

> and accreditation standards, and the increased costs of meeting them. These are facts, not opinions.[150]

The court also noted that the State controlled the expenditure of $1 billion per year of recaptured funds, and "the state's control of this local revenue is a significant factor in considering whether local taxes have become a state property tax."[151]

After noting that a very high percentage of districts were taxing at or near the maximum tax rate of $1.50, the court found that districts had lost "meaningful discretion" to tax at rates lower than the maximum rate.[152] Thus, only a few pages after it held that the system was efficient, suitable and adequate, the court held that districts are being forced to tax at the maximum rates just to provide an adequate education. So the real problem, according the supreme court, is that wealthy districts are not able to supplement their systems, which are already much better funded than the poor districts- but all the districts have enough. Possibly realizing the inconsistency of their holdings, the court did not just invalidate the tax cap,[153] which they acknowledged would be incredibly disequalizing and lead to an inefficient system.[154] Instead, the court enjoined the entire system and gave the State six months to cure it.

Legislative Reaction

In response to *Edgewood VI*, the Legislature reduced local property taxes and put significant additional state funds into the system.[155] This did slightly increase the equity of the system, but did not raise the levels of funding to any significant extent. The new system did indirectly reduce the amount of recaptured funds and will greatly extend and broaden the hold harmless provisions of the system. The system passed in 2006 and slightly amended in 2007 does allow some more school district discretion to raise tax rates, and almost guarantees another *Edgewood* lawsuit as even wealthy districts run out of funds to run their schools and maintain their advantages over the remainder of the state's children.

Analysis

Though this chapter has criticized the changes in the Texas Supreme Court's jurisprudence in the area of school finance, there is no doubt that the courts, both the trial courts and the supreme court, have had a very significant and positive effect on the equity and funding levels of the Texas school finance system. Of course, that effect was only realized because of the hard work and bravery of community members, advocacy groups, legislators and attorneys.

Importantly, the *Edgewood* cases directly led to a great decrease, but not complete removal, of the link between property wealth per student and revenue per student. One summary of the data on this concluded:

> To a large degree, the new finance scheme has significantly reduced the link between local property values and access to revenues. During the 1988-1989 [the year before the first Edgewood Supreme Court decision] school year, the correlation between tax effort and revenue was only 0.37 while the correlation between wealth and revenue was 0.75. By 1994, the correlation between tax effort and revenue was 0.81 and the correlation between wealth and revenue was only 0.34. Put another way, in 1989, wealth explained 56% of the variation in revenue for local districts, while tax effort explained only 13.5%. By 1994, wealth only explained 18% of the variation, while tax

effort accounted for 65%.[156]

In other words, now the wealth of the district in which a student lives has much less effect than the tax rate on the revenues available. Moreover, the overall funding for facilities and programs in low-wealth school districts has significantly improved. Unfortunately, the conditions in Texas had been so bad for so long — and are still not completely fair — that we have not yet achieved our goal of true equal educational opportunity for all students.

---

1 Assistant Professor of Law, St. Mary's School of Law, San Antonio, Texas. B.S. Massachusetts Institute of Technology, J.D., University of Texas at Austin. I want to acknowledge my teachers in school finance, Dr. Jose A. Cárdenas, Dr. Albert Cortéz, Craig Foster and James Vasquez. They have been my technical, political and emotional models as well as friends. I also want to thank my law clerks, Debra Elzner and Diana Cavazos, St.Mary's law school students, for their research and comments. And the chapter was improved by the comments of my co-workers on the case, Dr. Albert Cortez, Roger Rice, Peter Roos and David Hinojosa. I have written a much more detailed and critical description of the changes in legal doctrine through the six cases in Albert H. Kauffman, *The Texas School Finance Litigation Saga: Great Progress, Then Near Death by a Thousand Cuts*, 40 St. Mary's L.J. 511 (2008).

2 *Edgewood Indep. Sch. Dist. v. Kirby*, 777 S.W.2d 391 (Tex. 1989) (*Edgewood I*).

Edgewood Indep. Sch. Dist. v. Kirby, 804 S.W.2d 491 (Tex. 1991) (*Edgewood II*).

Carrollton-Farmers Branch Indep. Sch. Dist. v. Edgewood Indep. Sch. Dist., 826 S.W.2d 489 (Tex. 1992) (*Edgewood III*).

Edgewood Indep. Sch. Dist. v. Meno, 917 S.W.2d 717 (Tex. 1995) (*Edgewood IV*).

W. Orange-Cove Consol. Indep. Sch. Dist. v. Alanis, 107 S.W.3d 558 (Tex. 2003) (*Edgewood V*).

Neely v. W. Orange-Cove Consol. Indep. Sch. Dist., 176 S.W.3d 746 (Tex. 2005) (*Edgewood VI*).

3 The author of this chapter wrote the original petition in Edgewood I in 1984 and was lead attorney for the Edgewood plaintiffs from 1984 to 2002. He was lead trial counsel for the Edgewood plaintiffs in Edgewood I-V, and argued Edgewood I, II and IV before the Texas Supreme Court.

4 Tex. Const. art. VII §§ 1-9 (2008).

5 See HB 1, 80th Session Texas Legislature (2007).

6 Cardenas, Jose A., TEXAS SCHOOL FINANCE REFORM, AN IDRA PERSPECTIVE, (Intercultural Development Research Association (IDRA 1997) (Cardenas); J. Steven Barr & Mark Trachtenberg, THE EDGEWOOD DRAMA: AN EPIC QUEST FOR EDUCATION EQUITY, 17 Yale L. & Policy Rev. 607 (1999) (Farr and Trachtenberg);

7 Walker, Billy D., and Kirby, William, THE BASICS OF TEXAS SCHOOL FINANCE, (Texas Association of School Boards (Austin, Texas 1986) (Walker and Kirby); Cardenas, supra at 1-5; Farr and Trachtenberg, supra, at 607-621.

8 Farr and Trachtenberg, supra at 621-626.

9 *Demetrio P. Rodriguez, et al. v. San Antonio Independent School District, et al.*, 337 F. Supp. 280 (W.D. Tex. 1971), *rev'd* 411 U.S. 1 (1973). The judges in that case were Goldberg, Roberts and Spears from Dallas, Austin and San Antonio respectively.

10 *Rodriguez, supra* at 58-59.

11 *Rodriguez, supra* at 36-37.

12 See Cárdenas, *supra*, pp. 1-5.

13 Mr. Rodriquez was also a plaintiff in the Edgewood cases filed in 1984. Mr. Rodriquez was only one of several individual plaintiffs in the *Rodriquez* case.

14 Willie Velasquez (1944-1988) was founder and first director of the Southwest Voter Registration Project.

15 Justice Spector was the first woman elected to the Texas Supreme Court, where she served from 1993 to 1998. She wrote a strong dissent in *Edgewood IV* supporting the claims of low-wealth districts for more equity.

16 Mark Yudof worked on the case as an attorney for the Harvard Center on Law and Education and continued work on the case as a University of Texas law professor. He has been the Chancellor of the University of Texas System, and in 2008 became the President of the University of California system.

17 Frank Herrera is the former chair of the board of the Mexican American Legal Defense and Educational Fund, Inc. and a leading Texas trial lawyer.

18 Warren Weir is a leading trial lawyer and antitrust lawyer in Texas and is former president of the San Antonio Bar Association.

19 *San Antonio Indep. Sch. Dist. v. Rodriguez*, 411 U.S. 1, 25-27 (1973).

20 Walker and Kirby, *supra* n. 7.

21 IDRA has been a leading national advocacy and research organization in San Antonio, Texas for 35 years (see http://www.idra.org/description).

22 Dr. Richard Hooker was a long term professor at the University of Houston and the author of many reports and legislative plans in Texas school finance. He was the lead witness in the first Edgewood trial.

23 See Cárdenas, *supra* at 199-216.

24 *Edgewood I*, supra, at 392-93.

25 Mexican American Legal Defense and Educational Fund, Inc. was started in San Antonio, Texas in 1968 and is now a national organization with headquarters in Los Angeles. See www.maldef.org.

26 Ms. Cantú, now a professor at the University of Texas' School of Law and School of Education, later became the Assistant Secretary of Education in charge of the Office for Civil Rights, 1993-2001.

27 Dr. Cortez has been a consistent expert and advocate on Texas school finance and has served as an expert in several of the Edgewood trials.

28 The Equity center was formed in 1982 by Jimmy Vasquez, José Cárdenas, Jimmy Lehman and Craig Foster. See http://www.equitycenter.org/about.asp

29 Multicultural Education, Training, and Advocacy, Inc. (META)

30 Roger Rice is the only attorney who has actively worked on the litigation and trial of both *Edgewood I* and *Edgewood VI*. He has been a national leader in education litigation for Latinos for 40 years, especially is cases involving English Language Learners and immigrant children. He has served as a mentor to me and succeeding MALDEF education lawyers since 1974.

31 Peter Roos has also been a national leader in education litigation for Latinos for 40 years and has been especially involved in issues of immigrant children in public and higher education.

32 After he read the first draft of the *Edgewood* petition, META attorney Roger Rice commented to Kauffman, the author of the first draft, "Where's the harm?," noting the lack of allegations of educational inadequacy and the focus on the financial system.

33 Texas venue provisions would have supported the filing of the case in any of these three cities as well as almost any other county in Texas.

34 *Serrano v. Priest*, 487 P. 2d 1241 (Cal. 1971)

35 I will defer to another day the inconsistency of Texas's approach to education in 1984 with the developing centralization of control manifested by the Texas testing regimen, the basic model for the No Child Left Behind Act accountability provisions.

36 § 1 - SUPPORT AND MAINTENANCE OF SYSTEM OF PUBLIC FREE SCHOOLS

A general diffusion of knowledge being essential to the preservation of the liberties and rights of the people, it shall be the duty of the Legislature of the State to establish and make suitable provision for the support and maintenance of an efficient system of public free schools.

37 § 3 - EQUAL RIGHTS

All free men, when they form a social compact, have equal rights, and no man, or set of men, is entitled to exclusive separate public emoluments, or privileges, but in consideration of public services.

38 § 3a - EQUALITY UNDER THE LAW

Equality under the law shall not be denied or abridged because of sex, race, color, creed, or national origin. This amendment is self-operative.

39 Edgewood, San Elizario, Socorro, Brownsville, Pharr-San Juan- Alamo, Eagle Pass, LaVega school districts were the original school district plaintiffs in the case. North Forest, Harlandale, Kenedy, Laredo, and Milano joined the lawsuit soon after it was filed.

40 In 1985-86, Mexican Americans comprised 30% of Texas public school students, but Mexican Americans comprised 95% of students in the poorest districts (with 5% of the total students in the state).

41 MEXICAN AMERICAN EDUCATION IN TEXAS: A FUNCTION OF WEALTH, Report IV of the Mexican American Education Study (U.S. Commission on Civil Rights, August 1972); Cardenas, *supra* at 124-132.

42 Since its inception in 1968, MALDEF had filed a series of lawsuits against Texas school districts and the state of Texas regarding segregation of Mexican Americans, bilingual education, the rights of undocumented children to attend Texas school districts as residents, redistricting and employment discrimination.

43 See Farr and Trachtenberg, *supra*, at 643-644.

44 David Richards was a successful U.S. Supreme Court advocate and the former first assistant attorney in the Texas Attorney General's office; he had a reputation as the top civil rights attorney in Texas. See David's autobiography: Richards, David, Once Upon a Time in Texas: A Liberal in the Lone Star State (Focus on American History Series, Center for American History, University of Texas at Austin, 2005) (Hardcover - April 15, 2002)

45 Richard Gray was a former First Assistant Attorney General, and had represented the state of Texas in difficult litigation regarding the state's prison system and redistricting efforts.

46 Section 3 - TAXES FOR BENEFIT OF SCHOOLS; SCHOOL DISTRICTS

(a) One-fourth of the revenue derived from the State occupation taxes shall be set apart annually for the benefit of the public free schools.
(b) It shall be the duty of the State Board of Education to set aside a sufficient amount of available funds to provide free text books for the use of children attending the public free schools of this State.
(c) Should the taxation herein named be insufficient the deficit may be met by appropriation from the general funds of the State.
(d) The Legislature may provide for the formation of school districts by general laws, and all such school districts may embrace parts of two or more counties.
(e) The Legislature shall be authorized to pass laws for the assessment and collection of taxes in all school districts and for the management and control of the public school or schools of such districts, whether such districts are

composed of territory wholly within a county or in parts of two or more counties, and the Legislature may authorize an additional ad valorem tax to be levied and collected within all school districts for the further maintenance of public free schools, and for the erection and equipment of school buildings therein; provided that a majority of the qualified voters of the district voting at an election to be held for that purpose, shall approve the tax. (Amended Aug. 14, 1883, Nov. 3, 1908, Aug. 3, 1909, Nov. 5, 1918, Nov. 2, 1920, Nov. 2, 1926, and Nov. 2, 1999.)

47 Dr. Cárdenas's school finance volume, see Cárdenas, *supra* fn. 3, includes the full texts of the original decision, pp. 221-224, judgment, pp. 224–226 and Findings of Fact and Conclusions of Law pp. 226-254.

48 June 1, 1987 judgment of district court, see Cárdenas, *supra*, fn 3 at 224.

49 *Kirby v. Edgewood Independent School District*, 761 S.W. 2d 859 (Tex. App. – Austin 1988), *rev'd*, 777 S.W. 2d 391 (Tex. 1989).

50 *San Antonio Independent School District v. Rodriquez*, 411 U.S. 1 (1973).

51 See fn 36, *supra*.

52 See fn 46, *supra*.

53 *Kirby*, *supra* fn. 49.

54 *Edgewood Indep. Sch. Dist. v. Kirby*, 777 S.W.2d 391 (Tex. 1989) (*Edgewood I*).

55 See fn 27, *supra*.

56 *Edgewood I supra* at 394.

57 *Id.*

58 *Id.*

59 The Judgment is included in Cardenas, *supra* pp. 224-226.

60 *Edgewood I*, *supra* at 398.

61 For a more detailed description of the equal rights-equal protection issues in the case, see Albert H. Kauffman & Carmen Maria Rumbaut, *Applying Edgewood v. Kirby to Fundamental Rights Under the Texas Constitution*, 22 St. Mary's L.J. 69 (1990).

62 *Edgewood I*, *supra* at 397.

63 *Id.*

64 *Id.*

65 *Edgewood I*, *supra* at 398.

66 *Edgewood I*, *supra* at 393.

67 *Edgewood I supra* at 398.

68 *Edgewood Indep. Sch. Dist. v. Kirby*, 804 S.W.2d 491 (Tex. 1991) (*Edgewood II*), at 499-500.

69 Senator Uribe's plan was filed as Tex. S.B. 9, 71st Leg., 3d C.S. (1990).

70 Representative Luna's plan was filed as Tex. H.B. 34, 71st Leg., 3d C.S. (1990).

71 Texas school district rates are based on a tax rate of $.01 per $100 of property value, i.e. .0001 of the value of the property. The inequality is manifested by the ability of a wealthy district with $1,000,000 property per student (e.g. the Highland Park school district in Dallas) to raise $10,000 per student with a $1.00 tax rate, while a district with $20,000 property per student (e.g. the Edgewood school district in San Antonio) can raise only $200 per student with a $1.00 tax rate.

72 The Uribe-Luna plan is described in more detail in Cárdenas, *supra*, n. 6 at 291-292.

73 Act of June 7, 1990, 71st Leg., 6th C.S., ch.1, 1990 Tex. Gen. Laws 1. However, this bill was not nearly as strong as the Equity Center 95-95 plan.

74 See Cárdenas, *supra*, 293-302.

75 Judge McCown was the trial judge in *Edgewood II, III. IV*, and *V*. He is now executive director of the Center for Public Priorities (see http://www.cppp.org/index.php) in Austin Texas and he is a very active and effective advocate for school finance and tax reform in Texas.

76 *Edgewood II*, *supra* at 496.

77 *Edgewood II*, *supra* at 497

78 *Id.*

79 *Love v. City of Dallas*, 120 Tex. 351, 40 S.W. 2d 20 (1931)

80 *Edgewood II*, *supra* at 497-498.

81 *Love*, *supra*,n.66.

82 Almost all of the attorneys and advocates for low-wealth districts involved in the *Edgewood* case, including the lawyers who filed it, think this rehearing motion was a tactical error. Of course, "retrospect is 20-20."

83 *Edgewood II*, *supra* at 499-500 (Edgewood IIa).

84 *Id.*

85 *Edgewood II*, *supra* at 499.

86 *Id.*

87 See Farr and Trachtenberg, *supra* n. 6 at 660-662; Cardenas, *supra* at 318-319.

88 *Edgewood I.S.D. v. Meno*, No. 362516A, (Travis County Dist. Ct. 250th Jud. Dist. Of Tex., Aug. 7,1991)

89 *Edgewood II*, *supra* at 498.

90 Though implicitly embraced in *Edgewood* IIa, see n. 83 *supra*.

91 Tex. Const. art. VII § 3a, *supra* n. 38.

92 Tex. Const. art. VIII § 1-e;.

§ 1-e – ABOLITION OF AD VALOREM PROPERTY TAXES

No State ad valorm taxes shall be levied upon any property within this State. (Added Nov. 5, 1968; amended Nov. 2, 1982, and Nov. 6, 2001).

93 *Edgewood III*, *supra* at 494-498.

94 Act of April 11, 1991, 72nd Leg. , R.S. , ch. 20, 1991 Tex Gen. Laws 381, amended by Act of May 27, 1991 Tex. Gen. Laws 1475.

95 *Edgewood III*, *supra* at 498-500.

96 *Edgewood III*, *supra* at 500.

97 *Id.*

98 *Edgewood III*, *supra* at 503.

99 *Id.*

100 *Id.*

101 See *Edgewood Indep. Sch. Dist. v. Alanis*, 917 S.W. 2d 717, 725 (Tex. 1995) (*Edgewood IV*).

102 *Edgewood III*, *supra* at 503.

103 *Edgewood III*, *supra* at 510.

104 *Edgewood III*, *supra* at 537-576

105 Rep. Doggett (D.-Tx.) has been a U.S. Representative from Texas since 1995. He was a former state senator from Austin.

106 Justice Mauzy was the author of the unanimous decision for the Court in *Edgewood I*. He was a former state senator from Dallas.

107 *Edgewood III*, *supra* at 513-514.

108 Senator Cornyn (R.-Tx.) later became the Texas Attorney General and has been a U.S. Senator from Texas since 2002.

109 There is a plethora of excellent literature on the difference between adequacy and equity school finance cases, e.g. see Rebell, M.A. (2002). Education adequacy, democracy, and the courts. In Ready, T., Edley, C., & Snow, C. (Eds.), *Achieving high educational standards for all* (pp. 218-267). Washington, D.C.: National Academy Press. and Kauffman, Albert, A Comparison of the Adequacy and Equity School Finance Cases (Rockefeller Foundation, 2003) see http://finance.tc-library.org/Content.asp?abstract=true&uid=832 (accessed May 1, 2008)

110 *Edgewood III*, supra at 529.

111 *Edgewood I*, *supra* at 393.

112 See for example *Edgewood III*, *supra* at 531, n. 12

113 *Neely v. W. Orange-Cove Consol. Indep. Sch. Dist.*, 176 S.W.3d 746 (Tex. 2005).

114 See n. 94, *supra*.

115 *Edgewood III*, *supra* at 540.

116 *Edgewood III*, *supra* at 540-543.

117 *Edgewood III*, *supra* at 570.

118 See Cardenas, *supra* at 331-345; Farr & Trachtenberg, *supra* at 672-677.

119 Act of May 28, 1993, 73rd Leg., R.S., ch. 347, 1993 Tex. Gen. Laws 1479.

120 Senate Bill 7 is described in the *Edgewood IV* decision, *Edgewood Indep. Sch. Dist. v. Meno*, 917 S.W.2d 717, 727-729 (Tex. 1995) (*Edgewood IV*).

121 See Neely v. W. Orange-Cove Consol. Indep. Sch. Dist., 176 S.W.3d 746, 760 (Tex. 2005).

122 The $1.50 tax rate in Texas is based on a tax per $100 of value of real property, i.e. 1.5% of the value.

123 *Edgewood I, supra* at 397.

124 I wrote a very critical essay about this change in the IDRA Special Bulletin of March 1995, See Cardeans, *supra*, pp. 347-350.

125 I will explain the method used to distort the *Edgewood I* opinion in an upcoming law review article in the St. Mary's Law Journal, November 2008.

126 *Id.*

127 *Id.*

128 *Edgewood IV, supra* at 738.

129 These facilities claims were upheld by the district court which issues an injunction against the issuance of bonds until a constitutional facilities system was implemented.

130 *Edgewood IV supra* at 747.

131 *Edgewood IV supra* at 725.

132 *Edgewood IV, supra* at 738.

133 *W. Orange-Cove Consol. Indep. Sch. Dist. v. Alanis*, 78 S.W.3d 529 (Tex.App.—Austin 2002), rev'd 107 S.W. 3d 558 (Tex. 2003)

134 *W. Orange-Cove Consol. Indep. Sch. Dist. v. Alanis*, 107 S.W.3d 558 (Tex. 2003) (*Edgewood V*).

135 *Edgewood V, supra* at 582.

136 *Edgewood V, supra* at 579.

137 *West Orange-Cove Consol. Indep. Sch. Dist. et al. v. Neeley et al.*, No. GV-100528 (250th Dist. Ct., Travis County, Tex., Nov. 30, 2004) (Edgewood VI).

138 The findings and conclusions and judgment of the district court are available at http://www.tea.state.tx.us/legal/FindingsofFactandConclusionsofLawWOC.pdf#xml=http://www.tea.state.tx.us/cgi/texis/webinator/search/xml.txt?query=Edgewood+case&db=db&id=389800dbd869dc64 . The facts of the case are summarized in the Supreme Court's Edgewood VI decision, *Neely v. W. Orange-Cove Consol. Indep. Sch. Dist.*, 176 S.W.3d 746, 755-770 (Tex. 2005) and in the briefs of the parties available on WestLaw, https://web2.westlaw.com/find/default.wl?fn=_top&rs=WLW8.04&rp=%2ffind%2fdefault.wl&mt=LawSchoolPractitioner&vr=2.0&sv=Split&cite=176+S.W.+3d+746

139 I will discuss the district court opinion in more detail during the discussion of

the *Edgewood VI* Supreme Court decision, *infra.*

140 *Neely v. W. Orange-Cove Consol. Indep. Sch. Dist.*, 176 S.W.3d 746 (Tex. 2005).

141 *Edgewood VI, supra* at 784.

142 *Edgewood VI, supra* at 785.

143 *Id.*

144 TEX. EDUC. CODE §§ 4.001 (a) and 28.001

145 Edgewood VI, *supra* at 787.

146 *West Orange-Cove I.S.D. v. Neeley*, No. GV-1000528 (250th dist Ct., Travis County, Tex. Nov. 30, 2004), at 14-15.

147 *Edgewood VI* district court opinion at 9-14; also see more accurate attrition rates for Texas schools of 33 % total, 40% for African American and 45% for Hispanic in 2005-2006, Roy Johnson, *High School Attrition Rates Across Texas Education Service Center Regions* (IDRA May 22, 2008)

148 *Edgewood VI, supra* at 789.

149 For an analysis of *Edgewood VI* from an educator's perspective, see Dr. Albert Cortez, in IDRA newsletter at www.idra.org/IDRA_Newsletter/February_2006_Fair_Funding/A_Decision_Neither_Adequate_nor_Equitable/

150 *Edgewood VI, supra* at 796.

151 *Edgewood VI, supra* at 797.

152 *Id.*

153 The SB 7 system did not allow recapture of funds at taxes above $1.50 and did not supplement local funds above $1.50, so the inequalities would again be in the range of 100-1 or 200-1, i.e. the richest districts could raise an additional $10,000 per student with the $.50 tax rate available above $1.50 and the poorest districts could raise only an additional $100 per student with the $.50 tax rate available above $1.50.

154 *Edgewood VI, supra* at 798-799.

155 See description of the new bill in the Equity Center newsletter, www.equitycenter.org/members/newsletters/June2006.pdf (accessed May 1, 2008)

156 J. Steven Barr & Mark Trachtenberg, THE EDGEWOOD DRAMA: AN EPIC QUEST FOR EDUCATION EQUITY, 17 Yale L. & Policy Rev. 607, 704 (1999).

6 The Leandro Case: Leandro v. State of North Carolina

by Robert W. Spearman

The *Leandro* case has been described by one commentator as perhaps "the most important in modern state history because it established a right not previously recognized and directed the state to assure its deliverance."[1] The litigation was hard fought by the State, which battled plaintiffs "for a decade but ultimately lost on key points."[2]

Introduction

Leandro v. State of North Carolina was filed in Halifax County North Carolina in May 1994. In 2008 it was still pending. In 14 years of litigation, it has resulted in two major State Supreme Court opinions. The first, a decision on the pleadings in 1997, ruled that North Carolina schoolchildren had a judicially enforceable constitutional right to a sound basic education. The second, in 2004, affirmed a series of later superior court decisions after trials, and held the State had wrongfully denied this right to many State schoolchildren.

Subsequent trial court proceedings focused on proposals, plans and progress to remedy the established constitutional violations. The litigation has resulted in creation of a new Disadvantaged Students Supplemental Fund for at-risk students, full funding of a separate Low Wealth Fund to enhance education opportunities in low-wealth counties, institution of a statewide pre-kindergarten education program for at-risk four-year-olds, significant reductions of class sizes in early grades, and a variety of other education reforms and new programs.

Filing Suit: 1994

Representatives of several poor and rural eastern North Carolina school districts consulted with outside counsel in early 1994. Their superintendents and school board members were concerned that these districts lacked sufficient resources to provide an adequate education to their schoolchildren. A small supplemental funding program to aid low-wealth districts had been adopted by the State legislature in 1991, but efforts to expand it significantly had failed. Low-wealth rural districts were unable to provide students with the number or the quality of teachers employed in more wealthy urban local education agencies (LEAs). Compared to the rest of the State, teacher turnover rates in the low-wealth districts were very high and student graduation rates and test scores were low. Outside counsel were asked to assess the likelihood of obtaining substantially increased resources for these schools by litigation.[3]

Counsel concluded that after the U.S. Supreme Court *Rodriguez* decision, any challenge to the North Carolina school finance system based on federal equal protection standards would likely fail. But possible claims brought in North Carolina state court, based on the expansive, detailed language in the state constitution's education clauses, appeared more promising. Analysis was made of the pros and cons of various potential plaintiffs for reasons both of venue and standing. Ultimately the plaintiffs were the school boards of five low-wealth eastern North Carolina counties and parents and schoolchildren from those counties. The counties were Cumberland, Halifax, Hoke, Robeson and Vance. The counties had per capita incomes below the state average and all had significant percentages of minority students (African-American and/or American Indian). Many of their students participated in the free and reduced lunch program.

On May 25, 1994, the plaintiffs sued the State of North Carolina and the State Board of Education. Plaintiffs sought judicial relief directing the defendants to make available sufficient resources to allow the plaintiff school districts and other low-wealth North Carolina districts to provide their schoolchildren with adequate and equal educational opportunities. In the following summer of 1994, a number of urban school districts met and considered whether they should intervene in the suit, either to seek more funding themselves or to oppose possible judicial relief that might reallocate funds from wealthier to poorer districts. After extensive consultation with the original plaintiffs, six urban North Carolina school districts and individuals from those districts intervened as additional plaintiffs in October 1994, asserting that their large numbers of at-risk students needed more resources in order to have an adequate education.

The low-wealth plaintiffs' complaint filed in May asserted claims under State education statutes and the state constitution, but none under federal law. It emphasized the strong State constitutional language that: "[t]he people have a right to the privilege of education, and it is the duty of the State to guard and maintain that right."[4] It also relied on the constitutional provision that "[t]he General Assembly shall provide by taxation and otherwise for a general and uniform system of free public schools ... wherein equal opportunities shall be provided for all students ...."[5]

Plaintiffs alleged that the State had breached its constitutional and statutory duties both (a) by not providing adequate educational opportunities to plaintiff schoolchildren and (b) by not providing substantially equal educational opportunities in all school districts. Court decisions in an earlier lawsuit had held that the "equal opportunity" language in the State Constitution was intended to address racial desegregation, not to mandate equal programs and facilities in public schools throughout the State.[6] However, no prior North Carolina case had squarely ruled on an "adequacy theory."

The complaint described some of the consequences of the State's failures in the plaintiff districts, including serious shortages of qualified teachers, severely limited programs, and inadequate classroom space.[7] In addition to such "input" evidence, plaintiffs alleged that the inadequacies in the State's educational system in their school districts were also shown by the "outputs"; these included poor student performance on the State's standardized ABC tests, high drop-out rates, and poor performance by those students who sought community college or university opportunities.

In November 1994, defendants moved to dismiss the plaintiffs' claims, arguing that no claims for relief were stated and that the underlying education issues were political questions. The trial judge granted a motion to transfer the case to Wake County, site of the State capital, but denied the motion to dismiss. Defendants appealed. Plaintiffs' counsel, considered moving to dismiss the interlocutory appeal as premature, but we concluded that appellate review in which all our factual allegations had to be taken as true could place us in a strong position. The State Court of Appeals reversed the trial court and directed that all plaintiffs' claims be dismissed, ruling that the right to education set forth in the State Constitution embraced no qualitative standard.[8] Plaintiffs then appealed to the North Carolina Supreme Court, prepared new briefing and presented oral argument in October 1996.

Supreme Court Decision in Leandro I

In the summer of 1997, more than three years after plaintiffs filed suit, their efforts resulted in the *Leandro I* ruling, a unanimous decision holding that the North Carolina Constitution entitles each child to the opportunity to obtain a sound basic education.[9]

The state Supreme Court first rejected defendants contention that plaintiffs' claims presented non-justiciable political questions beyond the court's power to adjudicate. Instead it held it was "the duty of the courts to determine the meaning of the requirements of our Constitution."[10] In so doing, it relied on a North Carolina precedent approving judicial review of legislative action in a case decided in 1787, before *Marbury v. Madison* and even before adoption of the United States Constitution.[11]

The Court continued: "[t]he principal question presented by this argument is whether the people's constitutional right to education has any qualitative content, that is, whether the state is required to provide children with an education that meets some minimum standard of quality."[12] The Court unanimously concluded that the answer was in the affirmative, and that the State "has the duty of providing the children of every school district with access to a sound basic education."[13]

This Court defined a "sound basic education" in terms of particular substantive content and specific skills needed for a child's future success in higher education, employment and civic involvement.[14] The Court said,

> For purposes of our Constitution, a "sound basic education" is one that will provide the student with at least: (1) sufficient ability to read, write, and speak the English language and a sufficient knowledge of fundamental mathematics and physical science to enable the student to function in a complex and rapidly changing society; (2) sufficient fundamental knowledge of geography, history, and basic economic and political systems to enable the student to make informed choices with regard to issues that affect the student personally or affect the student's community, state, and nation; (3) sufficient academic and vocational skills to enable the student to successfully engage in post-secondary education or vocational training; and (4) sufficient academic and vocational skills to enable the student to compete on an equal basis with others in further formal education or gainful employment in contemporary society.[15]

On plaintiffs' claim for *equal* (as opposed to *adequate*) education opportunities, the Court, with one Justice dissenting,[16] affirmed the court of appeals and determined that equality in funding between districts was not required because the Constitution permitted local districts to supplement State programs and State funding.[17]

The Court unanimously concluded that plaintiffs' claims regarding educational adequacy stated a claim for relief "if ... supported by substantial evidence."[18] The Court listed three "factors which may be considered on remand to the trial court."[19] The first was "[e]ducational goals and standards adopted by the legislature."[20] The second was "the level of performance of the children of the State and its various districts on standard achievement tests.[21] The third factor was "the level of the state's general educational expenditures and per-pupil expenditures."[22] The Court cautioned against treating standardized test scores as "absolutely authoritative" and against reliance on "the single factor of school funding."[23] It noted that "'output' measurements [i.e. test scores] might be more reliable than measurements of 'input' such as per-pupil funding or general educational funding provided by the state."[24]

The *Leandro* Court concluded,

> If on remand of this case to the trial court, that court makes findings and conclusions from competent evidence to the effect that defendants in this case are denying children of the state a sound basic education, a denial of a fundamental right will have been established. It will then become incumbent upon defendants to establish that their actions denying this fundamental right are 'necessary to promote a compelling governmental interest.' ... If defendants are unable to do so, it will then be the duty of the court to enter a judgment granting declaratory relief and such other relief as needed to correct the wrong while minimizing the encroachment upon the other branches of government.[25]

The state Supreme Court remanded the case to the trial court to determine whether children in the State had been denied their rightful opportunity to obtain a sound basic education. Superior Court Judge Howard E. Manning, Jr. was designated by Chief Justice Burley Mitchell as a special judge under state procedural rules to preside over all subsequent proceedings. Judge Manning had a reputation for high intelligence and hard work. He was the first Republican since the 19th Century to have won a North Carolina statewide judicial election, and was known to probe deeply and meticulously into the details of cases presented to him.[26]

Pretrial and Trial before Judge Manning: 1997-1999

From 1997 to 1999, the parties engaged in extensive motion practice and discovery, taking dozens of fact, 30(b)(6), and expert depositions and producing and analyzing tens of thousands of documents. In this period, Judge Manning held numerous conferences and hearings on discovery issues, pleadings amendments, student confidentiality issues and other pretrial matters. At the trial court's suggestion, plaintiffs amended their complaint to add a claim that the absence of pre-kindergarten education programs for "at-risk" four year olds deprived them of an opportunity to a sound basic education.

At one pretrial conference, Judge Manning suggested that a trial involving the educational opportunities in five rural districts and six urban districts would be prolonged, complicated and unwieldy. He asked that the parties agree on one district as the principal subject matter for an initial trial, with other districts to be focused upon in later proceedings. Plaintiffs proposed that Hoke County be selected for the first trial, largely because its high levels of poverty and at-risk children and low levels of local funding were representative of education problems in low-wealth counties. Other relevant factors in this selection were the accessibility and availability of administrator and teacher witnesses willing and able to devote sustained attention to the litigation and the relative absence in Hoke of particular organizational issues not common to most North Carolina low-wealth counties. (For example, unlike Hoke, Halifax County had three separate school systems and funding and managerial issues were arguably one cause of that district's problems.) Defendants agreed to the proposal that Hoke serve as a sample county.

The case was tried before Judge Manning for five weeks in the fall of 1999 with closing arguments in December. It was interrupted briefly when the State courts were closed due to Hurricane Floyd. After the time scheduled for the trial in a state courtroom had expired, it was continued in a borrowed courtroom in federal court.

The trial focused particularly on Hoke County, but included extensive evidence on other North Carolina districts as well. Twenty-four live witnesses testified at trial and testimony of fifteen others was presented by deposition. Plaintiffs' trial exhibit list had 485 exhibits, plaintiff-intervenors listed 89 exhibits and defendants listed 681. Most of these were introduced at trial.

Plaintiffs' witnesses included Hoke school administrators, county finance officers, teachers, parents and schoolchildren as well as outside experts on test scores, pre-kindergarten education and special programs shown to benefit at-risk children. Plaintiffs' evidence emphasized the particular facts about Hoke County and its students — located in a rural area with no major shopping center, no university campus, and no hospital. The county student population was more than half African-American and Native-American; most students, blacks, whites and native- American alike, came from poverty backgrounds and almost two-thirds were eligible for the federal free and reduced lunch program.

Relying on the state Supreme Court's 1997 opinion, plaintiffs' evidence emphasized the stark disparity between student standardized test score results in Hoke County and the results statewide and from other more affluent counties. The evidence also showed very low academic performance by Hoke students in the State's community college system, and in admission rates to the University of North

Carolina system. A number of Hoke County employees testified that many graduates of the county's only high school had insufficient reading and math skills to be hired or to perform adequately even in relatively unskilled jobs.

The urban district plaintiff intervenors cooperated fully at trial with the plaintiffs. Both sought to show through expert and fact witnesses that at-risk children from all districts lacked opportunities for pre-kindergarten programs, tutoring and the smaller classes that they needed for reasonable academic achievement.

The defendants' evidence pointed to various possible causes of the Hoke and at-risk students' low academic performances, including inadequate local education leadership, lack of parental involvement and student failure to diligently perform homework. The defendants called no witnesses from the Hoke County School System. They relied in part on a national expert, Eric Hanushek, who offered the opinion that money was not a principal determinant of educational quality. Dr. Hanushek had not visited or studied Hoke Schools and relied principally on studies performed by other experts on other states' school systems.

Decisions and Further Hearings by the Trial Court: A "Beneficial Nag": 2000-2002

After trial, the parties submitted detailed proposed findings of fact and conclusions of law. Plaintiffs' submission was more than 200 pages. Following closing arguments, the court issued three detailed Memoranda of Decision comprising hundreds of pages, dated October 12, 2000, October 26, 2000 and March 26, 2001. These addressed in detail many issues that have repeatedly arisen in school finance litigations in a number of states.

The court's first memorandum concluded that certain components of the State education system, including teacher licensure, curriculum, the State's standardized test ABC accountability system, and student performance standards were not themselves unconstitutional. The court stated that the basic structure of the State's funding delivery system was valid, but reserved judgment on whether the State was providing sufficient funds to Hoke or to other counties to ensure all children were receiving an equal opportunity to obtain a sound basic education.[27] The court also concluded that whether students were — or were not — performing at grade level on the standard State ABC tests (Level III or above) were highly probative evidence of whether they had an opportunity for a sound basic education.[28]

Section Two (October 26, 2000): Pre-kindergarten.

In its second memorandum, the trial court addressed the special educational needs and programs for students at-risk of academic failure. Drawing on the State's own standards and documents, the court described the factors that place a child at-risk of academic failure, including poverty, low parental education, minority status, inadequate housing, and poor health.[29] The court described the vicious cycle for many at-risk children of school failures, drop-outs, crime, prison, and bringing more children into a world of poverty and hopelessness.[30] The court noted that many at-risk children perform below grade level.[31]

The court stated that educators and education experts at trial had all agreed that "given the proper resources, the educational needs of at-risk students (such as students living in poverty) can be met. All children can learn, even children with substantial disadvantages."[32] The court observed that counsel for the State had attempted to blame at-risk children for their failures and to attribute those failures to "lack of effort, too much television, lack of homework and lack of innate ability."[33] The court concluded that this defense argument was inconsistent with the positions taken by the State Board of Education and the Department of Public Instruction (DPI) that "[h]igh achieving schools accept their responsibility for enhancing student achievement and do not look for 'scapegoats'…."[34]

The court found that the evidence was "clear and convincing that at-risk students require additional help, programs and resources in order to perform at a level satisfactory for them to obtain a sound basic education …."[35] It noted that witnesses for all parties agreed that smaller class sizes, tutoring, more time on task, and competent and well-trained teachers were all important in educating at-risk children,[36] and that "providing a quality pre-kindergarten program is an effective means of increasing the performance of low-income and otherwise at-risk students."[37]

The court concluded that by age five (the age children may begin State public school kindergarten), many at-risk children are already far behind and not ready to learn.[38] Without early intervention, these children do not have an equal opportunity to obtain a sound basic education, because from the beginning they lack the basic skills needed to prepare for academic success.[39] These children generally fail to master basic reading and math by the end of grade three and continue to lag behind other children as they progress through the middle grades.[40]

The court held that the "common-sense" remedy for this problem was to offer at-risk children the opportunity for pre-kindergarten.[41] The reason for providing pre-kindergarten to at-risk students "is to prepare the student[s] to come to kindergarten with the skills and knowledge to be able to equally obtain the benefits of a kindergarten and early elementary education on as similar terms as possible" as children from more privileged circumstances.[42] The court also found that the State had provided some at-risk children with effective pre-kindergarten programs, but many more such children had no access to such programs.[43]

It concluded by directing the State to expand pre-kindergarten programs to serve all qualifying at-risk four-year-old children in North Carolina.[44] It left the details of implementation of this expansion to the executive and legislative branches.[45]

Section Three (March 26, 2001): At-risk students and Hoke County.

In his third memoranda of decision, Judge Manning found that at-risk students in Hoke County and at-risk children generally across the State were not receiving a sound basic education.[46] The court described the impoverished circumstances in Hoke County, which lacks universities, museums, shopping centers, or hospitals, and the economic and other disadvantages of the majority of its children.[47] The court analyzed the State's end-of-grade and end-of-course test data and found that substantial numbers of the Hoke students were failing to meet the State's proficiency standard of performing at grade level on ABC tests.[48]

The court considered several other indicators of whether students were receiving the opportunity for a sound basic education. These included the drop-out rate.[49] A large percentage of Hoke students were leaving the school system without graduating, and they were unlikely to have the language, mathematics, and other skills specified in *Leandro* as needed to function in a changing society.[50] It found that many Hoke schools' graduates lacked the skills needed to work in local businesses, including textile manufacturing, consumer products manufacturing, and agriculture-related businesses.[51] He noted that an additional indicator was the performance of Hoke schools' students at community college and the university system.[52] Large percentages of those Hoke students who went to community college or university had to take remedial courses, and their performance in non-remedial courses was far below the State average.[53]

Based on all these factors, including statewide test score data, the court found that at-risk students in both Hoke and statewide were not receiving the opportunity for a sound basic education. The court observed that poverty, low parental education levels, unstable home environments, and other factors that put children at-risk of academic failure were not the fault of the public schools.[54] Nevertheless, he concluded, the schools must provide these children with the equal opportunity to obtain a sound basic education. "[I]n the eyes of the law, these at-risk children are citizens of North Carolina, and, as citizens, they have the same constitutional rights" as those children who are better off.[55]

He also emphasized: "[t]he evidence is clear and convincing that children from economically disadvantaged backgrounds can learn. However, in order for them to perform well in school it may take 'more time or different kinds of intervention' and more resources than those needed for children from middle class backgrounds."[56]

Aside from the pre-kindergarten issue, the court stated that it was persuaded that at-risk children in Hoke and elsewhere were not receiving a sound basic education. But he noted he was not satisfied by clear and convincing evidence at that point that this failing resulted from lack of sufficient funding by the State.[57] He noted that at-risk children generally did not perform well on standardized tests even in more affluent districts, where local education spending levels were relatively high.

This third Memoranda of Decision ended by directing defendants and the other parties to examine the strategic allocation of resources and produce a rational comprehensive plan to enable all children in the State, including at-risk children, to obtain a sound basic education.[58]

But defendants then declined to cooperate in framing a plan. Instead, they filed an interlocutory appeal from the court's March 26, 2001 decision and sought a stay.[59] The stay motion was denied by the trial court and the court of appeals also denied defendants' request for a stay pending appeal. Thereafter, on May 29, 2001, the trial court amended its March 26, 2001 decision and directed the taking of additional evidence. Beginning September 15, 2001, a second trial, or series of hearings, was held, lasting ten trial days and ending on October 5, 2001. Sixteen live witnesses testified, and numerous additional exhibits were introduced. These hearings focused largely upon particular schools in districts that appeared to have been successful in improving significantly the performance of at-risk students.

On April 4, 2002, the trial court issued a Fourth Memorandum of Decision and Judgment. The court held that it was incumbent upon defendants to provide the State's children with the opportunity to obtain a sound basic education and that such responsibility could not be avoided by defendants blaming LEAs because the LEAs were themselves agencies of the State. The court held that defendants had failed to carry out their constitutional duties, including their duties with respect to at-risk preschoolchildren. The April 4, 2002 decision incorporated the trial court's three prior Memoranda of Decision, which had themselves set out many other findings of fact and conclusions of law. Among other holdings, the court ruled that:

- every child is entitled to a competent, certified, well-trained teacher;

- in a school led by a well-trained principal;
- where sufficient resources are available to support the instructional program to provide an equal opportunity for a sound basic education.

In this Fourth Memorandum decision, the trial court held that children were not receiving an equal opportunity for a sound basic education because the State was not providing the "minimum necessary educational resources."[60]

Defendants' Second Appeal: 2002-2004

Defendants then appealed again, this time from the court's April 4, 2002 Judgment, as well as from the court's previous orders. This time, under pressure from public opinion and many education groups, the Governor's office decided not to seek a stay of the trial court's orders during the appeal.

While the appeal was pending, the trial court, through a series of memoranda orders, effectively directed the State to send an assistance team to Hoke County schools to determine what assistance and new programs were needed to provide constitutionally adequate education opportunities. In a July, 2002 letter to defendants the court noted: "the Court's Orders on this case are not advisory and require action on the part of the State of North Carolina." Ultimately the State reported to the court that various new programs really were needed in Hoke and that the local system lacked the resources to provide them.

In May 2004, with defendants' appeal still pending but the judgment not stayed, the State Board of Education proposed to the court that to assist at-risk students a Disadvantaged Students Supplemental Fund (DSSF) should be established, funded initially at $22.3 million annually and ultimately at $223 million a year. The trial court set a hearing for July 2004 on whether the State was complying with its (unstayed) judgments. Just before the hearing, the governor announced he had found $12 million in funding to commence funding of the proposed DSSF.[61]

Meanwhile, on its still pending appeal, the State principally was arguing that the trial court had improperly relied on State test score data to conclude that students were not receiving a sound basic education, that plaintiffs had failed to prove causation because any educational deficiencies stemmed largely from the actions of local school officials, not the State, and that pre-kindergarten programs for at-risk four-year-olds were not constitutionally required.

Leandro II Supreme Court Decision

On July 30, 2004, almost ten years after plaintiffs had filed suit, a unanimous State Supreme Court issued its opinion in *Leandro II*, upholding the trial court's ruling that children in North Carolina had been denied the opportunity to obtain a sound basic education and that the responsibility for this constitutional violation rested with defendants.[62] This new opinion was authored by Justice Robert Orr, who in the 1997 decision had been the only Justice to conclude that Plaintiffs had properly stated "equal opportunity" claims as well as "adequacy claims."

In reaching its conclusions, the Court ruled, among other holdings, that:

- The trial court had been correct to reject defendants' contention that below-grade level student performance showed students were obtaining a sound basic education.[63]
- Defendants had failed in their constitutional duty to provide students with the opportunity to obtain a sound basic education.[64]

- The trial court had correctly concluded that State efforts toward providing remedial aid to prospective at-risk enrollees was constitutionally inadequate. However it also ruled that directing pre-kindergarten classes as the "narrow" or "sole" remedy to assist at-risk prospective enrollees was inappropriate or premature at the time.[65]

The state Supreme Court observed that the 1999 trial had been focused principally on at-risk children in Hoke County; it affirmed the trial court's findings concerning Hoke, noting that further proceedings could be needed in the trial court with respect to the opportunity for a sound basic education in other state school districts.

After ten years of litigation, the *Leandro II* opinion was enthusiastically received by the press and in public opinion. Gene Nichol, UNC Law School Dean, wrote in an op-ed piece:

> What I find surprising — and hugely encouraging — about these rulings is that they came from Manning and Orr. These are hardly wide-eyed social engineers or Warren Court enthusiasts. They don't believe in government by judiciary or in updating the constitution to serve the "felt needs" of the day. They aren't softies or whiners. Not liberals or bleeding hearts. They aren't ideologues or utopians. They aren't even Democrats.
>
> They are, instead, old-fashioned craftsmen who followed where the cases led. They faced the facts of our educational disparity and refused to flinch. They determined that our constitutional mandates are to be taken seriously, not ignored. They realized that we

> define ourselves by the opportunity that we provide. And they reminded us that our most fundamental value is that we're all in this together.
>
> Not bad for a couple of conservatives. Perhaps somewhere they read that all children are equal in the eyes of God.[66]

Interestingly, the opinion was also applauded by much of the State's educational establishment and by state legislators. The elected State Superintendent of Public Instruction, Mike Ward, told the press:

> This is a case where I personally think we win by losing, because it's good for the kids. The legislature ignored that request [for DSSF funding] this time. I don't think they can do that again.[67]

And the co-chairman of the State House Committee on Education Appropriations, whose district included Hoke County, predicted with satisfaction that next year legislators would find the money:

> They'll be on board.... The big obstacle was waiting on this [Supreme Court] decision.[68]

Marc Basnight, President Pro Tempore of the State Senate, remarked of Judge Manning:

> He's a bit of a nag, but it's a beneficial nag. . . . Without him we wouldn't be addressing the problem the way we should.

Further Leandro Proceeding: Steps toward Effective Remedies

After the North Carolina Supreme Court decision in *Leandro II*, the defendants were asked to appear in court and set out their plans for compliance with the decision. They did so, noting that their plan included expansion of the Disadvantaged Students Supplemental Fund, full funding of the Low Wealth Fund for poor school districts, continued expansion of the More at Four pre-kindergarten program to serve more at-risk schoolchildren, more funding for early grade class size reductions, new teacher salary increases and professional development expenditures to boost teacher recruitment and retention.

Significantly, it was accepted by all parties that *Leandro* compliance should be addressed on a statewide basis, without further "liability" trial for additional school districts. [69]

To force the pace of the States' response, plaintiffs filed a motion to show cause or for approval of plan. Among other relief, it sought court approval of a *Leandro* compliance plan that involved immediate full funding of the Low Wealth Fund, a $300 million annual DSSF and increased spending for teacher recruitment and retention.

However at no time during the proceedings subsequent to the supreme court *Leandro II* decision did the trial court specifically order adoption of plaintiffs plan or direct expenditure of funds for a particular program. This may have been due, at least in part, to the Supreme Court having approved the trial court's conclusion that defendants were not providing a constitutionally adequate education, but, in the same opinion, having reversed the trial court's order specifically mandating a pre-K program for at-risk four-year-olds.

The remedy phase of *Leandro* involved not only motions by the parties, but a complicated interplay of executive, legislative and judicial action. On many occasions the governor relied on judicial opinions to support unusual executive orders and actions that effectively funded new initiatives for at-risk students, including directing initial funding of the DSSF by executive order in 2004. And legislative debate on proposed *Leandro* education reform efforts and increased funding proposals often cast the arguments in terms of what would likely be acceptable, or not acceptable, to Judge Manning.

From 2004 to 2007 the plaintiff LEAs themselves, assisted by a broader Low Wealth Schools Coalition and their legislative counsel, joined with other education groups and engaged in an extensive legislative lobbying campaign, principally seeking more funding for the Low Wealth Fund and the DSSF.

Beginning in 2004, despite the absence of a specific new remedial order by the trial court, the State began to take some substantial steps to implement the courts' decisions. The Low Wealth Fund was first substantially increased and then, in the 2006-2007 State budget, it was fully funded at a level of $173 million on a recurring annual basis. The new DSSF was initially funded at a level of $22 million by two gubernatorial executive orders in 2004. It then was repeatedly increased by the General Assembly, reaching a level of $67 million annually in 2007–08. This meant that the total cumulative, new DSSF expenditures since the program's 2004 inception had reached $234.6 million by the end of 2008.

By 2007 a pre-K "More at Four Program" for at-risk four-year-olds had been expanded to provide 28,000 available slots for students, and the annual spending on it had reached $140 million. Although the Supreme Court opinion had not required this program, it was strongly supported by the governor and by the legislature after the trial court had directed mandatory pre-K in its October, 2000 order. The cumulative increased spending stemming from *Leandro* from 2004 through 2009 exceeded $2 billion, most of which was for the DSSF, the Low Wealth Fund, pre-K and early grade class size reductions. And other significant new education programs were initiated largely in response to *Leandro*, including the restructuring of many state high schools under a New School Program partly funded by the Gates Foundation, a Learn and Earn high school program involving State community colleges, and various education reform pilot programs for schools with large at-risk student populations.

The remedial phase of *Leandro* also led to increased court and State Board of Education focus on the quality of education provided at-risk children in State high schools, and middle schools, including those in the State's urban centers such as Durham, Greensboro and Charlotte. Largely based on a review of student test score performances, the trial court had concluded in memoranda opinions that the test scores and other indices of educational achievement were cause for serious concern even where, in the court's view, the problem was not principally one of a lack of local funding or local resources. The court did not issue mandatory orders involving specific increased funding, but it successfully encouraged the legislature to do so. The court also effectively required a number of school reform efforts for low performing schools. These included the dispatch of State education assistance teams, monitoring the effectiveness of school leadership, and supplemental training programs for principals and superintendents at the University of North Carolina at Chapel Hill.

The court also held numerous hearings, requiring testimony in open court on school performance problems from State Board of Education and DPI personnel as well as testimony from leaders of non-profit education reform organizations. Based on this testimony and analysis of test score results, the court issued a series of additional memoranda opinions detailing problems in schools and identifying and describing plausible reform programs.

Some Lessons Learned

School finance litigation is often protracted with battles on multiple fronts. A number of lessons can be drawn from the *Leandro* efforts in North Carolina.

A parallel political and lobbying effort needs to accompany any litigation. Many such cases, even successful ones, do not end with a detailed court order directing a State or its legislature to provide specific new school reform programs or certain levels of increased appropriations. Achieving school finance reform always requires legislative and executive action as well as judicial action. Coalitions that will both support the litigation and continue to push politically for school reform need to be built before any suit is filed.

In *Leandro*, the early alliance between the wealthier urban school districts and the relatively poor rural districts was critical to success in court and in the legislature. The alliance effectively provided two teams of plaintiffs' lawyers and two sets of experts to litigate against the State defendants. At many points in the suit, supportive amicus briefs filed by non-party civil rights, law school and business groups were a great assistance. On the first *Leandro* appeal to the North Carolina Supreme Court, seven organizations, ranging from the Eastern North Carolina Chamber of Commerce to the ACLU, submitted amicus briefs supporting the plaintiffs' position. No amicus brief was submitted supporting the defendants' view that the adequacy of the education provided by the public schools could not be challenged in court.

Relations with the media in school finance cases are far more critical than in most civil litigation. Almost all the major North Carolina media, television, radio and print, were sympathetic to the plaintiffs' aim and gave the case extensive and sympathetic coverage as it progressed.

In some ways, school finance cases are sui generis. But for plaintiffs to prevail, they and their attorneys need to employ also the classic tools of civil litigation used in other significant civil, business or tort cases. These include a careful analysis of state legal precedents; a consideration of potential plaintiff and defendant parties to deal with standing and venue issues; the selection of a favorable forum; and careful evaluation of the strengths and weaknesses of possible fact and expert witnesses.

Plaintiffs must also be ready for a long struggle and determine in advance how funds can be raised to pay experts, court and deposition costs, attorney's fees and other litigation expenses. In *Leandro*, the suit was financed principally by the five plaintiff boards of education. The state Low Wealth Schools Consortium, a broader group of state low-wealth schools, also helped to fund it.

In framing a complaint, it is important to maintain flexibility and to advance plausible alternative legal theories. The *Leandro* complaint, based entirely on North Carolina state law, advanced claims based on constitutional equal opportunity and educational adequacy provisions as well as on state statutes. The first supreme court decision in 1997 rejected the "equal opportunity" theory, which many had thought relatively simple and most promising. The court instead remanded the case for trial to decide whether the "opportunity for a sound basic education" had been denied. This decision complicated the plaintiffs' case and shifted its focus somewhat from educational "inputs" to "outputs" such as standardized test scores, college and community college admission rates and students' post public school employment opportunities and accomplishments. And as the case continued, increasing attention was focused on the special needs of at-risk children everywhere, in both rural and urban districts.

The Litigation Team

The principal attorneys for the low-wealth plaintiffs through the 1999 trial were litigation partners at the North Carolina firm Parker Poe Adams & Bernstein of Raleigh and Larry Armstrong of Enfield, North Carolina. The Parker Poe attorneys were **Robert W. Spearman** (a graduate of UNC-CH and Yale Law School); Robert H. Tiller (a graduate of Oberlin and the University of Virginia Law School); and Melanie Black Dubis (a graduate of UNC-CH and Vanderbilt Law School). Mr. Armstrong is a graduate of UNC-CH and its law school. Additional biographical information on Mr. Spearman and Ms. Dubis is available at www.parkerpoe.com.

The attorney and legislative counsel for the North Carolina Low Wealth Schools Consortium, which supported the suit, and the low-wealth schools' lobbying effort was William G. Hancock (a graduate of UNC-CH and Duke Law School). Further biographical information on Mr. Hancock is available at www.eghs.com.

Law firms that represented the urban intervenor plaintiffs at various stages included Smith Helms Mullis & Moore, Hogan & Hartson and Tharrington Smith. Other attorneys involved in the litigation are listed in the North Carolina Appellate opinions. The case was defended by the North Carolina Attorney General's office. Its principal attorneys were Edwin M. Speas and Thomas J. Ziko.

Copies of the principal legal documents from the *Leandro* case, including pleadings, briefs and trial and appellate court decisions, are available on a CD from the Institute for Educational Equity and Opportunity, 1200 G St., NW, Suite 800, Washington, DC 20005. Copies of the *Leandro* trial transcripts are available on a CD from the Institute. Copies of the trial court decisions in the *Leandro* case are also available on the Internet at www.schoolfunding.info/states/nc/lit_nc.php3.

1 See Jack Betts, Op-Ed, "Leandro's Lesson: Still Not Enough Money," Charlotte Observer, January 15, 2006.

2 Id.

3 Prior to the *Leandro* litigation there were significant disparities in education spending among different North Carolina counties although these disparities were not as stark as those existing in some other states. State appropriations, derived largely from State income and sales taxes, provided more than 60% of the current operating budgets of the North Carolina public school system, federal funding provided approximately 10% and local funding provided over 24%. Any local funding is provided by county commissioners, which have taxing authority, not by school boards, which have no such power.

In the 1980s, the North Carolina General Assembly had directed the State Board of Education to develop a standard course of study to be offered to every public school student and that program was funded largely by the State, as were teachers' base salaries. Despite the relatively high percentage of total funding derived from the State, stark disparities in teachers' salaries and student teacher ratios resulted from the much higher local spending engaged in by wealthier urban counties in contrast to rural poorer counties.

In 1991, the State General Assembly had begun providing funds to low wealth and small school units that because of their relatively low property tax bases or low enrollments had difficulty in adequately supporting schools. However, before the litigation, this program was funded at a level of less than $10,000,000 a year statewide and it had relatively little impact.

4 N.C. Const. art. I, § 15.

5 N.C. Const. art. IX, § 2.

6 *Britt v. North Carolina State Board of Education*, 86 N.C. App. 282, 357 S.E.2d 432 (1987).

7 Complaint filed 5/25/94, pp. 16-17, 19-20.

8 *Leandro v. State*, 122 N.C. App. 1, 11, 468 S.E.2d 543, 550 (1996).

9 *Leandro v. State*, 346 N.C. 336, 488 S.E.2d 249 (1997) ("*Leandro I*"). The North Carolina Supreme Court at the time was comprised of five Democratic and two Republican judges. When the second supreme court decision was issued in the case in 2004, the court was comprised of six Republicans and one Democrat.

10 *Id.* at 345, 488 S.E.2d at 253.

11 *Bayard v. Singleton*, 1 N.C. 5, (1787).

12 346 N.C. at 345, 488 S.E.2d at 254.

13 *Id.* at 345, 353, 488 S.E.2d at 254, 258.

14 346 N.C. at 347, 488 S.E.2d at 255.

15 *Id.*

16 Justice Robert Orr joined the portion of the majority opinion recognizing the

right to an opportunity to a sound basic education but dissented from the court's conclusion that plaintiffs' equal protection claims had properly been dismissed. Judge Orr later authored a unanimous opinion upholding the trial court's later decision, after trial, that plaintiffs had proved defendants had failed in their duty to provide students with the opportunity to obtain a sound basic education. *Leandro II*, 358 N.C. 605, 599 S.E.2d 365 (2004).

17 346 N.C. at 348-51, 488 S.E.2d at 255-57.

18 *Id.* at 355, 488 S.E.2d at 259.

19 *Id.*

20 *Id.*

21 *Id.*

22 *Id.* at 355, 488 S.E.2d at 260.

23 *Id.* at 355, 357, 488 S.E.2d at 260.

24 *Id.* at 355, 488 S.E.2d at 260.

25 *Id.* at 357, 488 S.E.2d at 261 (citations omitted).

26 As plaintiffs' counsel we had anticipated that our equal protection claims might be more readily accepted by an appellate court than our "adequacy" claims. We certainly believed that the equality claims would be easier to prove in a trial because the stark disparities in education spending between poor, rural districts and more affluent, urban districts were not in dispute. We had expected that an appellate court might well consider equality claims to provide a more manageable judicial standard that would not require examination of issues such as teacher quality and the details of curriculum.

27 Mem. Decision, October 12, 2000 at pp. 118-119.

28 *Id.* at pp. 191-192.

29 Mem. Decision, October 26, 2000 at pp. 4-10, 12-13.

30 *Id.* at pp. 2-3.

31 *Id.* at pp. 1, 12-15.

32 *Id.* at p. 15.

33 *Id.* at p. 11.

34 *Id.* at pp. 11-12.

35 *Id.* at p. 15.

36 *Id.* at pp. 16-17.

37 *Id.* at p. 27.

38 *Id.* at p. 24.

39 *Id.* at pp. 24-25, 40.

40 *Id.* at pp. 19-24.

41 *Id.* at pp. 26-27.

42 *Id.* at p. 32.

43 *Id.* at p. 40.

44 *Id.* at p. 43.

45 *Id.*

46 Mem. Decision, March 26, 2001 at p. 3.

47 *Id.* at pp. 1, 6-9.

48 *Id.* at pp. 12-16.

49 *Id.* at p. 17.

50 *Id.*

51 *Id.* at pp. 22-25.

52 *Id.* at pp. 26-30.

53 *Id.*

54 *Id.* at p. 69.

55 *Id.* at p 70.

56 *Id.* at p 71.

57 *Id.* at p 79.

58 *Id.* at pp. 83-84.

59 Some newspaper and political commentary suggested that this appeal by the State was due to a concern that the trial court's order was effectively directing a reallocation of existing resources to meet the needs of at-risk students and that serious steps in this direction might erode political support for the public schools by the parents of middle class children.

60 Mem. Decision, April 4, 2002, p. 104.

61 July 29, 2004 Press Release, Office of the Governor, NC.

62 *Hoke County Board of Education v. State*, 358 N.C. 605, 599 S.E.2d 365 (2004) (This decision is often referenced as "*Leandro II*").

63 *Leandro II*, 358 N.C. at 624, 599 S.E.2d at 382.

64 *Id.* at 647, 599 S.E.2d at 396.

65 *Id.* at 642,643, 599 S.E.2d at 393.

66 See, Gene Nichol, Op. Ed. , News & Observer, August 20, 2004.

67 Charlotte Observer, August 9, 2004; Plaintiffs' Memorandum in Support of Motion for Attorneys Fees and Costs, Ex. H. Ward posted the following on the State Board of Education website. "On Friday July 30 the NC Supreme Court issued its decision in the Leandro case, and what was a loss for the state was a win for vulnerable children in challenged school districts."

http://www.ncpublicschools.org/teachersarchive/messages/2004/20040812?&print=true.

68 *Id*. See also, Reidsville Review, September 12, 2004.

69 Subsequent to the 2004 supreme court decision, the lineup of parties in the suit changed. A class of students from the Charlotte-Mecklenburg system intervened, asserting that both the original State defendants and the CMS school system (one of the plaintiff urban intervenors) had deprived CMS students of *Leandro* rights. Thereafter, all the urban plaintiff intervenors (except CMS) dismissed their claims without prejudice, stating they believed they could pursue school reform more effectively without additional trials concerning the urban districts.

7 A Quest For Educational Equity In Massachusetts: The Case Of Hancock v. Driscoll

by Michael Weisman and Rachel Lipton

Introduction

As the birthplace of John Adams and American public education and home to some of the world's finest universities, to some, Massachusetts is synonymous with academic excellence. And truth be told, it certainly holds some beacons deserving of this reputation. But, the question plaguing educational adequacy and equity activists for over three decades is: what kind of public primary and secondary school education does Massachusetts have to offer its residents and future leaders, particularly those living in its property-poor cities and towns?

Beginning in 1978, Massachusetts residents began their appeal to the judiciary to help answer this question. After fifteen years of start and stop litigation, the supreme judicial court issued its 1993 landmark decision in the case of *McDuffy v. Secretary of the Executive Office of Education*. The *McDuffy* court unequivocally held that the

State had an enforceable duty to educate *all* of its children, regardless of the wealth of the community in which they lived and to provide *all* public school students with an "adequate" education. The court also directed the single justice, in his or her discretion, "to retain jurisdiction to determine whether, within a reasonable time, appropriate legislative action has been taken."[1]

Six years later, public school students sought further relief from the single justice, alleging that the Commonwealth was continuing to violate its constitutional obligation to educate children as articulated in *McDuffy* because public education in their districts, again the poorer districts in the state, remain constitutionally deficient. This case, known as *Hancock v. Commissioner of Education*, was assigned to Superior Court Judge Margot Botsford,[2] who presided over discovery and trial and ultimately issued a 318-page report containing comprehensive findings of fact, conclusions, and recommendations. Judge Botsford found that students in the plaintiff districts (represented in this case by four "focus districts") were being denied their constitutional right to educational opportunity. Her findings and recommendations were then reported to the supreme judicial court, which heard oral arguments from both sides before issuing its ruling.

On February 15, 2005, twelve years after the initial *McDuffy* decision, and despite Judge Botsford's report which the court praised as "thoughtful and comprehensive" and "amply supported," the supreme judicial court ruled in favor of the defendants. The 5-2 ruling reaffirmed the 1993 adequacy decision in *McDuffy*, and found that "the process of education reform can and must be improved," but, nonetheless stated that this was "not a case where the Legislature reasonably could be said to have neglected or avoided a constitutional command."

While the court terminated the ongoing jurisdiction of the single justice, the plurality opinion nonetheless signaled its openness to a later challenge to the adequacy of the educational system by stating: "[n]othing I say today would insulate the Commonwealth from a successful challenge under the education clause in different circumstances." Thus, although unfavorable, the *Hancock* decision reaffirmed that *McDuffy* remains good law and that matters of constitutional adequacy are not exempt from judicial scrutiny in Massachusetts. As stated by Plaintiff's counsel in the aftermath of the decision, "the only thing the Legislature ought to take away from today's decision is that the court is going to give them some time to get the job done."

History of Education and Education Finance in Massachusetts

Prior to the 1990s, public education in Massachusetts was primarily a matter of local concern. By statute, the requirement to maintain schools is assigned to the towns and cities of the Commonwealth.[3] "General charge" of the public schools in each town, city or regional school district is assigned to a locally elected school committee.[4] While a State Board of Education is charged with setting state-wide policy and requirements, in practice, locally elected school boards directed the education policy in their districts.[5] Similarly, school financing was "governed by a loosely connected mélange of statutes, local regulations and informal policies."[6] While funding for the public schools came from three sources — local monies, State monies and federal monies — the main source of funding for a school was local monies, derived from the local property tax.[7]

Accordingly, not only were certain cities or towns hamstrung by the low property values in their districts, but also by the strict limits of Proposition 2 ½, which limits the amount of local taxes which any city or town may assess in any given year to two and one-half percent of the full and fair cash value of the real and personal property in such city or town. Any override of this limitation requires a two-thirds vote of the voters at a general election. Moreover, federal aid during the 1980s only accounted for four to five percent of school funding as was typically directed at specific programs. Some districts did not receive any federal funds at all. The "state aid" which was to be directed at promoting the equalization of educational opportunity across districts pursuant to a statutorily prescribed formula was routinely "unheeded, leaving cities and towns at the mercy of unpredictable annual appropriations from the Legislature".[8] Accordingly, districts could not count on any set amount of state or federal aid. As a result, wide financial disparities existed with respect to educational funding and the lack of fiscal support significantly impacted the quality of education students were receiving in the property-poor districts.

It was in this context, that *McDuffy*, the initial adequacy litigation in Massachusetts was filed, litigated and decided. *McDuffy* was actually comprised of two independent actions filed in two different state courts which were ultimately consolidated before the supreme judicial court, the highest court in the state of Massachusetts. The first case, *Webby v. Dukakis* was filed on behalf of students from 16 public schools seeking a declaration that the Commonwealth had failed to provide them an education as mandated by the Constitution.[9] During the pendency of *Webby*, the legislature passed two different statutes relating to public school finance and administration. Each time, activity in the case was suspended.

In 1989, a second case, *Levy v. Dukakis*, was filed on behalf of students from five other public schools challenging the constitutionality of the state's school-financing system.[10] In 1990, the constitutional counts alleged in *Levy* were consolidated with those of *Webby*. A year later, in 1991, and supplemented in 1992, the parties in the consolidated case of *McDuffy v. Secretary of the Executive Office of*

Education, filed a stipulation of agreed upon facts and a joint appendix consisting of six volumes of documents. In December 1992, the single justice referred the case to the full supreme judicial court for decision.

In 1993, the supreme judicial court decided the *McDuffy* case, holding unequivocally that the State had a duty to educate *all* of its children, regardless of the wealth of the community in which they lived and to provide *all* public school students with an "adequate" education. The court's language was clear and powerful:

[T]he Commonwealth has a duty to provide an education to *all* its children, rich and poor, in every city and town of the Commonwealth at the public school level, and that this duty is designed not only to serve the interests of the children, but, more fundamentally, to prepare them to participate as free citizens of a free State to meet the needs and interests of a republican government, namely the Commonwealth of Massachusetts.

This duty lies squarely on the executive (magistrates) and legislative (Legislatures) branches of this Commonwealth. That local control and fiscal support has been placed in greater or lesser measure through our history on local governments does not dilute the validity of this conclusion….They may delegate, but they may not abdicate, their constitutional duty.[11]

While the court was absolute in recognizing the duty of the State, it was hesitant to proscribe how that duty should be met. To the contrary, the court affirmed its confidence "that the executive and legislative branches of government will respond appropriately to meet their constitutional responsibilities."[12] Accordingly, the court left it to the Magistrates and the Legislatures to define the precise nature of the task which they face in fulfilling their constitutional duty to educate our children today, and in the future.[13] In addressing the funding of public education, the court stated clearly that it was not ordering equal per pupil expenditure across districts, but noted that "fiscal support, or the lack of it, has a significant impact on the quality of education each child may receive."[14] In addressing the curricular content of an adequate education, the court articulated broad guidelines. These guidelines included what are commonly known as the Rose factors (from the Kentucky equity litigation *Rose v. Council for Better Educ., Inc.*, 790 S.W.2d 186, 212 (1989)):

> An educated child must possess at least the seven following capabilities: (i) sufficient oral and written communication skills to enable students to function in a complex and rapidly changing civilization; (ii) sufficient knowledge of economic, social, and political systems to enable students to make informed choices; (iii) sufficient understanding of governmental processes to enable the student to understand the issues that affect his or her community, state, and nation; (iv) sufficient self-knowledge and knowledge of his or her mental and physical wellness; (v) sufficient grounding in the arts to enable each student to appreciate his or her cultural and historical heritage; (vi) sufficient training or preparation for advanced training in either academic or vocational fields so as to enable each child to choose and pursue life work intelligently; and (vii) sufficient level of academic or vocational skills to enable public school students to compete favorably with their counterparts in surrounding states, in academics or in the job market.[15]

Despite leaving the task of defining the specifics of the educational system to the legislature, the court permitted the single justice, in his or her discretion, "to retain jurisdiction to determine whether, within a reasonable time, appropriate legislative action has been taken."[16]

While the educational adequacy and equity debate was being hashed out in the courts, it was also proceeding on a parallel path through the legislature. In fact, the representative who chaired a special legislative committee to reform education expressed his hope that Massachusetts would become the first state to overhaul education financing before being ordered to do so by a court.[17] The Legislative efforts culminated in the Education Reform Act ("ERA") which was passed just three days after the court issued its *McDuffy* decision.

The ERA revamped the structure of funding for public schools and strengthened the power of the state Board of Education to establish and enforce statewide educational policies and standards. With respect to funding, the ERA established a "foundation budget" for each district in the state which was derived from a complex 32-step formula that accounted for the number and needs of the children residing in each district. The foundation budget was premised on the idea of identifying the minimum amount of money each district needed to provide its students with an adequate education. Further, the ERA guaranteed that each district receives its foundation budget with the shortfall between the foundation budget and the required local contribution.

With respect to academic standards, the ERA developed and implemented "curriculum frameworks" in the core subjects of mathematics, science and technology, history and social science, English language arts, foreign languages, and the arts, which "present broad pedagogical approaches and strategies for assisting students in the development of the skills, competencies and knowledge called for by these standards."[18] Lastly, the ERA required that every senior graduating from a public school attain competency in these core subjects as measured by the student's performance on the Massachusetts Comprehensive Assessment System examination ("MCAS").[19]

Despite the sweeping promises of the ERA, six years later, in December 1999, public school students sought further relief from the single justice, alleging that the public education in their districts, notably again the poorer districts in the state, continued to violate the Commonwealth's constitutional obligation to educate children. This case became known as *Hancock v. Commissioner of Education*.

Initiating the Litigation

Plaintiffs and counsel in the *Hancock* case faced a number of strategic challenges in initiating what has been deemed the remedial phase of the *McDuffy* litigation. These challenges largely came in the form of the fundamental questions of When?, How?, and What?.

The question of when?

Lead counsel for the plaintiffs in *McDuffy* remained committed to following the progress of the implementation of the *McDuffy* decision and the ERA. While they were hopeful that the constitutional mandate of *McDuffy* would incite the legislature to speedy and appropriate action, they were skeptical from the outset that the foundation budget would really be sufficient to enable the poorer districts to provide the now constitutionally mandated education to all children. In the mid-1990's, when it appeared the legislature was not going to fully fund Chapter 70 (the foundation budget), the plaintiffs quickly mobilized to file a motion for further relief in the courts. The legislature responded almost immediately by fully restoring the Chapter 70 funding, and plaintiffs did not prosecute their motion.

In the meantime, plaintiffs' counsel maintained regular, periodic contact with the educators, legislators and activists who had been instrumental in the success of the *McDuffy* case and active in the field. Despite acknowledging that significant additional resources were being allocated to education by the State, counsel and the interested parties were troubled by the rate of this progress and the continuing disparities between the wealthy and poor districts and the persistent achievement gaps. They acknowledged that the legislative process needed to be afforded reasonable time to meet the judicial mandate, yet they also knew that the State could not afford to do so at the expense of yet another generation of children. Counsel was keenly aware that while further action was likely to be necessary, they needed to wait sufficient amount of time before seeking further relief so that they could credibly argue that the Legislative response was insufficient to cure the constitutional violations found in *McDuffy*. However, as experienced litigators, counsel was also keenly aware of the speed of the judicial process and knew that any action filed would take years to reach an ultimate resolution.

Plaintiffs ultimately returned to court in 1999, six years after the *McDuffy* decision and as the seven year phase-in of the foundation budget as provided by the ERA was nearing its end. At this point, plaintiffs felt that they had sufficient evidence that the foundation budget, as presently conceived, was not enough and had waited long enough for the constitutional violations to be cured. Plaintiffs' counsel partnered with the state teachers unions, the Massachusetts Teachers Association and the Massachusetts American Federation of Teachers, the Council for Fair School Finance, and the Schott Foundation and filed *Hancock v. Commissioner of Education*.

The question of how?

After filing the Complaint, plaintiffs faced the daunting task of determining how best to present their case. An initial concern, which permeated throughout the case, was how to frame the proper legal question for the court. To plaintiffs, it was clear that *McDuffy* identified a constitutional violation which the Commonwealth was obliged to remedy. While *McDuffy* declined to specify precisely what curricular and financial frameworks were needed to cure such violations, the plaintiffs believed that the court's retention of jurisdiction "to determine whether, within a reasonable time, appropriate legislative action has been taken" meant that the court retained jurisdiction to ensure that within a reasonable amount of time the constitutional violations had been cured.

The Commonwealth, however, viewed the mandate of *McDuffy* very differently. To it, *McDuffy* mandated "appropriate legislative action" within a reasonable amount of time and nothing more, regardless of whether the constitutional violation had been cured.

The Commonwealth maintained that the ERA was appropriate legislative action. Moreover, in its view, the Commonwealth had made measurable effort and progress in the intervening years, as evidenced by the significant amount of money allocated to education and the programs developed by the Board of Education, which absolved it of any lingering constitutional violations, even if many of the ills identified by the *McDuffy* court persisted.

Next, *Hancock* presented a new set of evidentiary issues from those faced in *McDuffy*. While *McDuffy* was presented to the court on a stipulated record, containing affidavits from a variety of educators attesting to the conditions in the selected school districts and an agreed upon appendix of Department of Education records and public reports, it was clear from very early on in the *Hancock* case that the defendants were not willing to similarly proceed in this phase of the litigation. Accordingly, live testimony with cross-examination of witnesses would be necessary. Additionally, plaintiffs would have to be cognizant of how to ensure that all the necessary documentary evidence would be admitted into evidence through laying a proper foundational and that all necessary experts would be qualified as such if subject to a *Daubert* challenge.

Although nineteen plaintiffs were selected in an effort to present geographic and demographic diversity, it was readily apparent that presenting a picture of the educational offerings and deficiencies of all nineteen districts would be unwieldy. Accordingly, with the assistance of Judge Botsford, it was agreed between counsel for the parties that factual evidence on a group of districts fewer than the total would be presented.

Ultimately, the plaintiffs selected four districts which were thereafter referred to as the "focus districts": Brockton, Lowell, Springfield, and Winchendon. The first three districts represented urban districts (smaller and less complicated than Boston) and the last represented a rural district. The districts were chosen primarily for geographic diversity, but the plaintiffs also considered the willingness of the school administrations to participate in the litigation since amassing the documentary proof and selecting appropriate witnesses from each district would also be a critical task. In addition, it was agreed that limited amounts of evidence concerning three relatively affluent districts, Brookline, Concord/Carlisle and Wellesley, would also be presented for comparison sake. All three of these districts had also been considered a "comparison district" in the original *McDuffy* proceedings.

During the first several months of the case, plaintiffs' counsel spent a significant amount of time meeting with individuals in the focus districts to understand the conditions in each district and gathering compelling evidence of the districts' successes and weaknesses. Additionally, within each district, there were discrepancies among individual schools in that district. With the assistance and guidance of the superintendents, plaintiffs' counsel was able to understand the inner workings of each district and identify a number of important factual witnesses. Plaintiffs' counsel also spent considerable time reviewing the documentary evidence, much of it contained in official Department of Education records, to understand the demographic make-up, financial resources and MCAS performance of each of the focus districts. This evidence was then synthesized and analyzed for the best presentation to the court.

In evaluating the evidence obtained from each district, the plaintiffs were faced with the critical issue of framing for the Court the proper metric by which to measure whether a constitutional education was being provided the students in each district. To do so, plaintiffs had to define a constitutionally adequate education, a task specifically rejected by the court in *McDuffy*; in a footnote in *McDuffy*, the court stated:

We note that both parties engage in a clash of views that focuses on whether the constitutional language requires an "adequate" education, whether the State provides an education which is "adequate," and if not, who is to blame. We decline to enter into this aspect of the debate. To us the words "adequate" and "education" can be viewed as redundant as well as contradictory.... The word "adequate" does not appear in the constitutional language and the struggle of the parties reveals, with good faith on all sides, necessary biases as to meaning. Thus, we strive to ascertain, as we should, the intention of the drafters of the constitutional language and to provide a frame of reference for the implementation of that intent in a modern society.[20]

Accordingly, *McDuffy* articulated broad capabilities each child should have upon completion of his/her public school education and left it to the legislature to determine how to ensure that their capabilities were realized.

Plaintiffs argued successfully that the detailed curriculum frameworks enacted in response to the ERA constituted the State's definition of a constitutionally adequate education. It was understandably difficult for the State to argue to the contrary since the frameworks were its own work product. In the absence of any contrary definition from the State as to what constituted a constitutionally minimal education, the plaintiffs persuaded Judge Botsford that the curriculum frameworks should be that metric. In a pretrial order, Judge Botsford ruled that the defendants would not be permitted at the trial to define or offer evidence of a minimum educational standard that was less comprehensive than that provided by the frameworks.

Accordingly, the plaintiffs retained experts in each of the seven curriculum frameworks,[21] often individuals who assisted in the drafting of the frameworks, to serve as expert witnesses. These witnesses testified to the value and importance of each framework and how it was designed to implement the *McDuffy* capabilities. The defendants did not offer any contrary evidence.

In addition to the seven curriculum frameworks, the plaintiffs also presented specific evidence designed to present a comprehensive picture of the educational programs in the focus districts. The plaintiffs also chose to include in the district specific testimony evidence pertaining to the adequacy of their special education programs, facilities, and teacher recruitment and retention, viewing these as specific challenges impeding the success of the State's poorer districts. In addition, evidence regarding libraries and information technology was presented as those resources impact virtually all of the frameworks and more generally the delivery of an adequate education in today's information-based society. The recurrent theme implicit and explicit in all of the evidence presented was that a lack of resources prevented these schools from providing the constitutionally minimum required education to their students.

The question of what?

The next strategic question was determining what remedy to request from the court and what evidence was required to justify such a remedy. The plaintiffs knew that a new funding scheme would be required, as they all agreed that a lack of resources was their most pressing problem, but to justify such a remedy, they first had to tie the deficiencies they established in the focus districts to the inadequacy of the funding scheme (i.e. the foundation budget) established by the State.

To achieve this, the plaintiffs offered expert witnesses, each of whom studied and evaluated the funding adequacy in the focus districts through the use of a different analytical model; one expert used what is called a "successful schools" model,[22] the other a "professional judgment" model[23] and a comparison of actual spending with the foundation budget. Instead, their goal was to highlight the gap in the actual spending as compared a required level of spending and to convince the court that the State itself must conduct its own true cost-study. To rebut this evidence, the defendants presented a number of witnesses who criticized the methodologies used by plaintiffs' experts and one witness who presented his own "professional judgment" model and study.

With one exception, Judge Botsford, however, afforded little weight to any of the studies. She did, however, find persuasive plaintiffs' evidence that that the focus districts were on the whole spending just about 100% of foundation budget on their schools and were unable to implement the curriculum frameworks and achieve uniform success among their student bodies on the MCAS or graduation rates. By way of comparison, successful school districts were all spending significantly in excess of the foundation budget. Based in significant part on this evidence, Judge Botsford concluded that the foundation budget formula failed to reflect the real costs of educating all the varied types of children in the Commonwealth's public schools and as a result, districts like the focus districts, that are not able to spend much more than their foundation budget levels on education, are not receiving adequate funding to provide the constitutional minimum of an adequate education.

In addition to attacking the state funding scheme, the plaintiffs also specifically sought funding for universal preschool. Plaintiffs included universal preschool in their requested remedy because the curriculum frameworks designed by the Commonwealth were all designed from pre-K through grade 12. The plaintiffs believed that if the curriculum frameworks stated the constitutionally minimum education within the state, then their complete implementation required pre-K education. The plaintiffs supported this request for relief by presenting evidence concerning preschool programs in the focus districts as well as expert testimony and evidence on the value of early childhood education.

Liability Decision and Remedy

After 78 days of trial spanning the course of eight months, including testimony from 114 witnesses and over 1,000 exhibits, Judge Botsford, concluded that the State was not meeting its constitutional duty to provide an education to all children and generated a comprehensive, well-articulated report (the "Report") detailing her findings and presenting her recommendations to the supreme judicial court. The Report, issued in April of 2004, comprised 318 pages in total. Judge Botsford made comprehensive findings of fact with respect to the educational programs in each of the four-focus districts, using the seven capabilities articulated in *McDuffy* and the curriculum frameworks presented in the ERA as the applicable standards. While noting that the four districts are obviously different from one another, each with its own strengths and weaknesses, the Report concluded that none of the districts was adequately implementing the Massachusetts curriculum frameworks, nor equipping its students with the capabilities described in *McDuffy*. Therefore in every one of these districts, the students were not receiving the level of education that the Commonwealth has a constitutional duty to provide.

Next, the Report made findings with respect to the adequacy of the State's school financing mechanism, the foundation budget formula, which the Department of Education considers the minimum amount of funding necessary to provide an adequate educational program. The Report stated that "it is significant that in the school districts across Massachusetts that are considered to be performing well in terms of the Department's performance rating system, the average expenditure is 130% of the district's foundation budget, — the statewide average expenditure is about 115-117% of the district foundation budget and the comparison districts' group average expenditure is 161% of the foundation budget."[24] The focus districts, on the other hand, were uniformly at or around 100% of foundation budget. Accordingly, the Report concluded that the foundation budget does not presently provide sufficient funds to the focus districts to permit them to implement the curriculum frameworks or generally to meet the standards of *McDuffy*, and no other source of State funding fills the gap. Lastly, the report looked at the remedial issues presented during the case and made the following recommendations:

The first recommendation is that the Court enter an order directing the Commonwealth educational officials to: (1) determine the actual cost of providing to all the children in the focus districts' public schools the opportunity to acquire the capabilities outlined in McDuffy, which in essence means determining the cost to implement effectively the seven curriculum frameworks for all school children (the funding issue); (2) determine the costs associated with enacting measures to improve the educational leadership capacities of the focus districts (the leadership issue); and (3) implement whatever funding and administrative changes result from the first two determinations (the implementation issue). The report further recommends that the defendants be provided a definite but limited period of time to accomplish these tasks, and that the Court retain jurisdiction to be satisfied that the remedial efforts are progressing towards a timely, effective solution.[25]

The Report was then submitted to the supreme judicial court for further review. On February 15, 2005, the court issued its plurality opinion written by the Chief Justice Margaret H. Marshall.[26] While repeatedly reaffirming the *McDuffy* decision and accepting the findings of Judge Botsford, the court ultimately refused to order further relief. Chief Justice Margaret Marshall,, writing for a plurality, acknowledged that the "amply supported findings" of Judge Botsford "reflect much that remains to be corrected before all children in our Commonwealth are educated" and "stand as a compelling, instructive account of the current state of public education in Massachusetts." She further noted that "[n]o one reading the judge's decision can be left with any doubt that the question is not 'if' more money is needed, but how much."

Nonetheless, the Chief Justice found that the progress since 1993, in the focus districts and across the state, was enough to remove the legislature from constitutional culpability. Specifically, she stated: "No one, including the defendants, disputes that serious inadequacies in public education remain. But the Commonwealth is moving systemically to address those deficiencies and continues to make education reform a fiscal priority." Moreover, the court acknowledged that ""the plaintiff's frustration with the slow, sometimes painfully slow, pace of education reform in the focus districts is understandable.

I am cognizant that for the student whose special needs go unaddressed, for the student who sits in an overcrowded classroom or an ill-equipped school library, and for their parents or guardians, the prospect of better things to come in public education comes too late." Nonetheless, she maintained that "I cannot conclude that the Commonwealth currently is not meeting its constitutional charge to 'cherish the interests of... public schools. On the record before us, we cannot conclude that the Commonwealth presently is violating the education clause and that a remedial order is appropriate at this time."

The Chief Justice supported her decision by contrasting the situation in Massachusetts with that of other states in which there were "years of legislative failure" that led the judges in those cases to order more specific remedies. According to the Chief Justice, the actions of the Massachusetts Legislature and Governor were sufficiently substantial that they did not merit further court review at this time. Consistent with her ultimate conclusion, the opinion details the myriad reforms undertaken by the legislative and executive branches of the state government, as well as the improvements on all measures of student and school achievement witnessed across the state in the decade since the ERA was passed. In conclusion, the court terminated the ongoing jurisdiction of the single justice.

As a last glimmer of hope for educational equity activists, however, the Chief Justice was careful in her opinion not to undermine the precedent set up by *McDuffy* and the future role of the courts in education reform, writing "Nothing I say today would insulate the Commonwealth from a successful challenge under the education clause in different circumstances."

Lessons Learned

It is important for counsel both within the State and outside to take a critical look at the *Hancock* case to glean its important lessons.

In creating its record, the *Hancock* plaintiffs realized a number of successes which are key to any school finance case. First, it is essential to spend the time and effort understanding the intricacies of school districts before filing suit. To do this effectively and efficiently, building a relationship with key school officials, particularly the school superintendents, is imperative. The superintendents can provide access to the right individuals within their school systems to help you build your case and do much of the pre-screening of witnesses and relevant documentary evidence. They can also serve as unretained experts to help you analyze and understand the complex data collected by the State to evaluate educational progress. Working closely with the "focus district" superintendents in the *Hancock* case enabled counsel to create a detailed factual record and to support its claimed constitutional violations and requested remedy.

Deciding what evidence and how much evidence to present in a school finance case is a very difficult decision for counsel. It is important to balance the anecdotal evidence with the hard statistical evidence. While some have criticized the *Hancock* case for presenting too much anecdotal evidence, counsel for the plaintiffs disagree. The anecdotal evidence presents both context and color for the otherwise potentially unemotional statistical evidence. A court needs to be reminded that a school finance case is ultimately about students and not just numbers. The anecdotal evidence is a strong reminder of the importance of these issues. While the *Hancock* plaintiffs presented a number of teachers and administrators as witnesses, they did not present any students. In hindsight, a few carefully selected student witnesses may have been powerful anecdotal testimony.

Next, it is important to identify the right experts to use in any school finance case. School funding studies are inherently difficult to design and no one method is without its criticisms. Nonetheless, such expert testimony can be extremely useful in highlighting the funding inadequacies present in your case. In *Hancock*, the Plaintiffs sought to present the court with two different approaches to the funding issue, yet ultimately both were rejected by the court. In looking back at their strategy, the Plaintiffs learned that they were perhaps not involved enough in the design of each of the studies, leaving their experts vulnerable to easy cross-examination for being too aspirational and detached from the minimum requirements of the constitutional standard. Accordingly, it is important for counsel to be involved in the design, implementation and analysis of any expert study and to have regular check-ins with their expert with opportunities to change and mold the study to present defensible results from a legal standpoint to the court.

Importantly, the *Hancock* case also highlights the complexities of any school finance case as an interplay between law and politics and the necessity to continue to evaluate your case in both of these terms. The toughest pill for the *Hancock* plaintiffs and their counsel to swallow was acceptance of the fact that despite winning the case on its merits, it was nonetheless lost on its politics. After receiving Botsford's report in April 2004, the plaintiffs were hopeful that their pleas had been heard and would soon be answered. While not without its criticisms of certain aspects of management, or mismanagement, within the focus districts and the Board of Education, the report presented a comprehensive picture of the realities faced by educators in districts who were hamstrung by the lack of sufficient resources to meet the constitutional mandate. The report also made it abundantly clear that the constitutional violations identified in *McDuffy* persisted; despite its allocation of monies and development of beneficial programs, the Commonwealth had not "taken appropriate legislative action within a reasonable amount of time" and it was time for the judiciary to hold it to task.

The supreme judicial court, however, took a markedly different approach to the legal question presented. While deferential to the factual findings made by the Botsford report, to the SJC, reasonable effort and progress by the Commonwealth was enough to satisfy its constitutional obligation, even if that meant that another generation and countless generations thereafter that would graduate Massachusetts public schools with an education that fell below the constitutional minimum.[27] To understand this ruling, it is important to note that the court which heard and decided the *Hancock* decision was markedly different from that of *McDuffy*; in fact six of the seven justices who had comprised the *McDuffy* court had since been replaced by Republican appointees. The lesson learned is that politics plays a pivotal role in school finance decisions and despite our highest aspirations to the contrary, courts are not insulated from this political dimension. Accordingly, it is essential that litigators advocating a school equity or adequacy case take note of the political climate in their state and try to garner bi-partisan support for their remedy outside of the courthouse.

While counsel in *Hancock* made a concerted and successful effort to demonstrate to the court the broad based organizational support for its requested remedy, and accordingly had fifteen amicus briefs submitted in support their position,[28] they failed to incite and garner a similar level of sustained and broad based public engagement on an individual or grass roots level. Despite the critical importance of the school funding issues being decided in the *Hancock* case, most of the general public was unaware of the pendency of the litigation. In fact, many students, teachers and parents even in the focus districts were ignorant that the adequacy of the education provided in their very schools was being considered by the courts. There were no rallies or public outcries. While the local news media covered the issuance of each of the *Hancock* decisions, otherwise the public exposure of the case was relatively limited and short-lived. In hindsight, active and vocal public engagement might have helped instigate parallel action by the legislature and might have affected, even if not shifted, the political inclinations of the court. Accordingly, while the litigators themselves are likely not the right individuals to drive public engagement, it is worthwhile for litigators to seek out and partner with local activists and organizers throughout their case to help keep these issues in the forefront of the public consciousness.

Conclusion

As Massachusetts enters 2009, plaintiffs' counsel remains committed to the goal of providing every child within the state with the constitutionally required education. Heeding the lessons learned from *Hancock*, counsel is hopeful that the political climate has again shifted in its favor and the newly elected democratic governor will stand by his campaign commitment to improving educational equity and adequacy. At the time of writing this chapter, however, there is reason for concern. The Governor's proposed budget for Fiscal Year 2010 contains funding reductions that, if implemented, would cause some school districts to reduce their funding to below-foundation levels. The negative implications of this development are all the more alarming given that the foundation level is virtually universally recognized to understate the amount necessary to provide all children, particularly those at risk, with the constitutionally required education. It may well be that additional litigation will be necessary to enforce the rule of law as announced in *McDuffy* and affirmed in *Hancock*. [29]

Biographies

Michael Weisman is the founder and a principal of the Boston-based trial law firm Weisman & McIntyre. In two decades of legal practice, Weisman has represented clients in Massachusetts, Arizona, California, Indiana, Montana, New Hampshire, New York, Rhode Island, Texas, and Vermont, and has worked for clients located in France, Sweden, and Switzerland.

Prior to starting his current firm in 1997, Weisman spent 18 years at Hill & Barrow. Weisman served as chairman of the firm's Trial Department from 1987-1997, and also chaired Hill & Barlow's Tort Law Practice Group. Early in his law career, he clerked for the late Hon. Judge David S. Nelson, United States District Court for the District of Massachusetts and for the Justices of the Massachusetts Superior Court.

Weisman has taught on a variety of civil litigation and trial practice issues at Harvard Law School, Boston University School of Law, Massachusetts Continuing Legal Education, and the Massachusetts Bar Association, among others.

Weisman served as lead counsel on the McDuffy v. Secretary and Hancock v. Driscoll lawsuits. Weisman was the recipient of the "President's Award" from the Massachusetts Federation of Teachers in 1996, the "Distinguished Service Award" from the Massachusetts Association of School Superintendents in 2005, and the "Friend of Public Education Award" from the Massachusetts Association of School Committees also in 2005. He is currently serving as lead counsel in the Indiana school adequacy case and has consulted on school adequacy cases in numerous other states.

Weisman is a Fellow of the American College of Trial Lawyers and a Fellow of the International Academy of Trial Lawyers. He was a founding member as well as former treasurer and president of the Frank J. Murray Inn of Court, an association of judges and lawyers in Boston, modeled after the Inns of Court in Great Britan. For many years, Weisman has also served on the Steering Committee of the Lawyers' Committee for Civil Rights.

Rachel Lipton is a member of the Employment Counseling & Litigation group. She regularly counsels clients on issues relating to personnel manuals, non-competition agreements and discrimination laws. Ms. Lipton has defended clients in the Massachusetts Commission Against Discrimination against claims of religious discrimination and retaliation. She has also defended clients in the court against claims arising under te Massachusetts Wage Act and prosecuted claims of sexual discrimination and retaliation in Federal Court.

Prior to joining Brown Rudnick, Ms. Lipton worked at the Massachusetts Appleseed Center for Law and Justice and at Weisman & Associates in Boston, researching and writing legal memoranda and drafting the proposed findings of fact and rulings of law in the Massachusetts education finance reform case.

During law school, Ms. Lipton worked as a teacher fellow to Harvard Law School Professor Lani Guinier. She also assisted staff attorneys in the Hale and Dorr Legal Services Center Trauma and Learning Policy Initiative advocating on behalf of children affected by domestic violence in their special education needs.

---

1 *McDuffy v. Secretary of the Executive Office of Education*, 415 Mass. 545, 621 (1993).Id. at ___.

2 Subsequent to the *Hancock*Hancock decision, Judge Botsford was appointed by

Governor Deval Patrick to the sSupreme jJudicial cCourt.

3 Mass. Gen. Laws c. 71, § 1.

4 Mass. Gen. Laws c. 71, § 37.

5 <u>See</u> *Hancock v. Comm'r of Educ.*, 443 Mass. 428, 436 (2006).

6 *Id.*

7 *McDuffy*, 415 Mass. at 611.

8 *Hancock*, 443 Mass. at 446; <u>see also</u> *McDuffy*, 415 Mass. at 613 (discussing Mass. Gen. Laws c. 70).

9 <u>See</u> *Webby v. Dukakis*,

10 <u>See</u> *Levy v. Dukakis*,

11 <u>See</u> *McDuffy v. Sec'y of the Executive Office of Educ*, 415 Mass. 545, 606, 611 (1993)

12 *Id.* at 551.

13 *Id.* 620.

14 *Id.* at 614.

15 *Id.* at 618.

16 *Id.* at 621.

17 *Hancock*, 443 Mass. at 436 (citing Education, State House News Service, Jan. 4, 1993).

18 Mass. Gen. Laws c. 69, §§ 1B, 1D, 1E, 1I.

19 *Id.* at § 1D.

20 *Id* at 551, n. 8.

21 The seven curriculum frameworks include: Arts, English Language Arts, Foreign Languages, Comprehensive Health, Mathematics History and Social Science, Science and Technology/Engineering, and English Language Proficiency.

22 A "successful schools" model identifies high performing school districts in terms of a particular State's performance standards and distills what these districts spend for their core regular educational program on a per pupil basis. This base per pupil figure is then used to determine the necessary per pupil expenditure for an actual district by using that district's actual numbers of students and by making weighted adjustments to take into account the number of students who fit into specific populations such as LEP, low-income, special education, etc.

23 The "professional judgment" model convenes various panels of educators to determine the necessary resources for delivering the required education for various types of districts. An expert panel is thereafter convened to reviewed all the panel reports for consistency, and also to assign costs.

24 Summary of Report

25 *Id.*

26 The Courtcourt was deeply divided in its decision. While Chief Justice Marshall wrote the plurality opinion on behalf of herself and two other justices, there was

also a separate concurrence signed by two justices and two separate written dissents.

27 Specifically, Chief Justice Marshall, writing for the court, stated: "Here, the legislative and executive branches have shown that they have embarked on a long-term, measurable, orderly, and comprehensive process of reform "to provide a high quality public education to every child." G. L. c. 69, § 1. They are proceeding purposefully to implement a plan to educate all public school children in the Commonwealth, and the judge did not find otherwise. They have committed resources to carry out their plan, have done so in fiscally troubled times, and show every indication that they will continue to increase such resources as the Commonwealth's finances improve. While the plaintiffs have amply shown that many children in the focus districts are not being well served by their school districts, they have not shown that the defendants are acting in an arbitrary, nonresponsive, or irrational way to meet the constitutional mandate."

28 These included briefs submitted on behalf of State Senator Jarrett T. Barrios & others; the Massachusetts Alliance for Arts Education & others; the Massachusetts Health Council, Inc., & others; the Jewish Alliance for Law and Social Action & others; Jonathan Kozol; Centro Latino de Chelsea & others; the Lawyers' Committee for Civil Rights Under Law of the Boston Bar Association & others; the Massachusetts 2020 Foundation & others; the Massachusetts Teachers Association/NEA & others; the Massachusetts Urban School Superintendents; the Massachusetts Business Alliance for Education & others; MassPartners for Public Schools & another; The Civil Rights Project at Harvard University; the Federation for Children with Special Needs, Inc.; and Strategies for Children, Inc., & another.

8 Making the Case for Rural Schools: Lessons Learned from Finance Litigation in Five States: West Virginia, Arkansas, Tennessee, Alabama, and South Carolina

by Amanda Adler*

Rural students constitute a significant portion of the nation's public school attendees; one-fourth of United States school children go to school in rural areas or small towns of less than 25,000 population. In many states, nearly half of students attend schools in these smaller communities. These children remain largely invisible in the debate over school improvement because the communities in which they attend school are small, sparsely populated and widely dispersed.

Yet despite entrenched generational poverty and historic underfunding, schools are the central public institutions of hope for the rural poor. Education has always been the foundation for self-improvement and economic opportunity in rural places and is also essential to an effective rural development strategy because good schools produce a quality local work force for businesses and make the community they serve a good place to raise children. Committed to these beliefs, rural people are likewise committed to their local schools.

Financing these schools, however, is problematic. Rural areas are fiscally squeezed between three forces: an inadequate local tax base from which to build and support schools, local taxpayer resistance to property taxes, and a state policy environment in which rural schools are perceived as a burden on economically stronger areas. In some rural states, tax structures favoring corporate owners of large rural areas also limit school funding. To meet these challenges, rural people have used both legal strategies and policy-making processes.

Over the last century, legislators and courts have endeavored to address the inequalities in school funding across the nation including in rural communities. Many of these efforts have been spurred by the rural citizens who, in some cases, have initiated litigation to solve the problems of unequal and inadequate educational opportunities in their communities. Some of the most egregious examples of underfunded, crumbling schools are in rural areas, which has leant a moral imperative to claims by rural people seeking better schools. Often lacking political power within their states, rural plaintiffs have been forced to use the courts for redress. It is not an exaggeration to say that the majority of court cases involving the financing of schools had their origin in rural areas of the state. In the education finance litigation in many of the states, rural people have provided the leadership and impetus through years of legal wrangling, high legal costs, and increasing public disapproval and legislative delay to push for change through the courts. In the wake of favorable legal decisions, they have worked to influence public opinion and policymaking to obtain adequate remedies for rural schools.

This chapter seeks to view school finance and education adequacy litigation through the eyes of the rural students on whose behalf many of these cases have been brought, and from the perspective of the parents, families, and communities who have supported the lawsuits and lived with the results. While rural plaintiffs and schools have been the subject of evidence, pleadings, arguments, and court decisions, official court documents provide an incomplete view of the rural educational perspective. This perspective needs to include the impact of litigation not only on rural students' educational opportunities and academic outcomes but also on the political power and political capacity of rural people.

An analysis of school finance lawsuits and the resulting policy landscape in five rural states — West Virginia, Arkansas, Tennessee, Alabama, and South Carolina — identifies important considerations that should guide the work of improving rural schools. These states are also significant because they represent important milestones in school finance litigation history. For example, West Virginia and Arkansas, both set important precedent for subsequent cases that linked finance issues to state academic standards. Tennessee is an example of the extensive educational reforms that can result from litigation. Alabama and South Carolina illustrate the perseverance and multiple strategies needed to achieve real reform in the face of institutionalized racial discrimination.

Conversely, these decisions also illustrate some of the unintended and negative consequences of school funding litigation for rural schools. The focus of some of the litigation on increasing equity among schools — and therefore spending — has resulted in states looking for ways to save money. These have included the application of narrowly focused economy-of-scale principles, which have resulted in school and district consolidation to the detriment of rural students. Arkansas and West Virginia illustrate that a state may respond to a favorable court ruling with an attempt at wholesale consolidation of schools. Tennessee demonstrates the polarization that can occur between suburban and rural interests in the struggle for equitable funding and the need for vigilance over years to prevent erosion of systemic reform.

West Virginia

West Virginia has been described as a rich state with poor people. The conflict between the holders of mineral extraction rights and the citizens who live in coalfield communities dominates the state's economic policy and this conflict has been mirrored in school financing issues. The tax system heavily favors the massive corporate ownership of land and resources and makes it difficult for rural counties to obtain a fair share of property wealth for the schools. Coupled with an inadequate tax base overall, sparsely populated rural counties struggle to meet their students' needs. Over half of rural students in West Virginia are eligible for free or reduced price meals.[1] Students do poorly on academic achievement measures such as the National Assessment of Educational Progress (NAEP).[2] Rural West Virginia has the nation's second highest percentage of special education students, and rural adults in the state have the fourth lowest educational attainment in the nation.[3] Further, the state's schools and districts have the highest ratio of transportation costs to instructional spending of any state.[4]

The physical state of schools in the early 1970's was a major factor that drove parents in rural Lincoln County, West Virginia, to bring a class action lawsuit against state and local school district officials seeking a declaratory judgment that the school finance system violated the West Virginia Constitution. Named plaintiff Janet Pauley found deplorable conditions in her sons' elementary school including an open sewer running behind the school.[5] Pauley has reminisced: "[T]he seats were broken in the school. You couldn't even sit down. I bet there were 21 windows broken out in that school. And, most of all, the smell, oh, you couldn't stand it."[6] The plaintiffs claimed the state was denying their children the constitutionally required "thorough and efficient system of education" as well as denying them equal protection under the law.[7] Plaintiffs claimed that funding and educational opportunities in property-poor counties, such as Lincoln were highly unequal compared to those in more wealthy counties.[8]

The 1975 suit was dismissed by the Kanawha County Circuit Court in 1977, and plaintiffs appealed to the West Virginia Supreme Court.[9] In 1979, the state supreme court overruled the lower court's decision and sent the case back for trial,[10] finding that education is a fundamental right in West Virginia and that the complaint stated a claim under both the West Virginia Constitution's equal protection guarantee and the education article which guarantees a "thorough and efficient" education system.[11] In the majority opinion, Justice Sam Harshbarger wrote that a thorough and efficient system of education meant "the best that the state of education expertise allows."[12]

Then-Circuit Court Judge Arthur Recht was appointed special judge by the state supreme court to oversee the trial. For six weeks, experts and evidence spoke to the gap between what was being offered in some of West Virginia's lowest wealth school districts in comparison to educational opportunities in one of the state's better funded districts and best educational practices available at the time.[13] The trial also examined property tax mechanisms and collection in the state, and evidence showed severe inequities in rates and reassessment. In the 1982 circuit court decision — often referred to as the "Recht Decision" — the circuit court ruled that the West Virginia system of education must be entirely reconstructed. Judge Recht released a 244-

page *Opinion, Findings of Fact and Conclusions of Law and Order* with his order that found "broad and comprehensive constitutional inadequacies in the structure and composition of West Virginia's current educational system, and found the same constitutional infirmities in the financial mechanism that surrounds that system."[14]

The circuit court noted that the greater the property wealth in an area, the higher the quality of the education. Likewise, the circuit court found that the poorer the property wealth, the poorer the quality of education. The circuit court charged the state with failing in its constitutional and statutory duty to achieve high standards of education, and found that "inadequate and inequitable" funding is the predominant cause. Judge Recht also stated that allowing local voters to raise school taxes unfairly favored property-rich places, that the reappraisal of property was irregular, and that the tax system needed to be completely restructured. The decision noted that all county systems needed improvement and that many systems were "woefully inadequate."[15]

Lawyers for the state had argued that broad educational definitions by the state intentionally left standard making up to counties. The judge disagreed and placed the responsibility on the state for both standards and funding. This element of the decision integrated the adequacy approach by comparing educational opportunities in the poor districts to educational quality standards. Judge Recht outlined areas in state education policy that needed completion: curriculum, personnel, materials, equipment, and assessment.[16] In the epilogue of his order, the judge stated that "the when must be now and the who is the judicial branch, bringing together the energy and talents of all interested West Virginians for the benefit of our most precious resource — our children."[17]

The *Pauley I* decision included an order to develop a "master plan for a thorough and efficient education" within 120 days, to appoint a special commissioner to oversee its development, and to develop a plan to overcome the deficiencies in the current tax structure. Consequently, the court ordered the appointment of a special master to oversee "the development of a master plan for the constitutional composition, operation and financing of the educational system in West Virginia."[18] The 1982 decision was not appealed by the state, allowing this remedy phase to begin.

The process was questioned by rural advocates from its inception, however, because the State Department of Education, which had played a major role in defending the state in the case, was named special master over development and implementation of the plan. Linda Martin, a citizen of Lincoln County, ally of Janet Pauley, and education activist, was invited to be on the Master Plan Committee. She characterized their work as tightly controlled by the Department and learned in early stages that the Master Plan ultimately would result in large consolidated schools replacing small community schools across the state.

Martin and other plaintiff allies tried to block the Plan's implementation by seeking to intervene in *Pauley II*.[19] However, in March 1983, the circuit court entered its Final Order approving the Master Plan despite the plaintiffs' unsuccessful appeal claiming the trial court abused its discretion by not submitting a specific timetable for complete plan implementation.[20] The court found that retaining jurisdiction and the time limitation of "at the earliest practicable time" was sufficient.[21]

In that same year, a statewide reappraisal was completed but anti-tax opposition in the state prevented those new standards from taking effect. Further, in a special legislative session, a tax limitation amendment was passed, requiring all property to be assessed at only

60 percent of its market value.[22] A 1987 order said the state should confiscate excess property tax collections and redistribute them.[23] However, in November of 1988, the West Virginia Supreme Court ruled that Judge Recht erred when he ruled that a law permitting a county school district to seek excess property tax levies was unconstitutional.[24] On this point, the state supreme court stated a determination needed to be made whether the counties were getting all the funding to which they were entitled and as to why no reappraisal of property should occur.[25]

The court left intact the ruling that the current school funding system was unconstitutional, but ultimately the property tax issues went unresolved, leaving in place a system that kept the quality of rural schools tied to local property wealth and subject to the power of corporate owners of property in rural school districts who successfully prevented tax increases for schools. In 1990, when the "fair and equitable property valuation program," which required that the assessed valuation of all property be 60% of the true and actual market value, was implemented, rural school districts were further disadvantaged because they became responsible for a larger portion of the basic foundation program due to the mandated increase in assessed valuations.[26]

Consolidation Struggle Begins

The legislature's response to the Master Plan was an economies-of-scale approach. Greater funding was earmarked for school construction but was allocated through the School Building Authority, (SBA) created by the legislature in 1989 to comply with the Master Plan. It was authorized to sell bonds and distribute funding for school building and maintenance. Although multiple factors were considered in allocating funding for school construction, significant weight was given to whether the new or remodeled school facilities increased economies of scale. Consequently, a mass consolidation effort was implemented. This led to children being bused long distances throughout the state, including some preschoolers in Lincoln County, who had to travel one and a half hours each way.[27]

In 1995, Plaintiffs filed a motion in the circuit court to reopen *Pauley v. Kelley*, asserting that the state had failed to implement the Master Plan to reform West Virginia's education system, and asking the court to set a timetable for implementation and appoint a commissioner to oversee it.[28] As noted above, earlier, in 1984 the plaintiffs had appealed to the high court to compel the state to comply with the Master Plan of *Pauley I*.29 At that time, in the face of a state request for a compliance timetable of seventeen years, both the circuit court and supreme court had stated compliance must be implemented at the "earliest practicable time."[20] In 1997, the circuit court found that the State's Public School Support Plan, known as the foundation formula, was "constitutionally deficient."[31]

In 1997, the Governor appointed a Commission on Educational Quality and Equity to "examine the issues raised in recent court decisions in relation to current constitutional provisions, statutes, policies and programs, and craft solutions within the boundaries of fiscal responsibility that build upon and continue the progress underway on improving the quality and equity of education in West Virginia."[32] The commission prepared an update to the Master Plan. In addition, the Governor appointed a Fair Taxation Commission to review the system of taxation, and the commission established six objectives, including developing a constitutional method of funding education.[33] However, this goal was quickly abandoned in favor of providing ultimately unsuccessful support for removing judicial authority over the school finance case. In 1999, Judge Recht called attorneys together to discuss how the mandates of Pauley were being implemented. The negotiations lasted through 2000. In 2002, Recht called on the legislature and governor to develop a timeline for funding reform.

In response to the 1997 order, the legislature enacted West Virginia Code Section 18-2E-5 (1998), which changed the school model from a resource model to a performance model.[34] The performance-based approach is designed to allocate and spend resources where they are most needed.[35] However, in *Tomblin*, Circuit Court Judge Recht found that the 1997 order must be vacated because the formula must be measured within the context of the newly enacted § 18-2E-5, the performance model, giving the State Board of Education and the Superintendent of Education "an opportunity to identify specific deficiencies as contemplated by West Virginia Code § 18-2E-5."[36] Judge Recht ruled that the court would no longer maintain jurisdiction because "that would cynically suggest that the legislative and executive branches have no intention of fulfilling the destiny of public education endorsed in § 18-2E-5(a)."[37]

In the meantime, rural West Virginians challenged the state's efforts to tie school funding to school consolidation in various court actions. In 1998, Pendleton Citizens for Community Schools sued the state over the decision to close a local high school, Circleville High because when it closed, students would be bused to a new, county-wide school being built nearly 17 miles away.[38] The circuit court found that the Pendleton Citizens effectively argued "community-based schools produce significant benefits, especially for rural children with their higher rates of poverty, and that closing their school and the… insistence on consolidation threatened rural students statewide with irreparable harm."[39]

The circuit court cataloged all of the potential problems that consolidation creates, as proven by the plaintiffs: "Long commute(s) interfere with students' study time; larger schools mean lower participation rates ...in extracurricular activities; the level of parental involvement...diminishes; (it) creates a significant risk of substantially increasing the dropout rate among students."[40] The court found that the West Virginia school funding system, including the economies-of-scale requirement, forced local school districts into consolidation. The circuit court also held that this forced consolidation "violated the plaintiffs' fundamental right to an education guaranteed to them by Article XII, section 1 of the West Virginia Constitution."[41]

However, the West Virginia Supreme Court reversed the circuit court's decision in July 1998, siding with appellants, who argued "no jurisdiction has found that school consolidation and/or a state policy of incentives to consolidate result in… adverse effects that implicate a constitutional right to educational opportunities."[42] The court concluded that "there is no reasonably detailed identification… of alternatives to the policies complained of by appellees. It is not clear… that there are less discriminatory, feasible… alternatives to those policies."[43]

In 2000, the plaintiffs in the reopened *Pauley* case, now captioned *Tomblin v. Gainer*, asked once again for a specific timetable for implementation, specifically on the finance issues. Like many states, West Virginia's generally underassessed property values and variations among counties in local levies significantly limited tax revenue; however, these limitations effectively cut off the means for paying for the judicially-mandated systems change: the Master Plan. In a 2003 decision in *Tomblin*, issued by Judge Recht, the same trial judge who presided over the original *Pauley* trial, the court ordered the State Board of Education to evaluate and report on individual schools' specific needs, including personnel, curriculum and facilities, and request additional resources, if needed. [45] However, Judge Recht also ended the court's continuing jurisdiction, finding the finance and educational accountability systems implemented by the legislature constitutional, and dismissed the case.[xlv] A subsequent 2003 petition to reopen the lawsuit was denied.

Leading up to and following the conclusion of the state school finance case, citizens' groups, many partnering with or part of Challenge West Virginia, continued to mount challenges to the "bloody hammer" of consolidations.[46] Various legal approaches were tested, including challenging procedural violations of the West Virginia Constitution, Code, and State Rules as consolidations were planned and implemented without following legislatively mandated guidelines. Citizens also objected to the selling of bonds to finance consolidations without the agreement of the voters on the purpose of the bonds. New legislation was unsuccessfully proposed to require community votes on consolidation. Residents of affected communities faithfully attended and participated in the administrative process at the local and state school boards and worked to communicate the irreparable harm of long bus rides on children, as well as the enormous costs of building large consolidated schools. In the short term, the fight was lost, but long-term successes would eventually come.

The *Pauley v. Kelly* plaintiffs' arguments focused on both equity, citing disparities in resources among West Virginia school districts, and adequacy, referring to educational standards adopted by the state that low-wealth districts could not meet. This litigation took school finance litigation further than previous school finance cases.[47] As an equity case, it broadened "the notion of equity from one predominantly focused on financial inequalities arising from the structure of the school finance system, to one focused on equally providing all students what is required for them to have a fair opportunity to achieve desired educational outcomes."[48] The practical effect shifted the legal arguments in a new direction and also directed remedies more specifically at educational programs, not just revenues.[49]

Although no school funding litigation is currently pending in West Virginia, children in the state scored two long-needed victories in the legislature. As of July 2008, elementary students can no longer be bused more than forty-five minutes one-way. This non-retroactive legislation allows some room for special cases but any bus ride over an hour is absolutely prohibited.[50]

Also, during the 2008 legislative session, West Virginia passed a new school funding formula, the first since 1960.[51] Figures vary, but it is estimated that as much as S35 million per year in new funding will be added to education over the five-year phase-in period. The new formula ties the level of funded professional and service staff to student density in the state's counties, better supporting the ability of low-density rural districts to attract and retain teachers.[52] Per pupil funding is weighted accordingly, with sparser districts receiving more funding. The new formula also changes the way special education is funded in the state, an acute issue for rural districts. Formerly, adjusted enrollment counts effectively provided a financial incentive for identifying students as needing special education services, but the new formula eliminates that practice, protects districts with declining enrollment, and implements a special education account for high acuity special education students to be accessed by districts.[53]

Unified Advocacy

The *Pauley* litigation had the effect of unifying the advocacy efforts of rural activists in West Virginia. These efforts grew more sophisticated through the process and have yielded some important successes. Janet Pauley's concern for the conditions at her children's school and Linda Martin's leadership and grasp of the political landscape have paved the way for a statewide network. Challenge West Virginia evolved from these efforts. It is a school community leadership project that encourages grassroots participation in state education policy, and serves as an education forum to assist rural people in improving small rural schools. Linda Martin formed Challenge in 1998. This non-profit organization has led the fight against school consolidation and is active in 30 of the state's 55 counties. Early work of the organization also centered on the Appalachian Land Study conducted by the Highland Center, which revealed that the West Virginia tax structure heavily favors large industry in the state, especially coal companies.

Much of the work of Challenge was to fight school closings and the messaging strategies of those efforts bear documenting. Few states pursued consolidation more aggressively than West Virginia, and by some estimates, the state has spent $1 billion to close 320 small rural schools.[54] While the state touted cost savings and efficiency of larger schools and districts, rural advocates countered with the adverse effects of long bus rides on students and increased transportation spending. During this period of school closings, the state's cost per pupil for transporting students to school steadily increased. From 1991-2002, transportation costs per pupil nearly doubled, even though fewer students actually rode the bus.[55] West Virginia spends a higher percentage of school funding on transportation than any other state — seven percent.[56]

The motives of rural people were frequently challenged, as they are in many instances: those opposing consolidation are often accused of wanting to protect a sports program or some other special interest, of being provincial or anti-progress. But Challenge and its allies effectively kept the focus on the students who faced the hours-long rides to consolidated schools. From the vantage point of rural West Virginia, a significant outcome of the school funding litigation was the formation of Challenge of West Virginia, which created a solid political force and engaged the public in rural areas that had been effectively disenfranchised.

Arkansas

For over a century the Arkansas Constitution has recognized education as the primary source in providing "intelligence and virtue" that will safeguard "liberty and the bulwark of a free and good government."[57] To transform this ideal into reality, the Arkansas Constitution mandates that "the State shall ever maintain a general, suitable and efficient system of free public schools."[58] A tiny rural district in the eastern Arkansas Delta with only 200 students set out to enforce the constitutional standard, and as a result the education landscape in Arkansas was changed significantly. Lake View School District was extremely poor,[59] and all of its students African-American. Lake View was one of the 200 planned communities of the Resettlement Administration — later the Farm Security Administration — which enabled poor, landless people to become owners of homes.[60] Sixty of those communities, including Lake View, were planned farm communities where residents were also able to purchase quality farm land and outbuildings and to participate in cooperative management of community economic institutions such as cotton gins. The communities also had a school, community center, and health center. For Lake View, the litigation it initiated did not have a happy ending: ultimately, it cost Lake View its school.

In 1992, the plaintiffs, students and taxpayers of Lake View, sued then-Arkansas Governor Jim Guy Tucker, the State Board of Education, its members, the Speaker of the House, the Senate Pro Tempore, the State Treasurer, and the Director of the Department of Education, asserting that Arkansas' school funding system violated the equal protection and education clauses of the Arkansas Constitution.[61] In 1994, the circuit court held that the funding system violated both the Arkansas equal protection provision and its education clause, finding that the fiscal and educational disparity between the poor and wealthy districts had "no rational bearing on the educational needs of the district," and did not "provide a general, suitable, and efficient system of free public education."[62] The court in effect ordered that the school funding system was unconstitutional but stayed the effect of its decision for two years to allow the legislature time to implement a constitutional system.[63]

The legislature passed new funding laws, which effectively repealed the funding system at issue in the 1994 decision.[64] In addition, in 1996 Arkansas voters passed an amendment to the State Constitution "which fixed a uniform rate of 25 mills for each school district as the *ad valorem* property tax rate for the maintenance and operation of the public schools and permitted increases in the uniform millage rate as "variances" to enhance public education."[65] Consequently, the circuit court postponed a trial on the merits. In 1996, Lake View won approval to have the case designated a class action and that tiny district represented all school districts, students, parents and taxpayers in the state.[66]

The following year, Lake View lawyers negotiated a strange agreement to end the case. The proposed deal would have allowed them to collect legal fees from the state but obligated Lake View to drop its lawsuit and agree not to challenge the funding system again. This agreement was challenged by the Arkansas American Civil

Liberties Union, who successfully argued that members of the class would receive nothing in return for giving up their standing to challenge the constitutionality of the system.[67] The circuit court agreed, rejecting the deal.[68] That year, the circuit court also ruled that changes to the school finance system had rendered the case moot.[69] On appeal, the Arkansas Supreme Court ruled that the case was not moot because the 1994 decision was stayed for two years with no final order and should be considered by the circuit court.[70] Neither party had appealed from the circuit court's 1994 order at the end of the two years.[71]

In 2001, after a 19-day trial, the Pulaski County Chancery Court declared the state's education funding system unconstitutional because it was inadequate and because an equal opportunity for education was not being afforded to Arkansas students. In addition, the court found that an adequacy cost study was necessary to determine the amount of money needed to provide a constitutionally adequate educational system.[72]

The governor appealed the case to the Arkansas Supreme Court. Several groups representing rural interests participated in the *Lake View* litigation. The Arkansas Public Policy Panel and The Rural School and Community Trust filed an amicus brief urging the Arkansas Supreme Court to uphold the decision that the Arkansas school funding formula resulted in constitutionally inadequate education opportunities and was unconstitutionally inequitable.[73] The groups emphasized that the effects of poverty and the disadvantages of rural geography could be substantially mitigated for rural students by equal and adequate opportunities. The state supreme court affirmed the lower court's findings, giving the state until January 1, 2004, to perform a cost study and establish a constitutional funding system.[74]

Consolidation Struggle Begins

Despite the favorable decision, a subsequent shift in state education policy would ultimately harm rural schools that now had a mandate for adequate and equitable funding. State officials undertook to pass a massive plan of school consolidation, ostensibly to help meet the goals of adequacy and equity. Just two months after the *Lake View III* decision,[75] Governor Huckabee addressed the General Assembly to advocate for consolidation of school districts with less than 1500 students.

The response was a public outcry in opposition. Advocates from across the state formed the geographically and racially diverse Arkansas Grass Roots Network to fight the governor's push to close many rural schools.[76] The alliance offered a 10-point plan as an alternative to consolidation.[77] The grassroots plan required schools to be adequately funded and have the ability to offer courses through a variety of means, including distance education.

At the state supreme court's deadline, the legislature was still in session arguing largely over school consolidation. A highly controversial consolidation law, Act 60, was eventually passed that ultimately eliminated 57 districts in the state, including Lake View. A later lawsuit brought by Lake View about the long bus rides that resulted from consolidation contended that Act 60 racially discriminated against predominantly black districts that were not afforded options to closure.

In the 2004 *Lake View* busing case, plaintiffs asserted in federal court that the consolidation of their Arkansas district was unconstitutional and violated both federal constitutional rights and the Voting Rights Act by not allowing them to elect their school boards or be represented on budget matters.[78] Plaintiffs asserted that closing their local school would damage their children's "self-esteem, ethnic pride, psychological balance and ability to receive an education."[79] The plaintiffs argued that, following the school closing in 2004, children "suffered academic, social, and disciplinary problems".[80] A study completed by the Rural Trust and used by the plaintiffs confirmed that forced school district consolidation resulted in a 55% decrease in the number of African-American school board members in Arkansas.[81] The suit however, was ultimately unsuccessful.[82]

With respect to reform of school funding, when the state did not meet the court-imposed 2004 deadline, plaintiffs brought a compliance motion, resulting in the appointment of special masters by the court[83] and swift action by the legislature to make substantial increases to school funding.[84] The two special masters reported "laudable progress" to the state supreme court, and a divided court terminated its jurisdiction in June 2004.[85] The court stopped short of saying that the state's efforts met the requirements of the Arkansas Constitution but did say that further consolidation may be inevitable.[86]

However, after the 2005 legislative session, at the behest of the 49 plaintiff districts, the court issued a per curium order to recall the mandate and reappoint the earlier special masters.[87] In October of 2005 the special masters issued a report, which concluded that the legislature had not met its constitutional mandate.[88] In late 2005, the Arkansas Supreme Court ruled that the legislature had failed to comply with its own school funding statutes and had underfunded education and set a December 2006 deadline for legislative action,[89] which was met by the legislature in a special session.[90]

The reappointed masters issued a report in May 2007, which the Arkansas Supreme Court adopted.[91] The court closed the 15-year-old case, finding that the General Assembly had taken the required and necessary steps to assure that an adequate education and a substantially equal educational opportunity are provided to all school children.[92] The court noted that new statutory requirements for the state to undertake regular adequacy studies and to fund education as its first priority were reasons for confidence that the gains for students will not disappear in the future.[93] The court ruled that the legislature had complied with prior court rulings and established a constitutionally acceptable school finance system, including state support for facilities, and had processes in place to continue to provide adequate resources for schools in the future.[94] The court's unanimous decision was praised by most state officials, but some education experts cautioned that more systemic changes in the tax structure were also needed to accomplish equity.

During this time rural advocates were also attempting to stop other school closures brought on by consolidation. During the summer of 2006, patrons of Paron High School sought to prove in court the detrimental effects of school consolidation and busing; they produced documentation showing that students in 33 schools in the district had daily bus rides of 3 hours or more. They provided expert testimony regarding dropout rates, declining parental involvement, and illness created by long bus rides. Nonetheless, this lawsuit was unsuccessful and the school was closed.[95]

Rural advocacy efforts played a significant role in the *Lake View* case through the years of litigation. A stimulus was the Governor's consolidation plan which produced shock within the education community. Lavina Grandon, then a full-time teacher, was one of the advocates who crafted a response to Governor Huckabee's consolidation proposal, which would have lowered the number of school districts in the state from 312 to 75. Within days of the announcement of the plan, Grandon and fellow consolidation opponents mobilized the community to solicit support and to plan regional rallies. The immediate outcome was successful: the Governor, even with the support of the Senate and House Chairs of their respective education committees, was unable to obtain passage of consolidation legislation during that session. In the House, a sponsor could not even be found. During the summer, the Rural Grassroots Network held meetings throughout the state with legislators to garner public support and held a statewide rally with thousands of supporters on the capitol steps.

As a result of their efforts, many legislators supported the move to preserve small schools and the consolidation measure passed was much more limited than the original proposal.

Still, the effects of consolidation are being experienced in multiple ways by students. Some Arkansas children are traveling as much as seventy miles each way to school. School leaders in the state believe that lengthy commutes are causing some students to drop out and some families to opt to homeschool, and research confirms a trend of lower participation in school activities for students facing long rides.[96] Lavina Grandon's rural organization, Advocates for Rural and Community Education (ACRE) is providing transition support for students and communities that lost their schools, as well as working to ensure that students are able to learn in small classes with caring teachers. ACRE also works to ensure community involvement in the school budgeting process.

Progress

The *Lake View* case can be considered a significant victory for rural plaintiff districts in challenging inadequate and inequitable funding systems although this was accompanied by a consolidation plan that eliminated nearly 60 small rural districts, including Lake View. Before the suit, Arkansas' poverty rate was 16.4%, 63% greater than the national average[97] and the state relied on local property taxes to fund public schools, which seriously disadvantaged rural schools that are typically located in very low property wealth areas.[98] In fact, the state's per capita expenditure on education was the lowest in the nation and this was reflected in poor national and state test results, very low teacher salaries, and dilapidated and ill-equipped school buildings in rural districts.[99] In addition, there was a $1,800 difference in per-pupil annual spending between the Arkansas schools spending at the 95th percentile and those spending at the 5th percentile.[100] *Lake View* ultimately led to increased state funding for public education. Operating aid increased by over $400 million. And the state committed to an increase in facilities funding of over $846 million.[101]

The *Lake View* decision stated that equal educational opportunities must be provided to all students, including facilities that are "safe, dry, well-lit, and equipped." As a result, Arkansas developed an "equalized millage" plan that helps low-wealth districts that are unable to rely solely on local bond issues to improve and build the facilities they need. The state also directed school districts to provide a certain minimum of financial support to assist in meeting the mandate to provide adequate facilities. Failure of districts to comply with this directive could result consolidation since if districts do not meet certain standards in their facilities or if they are considered in "fiscal distress", they could suffer consequences ranging from forced changes in the budget to state takeover or consolidation.[102]

Since the suit was filed students have done better on state achievement measures. A greater proportion of Arkansas students are considered "proficient" on state tests, and the achievement gap between whites and minorities has decreased.[103] The work of rural advocates was critical at every stage of the process — driving the lawsuits, working to mitigate consolidation, and now, preventing further school closures and supporting students in newly consolidated schools. Those closest to the issues cite a mixed result from the litigation. Although some consolidation resulted from the successful school finance litigation, the consolidation plan adopted by the legislature was more limited than the Governor proposed. Importantly, education funding almost doubled, and education is now required to be funded as a first priority before any other state expenditure. As a result of rural political action, legislators are much more responsive to rural issues and concerns and the state today is less likely to be in conflict with rural interests.[104]

Tennessee

Tennessee is a state known for its regional geographic divides and is often called "the three Tennessees." Each of the three regions is distinct culturally and otherwise, and each has both a strong rural and urban presence. Another notable feature of the state is the economic rural-urban divide, which is growing, although Tennessee's rural counties have been growing more quickly than their urban counterparts. These population trends have helped maintain a strong rural representation in the legislature but urban legislators are fast closing the gap. Except that the state's political climate is mainly conservative, with a strong pro-business and anti-tax sentiment. It is one of only a few states without a personal income tax, except the state does tax personal income from dividends and interest. Tennessee's public schools serve a greater proportion of rural students than all but nine other states, and its rural areas tend to be some of the poorest in the country. Although Tennessee has a fairly equitable educational funding system, spending on instruction is among the nation's lowest.[105] Among rural states, Tennessee ranks fourth in its percentage of rural special needs students.[106] And, a significant proportion of rural adults — 73.3 percent — lack a high school diploma.[107]

In 1986, three school superintendents formed a coalition, Tennessee Small School Systems (TSSS) ("*System*" is the state term for district).[108] In 1988, the TSSS and other plaintiffs — including parents, students, rural school districts, superintendents, and board of education members — filed suit claiming that Tennessee's education funding system violated the Tennessee Constitution because the funding system denied public school students the right to equal education because of disparities in resources between rural and urban counties. With these arguments, the Plaintiffs combined adequacy and equity theories. Although many of these rural systems were poor, poverty was not confined to the plaintiffs' rural schools. At the time of the lawsuit, almost 50 percent of Tennessee's students eligible to participate in the federal lunch program were in nine large urban and suburban districts. And those districts intervened in the case to join the state as defendants out of concern for losing funding to rural districts.

The trial took six weeks and was held in Davidson County. Chancellor C. Allen High ruled on August 6, 1991, that the public education funding system violated the equal protection clause of the Tennessee Constitution. He found that students in rural schools did not have equal access to science laboratories, computers, current and new textbooks, adequate buildings, foreign language courses, state-mandated art and music classes, and other curricular opportunities.[109] When the state appealed, the Tennessee Court of Appeals reversed the trial court, said that it would not follow any blind trends — referring to recent school finance decisions in Kentucky and elsewhere — and set the stage for arguments before the Tennessee Supreme Court.

An *ad hoc* committee of state education officials had already begun analysis of the state education finance system in 1986. When the trial court ruled in 1991, legislative efforts were already underway to implement the committee's recommendations, as well as to make district management changes and impose accountability standards. The final legislation, the Education Improvement Act, (EIA) passed in 1992, adopted a new system of finance called the Basic Education Program (BEP), which was designed to fund a basic education and determine local funding share on the basis of fiscal capacity. Additional education funding needed under the BEP was estimated at $665 million to be phased in over six years.

BEP was designed to increase the state's share of education funding to 70 percent, from its then 50 percent share. Governor Ned McWherter unsuccessfully proposed that an income tax be adopted to pay for these education reforms. Instead, the Legislature passed a half-cent increase in the state sales tax to be dedicated to education. The EIA also gave the Commissioner of Education power to remove locally elected school boards and their superintendents from office if districts did not meet performance goals.

The Governor and Legislature hoped that the reforms would put an end to the litigation, but the rural plaintiffs were unsatisfied. Tennessee is reliant on sales, use and property tax receipts for education. However, the half-cent sales tax increase authorized by the EIA paid less than a fourth of the additional costs of equitably funding schools, and did not resolve how low-wealth rural districts would make up the difference. Lewis Donelson, the lawyer representing the districts, noted at the time that the phase-in aspect of the new funding formula left the rural systems without any immediate help to remedy their deplorable educational situations including decaying physical plants, inadequate heating, showers that did not work, buckling floors, leaking roofs, inadequate science labs, and outdated textbooks and libraries, which were common conditions in the state's rural schools, as had been noted by the trial court.[110] When crafting a response to the legislature, the *Small Schools* rural plaintiffs met with and agreed with suburban systems that the litigation should continue, focused on the issue of full funding of the BEP.

From its inception the BEP faced legal and political pressure over how to raise the additional revenues. Members of the business community and other anti-tax forces opposed any tax increases and insisted on programmatic accountability provisions as well as appointment of local superintendents by school boards. Ironically, one of the "accountability" measures was a prohibition on new revenues being spent on teacher salary increases. The cost-based system otherwise offered a great deal of spending flexibility with components of the BEP falling into only two categories: classroom and nonclassroom expenses.

The Court of Appeals reversed the trial court's 1991 decision, and in 1993, the Supreme Court of Tennessee upheld the trial court and ruled that the state's education finance system did indeed violate the Tennessee Constitution's equal protection clause.[111] The court found that the system created impermissible disparities in the educational opportunities available to public school students, evidenced by significant differences in teacher qualifications, student performance, and basic educational programs and facilities. The court found that the educational disparities shown in the case did not result from a lack of local effort. There was much testimony about the "Wal Mart effect" by which the location of such a store drew sales tax collections from surrounding counties. The court stated that local control did not justify the disparities.

Subsequently, the legislature revised the funding system again, but the plaintiffs contended that the plan violated the state's equal protection clause because of the failure to equalize teacher salaries and the length of the phase-in of new funds. In 1995, the court upheld the reform timetable[112] but also held that teachers' salary increases must be included in the equalization formula in order to meet the objectives of the plan. As a result, the legislature passed the Teachers' Salary Equity Plan in 1995. However, the plaintiffs sought equalization of teacher salaries across the state by filing a successful motion with the Tennessee Supreme Court seeking assumption of jurisdiction because of the public importance and need for an expedited decision.[113] The plaintiffs claimed that teacher salaries are a significant factor in determining where teachers choose to live and work, asking the court to order a cost determination concerning what it takes to recruit and retain teachers for rural systems, and asking the court to rule the Salary Equity Plan a failure.[114]

In October 2002, the supreme court held that the 1995 Teachers' Salary Equity Plan failed to provide substantially equal educational opportunity.[115] The justices found no rational basis for excluding the largest and most important component of educational opportunities — a qualified teacher — from the equalization cost analysis required for other components of the school funding plan.[116] The court stated that there was no cost determination or annual cost review of teachers' salaries, even though other salaries were equalized through the BEP.[117] The court pointed out that relying on a salary schedule with training and experience factors for all districts is not the same as equalizing the salaries and in fact channels money to wealthier districts that can afford more experienced and better trained teachers.

After *Small Schools III*, revisions to the formula addressed the salary equity funding issue. These included incorporating real-world average salaries and requiring a BEP Review Committee to conduct an annual cost review of teachers' salaries. Changes in the formula for equalization purposes were required to be submitted to the Tennessee house and senate education committees for review and approval. In 2006, *Small School Systems* was closed by a Davidson County judge, Chancellor Carol McCoy, who ruled that there were no current issues for the court to decide. Plaintiff attorneys had asked the court to leave the case open, citing lobbying efforts by urban districts as a threat to the BEP. Judge McCoy agreed with the state's lawyers that the case could not be continued indefinitely on a "what if" basis, but she also said that she would consider reopening the case if the BEP were repealed or substantially changed.

Tennessee illustrates the need for political action to achieve positive outcomes following a good decision. From the outset, rural advocates worked through a multifaceted approach that included legislation, negotiation, and organizing. School funding in the state increased dramatically even in competition with other state spending that also increased during this period. For example, during the same period (1988 – 1992), Medicaid expenditures increased by 103.6% creating resistance from the business sector to additional investment in education.

As a result of the lawsuit, spending disparities were reduced among districts, classroom expenditures increased, and the public school curriculum was improved. Ninety-four percent of state funding to districts was equalized under the new system. The BEP's spending flexibility appealed to districts. Average total funding per student in the plaintiff districts increased 32% the year following implementation and funding increased 23% per student in other districts. Urban districts, however, criticized the BEP, saying that it ignored the needs of poor students in their schools.

Subsequently, in 2007, Tennessee's BEP was substantially revised by the legislature. The changes to the BEP are to be implemented over a three-year period with an infusion of $524 million in new spending and will be funded, in part, by a controversial 42-cent increase in the state's cigarette tax. The new BEP, dubbed BEP 2.0, increased education spending overall and increased the state share of teacher salaries from 65% to 75%. It provides additional funding to reduce teacher-student ratios for at-risk students, and for English Language Learners. As sought by suburban and urban districts, BEP 2.0 changed the fiscal capacity measure by removing personal income from the wealth measure, which had greatly diminished what those districts received from the state.

Despite these changes in the BEP, rural litigants still feel rural priorities are now better recognized by the state. Edd Diden, a rural superintendent in Cannon County who has been involved in the rural school finance litigation almost from its inception, notes that the rural-urban divide has abated some in recent years with regular full funding for at-risk student supports. Diden credits Governor Phil Breseden for his commitment to education through the process.[118] Lewis Donelson, the lawyer for *Small Schools* plaintiffs who is still monitoring the case and its aftereffects, characterizes any ill effects to rural districts as relatively minor.[119] However, urban systems continue to criticize even the revised BEP and are considering litigation of their own at this writing. The state's four major urban areas have claimed that the local capacity calculations, which govern the state and local shares of BEP, still limit their ability to serve their at-risk and ELL populations. Urban districts cite their concentrations of poverty, a common urban condition that is exacerbated by overly large schools that by many accounts do at-risk students a disservice.

Despite the gains, Tennessee's public schools face significant challenges. As in Arkansas and West Virginia, Tennessee's rural areas experience high rates of poverty and adult unemployment. [120] Further, rural spending on instruction is among the lowest and graduation rates and scores on the National Assessment on Educational Progress are among the worst in the country.[121]

In the *Small Schools* decisions, the Tennessee Supreme Court made significant rulings that have been widely cited on several points, including the justiciability of issues relating to educational funding inequities: that state courts have a responsibility to overturn school finance systems that are inequitable. *Small Schools* also serves as a landmark case for rural schools, standing for the responsibility of courts to address equity claims, particularly the claims of rural schools, and for singling out the need for ongoing commitment to ensuring that funding systems address teacher salaries as a critical component of good schools. The State of Tennessee was forced to mitigate the resource disadvantages faced by rural districts — disadvantages that affect rural districts across the country. The *Small Schools* litigation and ensuing legislative developments are unusual in that rural concerns dictated the manner in which the remedy was implemented. Because of the length of the litigation, plaintiffs and their allies had to commit to this struggle for the long-term. The lowest wealth districts organized, brought, and successfully supported the lawsuit for 20 years even in the face of conflicts with urban interests, a conflict that still exists in Tennessee.

Alabama

Like West Virginia, Alabama is characterized by significant corporate property holdings, which have heavily influenced the tax structure of the state, undermining education revenues. Alabama's property taxes are by far the lowest in the nation, and rural instructional expenditures are also very low.[122] The most powerful advocates for low property taxes in Alabama have traditionally been those entities and individuals, such as large timber companies, that hold huge tracts of "unimproved" — primarily forest — acreage that is mainly in rural places. Property tax restrictions are part of the 1901 state constitution and include constitutional amendments added in the 1970s that further restrict the capacity of localities to raise property taxes, especially in rural areas.

Property tax millages are limited and assessment rates are kept artificially low. Alabama local property tax rates are limited to 6.5 mills with an optional 1-mill county assessment. The unspoken intent of this limitation was to prevent white property owners from being taxed to pay for schools educating African-American children. Also, assessments are very low; for example, forest land, which makes up 70% of Alabama's land, can only be taxed at a 10% current use assessment value. As a result, forest land contributes only 2% of all property tax revenue. The resulting underfunding of schools falls disproportionately on African-American students, largely in rural areas.[123] As a result of these restrictions, local governments are forced to rely heavily on sales taxes to fund schools. However, rural counties generate low sales tax revenues, so they often lack the means of raising adequate revenues for schools.

In 1990, the Alabama Coalition for Equity (ACE), a nonprofit organization comprised of 25 school systems — 24 rural counties and one small town system — and a number of parents and children in the school systems, filed a suit in the Montgomery County Circuit Court seeking declaratory and injunctive relief, challenging the constitutionality of the state's education finance system on adequacy grounds and also claiming that the method of school funding violated the state's equal protection clause. That same year, the Alabama

Disabilities Advocacy Program brought a John Doe action in state court with additional claims on behalf of children with disabilities claiming the state failed to provide "appropriate education and special services" as required by statute. Their motion to intervene in the *ACE* case was granted in January 1991.[124]

That same month, the ACLU, filed a class action with Mary Harper, named plaintiff, alleging a violation of the state's education clause.[125] In *Harper* the Alabama Department of Education was a willing defendant and during the course of the litigation actually switched sides to join the plaintiffs. The *Harper* and Disability Advocacy Program complaints were certified as a class and subclass, and all three cases were eventually consolidated by the court into *ACE v. Hunt*, commonly referred to as the "Equity Funding Case."[126] The case was bifurcated into liability and remedy stages.[127]

One of the initial claims to be resolved in *Harper* concerned State Constitutional Amendment 111, added in 1956 following *Brown vs. Board of Education* which stated that Alabama has no responsibility for public education. Early in the *Harper* case, the court said the amendment was void under the 14th Amendment to the United States Constitution, reestablishing a child's right to an education under the state constitution. This partial summary judgment order was not challenged by the defendants.

At the 1992 trial in the consolidated cases on the liability issue, the plaintiffs examined the educational adequacy of inputs and outcomes and also emphasized the profound disparities affecting their districts and students.[128] In response, defendants argued that local control and — as an extension — local taxation caused the gaps and that court intervention was a violation of the separation of powers doctrine.[129] In August 1992, the court issued a declaratory judgment for the plaintiffs on the liability phase of the case.[130]

In 1993, the trial court entered the liability phase judgment and ruled that the Alabama Constitution requires that schools be adequately and equitably funded.[131] The court recognized that students have different educational needs and, thus, equal educational opportunity does not necessarily mean precisely equal funding.[132] The court judged equity in terms of "substantial equity and fairness in the way the state's system of public schools allocates educational opportunity to its students."[133] According to the court, because money provides opportunities and programs such as computers and field trips to students, equal opportunity is rooted in the equity in school funding.[134] For example, the Mountain Brook city school system had $4,820 in state and local revenues to spend per pupil where the Roanoke city schools had only $2,371 per pupil.[135]

The court did not agree with the state's assertion that it was local citizens who cause funding disparities because "by setting low requirements for local effort, and failing to equalize local funds with state dollars, the state has allowed educational opportunities for schoolchildren to hinge on local tax decisions."[136] The court then defined the right to an education and the essential principles and features of public schools in Alabama. The court laid responsibility for the school system in state officials' hands and enjoined them to create and implement a system that would result in an equitable and adequate education.[137] Following the ruling, the State Board of Education, Superintendent, and Speaker of the House realigned themselves as defendants in the action.

The Alabama Supreme Court was then asked by the legislature to issue an advisory opinion on whether the legislature was required to comply with the circuit court's order. The supreme court affirmed the lower court and required the state to comply.[138] When the court affirmed, the parties were ordered to work on a remedy plan to comport with the judgment. The parties worked under a court-appointed facilitator, and by October of 1993, a plan was offered to and preliminarily approved by the trial court. After the remedial plan was agreed upon, a public hearing was scheduled since the remedy would impact the certified class of students. The order said that there must be adequate and equitable funding of the education system including facilities, and that services must be offered to overcome social and economic barriers to learning. Before the public hearing on the reasonableness, fairness, and adequacy of the proposed remedy, three classes of persons sought to intervene: gifted students, students in schools already providing an adequate education, and parents. The trial court denied these motions, but on appeal the Supreme Court of Alabama reversed their denial and allowed these plaintiff intervenors into the remedy phase of the case.[139]

The plan was ruled final by the trial court in December of 1993. Important elements of the plan included the need for performance standards, a sound infrastructure, and equitable and adequate funding. After Governor Forrest (Fob) James was elected in 1994, he petitioned the court to vacate the orders of the trial court, dismiss the actions, and exercise no further jurisdiction. In 1995, the Alabama Supreme Court denied the governor's petition on liability but said he could appeal when the remedy became a final order, which it had not because the court retained jurisdiction. Later that year, the trial judge, Eugene Reese, was removed from the Equity Funding Case by the Judicial Inquiry Commission on questions regarding his impartiality after he campaigned for the Alabama Supreme Court by promoting his leadership in the case.

Governor James continued to petition the trial court to end the case and the new trial judge denied the motions but moved the jurisdiction over the remedy plan from the court to an independent monitor. In 1995, James and other defendants renewed their claim before the state supreme court and added other claims questioning the entire proceeding given the shifting of parties and subsequent removal of the trial judge which they argued had tainted the entire process. In 1997 the Alabama Supreme Court vacated the remedy order, stating that even though the separation of powers doctrine does not prohibit the judiciary from fashioning a remedy for constitutional violations, the judiciary should only do so if the legislature fails to take appropriate action.[140] Thus, the high court held the trial court abused its discretion not by trying to implement a remedy plan but by doing so before the other branches of government had a chance to create a valid plan. The court gave the legislature one year to come up with a plan.[141] On reconsideration, the court changed the time from one year to a "reasonable period."

Subsequently, remedy negotiations were held, in which no third party interests were permitted to participate. Various groups worked through the Governor's Task Force on Education Reform.[142] A plan was submitted to the trial court in October 2001 and a hearing on progress was scheduled for December 2001. The plan included a definition of an adequate level of education for Alabama, a phase-in schedule for implementing the adequate system, and an estimated funding cost. The hearing on the plan was rescheduled for July 2002, but before it could occur, the Alabama Supreme Court took an unexpected action that ensured that the plan would never be implemented

In January 2002, the Alabama Supreme Court put the Equity Funding Case back on its rehearing docket. It ordered the attorneys to discuss the original causes of action and consider whether the plaintiffs even had standing to sue.[143] In February 2002, the Alabama State Board of Education approved a list of required programs and initiatives to be funded, designed to comply with the liability and remedy orders. The Board also made recommendations about the needed reforms to the state tax system. In May 2002, the state supreme court dismissed the case,[144] stating that separation of powers principles dictated that its jurisdiction, and that of any trial court requiring disbursement of state funds, must end.[145] In separate concurring opinions, members of the court also undermined issues resolved by the trial court about the lack of a right to education in Alabama and of the presence of an equal protection clause in the Alabama Constitution.[146] The dissent pointed out that the court had not been asked to rule on any finding since 1998. After the case was dismissed, implementation of the State Board plan stopped and did not resume.

Following the extraordinary sequence of events in the School Equity Case, rural advocates worked in other venues to continue the fight for equity and fairness for rural students. For instance, in 2002 local residents of Millerville in rural Clay County organized to oppose the closure off Bibb Graves School. It appeared that the Board of Education was inclined to close the school because of information that leaving Bibb Graves open would create an $800,000 deficit for the district in the following school year. Rural advocates argued that this small K-12 school was the heart of the community and as a well-integrated school a good example of positive race relations.[147] Moreover, if the school were closed, many of its 400-plus students would have bus rides of over one and a half hours that would also provide obstacles to student and parent participation in school activities and achievement.[148]

After a multi-racial group of community residents fought back to keep Bibb Graves open, the U.S. Department of Justice reviewed the proposed consolidation and ruled that the county could not single out

Bibb Graves, a racially integrated school for closing. The county Board of Education then voted to leave Bibb Graves open for the 2002-03 school year, but to close it and one other school the following year. Following extensive organizing efforts by rural county residents, the Board reversed itself again in February 2003, deciding to leave all of the county schools open. A key factor in the decision was that the projected deficit of $800,000 did not materialize and instead the district ended the school year with a surplus of more than $250,000.

Olivia Turner, the Director of American Civil Liberties Union of Alabama, who was a key strategist for the plaintiffs and their attorneys in the state's school finance litigation, believes that the plaintiffs' initial success was a result of using an adequacy argument which clearly illustrated the denial of the state-guaranteed basic educational opportunity. A key component of plaintiffs' strategy was an exhaustive amount of analysis. Experts analyzed everything from the source of dollars to the materials in the schools. Another element was close working relationships with local community groups and schools.

Unlike some other states, in Alabama at the time of litigation, there was not a strong statewide network of public education advocacy groups. School finance litigation clearly motivated the creation and strengthening of this network. Liaisons from the plaintiff district group met and worked with other groups, including exchanging ideas about what the remedy should look like. A focus of community involvement in the Alabama litigation was to balance the input of citizens with client goals. The legal and legislative advocacy proceeded in parallel. This involved constant interaction to shape a consensus as to what the remedy should be.

The various groups involved in the litigation-related advocacy, however, did not coalesce and mobilize sufficiently to win legislative victories. As the Alabama ACLU's Turner observed, "You have to have more than litigation tools in your tool bag." After the court issued the liability order and before the remedy phase began, the governor and legislature developed a package of reform bills. What was missing from this mix was a strong organized public demand that the legislative package be adopted. Consequently, the legislative package was ultimately defeated. It is possible that developing public demand for reform a year or two prior to the litigation might have resulted in a more favorable legislative outcome. Alabama may be an object lesson of the pitfalls of approaching reform with a single-minded focus on litigation, and of the need to conduct public information and legislative advocacy efforts early on to create a demand for the reforms sought in the litigation.

In spite of the legal setbacks of the Alabama litigation, there has been some positive legislative reform of the school funding system in the state. For example, the ACLU's Turner does see numerous concrete benefits that have resulted from the filing of these cases. Because litigation lasted for years, the education system was a primary focus and in the public eye, and the lawsuit was a valuable educational tool for the policymakers and the public. The resulting exposure pressured the legislature, the Alabama State Board of Education, and governor to act. Turner is confident that if the lawsuit had not been brought, then the legislature would not have implemented a new finance scheme for the schools which ultimately resulted in the narrowing of the gap between high and low income students with the latter getting more state funds.

In addition, historically, local money funded transportation to public schools. Another indirect result from the litigation is that the state now fully funds transportation, which frees up local funds for other educational needs. Transportation funding also shifted to a state fleet renewal program. Another significant change was the addition of "at-risk" funding in the foundation program. The rate of school consolidation also slowed. Another positive outcome was that the Governor promoted and the legislature passed two large bond issues, which allowed for new buildings and renovations of old buildings.

Alabama's public schools still continue to struggle for success, however. Currently Alabama ranks second overall among the 50 states in need of rural education attention and improvement.[149] The state has very high rural poverty, low educational attainment among rural adults, some of the lowest student test scores, and the fifth lowest graduation rate in the country.[150]

Subsequent to the setbacks in the Alabama state courts described above, other Alabama plaintiffs have turned to federal court for relief with a new litigation strategy. Plaintiffs from two rural counties have asked a federal court in Alabama to suspend several provisions of the state's constitution, claiming that those provisions that place severe limits on property taxes are rooted in historic efforts to deny educational opportunity to African Americans and continue to severely restrict the capacity of rural and majority black counties to raise revenues necessary for schools.[151] The lawsuit charges that these provisions are purposefully discriminatory and violate Title VI of the Civil Rights Act and the U.S. Constitution. It alleges that Alabama's property tax revenues fail to adequately fund K–12 public schools and that this shortfall unconstitutionally shortchanges black public school students. The success of this action is yet unknown.

South Carolina

Rural South Carolina encompasses some of the greatest natural beauty in the southeast. From gentle foothills in the Upstate to the lush Coastal Plains, these portions of the state abound in historical significance, character, and sense of community. In these idyllic settings, however, rural schools have urgent needs and geography is still determining the educational destiny of thousands of students living in rural areas of South Carolina. Almost 40% of students are rural, and of these, 42% are members of minority groups.[152] More than half of the state's rural students qualify for subsidized meals, the sixth highest rate in the nation.[153]

In 1993, 40 mostly rural, low-wealth school districts, their students, and representative taxpayers filed suit seeking a declaratory judgment that the South Carolina education funding system violated the education and equal protection clauses of the South Carolina Constitution, the Fourteenth Amendment to the U.S. Constitution, and the South Carolina Education Finance Act.[154] In 1994 and 1995, defendants moved to dismiss, and in September 1996, the circuit court granted Defendants' motions and dismissed plaintiffs' complaint for failure to state a claim.[155]

The plaintiffs appealed to the South Carolina Supreme Court and achieved a partial reversal in 1999; the court found that the plaintiffs had stated a valid claim for inadequate educational opportunity under the education clause, which requires the state to "provide for the maintenance and support of a system of free public schools open to all children."[156] According to the state supreme court, this language requires a system that is at least "minimally adequate."[157] This is the standard that would be used throughout subsequent proceedings. The justices defined "minimally adequate" as "providing students adequate and safe facilities in which they have the opportunity to acquire: 1) the ability to read, write, and speak the English language, and knowledge of mathematics and physical science; 2) a fundamental knowledge of economic, social, and political systems, and of history and governmental processes; and 3) academic and vocational skills."[158] The state supreme court affirmed the equal protection holding of the trial court and remanded the case for further proceedings.

At the subsequent trial, plaintiff attorneys sought to demonstrate that the state had violated the state constitution's education clause and state statutes by failing to provide children in the plaintiff districts the opportunity for a minimally adequate education. Judge Thomas Cooper, the circuit court judge, heard the case in the historic Clarendon County Courthouse, where *Briggs v. Elliott*, one of the cases consolidated into *Brown v. Board of Education* was heard. Notably, one of the preliminary issues addressed by the court was that race would not be considered as a separate factor in the case, citing an expert who had stated race and poverty are collinear in the state and leading the court to conclude that student achievement is not a function of race, but of poverty. The court agreed to hear the claims of eight of the now 36 plaintiff districts, and the trial began in June of 2003.

During the 102-day trial, 70 witnesses testified and 23,000 pages of transcription were generated.[159] Testimony covered a wide range of serious problems in the plaintiff districts, including unqualified teachers, aging and dilapidated buildings, and the lack of funding to make changes in these and other areas. Plaintiffs worked throughout the case to establish a positive correlation between expenditures and educational opportunity.

The circuit court issued its order on December 29, 2005, holding that the State was not satisfying its constitutional obligation to provide each child in the plaintiff districts with the opportunity to acquire a minimally adequate education.[160] However, the court limited the state's liability to its failure to provide early intervention programs; consequently, the sole remedy ordered by the court was to require the state to fund and implement pre-K through grade-3 intervention programs designed to address the impacts of poverty on the educational abilities and achievements of the students in the plaintiff districts.[161]

Both sides moved for reconsideration in early 2007, and defendants asked Judge Cooper to reconsider his decision that a lack of comprehensive early education programs was causing violations of the rights of students living in poverty in the state.[162] Plaintiff attorneys sought a broader ruling that might address failings in facilities, teacher pay, and support for middle and high school students, while defense attorneys wanted the judge to remove the requirement that the state implement preschool and other programs for young children.[163] The judge refused both sides, and reiterated that the case had "never been about what is best" but only about meeting the state's "minimally adequate" constitutional requirement. In both of his rulings, Judge Cooper referred to a "constitutional floor" below which the state could not go, but stated that the only failure of the state in this regard was in not implementing early interventions for students living in poverty. Both sides decided to appeal.[164]

While the case was being finalized and appeals crafted, the legislature responded by funding a pilot K-4 (preschool) program in the eight trial districts. Some other preschool programs were already in place in the state, funded in part by private partnerships, but no statewide preschool or early elementary school interventions for students living in poverty were funded. The legislature's response was limited to a pilot program in eight districts. Interestingly, following the court's order to provide high quality preschool programs, consolidation plans immediately emerged as an alleged means to save money to meet the mandate. Although South Carolina has only 85 districts, mostly county-wide, legislators proposed a commission to recommend which districts to consolidate.[165] This proposal flew in the face of a recent Legislative Audit Committee study that found that little would be gained by consolidation and of an Education Oversight Committee report that concluded that consolidation could actually lower student achievement.[166]

Plaintiffs appealed to the South Carolina Supreme Court on all the issues raised at trial, and the state cross-appealed, saying that not only was it correct to find that all districts provided minimally adequate educational opportunities, but that Judge Cooper overstepped his judicial authority on the preschool ruling. Oral arguments were held in June of 2008. Plaintiffs' attorneys reiterated their case that inequities pervade the state's education system — in the disparities in facilities, in the ability to hire and retain qualified teachers, and in the ability to offer other interventions to students that would help ensure academic success. In a dramatic and at times heated exchange, the justices assured lawyers for plaintiff districts that they recognize the severe discrepancies in the quality of education in low-wealth and rural schools in the state. "But what would you have us to do?" asked Chief Justice Jean Toal. Attorneys from Nelson Mullins Riley and Scarborough, who worked *pro bono* on the case, assured the South Carolina justices that they would be well within their authority to declare the entire state education finance system unconstitutional and to order the legislature to make it constitutional. As of this writing, the supreme court has not issued a decision on this appeal.

Rural advocates have been a major part of the South Carolina litigation and legislative processes and have worked on a variety of fronts to inform public opinion about school finance issues. For instance, the South Carolina Rural Education Grassroots Group, (SCREGG) formed in 2001 by rural community members and leaders primarily from the plaintiff districts has worked on state education policy as the case has made its way through the courts. SCREGG members have worked in their individual communities to educate and build support for the lawsuit and to promote policy issues related to the plaintiff school districts. Members have worked at the state level on budget shortfalls, midyear cuts, and new testing and accountability requirements, the graduation rate, teaching quality, and other issues. In 2003, SCREGG released a major policy report detailing policy recommendations for ensuring that rural schools remain at the heart of their communities.[167] SCREGG also submitted amicus briefs to both the trial court and the state supreme court in the *Abbeville* case.

Other support efforts include *Corridor of Shame*, a documentary film about conditions in the plaintiff schools, which was widely cited during the 2008 presidential primaries in South Carolina, and a follow-up photography exhibit and campaign entitled, "What About Us?" that highlighted the needs of students not addressed in the court decision. Both of these campaigns were developed and carried out by a state public relations firm, which donated its services to the plaintiff districts to help get media attention for the trial. In addition, rural advocates helped plan a march to the state capitol steps and two town hall meetings to bring public attention to the lawsuit. Education First, a coalition seeking to keep pressure on policymakers to reform the school finance system, has put billboards up along interstates in South Carolina welcoming travelers to the "Home of Minimally Adequate Schools."

Another non-litigation strategy underway in South Carolina is a public petition being circulated to support a change to the state's constitution from its current language, which has been interpreted to mean "minimally adequate" to language that conveys a need for quality education for all children. Legislation has been introduced to amend the state constitution to guarantee "a high quality education, allowing each student to reach his highest potential." Currently, the constitution guarantees "a system of free public schools open to all children in the State." Supporters hope to garner one million signatures on the petition in support of the legislation.

Litigators, school leadership, and community activists in South Carolina all recognize the fortitude needed for school finance cases. The majority of plaintiff districts have participated in litigation for almost 30 years — the number of suing districts has decreased mainly due to consolidation. A few districts had to drop out of the litigation prior to the commencement of *pro bono* representation by Nelson Mullins because they could not afford the legal costs. The rural districts have been fortunate to have had free legal services at trial, for the appellate briefing, and at oral argument before the South Carolina Supreme Court. Nelson Mullins attorneys have maintained a close relationship not only with plaintiff group leadership, but other community leaders and organizations interested in the outcome of the suit.

In considering the strategy of the case, Laura Hart, Nelson Mullins partner and one of the *Abbeville* litigators, stresses the importance of sufficient staffing and the need for partnerships with others who will promote the arguments of the plaintiffs outside the courtroom. The significant contribution of time and talent by Nelson Mullins also makes the *Abbeville* strategy almost unique; by some estimates the firm has donated $5 million in billable time to the case.

The legislature's K-4 preschool funding is viewed to be the one small and incomplete success of the litigation in South Carolina thus far. No funding has been allocated for repairing buildings or helping rural schools attract and retain teachers. At this writing all parties eagerly await the South Carolina Supreme Court's ruling. Greater attention has been focused on rural districts as a result of the litigation, but the issues and problems around race and poverty in the rural portion of the state are deeply embedded. Although various policy efforts have been made to lessen the disparities, overall, the political will to make the systemic changes needed still appears to be weak.

Lessons Learned

Rural schools have a high stake in the outcomes of school finance litigation. And rural children, parents, school districts and school officials have been frequent plaintiffs in the many cases that have challenged inequitable and inadequate school funding systems. From the perspective of rural educational interests, the outcomes of these cases have been a mixed blessing in most states. As described, rural districts bear disproportionate burdens from inequitable and inadequate finance systems as they cope with high student poverty, obsolete and deteriorating facilities, and insufficient local tax bases

Rural school finance litigation in the five states reviewed here generally has benefited the litigants and contributed to the body of knowledge needed to successfully bring school finance cases elsewhere. Some of these state courts — Arkansas, Tennessee, and West Virginia — have acknowledged that higher spending provides greater educational opportunity. In Arkansas and Tennessee, the courts maintained jurisdiction over long periods of time in order to see their rulings become state policy.

Rural school finance litigants have also experienced unforeseen and unintended consequences of their challenges to the funding systems. West Virginia and Arkansas suffered the loss of many rural schools in districts that sought equity and adequacy of funding. Consolidation policies and accountability systems often ignore the historical underfunding of schools, the poverty of communities, and the academic consequences of forcing children to travel long distances. From the battle against consolidation, there has emerged a significant body of scholarly research that confirms that small schools work, and work well for students. Rural advocates continue to use that knowledge to protect small schools from consolidation, to build new small schools, and to promote downsizing of too-large schools.

It is one thing to win in court, but a very different one to achieve a timely remedy. Tennessee has had notably long battles on many fronts despite seemingly rural-friendly courts and allies, and has had to grapple with growing urban influence and overall inadequacy of funding. An ultimately failed court action, as in Alabama, can also be a setback to obtaining a political solution. In that state, after some improvement in school facilities, opponents redoubled efforts to block any court involvement in school equity and adequacy in the state. Any political solution must have broad public support.

These outcomes can inform future rural advocates on strategic planning issues, including the efficacy of these lawsuits and whether alternatives to litigation may exist, and how plaintiffs and others might mitigate unforeseen negative outcomes for rural schools. Several guiding principles emerge from examining these five states and the work of Rural Trust in other states.

First, to ensure rural public engagement on what is a fair and effective funding system, a rural agenda needs to be shaped from within rural communities. Knowing the issues most important in each state — teacher salary disparities in Tennessee, for example — results a better focus on rural needs.

Second, for a fair and effective school finance system, the issues that affect community confidence in public schools — tax system fairness, authority of the community in school matters, and efficient use of school funds — cannot be ignored. Alabama's tax system, for example, continues to prevent rural districts from adequately funding their schools.

Third, rural people can be effective and responsible participants in school funding issues in the democratic process. Building organizations that sustain efforts and consistently renew leadership can ultimately succeed, as in West Virginia, even after years of disappointment.

Fourth, to achieve reform, action strategies must be shaped to respond to the varying facts and circumstances rural people face. Working both within and without the judicial system is an important strategic decision. For example, where litigation remedies and rural interests diverge as in Arkansas where the real focus became consolidation, rural interests had to operate effectively in the legislature to prevent the consolidation remedy from being used against them.

Fifth, schools must be community institutions, and school funding must reflect that ideal. We believe that "equity" and a truly adequate education can only occur where children feel safe, valued, needed, and expected to do well. Good small schools close to home are an essential part of a quality education.

In a still challenging policy climate, rural citizens, educators, and community members share hope and strength for the continued battle. Rural people have not only committed to the long-term battle of legal challenges but also to the accompanying long-term public policy and public relations efforts. As school finance advocacy moves from the courtroom to the community meeting room, school board room, and legislative arena, The Rural School and Community Trust is partnering with rural leaders to impact finance policy issues affecting their schools and communities. Rural Trust builds civic capacity to engage in the policy debate, conducts scholarly research to support the positions of rural people, monitors and shares information about finance policy in the 50 states, and provides legal support when needed. This approach is unique not only in its rural focus, but also in the flexibility of service, which respects local communities, local issues, and local control.

The Rural Trust has served as both an active participant in litigation, and in a complementary role. The Rural Education Finance Center (REFC), a service of Rural Trust, has co-authored and filed amicus briefs, submitted expert opinion, and monitors remedy implementation in cases across the country. And, with the help of REFC, partner groups have written and released reports that have impacted state funding and informed policy changes. REFC is also connected to the academic and expert school finance community and has provided expert analysis on the rural perspective on equity and adequacy. In sum, REFC and The Rural Trust are making the case for rural schools.

As the REFC seeks to expand its work, we envision a groundswell of community partners who are attuned to the nuances of their state funding systems, who are advocates for their small and rural schools on these issues, and who are building support for those schools. The goal is to build a national network of rural organizations that are active stakeholders in their states' school funding process. Through timely research and analysis, the development of new legal theories, and the documentation of lessons learned, REFC is building and supporting just such a network across the country and helping to grow a new generation of advocates who can build on the groundwork skilled attorneys and advocates have lain.

Rural people have found avenues for participation in legislative and legal contexts, joining and forming coalitions, learning about funding opportunities, and writing about and sharing their experiences. Rural schools and communities are working together to be agents for change in state policy and advocates for equity and adequacy in school funding. Few challenges are as pressing as securing a quality education for every child in our country. The challenge is great, but not insurmountable.

Biographies

Amanda Gibson Adler is an attorney and Director of the Rural Education Finance Center, (REFC), a program of The Rural School and COmmunity Trust. REFC provides services to rural groups across the United tates that are working to improve funding for rural school and the children they serve. Ms. Adler's work includes policy monitoring ad analysis, scholarly research, and legal support. Working closely with state partners, she helps rural people and organizations advocate for equitable and adequate funding for all schools and she provides information on rural school finance issues across the U.S. She has filedamicus briefs in a number of school finance cases, including to the South Carolina Supreme Court in the Abbeville case.

Ms. Adler also works in the Nelson Mullins Student Advocacy Project at the South Carolina Appleseed Legal Justice Center. The Project was created to hel serve low-income special education students in South Carolina, and she provides case screening and placement, outreach, and training or families and advocates.

Ms. Adler began her legal career as an Equal Justice Works Fellow working on education policy in South Carolina, and also received the Nelson Mullins Riley and Scarborough Centennial Fellowshp in that capacity. She has written training materials and presented on education law and policy for a wide range of audiences, and her special interests include issues involving teacher policy, students in homeless situations, and English Language Learners. Ms. Adler is a former educator and worked in public schools in South Carolina and

Georgia. She has a law degree from the University of South Carolina and a B.A. from Emory University.

** Special thanks go to Caroline Ford, a law student at the University of South Carolina. This article would not have been pssible without her assistance.*

---

1 JERRY JOHNSON, ED.D. & MARTY STRANGE. WHY RURAL MATTERS 2007: THE REALITIES OF RURAL EDUCATION GROWTH, at 5. (Alison Yuanches, ed., Oct. 2007).

2 *Id.* at 98

3 *Id.*

4 *Id.*

5 BETH SPENCE. WHATEVER HAPPENED TO PAULEY VS. BAILEY? THE STORY OF THE POLITICS OF EDUCATION IN WEST VIRGINIA at 5. (Covenant House, 1998).

6 *Id.*

7 *Pauley v. Kelly*, 255 S.E.2d 859, 851 (W. Va. 1979). (*Pauley I*)

8 *Id.* at 851.

9 *Id.* at 863.

10 *Id.* at 884.

11 *Id.* at 877.

12 *Id.* at 877.

13 *Pauley v. Bailey*, 324 S.E.2d 128, 131 (W. Va. 1984). (*Pauley II*)

14 *Id.*

15 *Id.*

16 *Id.* at 132.

17 *Id.* at 131.

18 *Id.*

19 *Id.* at 135.

20 Education Week, EXCERPTS FROM THE OPINION IN THE WEST VIRGINIA CASE, May 26, 1982, http://www.edweek.org/ew/articles/1982/05/26/02270002.h01.html

21 See *Pauley I*, 324 S.E.2d at 132.

22 *Pauley v. Bailey*, 301 S.E.2d 608, 610 (W. Va. 1983).

23 See *Pauley*, 324 S.E.2d at 137.

24 *Id.*

25 *State ex rel. Boards of Educ. v. Chafin*, 376 S.E.2d 113, 121 (W. Va. 1988).

26 *Id.* at 115.

27 *Id.* at 120.

28 *Id.* at 121.

29 National Council for Education Statistics Study on West Virginia School Finance System, accessed at http://nces.ed.gov/edfin/pdf/StFinance/WestVir.pdf

30 See generally, Deidre H. Purdy, AN ECONOMICAL, THOROUGH, AND EFFICIENT SCHOOL SYSTEM: THE WEST VIRGINIA SCHOOL BUILDING AUTHORITY "ECONOMY OF SCALE" NUMBERS. Journal of Research in Rural Education, Winter, 1997, Vol., 13, No. 3, 170-182.

31 *Id.* In 2004, independent auditors confirmed this in a report which stated that the SBA had promoted consolidations, and noted that records making determinations about how SBA funding would be allocated had been shredded and not made public. See also, The Charleston Gazette, CLOSING COSTS: SCHOOL CONSOLIDATION IN WEST VIRGINIA, August 25, 1982, http://www.wvgazette.com/News/Closing+Costs.

32 *Tomblin v. West Virginia Board of Education*, No. 75-1268, slip op. at 4 (Cir. Ct. of Kanawha Co., W. Va. Jan. 3, 2003).

33 See *Pauley*, 324 S.E. 2d 128 at 132-133.

34 *Id.* at 132.

45 *Tomblin*, No. 75-1268, slip op. at 5 (referring to an Apr. 2, 1997 order of Cir. Ct. of Kanawha Co.).

36 See generally, Education Week, QUALITY COUNTS 1999: WEST VIRGINIA, http://rc-archive.edweek.org/sreports/qc99/states/policy/wv-up.htm

37 *Id.*

38 *Id.; see also*, W. Va. Code, § 18-2E-5 (1998).

39 *Tomblin*, No. 75-1268, slip op. at 6.

40 *Id.* at 7.

41 *Id.* at 13 – 14.

42 *Pendleton v. Marockie*, 507 S.E.2d 673 (W.Va. 1998), highlighting the circuit court case at 677.

43 Robert Bastress, THE IMPACT OF LITIGATION ON RURAL STUDENTS: FROM FREE TEXTBOOKS TO SCHOOL CONSOLIDATION, 82 Nebraska L. Rev. 9 (2003), discussing *Pendleton* at 41.

44 *Pendleton* at 677.

45 Bastress at 42.

46 *Pendleton* at 677.

47 *Id.* at 679.

48 *Tomblin v. Gainer*, No. 75-1268 (Cir. Ct. of Kanawha County, W. Va. Aug. 1, 2000)

49 *Tomblin v. West Virginia Board of Education*, No. 75-1268, slip op. at 13 (Cir. Ct. of Kanawha Co., W. Va. Jan. 3, 2003).

50 See generally, Interview with Thomas Ramey, Challenge West Virginia Director and Lincoln County School Board Member, July, 2008. See also, Rural Policy Matters, YOUNG SCHOOL BOARD MEMBER PREPARES FOR AFTERMATH OF THWARTED DEMOCRATIC PROCESS, February 2007.

51 Paul A. Minorini & Stephen D. Sugarman, *School Finance Litigation in the Name of Educational Equity: Its Evolution, Impact, and Future*, EQUITY AND ADEQUACY IN EDUCATION FINANCE: ISSUES AND PERSPECTIVES 49 (Helen F. Ladd et al. eds., 1999), accessed at http://www.law.berkeley.edu/faculty/sugarmans/Equity.htm

52 *Id.*

53 *Id.*

54 W. Va. Code § 18-2E-5d(b), (c), 18-9D-2(3). No new route can exceed the recommended one-way standard for elementary students by more than thirty minutes. The routes covered by this rule are those that transport pre-K through fifth grade students to and from a school included in a closure, consolidation, or new construction project approved after July 1 2008. One-way school bus transportation times to and from school in normal weather and operating conditions are thirty minutes for elementary students; forty-five minutes for middle school, intermediate school and junior high school; and sixty minutes for high school students. The state must provide technical assistance to county boards and facility plans must avoid excessive transportation time. W.Va. Code §§ 18-2E-5d(a), (d); 18-9D-2(5)(B).

55 West Virginia House Bill 4588, enrolled in Chapter 71, Acts 2008, repealing, amending, and reenacting various portions of W.Va. Code §18.

56 Amy Higginbotham, Dr. Tami Gurley-Calve, Dr. Tom Witt, STUDENT DENSITY AND ITS RELATIONSHIP TO PROFESSIONAL EDUCATORS AND SERVICE PERSONNEL, Bureau of Business and Economic Research, West Virginia University.

57 W.Va. Code §18-20-5 *et seq.*

58 The Rural School and Community Trust, CLOSING COSTS: A SUMMARY OF AN AWARD-WINNING LOOK AT SCHOOL CONSOLIDATION IN WEST VIRGINIA, A STATE WHERE IT HAS BEEN TRIED AGGRESSIVELY, available online at http://www.ruraledu.org/site/apps/nlnet/content3.aspx?c=beJMIZOCIrH&b=1073911&content_id={8692B89D-A06D-43B6-9DFB-F129B0EF3B95}&notoc=1.

59 The Charleston Gazette, CLOSING COSTS: SCHOOL CONSOLIDATION IN WEST VIRGINIA, August 25, 1982, http://www.wvgazette.com/News/Closing+Costs

60 *Id.*

61 A.R. Const. art. 14, §1

62 *Id.*

63 Prior to the litigation, ninety-four percent of students in the Lake View school

district qualified for free or reduced-price lunches.

64 Jane Adams and D. Gorgon, LEGACY ON THE LAND: NEW DEAL RESETTLEMENT IN THE MISSISSIPPI DELTA, Boston University.

65 *Tucker v. Lake View Sch. Dist. No. 25*, 323 Ark. 693, 696 (Ark. 1996). (citing footnote 2). (*Lake View I*).

66 *Id.* at 695

67 *Id.* at 697.

68 *Id.* at 695.

69 *Lake View School Dist. No. 20 v. Huckabee*, 91 S.W.3d 472, 478 (2002) (*Lake View III*); *see also*, AR Const. Amend. 74.

70 *Lake View III*, at 478.

71 *Lake View School Dist. No. 25 of Phillips County v. Huckabee*, 10 S.W.3d 892, 897-898 (2000) (*Lake View II*).

72 *Lakeview III*, at 478.

73 *Id.*

74 *Lakeview I*, 323 Ark. 693 at 697.

75 *Lake View School Dist. No. 20 v. Huckabee*, 91 S.W.3d 472, 477 (2002) (*Lake View III*).

76 *Lake View School District, No. 25 v. Huckabee*, No. 1992-5318 (Pulaski County Chancery Ct., May 25, 2001); *Lake View III*, 91 S.W.3d 472.

77 *Id.*

78 *Id.* at 511.

79 See *Lake View School Dist. No. 20 v. Huckabee*, 91 S.W.3d 472 (2002).

80 Background and related issues on school funding litigation in Arkansas, http://www.schoolfunding.info/states/ar/lit_ar.php3. This Network included Arkansans for Excellence in Education, Arkansas Communities Uniting for Results in Education, American Family Association of Arkansas, the Arkansas African American Administrators Associations, the Arkansas Public Policy Panel/Citizens First Congress, Save Our Schools, and the Arkansas Rural Education Association.

81 Under the proposal, once the schools were adequately funded they would be required to offer the core curriculum by a variety of means, including on site courses, Internet, concurrent credit, distance learning, shared teachers, transportation to another school, or independent study. The plan demanded a state funding formula to target resources to areas of greatest need based on poverty factors and historical lack of funding. The plan also called for "fair distribution of taxes" to pay for these reforms. See also generally, The Rural School and Community Trust, ALTERNATIVE WAYS TO ACHIEVE COST-EFFECTIVE SCHOOLS.

82 *Lakeview School v. Huckabee*, 2005 WL 2076478 (E.D.Ark.) (2005).

83 *Id.* at 2.

84 *Id.* at 3.

85 Lorna Jimerson, THE IMPACT OF ARKANSAS' ACT 60 CONSOLIDATION ON AFRICAN-AMERICAN SCHOOL LEADERSHIP AND RACIAL COMPOSITION OF SCHOOLS DISTRICTS, The Rural School and Community Trust.

86 Following the June 2007 closing of the finance case in state court, the federal complaint was reopened to consider if it could be pursued further. *Friends of the Lakeview School District No. 25 of Phillips County v. Huckabee*, 2:04CV00182WRW, filed October 11, 2007. But in April of 2008, in an unpublished opinion, U.S. District Judge William R. Wilson granted the state's motion to dismiss the lawsuit.

87 *Lake View School Dist. No. 25 of Phillips County v. Huckabee*, 142 S.W.3d 643 (2004).

88 Background and related issues on school funding litigation in Arkansas, http://www.schoolfunding.info/states/ar/lit_ar.php3.

89 *Lake View School Dist. No. 25 of Phillips County v. Huckabee*, 189 S.W.3d 1, 7 (2004).

90 *Id.* at 14.

91 *Lake View School Dist. No. 25 of Phillips County, Arkansas v. Huckabee*, 210 S.W.3d 28, 29-30 (2005).

92 *Lake View School Dist. No. 25 v. Huckabee*, 220 S.W.3d 645, 646 (2005).

93 *Id.*

94 *Lake View School Dist. No. 25 v. Huckabee*, 370 Ark. 139, 142 (2007).

95 *Id.* at 145-146.

96 *Id.*

97 *Id.* at 147.

98 See generally, *Lake View School Dist. No. 25 v. Huckabee*, 370 Ark. 139 (2007).

99 *Arkansas State Board of Education v. Moody*, 367 Ark. 181 (2006).

100 Lorna Jimerson, SLOW MOTION: TRAVELING BY SCHOOL BUS IN CONSOLIDATED DISTRICTS IN WEST VIRGINIA, The Rural School and Community Trust, 2007.

101 Groups Ask Arkansas Supreme Court for Decision Supporting Rural Schools, *Rural Policy Matters*, Vol. 4, No. 3, pg. 3 (March 2002), accessed at: http://www.eric.ed.gov/ERICDocs/data/ericdocs2sql/content_storage_01/0000019b/80/1a/96/14.pdf

102 *Id.*

103 *Id.*

104 *Id.*

105 *Id.*

106 Arkansas Annotated Code § 6-2-1901 *et. seq.*

107 John Lyon, *State test scores shows narrowing achievement gap*, ARKANSAS NEWS

BUREAU. Jun 21, 2008, accessed at http://www.arkansasnews.com/archive/2008/06/21/News/346780.html.

108 Interviews conducted with Lavina Grandon, Policy and Education Director, Advocates for Rural and Community Education and Jimmy Cunningham, former president of the Arkansas Rural Education Association, July 2008.

109 JERRY JOHNSON, ED.D. & MARTY STRANGE, at 82.

110 *Id.*

111 *Id.*

112 TSSS subsequently changed its name to Tennessee School Systems for Equity and grew to an unincorporated association of 77 of the 139 districts in the state.

113 *Tennessee Small Sch. Sys. v. McWherter*, 851 S.W.2d 139, 144 (1993). (*Small Schools I*).

114 *Id.* at 145.

115 *Id.* at 156.

116 *Tennessee Small School Systems v. McWherter*, 894 S.W. 2d 734 (1995) (*Small Schools II*).

117 *Tennessee Small School Systems v. McWherter*, 91 S.W.3d 232, 238 (2002) (*Small Schools III*),

118 *Id.*

119 *Id.*

120 *Id.* at 234.

121 *Id.*

122 Interview with Edd Diden, Director, Cannon County Schools, Woodbury, Tennessee, July, 2008.

123 Interview with Lewis Donelson, Shareholder, Baker Donelson, Memphis, Tennessee, July, 2008.

124 JERRY JOHNSON, ED.D. & MARTY STRANGE, at 82.

125 *Id.*

126 JERRY JOHNSON, ED.D. & MARTY STRANGE, at 41.

127 Further, public school systems must contribute ten mills or the equivalent into the state's funding system in order to remain eligible for state funds. This foundation program was established following the liability decision in Alabama's school funding lawsuit.

128 *Alabama Coalition for Equity (ACE) v. Hunt*, 1993 WL 204083 (Ala. Cir. Ct. 1993), appendix to *Opinion of the Justices*, No.338, 624 So.2d. 107 (Ala. 1993), at 111.

129 *Id.*

130 *Id.*

131 *Id.*

132 Ala. Const. §256 (1956).

133 *ACE*, at 112.

134 *Id.* at 113.

135 *Id.*

136 *Id.*

137 *Id.* at 114.

138 *Id.* at 115.

139 *Id.*

140 *Id.*

141 *Id.* at 119.

142 *Id.* at 220.

143 *Opinion of the Justices*, No. 338, 624 So.2d 107 (Ala. 1993).

144 The supreme court also allowed defendant intervenors representing taxpayer and citizens into the case. *Pinto v. ACE*, 662 So. 2d 894 (Ala. 1995).

145 *Ex Parte James*, 713 So. 2d 869, 881 (Ala. 1997).

146 *Id.*

147 The Task Force was a public-private group that weighed various proposals outside of the remedy deliberations. Other advocacy and outreach efforts across the state were well-received; in all, over 23,000 Alabamians came to town hall meetings and other events to discuss education reform. Jeffrey Scott Berman and Drew Dunphy, STUDIES IN JUDICIAL REMEDIES AND PUBLIC ENGAGEMENT, Campaign for Fiscal Equity, July 1998.

148 On January 10, 2002, the Supreme Court of Alabama issued the following order, which says in pertinent part: "The "Equal Protection provision" of the trial court's order dated March 31, 1993, is predicated upon the premise that ss 1, 6, and 22 of Article I of the Constitution of Alabama of 1901, combine to guarantee the citizens of Alabama equal protection under the law of Alabama. Opinion of the Justices No. 338, 624 S.2d 107, 156-61, 165 (Ala. 1993). The trial court ordered the state officers charged by law with the responsibility for the Alabama public school system to provide equitable and adequate educational opportunities to all school-age children in accordance with the constitutional mandates of Art. I, ss 1, 6, and 22. Therefore, the "Equal Protection provision" resulting from the combination of ss 1, 6, and 22 is a necessary component on which all phases of this ongoing litigation are founded. In 1999, after [several of] this Court's opinions..., this Court held that ss 1, 6, and 22 do not combine to provide equal protection and that the Constitution of Alabama of 1901 does not contain an equal-protection provision. Ex parte Melof, 735 S.2d 1172 (Ala. 1999). The parties in the above-styled cases have been notified that we have placed these cases on rehearing ex mero motu. Order of January 10, 2002, Ex parte Gov. Fob James, (Ala. 2002)

149 *Ex Parte Governor Fob James*, 836 So. 2d 813, 815(Ala. May 31, 2002).

150 *Id*, at 877-888.

151 The trial court had declared that there was an equal protection clause in §§ 1, 6, and 22 of the Alabama Constitution, but a 1999 ruling declared otherwise. *Ex parte Melof*, 735 So.2d 1172 (Ala. 1999).

152 Strength in Numbers: A Rural Community Fights School Closure, *Rural Policy Matters*, Vol. 4, No. 8, pg. 1 (August 2002), accessed at http://www.eric.ed.gov/ERICDocs/data/ericdocs2sql/content_storage_01/0000019b/80/1a/96/14.pdf

153 *Id.*

154 Jerry Johnson, Ed.D. & Marty Strange, at 41. This ranking is based on five gauges on which states are measured by Rural Trust. They are: the importance of rural education to the overall education performance of the state; socioeconomic challenges known to be barriers to academic achievement faced by rural schools; the level of student diversity among rural students; the rural educational policy context and student academic achievement measures. The high the ranking on a gauge, the more important or the more urgent rural education matters are in that state. Alabama ranks near the top on four of the five gauges. *Id.*

155 *Id.*

156 *Lynch v. Alabama*, CV-08-S-0450-NE, filed March 13, 2008.

157 Jerry Johnson, Ed.D. & Marty Strange at 90.

158 *Id.*

159 *Abbeville County School District v. State*, 335 S.C. 58, 63, 515 S.E.2d 535, 538 (1999).

160 *Id.*

161 Abbeville County Sch. Dist. v. State, 515 S.E.2d 535 (1999)

162 *Id.* at 540.

163 *Id.*

164 *Abbeville County Sch. Dist. v. State*, No. 93-CP-31-0169, slip op. at 2 (Cir. Ct. of Lee Co., S.C. July 12, 2007). (quoting Dec. 29, 2005 order).

165 *Id.*

166 *Id.* at 2-3.

167 *Id.* at 21-23.

168 See generally, *Abbeville County Sch. Dist. v. State*, No. 93-CP-31-0169, slip op. at 2 (Cir. Ct. of Lee Co., S.C. July 12, 2007).

169 *Abbeville County Sch. Dist. v. State*, No. 93-CP-31-0169, slip op. at 2 at. 23.

170 Rural Policy Matters, South Carolina Consolidation Proposal Raises Complex Issues, Vol. 8, No. 3, Mar. 2006, http://www.ruraledu.org/site/apps/nlnet/content.aspx?c=beJMIZOCIrH&b=1461901&content_id={E1D4745A-C4AE-4DCE-A4C7-9458D62DF412}&notoc=1

171 *Id.*

172 Building Rural Schools in South Carolina: The Foundations We Need, The South Carolina Rural Education Grassroots Committee, http://www.scjustice.org/pdfs/RuralReport.pdf, (2003).

9 Education in Alaska, The Last Frontier: An Analysis of Moore v. State

by R. Collin Middleton, Robert J. Sato and Howard Trickey

Introduction

The State of Alaska is geographically the largest state in the United States. It is twice the size of Texas, the second largest, and at 685,175 square miles, is one-fifth the size of the rest of the United States.[1] Fully one-third of the state is above the Arctic Circle where the production and sale of oil has enabled the State to amass a savings account of almost 40 billion dollars.[2]

But the area above the Arctic Circle and just below it, where plaintiff districts are, also contains children to whom the Alaska Constitution guarantees an education. These areas have only a small number of children, who are disproportionately Alaska Natives (Aleuts, Eskimos and American Indians. Indeed the state as a whole is sparsely populated, containing roughly 130,000 students statewide. However, surprising numbers of children are unable to pass the proficiency examinations and obtain diplomas. The children of the

Alaska Native peoples (Aleuts, Eskimos and American Indians) persistently score below even the national NAEP scores for American Indians as a subgroup. They are, in the words of plaintiff's expert witness, Ray Barnhardt, "the lowest of the low."[3]

There are only 53 school districts and one state operated school for Alaska's 685,175 square miles.[4] All 130,000 students attend these schools.[5] Some of these districts serve students in such remote, isolated villages, accessible only by boat or plane, they are beyond even the term "rural." It is difficult to overstate the challenge of delivering educational services to students in these remote locations: huge logistical challenges of providing teachers, facilities and supplies combined with schools that serve the neediest children in the state.

One of the three plaintiff districts, the Bering Strait School District, is just below the Arctic Circle. Bering Strait has 15 schools with a total of approximately 1700 students.[6] The district covers an area roughly the size of Minnesota.[7] From the school farthest west to the school farthest east is approximately 350 miles.[8] It is bounded on the west by the International Date Line, on the north by the Arctic Circle, and on the south by the Yukon River.[9] The school and community are almost 100 percent Alaska Native.[10] Most students are economically disadvantaged (eligible for free or reduced price lunches) and have limited English proficiency.[11] Most have had little if any exposure to reading and writing when they begin school.[12] Less than half of the students in Bering Strait are proficient in English language arts (reading and writing) according to state standards. Graduation statistics are equally abysmal. In 2005-06, a meager 34 percent graduated.[13]

Within the district itself, there is great variance in student performance. In Unalakleet, for example, where the district's central offices are located, 79 percent of the students tested proficient in language arts.[14] Savoonga, in comparison, is one of the district's most struggling school sites.[15] Savoonga is located on the northern coast of St. Lawrence Island in the Bering Sea, almost an hour and a half plane ride from Nome.[16] About 640 people live in Savoonga, most of whom speak Siberian Yupik; indeed until recently the Savoonga school phone was answered in Siberian Yupiit.[17] The local economy consists largely of subsistence hunting for walrus, seals, and bowhead whales.[18] In 2005-06, just 34- percent of the students were proficient in language arts.[19] Twenty-five percent graduated.[20]

Another struggling plaintiff district is the Kuspuk School District. Kuspuk covers over 12,000 square miles but has only approximately 430 students, most of whom are Yupik Eskimo or Athabascan Indian.[21] It serves children in eight villages along the Kuskokwim River, accessible only by air and river travel.[22] Three of these schools are K-12 schools with enrollments of less than twenty.[23] About 80 percent of the students are economically disadvantaged and 90 percent have limited English proficiency.[24] In 2005-06, only 35 percent of its students were proficient in language arts and 26 percent were proficient in math.[25]

Still, this is better than the performance in Yupiit School District, the third plaintiff district. Yupiit serves 445 children in three schools.[26] Like Bering Strait and Kuspuk, most of the students in Yupiit are Alaska Native,[27] most are economically disadvantaged,[28] and most have limited English proficiency ("LEP").[29] Most children speak Yupik, and consequently come to school needing to learn an entirely new language, as well as new rules and expectations.[30] In the Yupiit School District, only one in five students tested proficient in English language arts,[31] and 25 percent graduated.[32] After a year of State intervention, the number proficient in language arts declined to 6 percent, approximately one in twenty.[33]

We began our lawsuit with what seemed to be the undeniable premise that the educational system was in some way failing these and many other children. It seemed inconceivable that so many children could otherwise be failing to succeed. But despite these compelling statistics, the lawsuit faced an obstacle unique to Alaska: the school districts with the lowest performing students tended to receive the most funding. In 2005, for example, Yupiit received $22,578 in total funding per student; Anchorage, the largest district in the state, by comparison, received just $8,708 per student.[34] Of course, Yupiit also has much higher costs than Anchorage because it is smaller and extraordinarily remote, and the State has long funded all school districts by a geographical cost differential as well as a small school factor. But comparing a dollar in Yupiit to a dollar in Anchorage proved to be arduous and ultimately, at least in the court's view, unsuccessful.

Why then were the students in Yupiit failing, and, more importantly, who bore responsibility for that failure? Did the State's constitutional obligation include more than funding local school districts? The lawsuit eventually turned on this question of the extent of the State's responsibility.

Education and Education Finance in Alaska

Before Alaska became a state in 1959, it had a dual system of education.[35] The United States Bureau of Indian Affairs (BIA) operated one system for Alaska Native students, and the Territorial Legislature operated another system for non-Natives and those Natives leading a "civilized life."[36] The framers of Alaska's constitution recognized that this dual system must end and that the new state must establish a single, unified system for all children.[37] It was with this fundamental purpose that the framers proposed the adoption of Alaska's education clause, which directs the legislature to "establish and maintain a system of public schools open to all children of the State."[38]

Like most other states, Alaska has established an educational system based principally on a system of locally controlled school districts. The State has three basic types of districts. Alaska has 16 organized boroughs, each of which is a school district.[39] In addition, the State has 18 home rule or first class cities outside a borough, and each one of these is also a school district. [40] The rest of Alaska is divided into nineteen Regional Education Attendance Areas ("REAAs"), each of which is a school district.[41] The REAAs are unusual because they exist where no city or borough exists. Another unique aspect of REAA school districts is that they have no access to local funding. Each plaintiff district is an REAA.

The State funds school districts principally through a foundation formula. The foundation formula allocates funds to school districts based on the number of students enrolled to a district. Adjustments are made to each district's allocation to account for differences in district size and geographic location.[42] Smaller school districts with smaller schools receive more because they lack the economies of scale of the larger districts. In addition, schools in remote locations receive more funding to account for the extraordinarily high costs of attracting teachers, energy and transportation, and other operating needs for schools in these locations. This geographic location amount can be greater than double the regular foundation for certain schools. Each district's allocation is then multiplied by a special needs factor, set by statute at 20 percent.[43] All districts receive the same special needs adjustment regardless of the actual number of special needs students in the district. Finally, adjustments are made for students who require intensive services[44] and correspondence students,[45] based on the number of students actually receiving these services.

Alaska has developed educational standards, which define the knowledge and skills all students are expected to learn. These include content standards in English/Language Arts, Mathematics, Science, Geography, Government and Citizenship, History, Skills for a Healthy Life, Arts, World Languages, Technology, Employability, and Library/Information Literacy. These standards are broad statements of what children should know and be able to do as a result of their public school experience.[46] In addition, the State has adopted "grade level expectations" (or "GLEs") in reading, writing, math, and science, which define more specifically what students should know and be able to do at the end of a given grade level.[47] The State has developed assessments to test whether students are meeting the GLE's in reading, writing, and math.

The State expects all students to become "proficient" in reading, writing and math.[48] Ultimately, students must pass a graduation examination,[49] which is designed to test "the minimum competencies in essential skills in the areas of reading, English, and mathematics that a student should have to know in order to function in our society."[50] Students who do not pass this exam do not receive a diploma.[51]

Litigation Strategy

Our litigation strategy was straightforward. We first defined a constitutionally adequate education in Alaska through expert witnesses, superintendents and the heads of the organization plaintiffs. Once that was presented we then presented evidence that the State was not providing all children with an opportunity to receive that education. The State had already developed good standards, which made the job of defining an adequate education much easier. The purpose of our witnesses was to show that these standards could be relied on by the judiciary as standards of a constitutionally adequate education. An abundance of test data clearly showed that many students were not achieving these standards. Alaska Native students in particular tended to perform academically at levels far below these standards and their peers.

For example, in 2003-04, 81.8 percent of Caucasian tenth grade students tested proficient in reading on the graduation exam while only 43.5 percent of Alaska Native tenth grade students tested proficient, a gap of 38.5 percentage points.[52] These failing students tended to be concentrated in certain school districts, particularly those serving students in remote areas of the state. In 2003-04, the statewide passage rate for tenth grade students on the reading portion of the graduation exam was 70.1 percent. The passage rate for Bering Strait tenth graders was 21.7 percent; for Kuspuk, it was 27.6 percent; and for Yupiit, it was less than 20 percent — gaps of 40 to 50 percent. This was powerful evidence that the educational system was failing the children in these districts. But how would we prove that lack of funding had caused this failure?

We began ambitiously with the idea that no district in the state received adequate funding or provided all of its students with an adequate education. Historically, the politics of education funding in Alaska, as in other states, has pitted one district against another. We hoped to avoid this divisiveness and build a strong coalition of school districts with the political strength to raise the level of funding for all districts. To support this effort, one of the statewide organizations retained a team of experts to conduct a statewide cost study.

The team of experts used three separate methodologies to calculate the cost of an adequate education in Alaska. Dr. Nathaniel Cole, who had, on behalf of the state, directed one of the first cost studies ever performed in the early 1980's, analyzed the state's historical spending on education and calculated the amount necessary for the state merely to keep pace with inflation. Dr. Van Meuller and Dr. Mary Jo Smith performed a professional judgment assessment. First, they conducted an audit of curriculum and staff from a sample of schools across the state. Using this data, they then determined the cost of staffing every school across the state so that all students would receive an adequate education using the state standards. Finally, Dr. Richard Salmon and Lisa Driscoll used a statistical analysis to identify characteristics of successful school districts in Alaska and ascertain the resources necessary to provide all school districts with such characteristics. The team of experts concluded, in a 500-page report, that the State must roughly double its education funding in order to deliver an adequate education to all students in Alaska. Interestingly, each of the methods used came out with the same results, as had a professional judgment study of Alaska performed by Dr. Mueller six years earlier.

In addition to this cost analysis of the statewide system, we introduced evidence of the specific programs and resources that were lacking. Three plaintiff school districts were chosen for this purpose, Bering Strait School District, Kuspuk School District, and Yupiit School District. As described above, these districts served predominantly Alaska Native populations in remote, rural locations and were among the lowest performing districts in the state and had been for decades. Through the testimony of administrators and teachers, we showed the educational programs and resources required to address the needs of students attending these schools and the reasons for their present lack of such programs and resources.

While our inclusive, statewide approach helped draw together interests from across the state, it may have been too big for our limited resources. But whatever the reason, the court found numerous flaws with all of the studies and ultimately rejected most of their conclusions.

Liability Decision and Remedy

The trial court issued its decision on June 21, 2007, in what could be characterized as a "mixed ruling" for the plaintiffs. While the court found the State to have fulfilled its constitutional obligation to fund education, it found that the State, nevertheless, had violated the Education Clause because it "failed to exercise adequate supervision and oversight."[53] The court explained further by stating, "This Court finds that the [state's] efforts taken as of trial, particularly with respect to the Yupiit School District, are constitutionally inadequate."[54] Further, ". . . the Alaska Constitution sets some limits. If generations of children within a school district are failing to achieve proficiency, if a school or a district has not adopted an appropriate curriculum . . . if basic learning is not taking place for a substantial majority of a school's children, then the Constitution places the obligation upon the Legislature to ensure that the State is directing its best efforts to remedy the situation."[55] The decision was stayed for a year to allow the legislature an opportunity to remedy the constitutional violations.

Notwithstanding the court's findings that the State had violated its constitutional obligation, the State unabashedly claimed victory. The press release issued by the Office of the Governor was titled, "Court Rules in State's Favor on Education Case . . . Additional State Oversight of School Districts Required." According to the press release, the State was "very pleased that the court has reaffirmed that the state supplies adequate funding for education." In an Anchorage Daily News Article, Barbara Thompson, the deputy commissioner of education, was quoted as stating, "We truly are pleased with the ruling but we also know that we have a lot to do."[56] The plaintiffs' initial response was less enthusiastic. Bill Bjork, president of NEA-Alaska, stated in a press release, "We're pleased that the judge recognized that many of Alaska's children are not receiving an adequate education. But as far as the funding piece is concerned, this appears to be a disappointing setback."[57]

The State immediately called for a hearing to show that even while the decision was pending, they had clairvoyantly fixed all of the constitutional violations by intervening in four districts. As noted above, one of the schools in Yupiit where the State intervened actually declined in proficiency.

The court, however, was unconvinced that an early hearing before the legislature even met was useful, especially one where the state's interventions had focused on only a few districts. She stated:

> ... I came away with the sense that [the state] interpreted my decision to be limited solely to the Yupiit School District and perhaps Kuspuk, and I intentionally chose words to expand to state schools, not solely districts ... it is not solely a district-wide obligation; its an obligation that looks toward the child's ... each child's rights to an education.[58]

The court continued the stay of further hearings for a year. She also ordered that students in the Yupiit School district, and any other school identified by the State as not receiving an adequate education as defined in the opinion, be granted diplomas whether the child passed or failed the graduation examination. And she required that the State compile a list of schools where an inadequate education is occurring.[59]

As with all litigation, it remains to be seen what will be the ultimate impact of the court's decision, but there are several aspects that potentially hold great promise for the children of Alaska. First, and perhaps most significantly, the court concluded that the right to education was not an empty promise; it had a substantive component. Two decades earlier, in *Hootch v. Alaska State-Operated School System*, the Alaska Supreme Court had considered whether Alaska's Education Clause obligated the State to build local high schools for every secondary school age child to attend.[60] The plaintiffs were students from several small, rural villages.[61] There were no local high schools in these villages, so their only option was to attend one of several state operated boarding schools if they wished to receive a secondary education.[62] The plaintiffs contended that under Alaska's Education Clause, they had a constitutional right to be educated in their villages.[63]

The Alaska Supreme Court recognized that the Alaska constitution "confer[red] upon Alaska school age children a right to education."[64] It held, however, that this right did not encompass the right to attend high school in one's village of residence.[65] The court reasoned that the Education Clause permitted "some differences in the manner of providing education" and "that different approaches are appropriate to meet the educational needs in the diverse areas of the state."[66] Thus, following *Hootch*, although there was a right to education in Alaska, the substance of that right was uncertain. We now have a much clearer picture of the contours of that right.

The trial court in *Moore* identified four components to the State's constitutional obligation to provide education:

> First, there must be rational educational standards that set out what it is that children should be expected to learn. These standards should meet or exceed a

> constitutional floor of an adequate knowledge base for children. Second, there must be an adequate method of assessing whether children are actually learning what is set out in the standards. Third, there must be adequate funding so as to accord to schools the ability to provide instruction in the standards. And fourth, where, as here, the State has delegated the responsibility to educate children to local school districts, there must be adequate accountability and oversight by the State over those school districts so as to insure that the districts are fulfilling the State's constitutional responsibility to "establish and maintain a system of public schools" as set forth in Article VII, § 1 of Alaska's Constitution.[67]

The court found, and plaintiffs did not dispute, that the State had adopted adequate standards and assessments.[68] Further, the court found that while the Education Clause did not require the State to guarantee that each child achieve these standards, it did require, as to those tested, that the State insure that "each child in this state is accorded a meaningful opportunity to achieve" them.[69] As to all the remaining but untested standards, the court decreed that each child had a right to a "meaningful exposure" to all of those subjects and standards.[70] Thus, it defined educational adequacy as a meaningful opportunity to achieve state standards in reading, writing and math, and as a meaningful exposure to the remaining subjects and standards.

The court next considered whether the State had provided such an opportunity. The court found that existing resources were sufficient to accord children such an opportunity.[71] The court found it significant that there were many areas of the state, including small, rural locations, where children were being accorded a meaningful opportunity to achieve state standards.[72] Further, without a meaningful analysis of the geographical cost differential, the school size differential or the haphazard nature of federal funding when available, the court observed that REAAs, such as the plaintiff districts, received "considerably more funding per student than the average city or borough."[73] Surprisingly, in light of the violations the court found, it concluded that while spending more money may have an effect on outcomes, "funding for a public education system is constitutionally inadequate only if it is proven that the existing resources are not sufficient to accord to children a meaningful opportunity to be educated," and this, the court concluded, the plaintiffs had not proven.[74]

Even so, providing adequate resources, the court found, does not alone satisfy the State's constitutional responsibilities. The court recognized that the concept of local control over the delivery of education was "deeply ingrained in state educational policy and the history of education in Alaska and elsewhere,"[75] and that in fact there is a benefit in allowing local school districts the opportunity to direct their funds in the manner they believe will best meet the needs of students within their district.[76] However, the court concluded that the concept of local control must give way "[i]f a school, despite adequate funding, is failing to accord a child with a constitutionally adequate education."[77] The State has a duty to "insure that its educational standards are being implemented at the local level so that all children within this state receive their constitutional entitlement to the opportunity for an adequate education."[78]

The court elaborated on the nature of this duty. First, the State must "insure that each school district has a demonstrated plan to provide children a meaningful opportunity to achieve proficiency in the State's performance standards, and meaningful exposure on the remaining content standards."[79] Perhaps even more significantly, the State must insure that each district's plan "is fully implemented and actually in use in the district's classrooms."[80] Finally, "the State must exercise considerably more oversight and provide considerably more assistance and direction to those schools that are identified as failing to meet the State's constitutional obligation, in a concerted effort to remedy that situation."[81]

The court found that the State had not met its constitutional obligation because it had "failed to identify those schools within the state that are not according to children a meaningful opportunity to acquire proficiency in the subject areas tested by the State and a meaningful exposure to the other content areas in the State's educational standards."[82] Further, it found, "as to those schools that are deficient in that regard, the State has failed to provide adequate supervision and oversight in a concerted effort to remedy that situation.[83] The court found that the Yupiit School District in particular did not have "an educational plan and a well-grounded curriculum in use in its classrooms that together aim[ed] to insure that each child is accorded a meaningful opportunity to achieve proficiency on the State's performance standards and meaningful exposure to the State's other content standards."[84] Finally, as stated above, the court held that Alaska's due process clause prevented the State from imposing a graduation exam on its students until it had cured the constitutional infirmities in its education system.[85]

Lessons Learned and the Second Round

As anyone involved in these lawsuits knows, the standards movement has had a tremendous impact on school finance litigation. State standards have given plaintiffs a useful way to define what students must learn and then measure whether they are learning it. And, the test data quite starkly show that many students in Alaska and elsewhere, particularly those who are economically disadvantaged, do not meet these standards.

But the emphasis on outcomes also has drawn into focus what for the court in this case has been an elusive relationship between money and student achievement. How much money is required for a child to achieve? When educational adequacy is defined in terms of inputs, like pencils, books, and teachers, it is relatively easy to determine its cost. But when it is defined in terms of the opportunity to achieve certain outcomes, plaintiffs in some courts find its costs much more difficult to prove. In this case, even though the court found substantial violations of both the Alaska education clause and the Alaska due process clause, uncertainty about the relationship between outcomes and money led to the remarkable result that the court found that the need for additional funding even for the targeted educational programs such as pre-kindergarten, Reading First, teacher orientation to remote Alaska Native Villages was unproven and consequently denied funding that would have made these programs available.

However, this is but the first round. The summer of 2008 will begin the second round where the State will attempt to show it has cured the many constitutional violations and may have to defend whether such fundamental violations cost money to cure. The State has its rainy day savings account. For many children, it's raining.[86]

Biographies

R. Collin Middleton, plaintiffs' lead counsel, graduated from Yale University in 1963 with a B.A. in economics. He then graduated from Columbia University with a J.D. from Columbia Law School, and a

Master's degree from the Columbia School of International and Policy Affairs, both in 1967. He has attended a trial and appellate practice program for six months at Northwestern University, and he is admitted to both the Illinois and Alaska bars.

Mr. Middleton participated as *amicus curae* for the Alaska State Medical Association, the American Academy of Pediatrics and the local chapter of the American Psychiatric Association in *Hootch v. ASOSS*, mentioned in this article. With the other two authors, Mr. Middleton participated in *Kasayulie v. State*, which successfully found the funding of school facilities in the REAAs to be a violation of the education and due process clauses. The result of that funding was multiple new schools for many of the areas mentioned in the article. The *Moore* education case was a direct outgrowth of the *Kasayulie* case.

Robert J. Sato was Mr. Middleton's partner and co-counsel for the plaintiffs. He has had the unique opportunity to visit schools in each of the plaintiff districts and meet many of the dedicated teachers and administrators who work long hours in some of the most incredibly challenging conditions. Mr. Sato recently started his own practice, Sato & Sato, LLC, with his exceptional wife, Jeannie, who he met at U.C. Davis, where they both attended law school. He continues to represent NEA — Alaska and its members in the lawsuit and a variety of other education-related matters.

Howard Trickey is both an accomplished litigator and has practiced extensively in school law. He represents, and has for decades represented many of the rural school districts in the state, including the three palintiff school districts, and additionally the Anchorage School District, the largest school district and the most urban in the state.

Mr. Trickey graduated from Catholic University with a J.D.

degree and has received a B.A. from the University of Wisconsin at Madison. He ws the lead counsel in the Kasayulie litigation mentioned in the article, and continues to pursue the state's lack of compliance with the court's order in Moore, including most recently a hearing that ended in October of this year.

---

1 World Book Encyclopedia

2 www.pdf.Alaska.gov

3 Deposition of Ray Barnhardt. Used at trial, pp. 104-105.

4 Alaska Department of Education and Early Development, Report Card to the Public, 2005-2006, at 2; Ex 2364.

5 *Id.*

6 Trial Transcript at p. 150.

7 *Id.* at 147 and 213.

8 *Id.* at 147 and 213.

9 *Id.*

10 *Id.* at 215.

11 *Id.* at 215-216; AYP district worksheets.

12 *Id.* 321-22.

13 Exhibit 105 at 3-4; Exhibit 107 at 3-4; Exhibit 109 at 3-4; Exhibit 149; Exhibit 2373

14 2005-06 AYP school worksheets.

15 Tr. pp. 147-48, 161-62.

16 http://en.wikipedia.org/wiki/Savoonga%2C_Alaska.

17 http://en.wikipedia.org/wiki/Savoonga%2C_Alaska.

18 *Id.*

19 AYP school worksheets.

20 *Id.*

21 http://www.kuspuk.org/mod/resource/view.php?id=438.

22 Exh. 109; Exh. 438; Tr. 1934-35, 1977; http://www.kuspuk.org/mod/resource/view.php?id=438.

23 http://www.eed.state.ak.us/DOE_Rolodex/schools/SearchFormAction.cfm.

24 Tr. at 1934.

25 Tr. at 1938-39.

26 Exhibit 109.

27 Exhibit 69.

28 Exhibit 149.

29 *Id.*

30 Tr. at 1026-27.

31 Exhibit 149-52; 156-58.

32 Exhibit 105 at 3-4; Exhibit 107 at 3-4; Exhibit 109 at 3-4; Exhibit 149; Exhibit 2373.

33 Exhibit 1, p.3 of State's Motion for an immediate hearing that it had complied with all of the court's findings of Constitutional violations.

34 Exhibits 2365, 2366 (data from *Alaska Department of Education and Early Development*).

35 *Hootch v. Alaska State-Operated School System*, 536 P.2d 793, 800 (Alaska 1975).

36 *Id.*

37 *Id.* at 800-01.

38 *Id.*

39 AS 14.12.010.

40 AS 14.12.010(1); AS 29.35.260(b).

41 AS 14.08.031, 14.08.011.

42 AS 14.17.450, 14.17.460.

43 AS 14.17.420(a)(1).

44 AS 14.17.420(a)(2).

45 AS 14.17.430.

46 Exhibit 219, at 9; Exhibit 388.

47 Exhibit 219 at 41.

48 Exhibit 109.

49 AS 14.03.075.

50 Exhibit 2270.

51 Exhibit 389 and 2270; Tr. at 2946.

52 Exhibit 116-19; Tr. at 3007-17.

53 Decision and Order, at 194.

54 Opinion, p. 187 at para. 38.

55 Opinion, p. 188 at para. 39.

56 6/22/07 ADN article by Peznecker.

57 *Id.*

58 Transcript of October 11, 2007 hearing at 13.

59 There are 170 schools which failed to make AYP in 2007. The vast majority are at level 3 or higher (5 are at level 5 4 years including Savoonga). The state, however, has yet to compile its list.

60 536 P.2d 793 (Alaska 1975).

61 *Id.* at 796.

62 *Id.*

63 *Id.* at 799.

64 *Id.*

65 *Id.* at 804-05.

66 *Id.* at 803-04.

67 Decision and Order, at 174.

68 *Id.* at 175.

69 *Id.* at 176.

70 Opinion, p. 176 at para. 10.

71 Decision and Order at 183.

72 Decision and Order, at 179-81.

73 *Id.* at 180.

74 *Id.* at 183.

75 *Id.* at 184.

76 *Id.* at 188.

77 Decision and Order, at 185-86.

78 *Id.* at 186.

79 *Id.* at 189.

80 *Id.*

81 *Id.*

82 Decision and Order, at 194.

83 *Id.*

84 *Id.* at 188.

85 *Id.* at 195.

86

10 Montoy v. Kansas: The Fight for Educational Equity and Adequacy for All Kansas Kids in the Home of Brown v. Board of Education

by Alan L. Rupe and W. John Robb*

> "This case is truly one of a kind ... I have been a member of the Kansas Supreme Court for almost 30 years. Without doubt, this is the most significant case to come before the Court in my tenure. The issues presented are numerous and complex and their resolution is having and will continue to have far-reaching effects. . . . This case is not about winners and losers—it is about the children of Kansas. They will be better educated and better prepared to meet the challenges of our rapidly changing society. Kansas will be the ultimate beneficiary."
>
> — *Chief Justice Kay McFarland, July 28, 2006*

Introduction

Through Schools for Fair Funding, Inc., 19 Kansas urban and mid-sized school districts—representing more than one-third of

Kansas public school children—challenged the existing Kansas scheme for funding public schools. Schools for Fair Funding's lawyers, Alan Rupe and John Robb, and the Schools for Fair Funding governing board developed a strategy to challenge the scheme that included litigation, lobbying, and public relations. They sued the State of Kansas and argued the scheme, which was devised through a political auction among lawmakers and not based on any actual educational cost or rationale, provided inadequate and unfair funding to minority, foreign origin, high poverty, limited English proficient and disabled children. Plaintiffs won. And they won the largest increase in public school funding in Kansas history.

Pre-Litigation Status of Kansas Education and Education Finance

Kansas school finance litigation began in 1972 with *Caldwell v. State*[1] in which a Johnson County District Court ruled that unequal and unfair disparities among Kansas school district expenditures violated the Kansas Constitutions' equal protection clause. The Kansas legislature thereafter enacted the 1973 School District Equalization Act, mandating a minimum level of school funding for each student.

In 1990, 42 school districts, parents and students challenged the constitutionality of the School District Equalization Act in *Mock v. State.*[2] Plaintiffs argued that the school finance system resulted in smaller school districts receiving more money per pupil than larger districts. Plaintiffs also argued wealthier districts could support a better public school education than poorer ones. Shawnee County District Court Judge Terry Bullock issued a pretrial opinion that said the Kansas Constitution guarantees a public education to every child in the state. Judge Bullock said the finance obligation is owed "to each child to furnish him or her with an educational opportunity . . . equal to that owed every other child."[3]

The district court postponed a scheduled trial and gave the Kansas Legislature the opportunity to fund education within the constitutional parameters laid out by the court. In response, the legislature adopted the School District Finance and Quality Performance Accreditation Act ("the Act"). Many of the plaintiff districts dismissed their lawsuits hoping the new law would provide adequate and equitable funding to all Kansas public schools. But because the new funding law had not fixed all the existing problems, one group pushed forward claiming the Act was unconstitutional. Shawnee County District Court Judge Marla Luckert heard the trial and ruled that the 1992 Act was unconstitutional because it created funding disparities between large and small districts and the differences were not based on any rational educational reason.[4]

The Kansas Supreme Court disagreed and reversed Judge Luckert's decision, finding the Act constitutional.[5] The Kansas Supreme Court explained that the Kansas Constitution places the responsibility of determining the suitability of funding with the legislature and not the Court.[6] Recognizing that disparities might cause court intervention at some time, the Kansas Supreme Court determined that "plain common sense" explained the existing disparities and deferred to the wisdom of the Kansas Legislature.

Robinson v. State of Kansas and *Montoy v. State of Kansas*

Robinson in Federal Court

The lawyers representing Schools for Fair Funding, a non-profit corporation, filed *Robinson, et al.v. State of Kansas, et al.*, (No. 99-CV-

1193-MLB (D. Kan.), in 1999 in the United States District Court for the District of Kansas. Plaintiffs were the Dodge City, Kansas School District, the Salina School District, and a group of foreign origin, minority, at-risk, disabled, and limited English proficient public school children. Plaintiffs challenged the 1992 School District Finance and Quality Performance Accreditation Act under both federal and state law. The State filed a motion to dismiss the federal claims arguing that the United States Constitution's eleventh amendment provided them immunity from litigating state law claims in federal court. In response, Plaintiffs dismissed the state law claims from the federal lawsuit and filed a separate lawsuit in state court.[7]

Federal District Court Judge Monti Belot overruled the State's immunity defense in *Robinson* and held that the acceptance of federal education funds waived state immunity.[8] The State appealed to the United States Court of Appeals for the Tenth Circuit, attempted a rehearing before the Tenth Circuit *en banc* after losing, and unsuccessfully sought review by the United States Supreme Court. Plaintiffs' federal claims returned to Judge Belot, who put the case "on hold" until *Montoy v. State* was complete in Kansas state court.

Montoy in State Court

The state court lawsuit, *Montoy v. State*, was assigned to Shawnee County District Court Judge Terry Bullock. The immigrant, minority, disabled, foreign born, and at-risk plaintiffs alleged the School District Finance and Quality Performance Accreditation Act failed to provide a suitable and adequate education for them, pursuant to the Kansas Constitution's equal protection clause and education article.[9]

In November 2001—twelve days before trial—Judge Bullock, on his own motion, dismissed the case. In a one-paragraph opinion, Judge Bullock ruled that school funding adequacy and equity were within the prerogative of the Kansas Legislature and not an issue to be judged by the courts. Plaintiffs immediately appealed the dismissal to the Kansas Supreme Court, arguing that Judge Bullock's dismissal was procedurally improper. The Kansas Supreme Court agreed and ordered the case to proceed to trial, providing directions to the trial court on the issues of adequacy and equity.[10] The Kansas Supreme Court specifically directed Judge Bullock to examine both the adequacy and equity of school funding in Kansas to determine if the funding formula squared with the "suitability" provisions of Article VI and the equal protection clause of the Kansas Constitution. The federal case remained "on hold."[11]

While this first appeal to the Kansas Supreme Court was pending, the Kansas Legislature adopted a statute, K.S.A. § 46-1225, which provided that because of funding "inadequacies and inequities," a cost study should be commissioned to determine the actual cost of providing a suitable education in Kansas. John Augenblick and John Myers, operating under the business name Augenblick & Myers, conducted this study for the state utilizing three methods of determining the cost of a suitable education. Augenblick & Myers concluded that Kansas' school finance funding was, adjusted for inflation, more than $800 million dollars short per year of what was necessary to provide all Kansas children an adequate education.[12]

More than three and a half years after it was filed, the *Montoy* case proceeded to trial in September 2003. The trial lasted eight days and produced more than 1400 pages of trial transcript and hundreds of exhibits. The evidence at trial focused on test scores and an achievement gap between categories of Kansas kids. Plaintiffs demonstrated beyond any doubt that there were educational differences in Kansas between urban and mid-sized school districts with large concentrations of minority, at-risk, foreign born, English as a second language and disabled children, on the one hand, versus the wealthy, predominantly white, suburban school districts, on the other. The evidence clearly showed that Dodge City, Salina, and other urban and mid-sized school districts with a predominately minority, foreign origin, disabled, immigrant, and English as a second language population were chronically underfunded by the state of Kansas. And the evidence was clear that the chronic underfunding caused the Plaintiffs and those similarly-situated to be deprived of educational opportunities.

Representatives of the Kansas Department of Education, a defendant in the lawsuit, characterized the achievement gap in Kansas as a "brutal fact." Kansas Department of Education statistics showed that in 2002, over 80% of all African-American and Hispanic tenth graders in Kansas performed below satisfactory in mathematics. The evidence was similar in other grades and other subjects. Plaintiffs proved the Kansas Legislature—which knew from Augenblick & Myers the cost of a suitable education in Kansas—simply refused to provide Kansas public school children adequate and equitable education funding. Plaintiffs showed the inadequate and inequitable school funding caused the achievement gap. As one superintendent testified "[We educators] know how to fix it [the achievement gap], we just don't have the resources to do it."[13]

In December 2003, Judge Bullock ruled that the school finance formula "blatantly" violated both the Kansas Constitution's Article VI suitable financing provision and its equal protection clause. Judge Bullock deferred his final order until July 1, 2004 and told the Kansas Legislature to "just go fix it" before that date.

The Kansas Legislature ignored Judge Bullock's order and refused to approve a school funding plan by the close of its 2004 legislative session. On May 11, 2004, three days after the close of the legislative session, Judge Bullock issued an order closing all Kansas public schools until the legislature fixed the constitutional flaws within the school funding plan. Absent any statutory mechanism for appealing Judge Bullock's order, the legislature responded with special legislation allowing the State to immediately appeal the District Court's interim order. The State appealed and the Kansas Supreme Court suspended Judge Bullock's order to close the schools during the pendency of the appeal.

Kansas Supreme Court and Kansas Legislature

On January 3, 2005, the Kansas Supreme Court agreed with Judge Bullock and ruled the State's inadequate and inequitable school funding scheme did not provide a suitable education for all Kansas school children. The Court ruled the school funding mechanism violated Article VI of the Kansas Constitution. The Kansas Supreme Court retained jurisdiction, and, like Judge Bullock, told the legislature to fix the funding problem in Kansas using educational cost data to determine appropriate funding. The court gave the legislature 90 days to resolve the problem.[14]

The Kansas Legislature ignored the Court's order to utilize educational cost data and ignored the Augenblick & Myers study. Instead, through another political auction — not based on any educational costs or rationale — the legislature added only $142 million dollars during the Spring 2005 legislative session. The Kansas Supreme Court ordered both sides to brief whether the small increase fixed the problem.

The litigants provided oral argument to the Kansas Supreme Court on May 11, 2005. And on June 3, 2005 the Kansas Supreme Court unanimously declared the $142 million increase insufficient to render the school funding scheme constitutional. The Court ordered the legislature to increase funding by an additional $143 million dollars by July 1, 2005. The Court also mandated another cost study be completed by January 2006 and indicated that if the legislature failed to provide funding at the level recommended by the additional cost study or if the cost study was determined to be illegitimate, the Court would order funding to the level recommended by Plaintiffs, their experts, and Augenblick & Myers—an additional $568 million dollars.[15]

A defiant Kansas Legislature provided no additional state funding by the Court's deadline. The Kansas Supreme Court ordered Plaintiffs' and the State's attorneys to appear on July 8, 2005 for a hearing to determine if the Court should order the immediate closure of Kansas schools. At this juncture, in July 2005, the Kansas Legislature and the Kansas Supreme Court appeared to be on a constitutional collision course.

Each branch of government—the legislative and the judicial — claimed authority over public school funding. On July 6, 2005, in an effort to avert a constitutional meltdown and to avert the closing of public schools, the Kansas Legislature added an additional $148 million along with substantial local spending authority to the state's education funding system.

Thirty-six hours after the legislature increased funding, Plaintiffs and Defendants argued their positions before the Kansas Supreme Court. The Court then issued its opinion hours later. The Court held that the addition of new money brought the state's aggregate funding within the parameters previously ordered by the court. The schools were not closed. The Court retained jurisdiction, did not dismiss the case, and ruled it would continue to monitor public school funding.

". . . large, high-poverty districts were still

massively underfunded, especially those serving at-risk and bilingual students."

By late January 2006, the Legislative Post Audit Committee had completed two cost studies pursuant to the Kansas Supreme Court's order. The first, an "inputs" study, which focused on the cost of providing core curriculum, revealed that the State's school system required additional funding of $399 million per year to support an average class size of twenty five students without placing an inequitable burden on small districts. The second, an "outcomes" study, which focused on the cost of achieving performance goals mandated by state and federal law, revealed that an additional $470 million a year was needed for the Kansas school system to meet achievement requirements. Both studies firmly established that large, high-poverty districts were still massively underfunded, especially those serving at-risk and bilingual students.

On May 19, 2006, Kansas Governor Kathleen Sebelius signed Senate Bill 549, increasing funding to the Kansas school system by $466 million cumulative over the following three years. Although this legislation constituted a significant increase in school funding, it fell short of the constitutionally mandated $470 million *per year* increase required by the "outcomes" study.

On June 22, 2006, Plaintiffs returned to the Kansas Supreme Court to argue that the new funding plan was unconstitutional and that the Kansas Legislature had ignored both the mandate of the Court and the needs of Kansas school children. The oral arguments lasted nearly three hours. In a dramatic departure from ordinary procedure, on July 28, 2006, Chief Justice Kay McFarland made oral comments before issuing the Court's written opinion.

Clearly recognizing the monumental implications of the decision,

Chief Justice McFarland coined the case "the most significant case to come before the court in my [nearly 30-year] tenure." In a 4-2 decision, the Kansas Supreme Court held that the new funding plan substantially complied with the Court's prior orders but declined to consider whether the new funding plan violated the Kansas Constitution. Based on the perceived substantial compliance, the Court dismissed the *Montoy* lawsuit.[xvi] In the wake of the significant gains achieved in this state court lawsuit, Plaintiffs dismissed the remaining federal lawsuit, *Robinson*, as moot.

Lessons Learned

Commitment and Focus

Anti-tax political flack, the adversarial nature of litigation, and the publicity of a case in which public education is center stage can create a raft of second-guessing and diversions which—to the unfocused and uncommitted—throw efforts to increase public education funding off course. Certain lessons learned in Kansas provide guidance for future efforts of others.

"Never, Never Quit"

Six years of litigation is a long time. If litigation is an inherently risky business and with all the political fall-out in a fiscally conservative state, there is a temptation for clients, public supporters, editorial boards, witnesses, and litigants to throw up their hands and quit. The philosophy of never giving up and accepting litigation as part of the journey to improve public education is an important theme. Utilizing a grassroots public relations effort and lobbying the legislature are essential components of the strategy to remain centered and move forward to improve public education for all kids.

Expect the Unexpected

Co-counsel John Robb, a non-litigator, said it this way: "Litigation is really interesting. What you end up chasing is not what you—in the beginning—were pointed at." Schools for Fair Funding started this matter in federal court arguing violations of equal protection, due process, and a claim pursuant to Article VI of the Kansas Constitution. The State moved to sever the state law claims from the federal law claims. Schools for Fair Funding ended up with one lawsuit in federal court asserting federal claims and another lawsuit in state court asserting state claims.

In the state court case, Schools for Fair Funding asserted an equal protection claim, a due process claim, and a claim under the Kansas Constitution's education Article VI. The Kansas Supreme Court dismissed the equal protection and due process claims leaving only the Article VI claim. To the Article VI claim, the Kansas Supreme Court applied an equal protection-type analysis and Schools for Fair Funding prevailed. Schools for Fair Funding dismissed the federal court case as moot. Where Schools for Fair Funding started was not where it ended up.

"Goofy Stuff"

And with the unexpected, just plain goofy stuff occurs. The Kansas Legislature, on one hand, and the Kansas Supreme Court and public schools, on the other, were on a collision course. The Kansas Legislature tried to impose barriers and influence the litigation in a number of ways.

For example, during the course of the litigation, the legislature raised the mandatory retirement age for district court judges but declined to raise the mandatory retirement age for Kansas Supreme Court justices. The legislature also provided pay raises to all Kansas judges, *except* justices on the Kansas Supreme Court. A number of constitutional amendments were introduced by the legislature to change the way Kansas Supreme Court justices are appointed. Proposals ranged from election to legislative appointment, although no amendments ultimately passed.

The jurisdiction of the S courts to hear appeals of non-final orders in school finance cases was a specific piece of legislation adopted just for the school finance litigation. Likewise the Kansas Legislature passed a law limiting the power of judges to remedy school funding matters. The legislature also enacted a procedure requiring a 120-day "hold" on any lawsuit filed involving school finance and requiring the litigants to give notice to the State before filing any of those cases. School finance matters at trial must now be decided by a three-judge panel, and courts cannot close schools or affect distribution of money as part of the remedy in a school finance case.

The legislature also enacted a new record keeping requirement for non-profit organizations involved in school finance requiring those non-profit corporations to be subject to the Kansas open meeting and records laws. Additionally, the legislature passed a law limiting a school district's ability to utilize its funds to pursue school finance litigation against the State. The statute that authorized the Augenblick & Myers cost study was repealed, and another law adopted by the legislature stated that cost studies could not be "binding" on the legislature in any school finance litigation.

In discussions concerning the passage of legislation to authorize carrying concealed weapons, public schools were exempted and could opt out from concealed carry. During the discussion it was proposed that, because of the school finance litigation, superintendents' offices not be allowed to exempt out from concealed carry. The measure did not pass but certainly generated discussion.

One lesson emerged from this compilation of "goofy stuff"—favorable public opinion to the school finance cause is important to balance the actions of ornery legislatures since law makers can change the rules in the middle of the fight. This lesson holds true for protection of both the litigants and the courts.

> ***"From the Boston Tea Party through the Selma March to lawsuits concerning school finance, conflict has often been coupled with progress."***

Conclusion

The ultimate lesson learned is that the fight is worth it. From the Boston Tea Party through the Selma March to lawsuits concerning school finance, conflict has often been coupled with progress. The increase in public school funding, and the increase in educational opportunities for Kansas kids, certainly made the fight over school finance in Kansas worth it. It is hard to image how much poorer the quality of Kansas education would be today if avoiding conflict had been the most important guiding principle during the last seven years.

Biographies

Both Alan Rupe and John Robb are known nationally for their school finance law expertise. They speak frequently at the national Quality Education Conference, held annually in Washington, DC, and Alan Rupe is a member of the advisory board for the National Access Network at Teachers College, Columbia University, one of the co-sponsors of the conference. Alan Rupe and John Robb work extensively with professors and attorneys across the country in the area of quality education issues. Both have consulted with and advised schools in several states concerning school finance issues and trial strategies.

Alan L. Rupe, a partner in the Kutak Rock LLP, is the National Chair of the firm's Employment Law Group. A skilled trial lawyer, Mr. Rupe is described by Chambers USA as heading "formidable fighting unit ... [he is] excellent on his feet and a man who clearly relishes the trial process." He is an Advocate in the American Board of Trial Advocates, and a member of the Litigation Counsel of America, International Association of Defense Research Counsel, and Defense Research Institute. He has served as lead counsel in more than 130 civil jury trials and regularly handles employment matters including class/collective actions across the country. Mr. Rupe s a frequent presenter on topics including class actions, trial tactics and employment law.

Mr. Rupe earned a B.A., with honors, from the University of Kansas and a law degree from Washburn University School of Law, where he served as Comments Editor of the Washburn Law Journal. He is admitted to practice in Kansas, Missouri, Oklahoma, Arkasas, Texas, the United States Court of Appeals (Fifth, Sixth, Eighth and Tenth Circuits), a number of United States District Courts and the United States Supreme Court.

John S. Robb is a long-time Kansas lawyer with special expertise in school finance, governmental entities and education law. A close working relationship with clients and courts alike has made him one of Kansas' premier education lawyers. John Robb has been actively practicing law since 1978 when he joined his father as a third generation lawyer. An active school attorney, John has distinguished himself in the area of school finance litigation and negotiations as well as day-to-day advice for school administrators and Boards. He has also consulted with and advised schools in Missouri and South Dakota concerning school finance matters.

After growing up in Newton, Kansas, John attended the University of Kansas. John has a continuing interest in business issues and puts his undergraduate degree in Business Administration to use frequently for clients and in his civic activities. Serving regularly on various local organization Boards and particularly finance committees has been a real pleasure.

The authors would like to give credit to* ***Jordan J. Wills**, Washburn University, Topeka Kansas, law student for her contributions to this article.*

---

1 *Caldwell v. State*, Johnson County District Court Case No. 50616 (August 30, 1972).

2 *Mock v. State*, No. 91-CV-1009 (Shawnee County, Kan. Dist. Ct. Oct. 14, 1991).

3 *Id.*

4 Shawnee County District Court Case Nos. 92-CV-1202, 92-CV-1175, and 92-CV-2406. Opinion filed December 2, 1994.

5 *Unified School District No. 229 v. State of Kansas*, 256 Kan. 232, 885 P.2d 1170 (1994).

6 *Id.* at 256-57.

7 *Montoy v. State*, No. 99-C-1738, 2004 WL 1094555 (Shawnee County, Kan. Dist. Ct. May 11, 2004); *see also Montoy v. State*, 120 P.3d 306 (Kan. 2005); *Montoy v. State*, 112 P.3d 923 (Kan. 2005); *Montoy v. State*, 282 Kan. 9, -- P.3d -- (Kan. 2006).

8 *Robinson v. State*, 117 F.Supp.2d 1124 (D.Kan. 2000).

9 Section 2, Kansas Bill of Rights (Equal Protection); Article 6, Section 6(b) ("The legislature shall make suitable provision for finance of the educational interest of the state.").

10 *Montoy v. State*, 275 Kan. 145, 62 P.3d 228 (2003).

11 *Robinson v. State*, No. 99-1193-MLB (D. Kan. Jan. 12, 2004).

12 Augenblick & Myers, Inc., Calculation of te Cost of a Suitable Education in Kansas in 2000-2001 Using Two Different Analytic Approaches (May 2002) (prepared for Legislative Coordinating Council).

13 Brief of Appellees/Cross-Appellants, pp.2, 26, filed June 28, 2004, *Montoy v. State*

14 278 *Kan.* 769, 776 (2005).

15 279 *Kan.* 817, 846 (2005).

16 282 *Kan.* 9, 25-27 (2006).

11 Pennsylvania School Finance Litigation II: Powell v. Ridge

by Michael Churchill

Overview

The *Powell* case was one of the rare attempts to use federal courts to address school funding issues after the Supreme Court's decision in *San Antonio Independent School Dist. v. Rodriguez*[1] which held that the Equal Protection clause of the 14th Amendment does not prohibit a state from funding schools unequally. *Powell* was an attempt by Philadelphia educational advocates, the Philadelphia School District, and City, to find a litigation route independent of the Pennsylvania state court system which would create some leverage with the state legislature to change state funding for Philadelphia schools.[2] It was the first time a federal lawsuit attempted to use anti-discrimination civil rights legislation to address state school funding reform. The case ultimately did not proceed because the Supreme Court, in a non-school funding case, rejected all private suits to enforce the Civil Rights regulations which prohibit activities that have a disparate impact on minority groups. The case also graphically demonstrates how political changes affect any litigation strategy.

The Supreme Court drastically limited the availability of federal jurisdiction on school funding matters in *San Antonio Indep. School Dist. v. Rodriguez*[3] where it rejected any claim based only on unequal funding. Thus, a federal suit over inequality could only be based on a claim of racial discrimination arising out of the funding system. This, however, seemed to be supported by the facts in Pennsylvania. A study of the state finances by a University of Pennsylvania professor of economics, Anita Summers, revealed that Philadelphia, with the largest number of minority students in the state, was underfunded. More compelling, when all districts with a majority of minority students were considered, they had received less funding than white districts with a similar percentage of poverty students had received. Essentially, for two districts with an equal percentage of poverty students, for every one percent increase in minority students in a district, the district received $52.88 less from the state.[4] (This amounted to more than $400 million a year underfunding for the Philadelphia School District.)

Plaintiffs alleged this pattern was a violation of the disparate impact regulation under Title VI of the Civil Rights Act of 1964[5] which prohibits actions by an agency receiving federal dollars which have an adverse impact on minority beneficiaries compared to white beneficiaries[6]. The Plaintiffs also alleged this pattern violated Section 1983, 42 U.S. Code § 1983, which prohibits deprivation, under color of law, of any right secured by the laws of the United States, in this case Title VI and its regulations.

The Plaintiffs, educational organizations, ten parents, and the City and School District of Philadelphia, filed this federal suit in March 1998 against the Governor and state education officials two weeks after the state's Commonwealth Court had dismissed the *Marrero* case.[7] That case charged that the state funding system violated the Pennsylvania Constitution because it did not enable Philadelphia schools to provide an adequate education to their students.

The *Powell* case was assigned to Judge Herbert Hutton, an African-American Republican who had been appointed by President Reagan in 1988. Republican legislative leaders intervened to oppose the federal action and the U.S. Justice Department intervened for the limited purpose of upholding the constitutionality and enforceability of the federal civil rights regulations.

After extensive briefing, Judge Hutton dismissed the Plaintiffs' Title VI regulations discrimination claim for failure to state a cause of action because, in his view, the complaint failed to allege that the disparity in funding was on account of race, but instead was on account of poverty.[8] Judge Hutton also dismissed the claims of all parties under Section 1983 that their rights were violated. He held that state officials sued in their official capacity were not considered "persons" who had deprived plaintiffs of their rights within the meaning of Section 1983, and, therefore, could not be sued.[9] Judge Hutton, however, rejected several of the other reasons defendants had supporting dismissal, including their strongly argued claim that there was no private right of action to enforce the Title VI regulation.

On appeal, a panel of the Third Circuit Court of Appeals in June 1999 unanimously reaffirmed its position that there was a cause of action to enforce the disparate impact regulation. It also reversed Judge Hutton's holding that the Complaint alleged a disparity based on poverty. The Court of Appeals found that the Complaint stated a cause of action for disparate impact on account of race. Finally, it held that the State officials were subject to Section 1983 injunctive actions.[10]

The Defendants sought review by the US Supreme Court of the issue whether Title VI regulations were enforceable in a private action, noting that the Court had granted review of a similar question from an opinion of the Third Circuit three years earlier in a case which had become moot before it could be decided by the Supreme Court.[11] Plaintiffs suggested to the Court that review was untimely because of the need for a more developed factual record. In December 1999, the Court surprisingly denied review.[12]

When the case returned to the District Court for discovery, Plaintiffs believed they needed a record showing as much evidence as possible of knowledge by the legislators of the disparate impact and underfunding of minority districts in order to permit inferences of intention or reckless disregard of discrimination. They wanted the case to be as strong as possible because they expected the Supreme Court would review it after trial and knew several members did not believe the disparate impact regulations were valid. The legislators resisted almost all but the most perfunctory discovery. Judge Hutton ordered them to comply. Claiming legislative privilege and immunity from discovery, they appealed.[13] The case was briefed to the Court of Appeals and argued in January 2001. In April, the Court held that by intervening and then seeking discovery themselves, the legislative defendants had waived any right to object to discovery.[14] Again the Defendants sought Supreme Court review and at the beginning of the new term in October 2001 were turned down.[15] In theory the case could proceed.

However, at about the same time as the Third Circuit decision permitting the discovery, the case had completely unraveled, both on the legal front and in the status of the parties. On April 24, 2001 the Supreme Court in the *Sandoval*[16] case had held that there is no private right of action to enforce the Title VI regulations, declaring wrong the Third Circuit and all of the other courts of appeals that addressed the issue. Because the only remaining federal vehicle was the Title VI statute itself, requiring intentional discrimination, plaintiffs would have to amend their complaint and prove intentional discrimination if they were to continue.

The parties' political positions also had changed. The City, unable to keep the schools open on its own, was now willing to accept just enough money from the state to keep the schools open rather than seek substantial increases to reach equality with other districts. With the state willing to provide that more limited funding, the City, School District and State negotiated a stay to the litigation in May of 2000 which was continued until the parties agreed to end the litigation without prejudice in 2006.[17] The community advocates, under great pressure from the City and District and without significant likelihood of success, agreed not to oppose the stay.

The radical changes in the context of the litigation can be seen by the changing positions of several key players. In the Spring of 2002, the legislature and governor took over control of the Philadelphia School Board. As a result, the School District no longer supported suing the legislature and was unwilling to continue the litigation designed to provide it with additional resources. Moreover, in 2003 Edward Rendell, who was Mayor of the City of Philadelphia and a plaintiff when the suit was brought against the Governor, became the Governor and would now be the Defendant. Among the organizational plaintiffs, two had lost funding and disbanded. The only persons who were still in the same place were the students who continued to find themselves victims of inadequate funding.

The Context

The litigation arose in the context of a stalemate in an increasingly bitter war between political leaders in Philadelphia and the state capital Harrisburg, led by Governor Tom Ridge, which was causing great harm to the District's pupils. At the beginning of 1998, the school district's finances were on life support from the relentless refusal of Harrisburg to increase funding. A new budget was being prepared by the District for the 1998-99 school year, and it did not appear there was any way to balance the budget without severely cutting into programs for students. Although student test performance had been increasing, that trend was unlikely to continue if classroom services had to be reduced further. Studies by the District showed that when the *Marerro* case had been brought, the gap between expenditures on students in Philadephia and the average suburban student was $1,522 per student. Now, a year later, that gap had now grown to nearly $2,000 a year, $24,000 over the school life of a student, equivalent to three extra years of schooling.

The budget policies of the Ridge administration seemed clearly at the heart of the problem: a document drafted by the District showed that funding had not even kept pace with inflation. Dropping the state funding formula in 1991 had permitted the state to appropriate Philadelphia $100 million less in 1997-8 than the formula would have called for. The especial hostility to Philadelphia was apparent from the fact that State appropriations to the Philadelphia School District on a per student basis had increased a total of 2.1 percent over five years, but for the rest of the state appropriations had increased 10.9 percent per student. As a result, the school district appeared likely to have an $85 million deficit in the next budget.

Faced with that situation, Superintendent Hornbeck, Mayor Rendell, and Council President Street held a joint press conference in which they announced that they were "drawing a line in the sand." [18] They would not cut back services, but they would spend what money they had at the same rate until the money ran out somewhere in the late Spring and would then close the schools until the state provided the money to open them. This was a strategy of desperation born of the lack of any strong alternative, seeking to turn weakness into strength through the jujitsu of arousing public pressure. Filing a federal lawsuit was considered as an adjunct to that policy, providing the opportunity to display to the world the facts of the unequal and unfair state funding system.

By that time the State Supreme Court did not appear likely to provide any relief for Philadelphia in its myriad attempts to move the legislature. The Court had been sitting on the *Desegregation*[19] case without scheduling a hearing since August 1996 when Judge Smith Ribner had held the State was required to contribute more to paying the cost of desegregating Philadelphia schools. The *Marrero* case had been lost in Commonwealth Court.[20] Filing the *Powell* case in federal court, however, neither intimidated the state leadership nor induced cooperation. Their response to the "line in the sand" was first to pass legislation which made easier the ability of the state to take control of a district which was in "financial distress" and could not or would not keep its schools open. Their second response came in 2002 to pass new legislation creating the State Reform Commission to take over Philadelphia schools.[21]

Although the facts contained in the Complaint — taken from the state's own records or from Professor Summer's work based on state records — were quite dramatic, they received little to no public attention. Instead, the press and public focused on the "accusation" of the Complaint that the Governor and legislature had discriminated on the basis of race. This was quickly turned by the defendants into a claim that they were "accused of being racists." "Just because we didn't give Philadelphia everything it asked for," was the gist of what followed. The fact that all of the minority districts were receiving fewer state dollars per student was not discussed, nor that state audits of Philadelphia had not found large wasteful expenditures. Neither the public nor the press discussed how Philadelphia, with the largest class sizes in the state, could be expected to educate its students for 25 percent less than the average suburban district.

Polls taken in this period by Greater Philadelphia First, a business organization, showed that citizens in each suburban county believed by wide majorities that the state funding system was unfair to urban districts. Nevertheless, these views did not get translated into changed legislative votes. And Governor Ridge, during his 1998 re-election campaign, was not seriously challenged on any of the state's education funding disparities.

John Street succeeded Ed Rendell as Mayor in January 2000, right after the Supreme Court's refusal in December 1999 to interfere with the Court of Appeals decision to let the case go forward. With the approach of active discovery in the trial, the Ridge Administration wanted to find some way to halt the case. At the same time, the district's funding crisis grew acute. At the City's budget-making deadline at the end of May, Street and Ridge negotiated a deal whereby the state would provide assistance to keep the schools open, the District would reduce its budget by $30 million and the District and City would agree to stay the lawsuit.[22]

The spokesman for Governor Ridge stated that suspending the lawsuit was an essential part of the deal: "You can't be working hand in hand with someone at the same time you're saying that they're racist." The collapse of the "line in the sand" provoked the resignation of

Superintendent Hornbeck, who at the same time defended the necessity of the deal negotiated by the Mayor: "The only other choice was to trigger a takeover by precisely those who demonstrate year in and year out that education in general, and education for poor rural and urban children in particular, are simply not the priority."[23]

Nevertheless, two years later that takeover was triggered when the School District again needed additional funds. The Republican leadership, realizing that it might be faced with election of a Democratic governor in the fall of 2002, enacted legislation that summer replacing the School Board, which had been appointed by the Mayor, with a School Reform Commission (SRC). [24] A majority of the SRC was appointed by the Harrisburg Republicans and they locked that majority into place for five years. Faced with a deficit he could not fund, the Mayor acquiesced. Now that they had control, the state permitted the District to float a $300 million bond issue to finance operating expenses, and over the next five years, a Democratic Governor saw to it that state funding to the district increased along with state funding to all public schools.

The same state Constitutional Clause that directed the legislature to provide for a thorough and efficient system of public education gave the state government ultimate control over the fate of the Philadelphia School District through its power to create or abolish districts. A challenge to the legislation taking over the School District mounted by unions and some community groups fearful of privatization of the schools and loss of local control was rejected by the Pennsylvania Supreme Court in a one word order: "Denied."

Philadelphia legislators who voted for the take-over experienced no organized opposition, much less any serious reprisal. The Mayor, who had obtained the power to appoint the entire school board by a charter change in the preceding election, found the only power he had was to bargain for an extra minority seat on the SRC. There was no other option because the City, with the highest taxes in the state, was unable or unwilling to devote substantially more of its own tax revenues to the schools, which was the only alternative the District had to relying on additional state support. For the Mayor, it was easier to say to the state: if you won't pay us sufficiently to run the schools, then they are yours' to run.

Community groups were at that point faced with few litigation options. Because of the *Sandoval* decision the previous spring, the only federal avenue of attack on the lack of adequate funding to Philadelphia was to prove that it was on account of intentional discrimination in violation of Title VI itself. An amended complaint alleging intentional discrimination was drafted but never filed. Problems of proof were great, particularly because the Supreme Court had held that mere knowledge of a discriminatory impact is not sufficient to permit an inference of intentional discrimination.[25] There were no smoking guns of statements about race. The litigation would be long and difficult and the cost would have to be borne by the community advocates and the Law Center alone with the City and School District no longer supporting the litigation.

In addition, once the SRC was in place it took the position that it did not need additional funding. While that technically was not responsive to the question whether the District was receiving less funding than it should because of discrimination, it made the issue politically more difficult. Furthermore, it would be politically difficult to sue as Governor the very person who had brought the case originally as Mayor and claim that he was now intentionally discriminating. Although the possibility existed to allege that a former Governor and legislature had discriminated and this Governor and legislature merely failed to correct the continuing effects, the prospect of attacking the Governor even at that level was not attractive to the participants. For those reasons, the community participants were willing to allow the stay to continue, and then in 2006, to end the case rather than re-open it.

The Litigation

The actual litigation turned out to be exceedingly complex, involving areas of law which were undergoing rapid changes. The initial victory of Plaintiffs in the Court of Appeals was a very significant milestone in the use of the disparate impact regulations and an important precedential case, as shown by the participation of the Department of Justice and its wide citation. But, the opinion could not stand up to the increasingly hostile opposition of a majority of the U.S. Supreme Court to claims of disparate impact discrimination and to claims of rights of action by citizens unless explicitly authorized by Congress.

To show its seriousness about the civil rights claim, the School District added noted Republican civil rights attorney William T. Coleman, Jr. from the Washington firm of O'Melveny & Myers, to the legal team it already had assembled for the *Marrero* case. That team already consisted of Patricia Brannan from Hogan & Hartson and lawyers at the Dilworth firm in Philadelphia. Coleman, a former Philadelphian and senior partner in the Dilworth firm, had been a member of Thurgood Marshall's *Brown v. Board of Education* legal team and served as Secretary of Transportation in the Ford Administration. As in the state court *Marrero* case, the City was represented by Richard Feder in the City Law Department and the educational advocacy organizations by Michael Churchill from the

Public Interest Law Center of Philadelphia with the assistance of Thomas K. Gilhool.

The City of Philadelphia had engaged Professor Anita Summers to review the state system of funding and her report was devastating about the strength of the findings of discrimination which existed, whether she looked at African-Americans or all non-whites, and whether she defined poverty as on welfare or entitled to free and reduced lunch. Her conclusion on the discriminatory nature of the system existed if she looked only at state funding which the legislature directly controlled or all funding (state and locally generated) available under the state created system of funding education. Because the analysis involved all of the school districts with a majority of non-white students (totaling 12 at the time of the study) it seemed to be an effective answer to the expected defense that under-funding Philadelphia was not about race, but merely reflected an anti-big city bias, which is not a violation of federal law. Not only Philadelphia, but also many smaller communities which had nothing in common except heavy concentrations of minority students, were similarly discriminated against. The only problem with the analysis was that the discrimination only became apparent after a regression analysis, comparing districts with equal levels of poor students. Because the inequality in funding did not readily appear to an observer, it was difficult to infer knowledge and intention by the legislators.

In the initial discussions of the lawsuit, the plaintiffs' lawyers knew that starting in *Regents of the Univ. of Cal. v. Bakke*[26], the Court had said that Title VI in Section 601 itself only prohibited intentional discrimination. So how, critics asked, could regulations authorized under Section 602 to enforce Section 601 "reach further" to prohibit "unintentional" discrimination not prohibited by Section 601? In 1983 the Supreme Court had only narrowly, by one vote, upheld the validity of the Title VI regulation prohibiting activities which had an adverse discriminatory impact, on the grounds that Congress permitted agencies to protect a right by broadly regulating activities which might promote infringements of that right.[27] The Court, however, had since then undergone extensive changes in the justices on the bench.

Bill Coleman himself raised this problem several times during drafting sessions, and kept asking whether plaintiffs could not allege and prove that depriving minority students of school funding was part and parcel of historic school segregation and widespread discriminatory practices aimed at depriving Black persons of governmental benefits, such as redlining areas by government agencies which discouraged integration. None of the parties, however, were able to develop proof of the state's involvement, much less develop any link to the system of school funding.

Both Churchill, with extensive prior experience with Title VI regulation cases arising from the Chester environmental litigation in the Third Circuit, and Brannan, with experience in school litigation, were comfortable with going forward with the disparate impact claim, but agreed that it would be strengthened by including as many "effects plus" allegations about knowledge of the unmet needs of the minority districts as possible to bolster the claim.

The Complaint noted that 75 percent of the students in the District were minorities, compared to 11 percent in the rest of the state, that 80 percent were from low income families, and that the District had the highest incidence of students in poverty in the five county metropolitan region. It noted that these demographic facts were known to defendants as well as the higher cost of educating students with a high incidence of poverty.

The Complaint then recited facts showing the vast disparity in funding. In fiscal 1996 Pennsylvania school districts with more than 75% minority enrollment had $389 less in educational support per student than did majority white districts per student. State records showed the gap per student in total revenue between the School District and the average for the rest of the metropolitan area was $1,615 in 1996 and was approximately $2,000 for fiscal 1998. The complaint also alleged that when comparing Pennsylvania school districts with the same level of poverty (based on the percent of families on AFDC), districts with the higher minority enrollment on average received $52.88 less per pupil for each increase of 1 percent in minority enrollment.[28]

Immediately after the case was filed, interested parties sought to intervene. First came the teachers union, seeking to intervene on behalf of the plaintiffs. Their participation in the remainder of the case was minimal. On the defendants' side, however, the intervention of the Republican legislative leaders with their own very aggressive counsel, John Krill, clearly influenced the conduct of the case, both because of the extremism of the views expressed, and because of the multiplicity of filings. Although Plaintiffs always jointly filed a single brief on behalf of all plaintiffs, the executive and legislative defendants never did, and there were clear differences in emphasis in their filings.

The third additional party was the United States, which first sought to participate as amicus curiae to express its views on the proper interpretation of the Title VI regulations. Then when the validity of the regulations were challenged by the legislative interveners, it sought to intervene as a party. The Department of Justice was represented by Seth Galanter, an accomplished lawyer from the Appellate Division who was following attacks by states on the Title VI regulations and other federal statutes nationally and who previously had worked closely with Law Center attorneys on litigation defending the validity of Section 504 of the Rehabilitation Act[xxix], IDEA (Individuals with Disabilities Education Act), and the ADA.

Judge Hutton's grant of the motion to dismiss was a surprise since the principle legal issue had been decided by the Court of Appeals in the Chester environmental case two years earlier. That issue was enforceability by private parties of the Title VI disparate impact regulations. In fact, Judge Hutton followed that ruling, but he went on anyway to dismiss the Complaint, by misconstruing it to state that it was not a claim about race but a claim about poverty, which did not violate the law. He also dismissed the Section 1983 claims on the grounds that the defendants were not persons who could be sued under that statute, a rather clear error of law.

The Appeal was briefed by the full team of lawyers working on the case. Oral argument was presented initially by William Coleman, while Patricia Brannan handled the rebuttal for plaintiffs. The principle contributions of the Plaintiffs' briefs, in addition to a strong analysis of the cases, was an extensive history of the Title VI legislation, the specific Congressional testimony of administration spokespersons that if they were empowered to adopt regulations they would include prohibitions on practices producing racially unbalanced outcomes, the subsequent refusal of Congress to repeal the regulations, and the subsequent Congressional incorporation of those regulations in directives to agencies under other statutes. These sections were based on extensive research of the legislative history by Churchill and Brannan. To the extent there was an issue about Congressional intention, plaintiffs felt they had made a strong case.

The Appeal raised issues which were at the heart of the civil rights enforcement debate at that time. The first was the legitimacy of federal disparate impact regulations, which had been uniformly adopted by nearly every federal agency and, therefore, applied to every aspect of federal financial assistance, not just education. Title VI disparate impact regulations were highly controversial because, unlike intentional discrimination, they were about disproportionate impacts on minorities, which for conservatives implied thinking of persons as racial groups, statistical disparities, and representation in accordance with numerical measures. Civil rights advocates, however, regarded the use of disproportionate numbers as a means of proving discrimination as absolutely vital, since smoking gun statements showing disparate treatment were becoming so rare. Moreover, intent to discriminate is almost impossible to determine when there is not a single decision maker but a collective body such as a legislature, with presumably a variety of intentions of individual legislators. With disparate impact, one can instead just look at results.

Another part of the unease with disparate impact was its breadth, expressed by critics who called it unintentional discrimination. When the Justice Department, which was historically committed to defending the Title VI regulations, consulted the Clinton Administration Department of Education, there was some hesitancy about its position in the *Powell* case. That hesitancy was based on fear that the regulations could reach past the situation alleged in *Powell* — that state funds were discriminatorily distributed — to include the impact of using local property taxes to fund schools, since that method of funding education undoubtedly would also have a disproportionate impact. Because of the narrow focus of the *Powell* Complaint, the two Departments agreed to support the litigation.

Although disparate impact cases are well accepted in employment cases under Title VII of the Civil Rights Act of 1964, the Supreme Court since 1976 had been struggling to reduce the role of disproportionate impact analysis in other areas.[30] The Court in *Regents of the Univ. of Cal. v. Bakke*[31] stated that Title VI extended only as far as the intentional discrimination reached by the 14th Amendment, immediately calling into question the validity of the regulations, because now there was an issue whether Congress intended to authorize regulations which reached further, and whether it had the power to do so.[32] In the Guardian Civic League case, the Court, in a very fractured voting pattern, appeared to uphold the validity of the regulations, *Guardians Ass'n v. Civil Serv. Comm'n of New York*[33]. But it did not explicitly conclude that there was a private right of action to enforce the regulations, nor did it decide if the regulations created an individual right protected from deprivation under color of law by Section 1983.

Both of those issues presented in the *Powell* case, implicated litigation in many areas in addition to education funding. It was those two issues which the Third Circuit addressed in a thorough opinion by Judge Doris Sloviter joined in by Judge Lois Mansmann and Visiting District Judge Robert Ward.[34] The importance of the issues addressed by the *Powell* opinion can be gauged by the 76 law review citations to the decision, even though only two years later it was superceded by the Supreme Court's *Sandoval* opinion on the private right of action question and by *Gonzaga Univ. v. Doe*[35] on the Section 1983 enforcement issue.[36]

Plaintiffs feared the Defendants had a high probability of getting Supreme Court review, but in their response to the Petition for Certiorari, they suggested that review would be more appropriate after development of the factual content of the case, since much of the harm Defendants predicted might not actually occur. The Court denied review of the decision, allowing the case to go forward to trial.

The *Powell* case in its second phase was a legal fight over the scope of discovery of documents from legislators and the scope of their immunity. This fight detoured the case for two years. The primary work at that stage was handled by the Dilworth firm, with Jim Rogers and Lynn Rauch taking the leading roles. A Third Circuit opinion by Judge Barry concluded:

"as the Legislative Leaders conceded at oral argument, the privilege they propose would enable them to seek discovery, but not respond to it; take depositions, but not be deposed; and testify at trial, but not be cross-examined. In short, they assert a privilege that does not exist."[37]

The principle impact of this phase of the litigation was that it delayed a trial on the merits until after the Supreme Court's decision in *Sandoval* permanently ended any threat of a trial on the disparate impact claim. [38]

Lessons Learned

The litigation had very limited results. If the goal of the litigation was to end Pennsylvania's discriminatory funding across the state, it clearly did not succeed. Pennsylvania was not forced to deal with its system of funding schools, which continued on an ad hoc basis, year by year. If the goal was to increase funding for the Philadelphia School District, the litigation may have succeeded to some limited extent. As part of the negotiations of the initial stay of the law suit, the state agreed to increase support for the District. Two years later, in connection with the state takeover, the district was allowed to float new bonds to permit additional operating expenditures. It is difficult to know the role of the law suit in these negotiations because the precarious financial plight of the district was another factor in the negotiations and the law suit was not near conclusion.

Nevertheless, cessation of the law suit was obviously important to the state negotiators and was one of their key demands. The amount of assistance offered by the state was not anywhere near the estimated $400 million underfunding, but the district did not have the financial stability to wait until final resolution of the litigation. In this sense, it was another example of the familiar story that litigation works best for the strong: the high expense and delay in obtaining a decision forces weak litigants to compromise in order to survive.

Racial discrimination claims are vulnerable in the court of public opinion if not fully explained. Philadelphia leaders were ambivalent about the issue of race discrimination. They clearly thought the state underfunded Philadelphia schools. Neither Mayor Rendell, a white man, nor Mayor Street, an African-American man, however, publicly charged the state with racial discrimination in any speeches apart from filing the complaint. They never held a press conference with Professor Summers to discuss the charges in public. They never met with the mayors of the other cities whose school districts enrolled predominately minority students to bring a concerted focus to the charges of underfunding minority schools. They never said, well if this underfunding is accidental, fix it for all minority districts. Although they said that Philadelphia did not receive enough money from Harrisburg, they never linked it to race, but in public discourse seemed to attribute it to an anti-urban bias. It was as if they thought the discrimination claim was a ploy, to get into federal court, but not the real issue. Perhaps they thought that reminding voters in the rest of the state that Philadelphia was heavily minority in population would be counter-productive to the attempt to get more funding.

By contrast, defendants did not have any hesitancy in reminding listeners that the case charged racial discrimination, as if that were absurd on its face. They never tried to explain the evidence of statewide underfunding or even to deny it; they just ignored it and professed their horror at being accused of being racially biased. With minorities approximately only 12 percent of the state, they did not feel any pressure to answer to a minority constituency. Defendants' counterattack focused on whether Philadelphia paid enough school taxes and that the fact that the state pays a higher share of Philadelphia's education budget than it does of wealthy suburban school districts. Philadelphia officials then engaged in a debate on those matters, without any attempt to link the underfunding to a racial pattern. This minimized support in the minority community and eliminated any public awareness of the basis for the claim.

Litigation is not an end in itself, it is only a part in a larger war, a war for public opinion. It is a familiar point in public interest litigation that a strong public relations strategy is necessary to accompany any litigation where the real goal of the litigation is a change in public policy. Public opinion is critical to whether public officials will facilitate the goal of the litigation or seek new ways to obstruct it. The civic groups bringing the law suit had little ability to control or influence the public dialogue about school funding. While the City and School District initially expended considerable effort to establish that the School District was underfunded, it was not clear to what audience such evidence was addressed. Their efforts seem to have been successful to the extent they were addressed to suburban voters, for public opinion polls showed people wanted to fix underfunding. The efforts do not seem to have been successful to the extent addressed to suburban legislators who voted in complete opposition to the polling results. Nor were the efforts successful in addressing the concerns of business leaders who did nothing to support increased funding for Philadelphia schools in this period. Business leaders acted as if they thought either that they had no stake in whether Philadelphia students performed better or that increased funding would have no impact on improving school performance, even though there was some improvement in Philadelphia students' test scores at this time. In either event, public opinion made no strong demands for political accountability for unequal, inadequate and discriminatory school funding.

It takes a crisis to arouse and mobilize public opinion. As long as Philadelphia public schools were open and functioning, it was difficult to mobilize support for the litigation or for better school funding. It was only when the district threatened to be unable to keep schools open in the summer of 2000 that the state stepped in with any assistance. And it was only when the State Reform Commission threatened to turn over the majority of the schools to a private enterprise in 2002 that the school unions and many parents became concerned enough to start political rallies around funding and governance issues. Spending $2,000 a student less on a Philadelphia child was not enough to provoke protests, but not having a school open was. When the crisis did come, the focus of public opinion was on the immediate issue of keeping the schools open, rather than to the long term issue of adequate funding.

This case never got to the stage where there was an opportunity to see the impact of a public airing at a trial of the differential racial funding of predominately minority school districts compared to predominately white districts in the state. That might have provoked some intense reaction if widely disseminated. Instead, the case became a victim of the Supreme Court's trend to undercut substantive rights (to be free from discrimination) by procedural barriers (no private right of action) which are so complex that most persons do not understand or protest. The ruling that private parties cannot enforce civil rights legislation unless the congressional intent is clearly spelled out, and then holding that it was not sufficiently spelled out 35 years earlier, was much too technical to excite widespread public interest.

Litigation organized around the interests of a single city is not sufficient to move state wide policies in Pennsylvania. Philadelphia officials brought this case because they lacked sufficient political power to solve their school funding problems in Harrisburg. The litigation did little to advance the development of that power. Although it was ostensibly based on underfunding 16 minority districts around the state, the Philadelphia city and school district leaders never sought to mobilize support in any of the other 15 communities or from their legislative delegations. The litigation, therefore, did nothing to increase the number of state legislators who were willing to vote for increased funding. By itself, Philadelphia did not have enough critical votes so that other legislators would support Philadelphia interests.

Although over-reliance on local taxes for funding schools and insufficient state support was a widespread problem in the state, Philadelphia did nothing to promote a common solution, and the litigation, by focusing on race discrimination common to only 16 out of 501 districts, did not promote any constituency for a legislative solution which would benefit other districts. Unfortunately, in this regard the litigation was perfectly aligned with the City's and School District's legislative strategy, which was to seek funds for the Philadelphia District alone, without mobilizing a constituency for changing the funding system for other districts too. Consequently, there were few allies in the rest of the state and little understanding that Philadelphia's problem arose out of a broken Harrisburg system rather than from uniquely Philadelphia sins.

He who pays the piper calls the tune. Philadelphia wanted the state to provide more funding for its schools, and, at the same time, to maintain its independent control of those schools. When it became apparent to the state that it would have to provide more money, it first attached significant strings to control how the money was spent and then took direct control of the district itself. Litigation was not able to avoid this result.

Finally, and not to be overlooked: **There is a need for enforcing disparate impact regulations.** Whether or not discrimination against minorities was intended by the state legislature, whether or not there was just an anti-urban anti-Philadelphia bias at work which existed when the city was white as well as when it was substantially minority, there was never any justification offered for why the state should continue to distribute its money in a manner which resulted in less money going to a district with poor minority kids than to a district with poor white kids. Even it there are other problems with how Pennsylvania funds its schools, there is no reason why the legislature should not be forced to correct this result. Once the facts are made known, and the state allows it to continue, it should not matter whether the cause is "intentional" or "unintentional"; it is fixable.

This was not a case requesting damages for past unintended acts: it demanded only that government no longer be allowed to continue with the unequal results. That is what Justice White voted for in the *Guardians* case and what all of the Courts of Appeals to decide the issue prior to *Sandoval* thought was the law. But it will take Congressional action to make it once again the law, so that minority students — through no fault of their own — do not have to live with fewer governmental resources than their companions in predominately white districts.

Biography

The author, **Michael Churchill**, was lead attorney for the community groups in both the Philadelphia Desegregation litigation and then in the *Marrero* case. He was Co-Chief Counsel at the Public Interest Law Center of Philadelphia, where he has practiced since 1976, except for 1984, when he served as Acting General Counsel for the Philadelphia School District. A 1965 cum laude graduate of Harvard Law School, he clerked for Chief Judge Lumbard in the Second Curcuit and became a partner in a Philadelphia law firm before joining the Law Center. His colleague, **Thomas K. Gilhool**, who participated in conceptualizing the suit and in drafting the Law Center's independent reply brief to the Supreme Court, had been the Commonwealth Secretary of Education in 1986-89. Mr. Gilhool, who graduated from Yale Law School in 1964, was an editor of the Law Journal, has practiced with a Philadelphia firm, was Consumer Advocate at Philadelphia Community Legal Services, and was an Associate Professor at the University of Southern California Law School before returning to Philadelphia to head the Law Center in 1975. Mr. Gilhool's work on behalf of persons with disabilities has included the landmark cases of *PARC v. Commonwealth of Pennsylvania*[24] and *Halderman v. Pennhurst Center.*[25]

---

1 *San Antonio Indep. School Dist. v. Rodriguez*, 411 U.S. 1 (1973).

2 In addition to the City and School District, the Plaintiffs in the case included The

Black Clergy of Philadelphia, the Philadelphia NAACP, ASPIRA, Parents Union for Public Schools, the Citizens Committee on Public Education in Philadelphia, and Parents United for Better Schools, as well as 10 families attending Philadelphia public schools, including African-Americans, Hispanics, Chinese Americans and Caucasians.

3 *San Antonio Indep. School Dist. v. Rodriguez*, 411 U.S. 1 (1973).

4 The Complaint did not identify plaintiffs' expert but recited the facts set out here Professor Summers had a distinguished career and had published extensive research on school finance matters.

5 42 U.S.C. §2000d (2008); 34 C.F.R. §100.3(b)(2)

6 "(2) A recipient, in determining the types of services, financial aid, or other benefits, or facilities which will be provided under any such program, or the class of individuals to whom, or the situations in which, such services, financial aid, other benefits, or facilities will be provided under any such program, or the class of individuals to be afforded an opportunity to participate in any such program, may not, directly or through contractual or other arrangements, utilize criteria or methods of administration which have the effect of subjecting individuals to discrimination because of their race, color, or national origin, or have the effect of defeating or substantially impairing accomplishment of the objectives of the program as respect individuals of a particular race, color, or national origin." (Emphasis added.)

7 *Marrero v. Commonwealth*, 709 A.2d 956 (Pa. Commw. Ct. 1998).

8 *Powell v. Ridge*, 1998 U.S. Dist. LEXIS 22328 (E.D. Pa. Nov. 18, 1998).

9 He also dismissed the Title VI claims of the School District and City on the grounds that they are not "individuals [subjected to] discrimination" protected by the Title VI regulation and, therefore, did not have standing. *Powell v. Ridge*, 1998 U.S. Dist. LEXIS 22328 (E.D. Pa. Nov. 18, 1998).

10 *Powell v. Ridge*, 189 F.3d 387 (3rd Cir. 1999).

11 *Chester Residents Concerned for Quality Living v. Seif*, 132 F.3d 925 (3d Cir.1997), *vacated as moot*, 119 S. Ct. 22 (1998).

12 *Ridge v. Powell*, 528 U.S. 1045 (1999).

13 The legislators sought interlocutory appeal on the grounds that the immunity privilege would be irreparably lost if the issue were not reviewed until after trial. *Powell*, 247 F.3d at 524.

14 *Powell v. Ridge*, 247 F.3d 520 (3rd Cir. 2001).

15 *Ryan v. Powell*, 534 U.S. 823 (2001).

16 *Alexander v. Sandoval*, 532 U.S. 275 (2001).

17 The stay was negotiated shortly after Judge Hutton ordered the state to comply with the discovery and the legislative defendants had appealed. The stay applied only to activities in the District court and permitted the legislative leaders' appeal

from the denial of their claim to immunity from discovery to continue.

18 Dale Mezzacappa, *Bias Alleged in Pa. School Aid Formula/In a Suit, the City and School District Say Poor White Districts Get More than Poor Minority Ones*. PHILADELPHIA INQUIRER, March 10, 1998; Kevin Haney, *City, Schools Base Funds Suit on Race/The Action is a New Approach to an Old Problem*, PHILADELPHIA DAILY NEWS March 10, 1998.

19 *Pa. Human Rels. Comm'n v. Sch. Dist.*, 681 A.2d 1366 (Pa. Commw. Ct. 1994).

20 *Marrero v. Commonwealth*, 709 A.2d 956 (Pa. Commw. Ct. 1998).

21 Act 1998-46, P.L. 270, approved Apr. 27, 1998; Act 2002-88, § 7, approved June 29, 2002.

22 The "assistance" was an agreement to delay repayment of $59 million the District owed the state for past overpayments and advancement of the state's regular payments for the next year saving the district $10 million in interest expense. The City agreed to provide $20 million in new money and the District agreed to cut $30 million in program expenses. Susan Snyder, *City Pa. Reach School Accord the One-Year Deal Will Avert a State Takeover of the Phila. District. The City will have to Suspend Lawsuit*. PHILADELPHIA INQUIRER, June 1, 2000.

23 Susan Snyder, *Hornbeck: Too Little Money the Phila. Superintendent Blamed Funding Woes and an Adversarial Relationship with Harrisburg for his Resignation after Six Years*, PHILADELPHIA INQUIRER, June 5, 2000.

24 Philadelphia voters in the preceding election had just revised the City's Home Rule Charter to give Mayor Street and his successors authority to select the entire Board rather than continue staggered terms of Board members selected by former mayors.

25 *Personnel Administrator of Massachussets v. Feeny*, 442 U.S. 256 (1979).

26 *Regents of the Univ. of Cal. v. Bakke*, 438 U.S. 265 (1978).

27 *Guardians Assn.* v. *Civil Serv. Comm'n of New York City*, 463 U.S. 582, 607 n.27 (1983). In *Alexander* v. *Choate*, 469 U.S. 287, 293 (1985) they unanimously agreed that was what they had done.

28 A follow up study covering the period FY1996 through FY2004 conducted by one of the economists who worked on the original study found that the per student "penalty" in state aid to districts for each additional percent of minority student, based on free and reduced lunch rather than AFDC, had increased over the nine years from $16 to $40 and that "As a fraction of average state aid per pupil across the Commonwealth, this penalty has **nearly doubled over the past decade,** increasing from 21 percent to 39 percent."

29 29 U.S.C. § 794 (2009).

30 It was not until *Washington v. Davis*, 426 U.S. 229 (1976) that the Court definitively held the Equal Protection clause of the 14th Amendments only prohibited intentional discrimination. The Court also tried to reduce the application of disparate impact regulations in the employment area in *Watson v. Fort Worth Bank & Trust*, 487 U.S. 977 (1988) and *Wards Cove Packing Co. v. Atonio*, 490 U.S. 642

(1989). Those decisions provoked Congressional reversals in the Civil Rights Restoration Act of 1991, 42 U.S.C. § 1981 (2009).

31 *Regents of the Univ. of Cal. v. Bakke*, 438 U.S. 265 (1978).

32 For a fuller analysis by the author of the legislative history of Congressional intent behind the regulations first created by the Robert Kennedy Justice Department, see 1 Rutgers J.L. & Urb. Pol'y 5 (2003).

33 *Guardians Ass'n v. Civil Serv. Comm'n of New York*, 463 U.S. 582 (1983).

34 *Powell v. Ridge*, 189 F.3d 387 (3d Cir. 1999), *cert. den.* 528 U.S. 1045.

35 *Gonzaga Univ. v. Doe*, 536 U.S. 273 (2002).

36 In *Alexander v. Sandoval*, 532 U.S. 235 (2001), Justice Scalia, for a majority of five, declared that although Section 601 of the 1964 Civil Rights Act created a private cause of action, Section 602, which authorized regulations to carry out the objectives of Section 601, did not have any "rights creating" language, was directed to the agencies, and was not directed to individuals. Consequently, he held that there was no congressional intention for Section 602 to be enforceable by private parties, much less any intention that the regulations created thereunder be enforceable. In *Gonzaga* the Court held that only statutes with unambiguous rights creating language like Section 601 were enforceable under Section 1983. According to the decision in *Sandoval*, Section 602 had no such language.

37 Judge Roth agreed with this analysis but wrote a concurring opinion on the even more technical issue whether the court had jurisdiction of this interlocutory appeal under the collateral order doctrine. *Ridge v. Powell*, 247 F.3d 520, 525 (3d Cir. 2001), cert. den. sub nom. *Ryan v. Powell*, 534 U.S. 823.

38 The only other school funding litigation to use the Title VI regulation was the New York litigation in state court which also included a federal Section 1983 claim that the New York system of funding violated the Title VI disparate impact regulation. This claim was initially upheld at the trial court level, but it was overshadowed by the state law claims. *Campaign for Fiscal Equity v. State of New York*, 187 Misc.2d 1 (Sup.Ct. N. Y. County, 2001). By the time of final appellate review, the Section 1983 claim also succumbed to Scalia's *Sandoval* opinion, but the plaintiffs had prevailed on their state law claims. 100 N.Y.S.2d 893 (2003).

12 New York Civil Liberties Union v. New York: Reflections on Promises Unfullfilled

by Arthur N. Eisenberg

Introduction

In 1968, the National Advisory Commission on Civil Disorders, commonly known as the Kerner Commission, offered a pessimistic projection. "Our nation," the Commission warned, "is moving towards two societies, one black, one white — separate and unequal."[1] This projection rested, to a significant degree, upon a well-recognized cycle of discrimination and disadvantage: Racially segregated schooling resulted in unequal educational opportunity, which led to disparities in employment skills, which, in turn, resulted in disparities in income, which reinforced segregated housing patterns, which led to segregated schools, resulting in unequal educational opportunity. So it went. And so it goes.

The push to improve educational opportunity has rested, in large part, on the compelling need to break this invidious cycle of discrimination and disadvantage. It has rested on the recognized need to redress abysmal conditions experienced by racial and ethnic minorities confined by economic circumstance to racially segregated and impoverished communities. It has also rested, in part, on the educational deficits experienced by children, regardless of color, from economically poorer communities. And, of course, the push to improve the quality of public education has also rested, more broadly, on the recognition of the importance of education in fostering individual competence, cultivating an informed and engaged electorate so necessary to the functioning of our democracy, and developing a skilled and productive workforce. All of these considerations coalesced to drive the school reform movement over the past 30 years.

Important Groundwork in the Levittown and CFE cases

The particular concern over the disparities in educational opportunity among school districts in New York State and the long-term consequences for poorer communities already facing many disadvantages provided the primary impetus for a lawsuit, brought in the 1970s, challenging New York State's method of financing public education. The suit, entitled *Board of Education, Levittown Union Free School District v. Nyquist*,[2] was initiated in Nassau County, in the state Supreme Court, the trial level court in New York, by a group comprised of 27 school districts situated in 13 counties and 12 school children represented by their parents. After the original plaintiffs initiated the suit, a second group of plaintiffs consisting of the Boards of Education of New York City, Rochester, Buffalo and Syracuse was permitted to intervene in the case.[3]

At the heart of the *Levittown* case was the claim that, under the State's funding regime, property taxes were the primary source of revenue for the support of public elementary and secondary education; that districts "poorer in real property wealth, such as the plaintiff districts, lev[ied] taxes at substantially higher rates than neighboring districts having greater real property wealth but [were] unable to match the latter in expenditures per child or in the provision of educational services"; that the "disparities in expenditures per pupil resulting from variations in local real property wealth produce[d] substantial differences" in the ability "to offer education advantages such as small class size, experienced and effective teachers, low pupil-teacher ratios, curricular breadth, extensive extracurricular programs, modern equipment, and special programs for the disadvantaged or the specially gifted."[4]

The *Levittown* suit advanced three legal arguments: first, that the inequalities created by the State's school financing regime violated the equal protection clause of the state constitution; second, that such inequalities violated equal protection principles of the federal constitution; and, third, that this statutory regime produced educational deficiencies that failed to satisfy the constitutional obligation, under the education article of the state constitution, to "create a state-wide system of free common schools in which all children may be educated."[5]

After extensive factual development of these claims, the trial court in the *Levittown* case found that the State's school funding regime violated the state constitution's equal protection clause as well as the education article of the state constitution. Distinguishing the U.S. Supreme Court decision in *San Antonio School District v. Rodriguez*,[6] the trial court further found that the statutory regime violated the equal protection clause of the federal constitution, at least as applied to the discriminatory treatment of the large urban school districts.[7]

The *Levittown* case ultimately reached the New York Court of

Appeals, the State's highest court, in 1982. The Court of Appeals concluded that New York's school funding scheme did not violate the equal protection clauses of the state or federal constitutions and did not violate the education article of the state constitution.[8] In doing so, however, the court's decision recognized that the education article of the state constitution required that the State provide "a sound basic education."[9] In this regard, the court noted that the *Levittown* suit did not present the claim that "the educational facilities or services provided in the school districts … fall below the statewide minimum standards of educational quality and quantity fixed by the Board of Regents."[10]

It was that phrase — "a sound basic education" — and the constitutional commitment to ensure "minimum standards" that the Campaign for Fiscal Equity (CFE) seized upon in asking the courts to revisit the adequacy of the educational services being provided to New York City schoolchildren. CFE was a coalition of parents, educators and organizations devoted to school reform. In a suit filed in 1993, CFE alleged "a widespread failure of the New York City public schools to meet minimum standards of Regents and the [State] Commissioner of Education."[11]

The *CFE* case reached the New York Court of Appeals in 1995 and, in a landmark decision, the court held that the education article of the New York Constitution requires the State to offer all children "the opportunity" to receive "a sound basic education."[12] It further suggested that in evaluating whether the State has fulfilled this constitutional obligation, courts should consider both the curricular, pedagogical and administrative resources of schools and the performance level of children within the schools.[13]

Taking a "Sound Basic Education" Beyond New York City

The New York Civil Liberties Union (NYCLU) strongly supported the *CFE* litigation and filed *amicus* briefs in support of *CFE* in that case. But, we also believed that the principles established in that case and, more importantly, the promise of educational opportunities created by the Court of Appeals in that case needed to be extended beyond New York City to other communities around in the state. We reached this conclusion for several reasons. First, we were concerned that a suit limited to the conditions of schools in New York City might result in judicial relief limited to New York City children and that upstate New York legislators might be reluctant to provide additional funding to satisfy any remedial decree if such a decree were limited to New York City schools. Second, we were concerned about the apparent emphasis on school funding suggested by the title of the organization — the Campaign for Fiscal Equity — that initiated the lawsuit. In that regard, we believed that while money well spent would go a long way toward improving educational opportunity, effective school reform would require non-monetary resources in addition to the infusion of additional money. Third, and most significantly, we believed that children outside of New York City were also experiencing inadequate educational opportunities and were equally deserving of additional resources and remediation.

Consequently, lawyers at the New York Civil Liberties Union began considering the possibility of a lawsuit on behalf of New York State children in areas of the state beyond New York City. We had heard about horrible conditions and abysmal academic performance in communities on Long Island and in Westchester County and upstate New York. And we began to examine the data on the academic performance of school districts beyond New York City. To our initial surprise, when we looked at the performance data in a variety of school districts, the test scores and graduation rates were not overwhelmingly dismal. And then we realized that an examination of district-wide averages masked the failures taking place at individual schools. Consequently, we next obtained student performance data on a school-by-school basis. When we looked at this data it was apparent that individual schools within districts displayed an abysmal level of failure. The school-by-school data demonstrated that in some schools approximately 30% of the children were functionally illiterate and between 60% and 70% of the children were failing the state competency tests.

Such data strongly suggested that many schools outside of New York City were experiencing serious and systemic educational failure. But, the 1995 Court of Appeals decision in *CFE* held that to establish a violation of the State constitutional commitment to "a sound basic education," it would not be sufficient to examine only the levels of academic performance within schools. It would also be necessary to demonstrate inadequacies in resources, facilities and pedagogical services. In this regard, we began talking to school reform experts in order to decide what to consider in assessing the resource inadequacies in these abysmally performing schools. We ultimately convened a meeting at Columbia Teachers College with a number of national school reform experts. The meeting included lawyers from the New York Civil Liberties Union and Gary Natriello of Columbia Teachers College, Linda Darling Hammond of Stanford University, Bob Slavin, then at Johns Hopkins University, and Tom Sobol, former New York State Commissioner of Education and also a member of the faculty at Columbia Teachers College.

We began the meeting by asking two basic questions: What makes for successful schools; and what factors cause schools to fail? Perhaps unsurprisingly, each of the experts interviewed advanced his or her theories regarding educational inadequacy and school reform. One expert emphasized teacher training and the stability and competency of the teaching staff; a second expert emphasized the need to focus on a "core curriculum." Others identified class size. As the conversation continued, others talked about school size, suggesting that the schools needed to be small enough to create a sense of community among students and parents and teachers. Some went on to focus on administrative leadership. Still others looked to parental involvement.

At the conclusion of the meeting, our school reform experts had identified approximately 11 common characteristics of school failure. These characteristics included a highly transient teaching staff, inadequately trained teachers, inadequate textbooks and computers, decrepit facilities, overcrowded conditions, a failure to give adequate attention to the core-curriculum, a lack of administrative leadership, classes that are too large for the many "high need" children in the classes, school buildings that house too many students to give children and parents a sense of community, an inability to involve parents in the activities of the schools and inadequate programs in art, music and athletics.

We followed these conversations with school reform experts and our examination of school performance data by meeting with community advocates, teachers, parents and students in various upstate communities, in Westchester and on Long Island. And these meetings led, in turn, to visits at individual schools and conversations with school administrators and community school superintendents. At the conclusion of this process, we came to understand that not every failing school would present precisely the same characteristics of failure. But, all failing schools shared a critical mass of these deficiencies.

On the basis of these interviews, we developed a litigation strategy that was school-based in its approach. We identified 27 schools, from 12 different communities from Long Island, Westchester and upstate New York,[14] which by virtue of inadequate resources and abysmal levels of student performance would, by any measure, be regarded as "failing schools." We then filed a lawsuit against state officials on behalf of children in these schools in which we asserted that the State was failing to fulfill its constitutional obligation to provide children with "the opportunity to receive a sound basic education."

The suit against the State was filed in the state Supreme Court of Albany County. Our legal argument with respect to these "failing schools" rested upon a simple and straightforward syllogism: Under the state constitution, the State was obligated to provide children with the "opportunity" to receive "a sound basic education"; and yet each of these "failing schools" presented an educational environment that was so inadequate that any child consigned by economic or residential circumstance to one of these schools was being denied the "opportunity" to receive "a sound basic education." We further asserted that the 27 schools were representative of a larger class of "failing schools" around the state that included upwards of 150 schools.

An amended complaint that exceeded 125 pages was filed in the case.[xv] It specified in great detail the deficiencies in resources, pedagogical services, materials and facilities in each of the schools. Thus, for example, as alleged in the amended complaint, of the 27 schools, six were built before 1925 and twelve were built before 1935. Most of these schools experienced serious overcrowding. Computer access in 20 of these schools was severely limited or virtually non-existent. The complaint also identified the desperately low performance levels of the children at these schools indicating that significant numbers of students failed to demonstrate even basic literacy and computational skills. As alleged, more than 40% of the students in each of the fifteen elementary and middle schools identified in the complaint could not achieve "minimum competency" on either the state language arts or mathematics tests. In five of the high schools identified in the compliant, the percentage of students receiving Regents diplomas ranged from a high of 27% in the Mount Vernon and Hempstead high schools to a low of 4% in the Roosevelt High School. And the complaint alleged that the State had failed to provide resources sufficient to permit these schools to provide children with the opportunity to receive a "sound basic education."

The inadequate resources, conditions, and performance levels set forth in the complaint were further dramatized by examining more specifically the detailed allegations with respect to a few illustrative schools. During the 2000-2001 school year, for example, 604 students attended the James A. Shea Middle School in Syracuse, which was originally built to accommodate 550 students. Consequently, classroom space was insufficient and inadequate. A trailer had been attached to the school for the preceding 12 years, but classrooms remained in disrepair with exposed electrical wires and chipped paint. Some classrooms had no windows and there was no air conditioning system in the school. The cafeteria could accommodate only 188 children. Therefore, the school was required to have three lunch periods and even then the lunchroom was seriously overcrowded.

The library collection at the school was inadequate. The school did not have enough textbooks for all of its students and textbooks were, therefore, photocopied. The school did not have enough desks for all the students and to accommodate its needs it had to borrow 50 desks from another school. Nevertheless, many of the borrowed desks were broken and were unusable. The school's curriculum was fragmented and out-of-date. And the school experienced high rates of both student and teacher absences. Not surprisingly, student performance was seriously deficient. On the May 2000 grade eight English Language Arts examination, 90% of the eighth graders tested failed to meet the state's standards of minimum competency. And on the May 2000 grade eight Mathematics examination, 97% failed to meet the state standards.

Public School 69 in Buffalo, New York, known as the Houghton Academy, was a third through eighth grade school that was built in 1924. The building was also in desperate need of repair. Structural additions to the original building consisted of two trailers with deficient cooling systems. The school experienced serious overcrowding: classes commonly exceeded 25 students yet classroom space was inadequate for classes of that size. The girls' locker and shower room had been converted to office space for the school's three part-time guidance counselors. Inside the school, children had been burned because radiators had no protective guards. Outside the school, the grass playground had been paved over into an asphalt parking lot that surrounded the school and that provided no real opportunity for outdoor recreation during the school day or an outdoor, after-school recreational facility. There were no full-time guidance counselors, librarians, or nurses at Houghton. The library was closed every other day. The absence of a full-time nurse forced the parents of children on daily medication to modify the medication administered to their children from recommended periodic dosages to once-a-day dosages.

The library at Houghton had books only appropriate for children in grades three through six although the school included seventh and eighth grade students. Textbooks were inadequate. Many teachers contributed personal money (some as much as $1,000) to assure that students were provided with minimum resources. The school had eight functioning computers, only one with internet access. Each student was allotted 45 minutes every five weeks to work on a computer. Again, sadly, performance at the school was abysmal. On the January 1999 grade four English Language Arts examination, 78% of fourth-graders tested failed to meet state standards of minimum competency. On the June 1999 grade four Mathematics examination, 55% of the students failed to meet the state standards. On the January 2000 grade four English Language Arts examination, 93% of the students failed to meet state standards. Finally, on the May 2000 grade four Mathematics examination, 84% of the students failed to meet state standards.

The other schools identified in the amended complaint experienced similar deficiencies in resources and conditions. And these deficiencies were set forth in fact-laden "allegations of inadequacies in physical facilities, curricula, numbers of qualified teachers, availability of textbooks and library books."[xvi] Moreover, as alleged in the amended complaint, the State had, over the years, known of these inadequacies and had failed to provide the resources (both fiscal and non-fiscal) necessary to permit these schools to perform their pedagogical functions properly and to provide children with "the opportunity" to receive a "sound basic education."

The complaint sought declaratory and equitable relief in response to these constitutional violations. Recognizing that the precise conditions of failure would vary from school to school, the suit did not seek to compel the State to provide resources on a uniform basis without regard to the particularized needs in each school. Rather, plaintiffs sought an injunction to compel state officials to conduct individualized assessments of the conditions in these "failing schools," to fashion remedial plans to address the particular sources of failure on a school-by-school basis and to provide the resources to implement the remedial plans.

This remedial approach comported with obligations that we believed the State had already partially assumed. Well before the suit was filed, the State Education Department (SED) had promulgated regulations that required the State Commissioner of Education to identify those public schools that were so deficient as to be at risk of having their registration as public schools revoked. With respect to these schools, the Commissioner was obligated to "appoint a team to undertake a resource, planning and program audit of the school," and, based on the results of such an audit, required to ensure that "a corrective plan" was "developed by the superintendent of the district … in consultation with the school staff, persons in parental relation of children attending the school and members of the community." Furthermore, the Commissioner and SED were required to secure implementation of the corrective plans.[17]

Accordingly, in addition to challenging the States' failure to provide the "opportunity" to receive "a sound basic education" as a violation of the state constitution, the NYCLU asserted, as a second cause of action, that the SED regulations required implementation of remedial plans for these "failing schools" and that SED had failed to adhere to these regulatory requirements. In these respects, the NYCLU was seeking to implement school-based school reform.

Our school-based approach differed from that set out in the SED regulations in two respects. First, we had been informed that when the SED conducted audits of failing schools it, typically would develop "corrective plans" but leave the local school districts with the obligation to find the resources, fiscal or otherwise, to implement such plans. In such circumstances, rather than assuming the responsibility imposed by the state constitution on the State, the SED approach deflected responsibility to local school districts in poor communities that were already taxing themselves heavily and were otherwise incapable of assuming such financial burdens and ill-equipped to provide additional pedagogical or administrative resources. The NYCLU asserted that the State was capable of bringing greater fiscal and non-fiscal resources to the remediation process than it had done to date and that it must bear the ultimate responsibility for the implementation of corrective plans.

Second, we urged that, when the SED conducted its audit and developed corrective plans, children as well as local administrators, teachers and parents should be consulted as part of the auditing process. In this respect, Jonathan Kozol has wisely observed that children are often "a great deal more reliable in telling us what actually goes on in public schools than many of the adult experts who develop policies that shape their destinies." Kozol has noted: "Unlike these powerful grown-ups, children have no ideologies to reinforce, no superstructure of political opinion to promote, no civic equanimity or image to defend, no personal reputation to secure. They may err sometimes about the miniscule particulars but on the big things children rarely have much reason to mislead us. They are … pure witnesses …."[18] We urged, therefore, that the auditing process be undertaken in consultation with all the stakeholders in the local communities, including the children as the most immediate beneficiaries of the educational experience.

The State's Motion to Dismiss

In October 2001, the State moved to dismiss the suit. In support of their contention that the plaintiffs' cause of action under the education article of the state constitution should be dismissed, defendants asserted that the State's obligation under the education article of the New York State Constitution is quite limited. In this regard, defendants contended that the State was required simply to "maintain and support" a system of public education and had no obligation to provide more than minimal financial support. Defendants further asserted that the principal responsibility for educating school children rested with the local school districts, and, therefore, the court could not find the State responsible for the specific failures taking place at particular schools, so long as the legislature provided minimal funding for public education. In moving to dismiss the second cause of action, the State contended that the administrative regulations that plaintiffs were seeking to enforce imposed discretionary and not mandatory obligations on state education officials and, therefore, such discretionary conduct was beyond the reach of judicial supervision.

In a decision rendered in June 2002, state Supreme Court Justice Joseph C. Teresi largely agreed with the State.[19] Justice Teresi concluded that "the plaintiffs have failed to allege or show any constitutional violation by or right to any relief from the named defendants …."[20] In reaching this conclusion, the court relied substantially on a decision of an intermediate appellate court in the *CFE* case[21] that had been issued by the appellate court one day before Justice Teresi rendered his decision in the *NYCLU* case. Justice Teresi concluded that the level of educational opportunity to which children were entitled under the state constitution "was indeed very low," so low, in fact, that evidence "of significant overcrowding and very poorly maintained buildings" would not be sufficient to establish constitutionally deficient physical facilities. Similarly, he ruled that "[t]he fact that very significant percentages of students did not obtain [a sound basic] education did not constitute evidence of a constitutional violation," and held that plaintiffs had failed adequately to allege that the State was "causally" responsible for the inadequate facilities and staffing found in the identified schools.[22]

In this decision, Justice Teresi also rejected plaintiffs' contention that the State Education Department has failed to adhere to its own regulations and rejected the claim that this failure warranted declaratory and injunctive relief. Justice Teresi concluded that a challenge to administrative misconduct cannot be pursued in an action seeking declaratory and injunctive relief, but only in a mandamus action, and that a mandamus action could not be brought to challenge the administrative conduct at issue in this case because such conduct involved discretionary decisionmaking not subject to mandamus. The court further concluded that even if an action for declaratory judgment were appropriate in this case, "plaintiffs failed to show any violation of the State regulations," even though such violations had been alleged and proof of such allegations was not required at that preliminary phase of the lawsuit.[23]

The NYCLU was entitled to appeal from Justice Teresi's decision to an intermediate appellate court known as the Appellate Division, Third Department. The NYCLU filed such an appeal. But, the parties agreed, with the approval of the Third Department, to delay the appeal to allow time for the Court of Appeals to review the decision of the Appellate Division in the *CFE* case upon which Justice Teresi had relied so significantly. In June 2003, the Court of Appeals rendered its second decision in *CFE* and rejected each of the central tenets of the Appellate Division decision in that case. Thus, the Court of Appeals decision in *CFE II* reversed the Appellate Division's conclusion that the constitutional commitment to "a sound basic education" was limited to a very low level of educational opportunity.[24] The court similarly rejected, as it had in 1995, the proposition that desperately low levels of student performance were irrelevant to the question of whether the State was providing the "opportunity" for a "sound basic education."[25] And, in *CFE II*, the Court of Appeals further rejected the "causation" analysis relied upon by the Appellate Division. In *CFE II*, the Court of Appeals made clear that plaintiffs' obligation to prove a causal link between the State's failure to provide resources and the poor performance of New York City schools "could be established by a showing that increased funding can provide better teachers, facilities and instrumentalities of learning" and that "such improved inputs yield better student performance."[26]

The Court of Appeals decision in *CFE II* should have resulted in a reversal by the Third Department of Justice Teresi's decision in the NYCLU case. Each and every conclusion drawn by Justice Teresi from the Appellate Division decision in *CFE* and used by him to reject plaintiffs' constitutional claim in the *NYCLU* case was expressly repudiated by the Court of Appeals in *CFE II*. Nevertheless, the Third Department affirmed the dismissal, even though it was unable to do so on the grounds offered by Justice Teresi.[27] Instead, the Appellate Division rested its decision on new and different grounds.

The Third Department read the Court of Appeals decision in *CFE II* as requiring allegations of "a systemic failure" within a school district. The Appellate Division then equated the term "systemic failure" with "district-wide failure" and concluded that "the amended complaint was properly dismissed, for it did not allege a district-wide or systemic failure."[28]

The Third Department reinforced this conclusion on the ground that the remedial relief the *NYCLU* plaintiffs sought differed from the relief ordered in *CFE II*. In this respect, the Appellate Division confused the issue of remedy with the question of what factual elements were necessary to allege a violation of the education article.

And the Third Department ignored the fact that the NYCLU, in its case, advanced allegations regarding deficient "inputs" and "outputs" that were quite similar to those found legally sufficient in *CFE II*.[29]

The Third Department decision also affirmed the dismissal of plaintiffs' second cause of action involving the failure by state officials to adhere to their own administrative regulations. In this regard, however, the Appellate Division affirmed on the same grounds employed by Justice Teresi, namely, that the regulations do not impose mandatory obligations and that discretionary administrative decisionmaking is not subject to judicial intervention.[30]

On appeal, the New York Court of Appeals affirmed the decision of the Appellate Division.[31] A unanimous Court of Appeals held that the NYCLU suit had failed to allege a violation of the education article because the suit focused on the deficiencies in individual schools and did not allege "any district-wide failure." In this regard, the court expressed concern that the NYCLU approach would "subvert the important role of local control in education."[32] The court further rejected the NYCLU's challenge to the administrative failures of the State Education Department on the ground that such failures involved discretionary decisionmaking which were not susceptible of judicial review.[33]

The Case in Retrospect

The Court of Appeals' suggestion that the NYCLU approach would have "subvert[ed] … local control" was misdirected for several reasons. First, the NYCLU school-based approach toward school reform would have actually enhanced "local control." As noted above, the NYCLU approach contemplated a process in which state officials would meet with local educators, parents and children to fashion collectively reforms that would be tailored to the needs of individual schools. Moreover, under the current regime, "local control" is more myth than reality, at least with respect to the capacity to fix failing schools. The school districts, whose schools were identified in the NYCLU lawsuit, lacked sufficient financial resources and human capital to bring meaningful reform to these seriously deficient schools. The NYCLU's insistence that the State provide supplemental resources to these schools would have enabled local school officials to develop remedial measures and would have created a realistic prospect that such measures could be implemented. In providing local school districts with the capacity to actually fix failing schools the NYCLU approach would have empowered these districts and advanced "local control."

Second, while community engagement is clearly a virtue in regard to any system of governance, "local control" is not, in all circumstances, the appropriate vehicle for addressing inadequate government performance. The Court of Appeals concern for "local control" harkens to a century-long debate about school reform in New York City that has looked to the structure of school governance as a vehicle for improving education. In the 1890s, school reformers asserted that the school system was too decentralized and that greater professionalism and accountability could be achieved if the school system were centralized. Following the consolidation of the five boroughs into New York City in 1898, New York City moved decidedly in the direction of a centralized school system.[34] By the 1960s, however, New York City's schools were seen, by important segments of the community, as largely unresponsive to the needs of children and parents, particularly children and parents of color. Consequently, in 1969 the state legislature adopted a hybrid decentralized system of school governance with the creation of 32 school districts for elementary and middle schools with a city-wide school district for the administration of the high schools.

Those pressing for school decentralization in the 1960s argued, first and foremost, that structural reform of the school system was necessary as a means of providing black and Latino communities with "equal access to the process of making decisions vitally affecting the education of their children."[35] But beyond the compelling demand for school decentralization in the service of racial justice, the movement toward decentralization also offered an example of cyclical social reform not uncommon in this country. The impulse toward reform rested upon the sense that bureaucratic and political institutions tend, over time, to arrogate power; that this arrogation of power often renders these institutions less responsive and, in some instances, unresponsive to the individuals that the institutions were created to serve; and that the most effective way to render such institutions more responsive is to reduce the accretion of bureaucratic or political power through a process of decentralization. By the 1960's, the New York City school system had, through the accretion of bureaucratic power, become unresponsive to communities of color within the City. Decentralization of the system was seen as the corrective to that dysfunction.

But, over time, decentralized institutions can also become inefficient, unresponsive and narrow in their administration. The reformative reaction to such narrowness often requires centralization. Seen in these terms, neither centralization nor decentralization represent permanent solutions. At times in the development of a political institution, social change must be brought about through decentralization. At other times, reform is accomplished through centralization. The mechanisms of decentralization and centralization are simply engines of social change, available to reformers seeking to challenge the arrogation of power by existing bureaucracies or political entities. So understood, the cyclical fluctuations between centralization and decentralization are a common theme of American political reform.[36] And so, at the beginning of the 21st Century, the decentralized New York City school system was regarded as dysfunctional and seen as failing too many children. This perception led to the resumption of a centralized system.

Finally, the elevation by the Court of Appeals of the concern for "local control" as the basis for rejecting the NYCLU suit discounted the fact that the education article places the ultimate constitutional responsibility for providing adequate educational opportunity on the State, not the local school districts.

At bottom, the NYCLU suit identified heartbreaking deficiencies in the provision of educational services to countless numbers of children in New York State. The NYCLU remedial approach toward those deficiencies offered the virtue of school-based reform that would have provided children with "the opportunity" for a "sound basic education" and would have done so by providing supplemental resources to local school districts in a realistic and narrowly tailored way. Instead, this drive for school reform was stopped before it could begin, and the cycle of limited opportunity and disadvantage continues to reinforce and perpetuate a nation divided, separate and unequal. Unfortunately, for the children attending many of the schools identified in the NYCLU suit, the state constitutional commitment to educational opportunity — remains a promise unfulfilled.

Biography

Arthur N. Eisenberg is Legal Director of the New York Civil Liberties Union, served as lead counsel in *New York Civil Liberties Union v. State of New York*. Mr. Eisenberg would like to thank others for their contribution to the suit. **Christopher Dunn** and **Donald Shaffer** served as co-counsel in the case. The suit was also supported by Norman Siegel and Donna Lieberman as Executive Directors of the NYCLU during the litigation. Sincere gratitude is also extended to the Schott Foundation and the Overbrook Foundation for their support in connection with this litigation. Finally, Mr. Eisenberg would like to thank **Jeremy Shweder**, a graduate of Fordham Law School, for his insights, research and editorial suggestions in the preparation of this essay.

---

1 Report of the National Advisory Commission on Civil Disorders, Summary of Report (1968) at 1.

2 94 Misc.2d 466, 408 N.Y.S.2d 606 (Sup. Ct., Nassau Cty, 1978)

3 *Levittown*, 94 Misc.2d at 475-476.

4 *Levittown*, 94 Misc.2d at 476-477.

5 *Levittown*, 94 Misc.2d at 477-479.

6 411 U.S. 1 (1973).

7 *Levittown*, 94 Misc.2d at 529-536.

8 *Levittown*, 57 N.Y.2d 27 (1982).

9 *Levittown*, 57 N.Y.2d at 48.

10 *Levittown*, 57 N.Y.2d at 38.

11 *CFE v. State of New York*, 162 Misc.2d 493, 498, 616 N.Y.S.2d 851, 355 (1992).

12 *CFE v. State of New York*, 86 N.Y.2d 307, 315 (1995).

13 *CFE*, 86 N.Y.2d at 316-318.

14 The 12 communities were Albany, Buffalo, Hempstead, Lackawanna, Mount Vernon, Roosevelt, Schenectady, Syracuse, Utica, Westbury, Wyandanch and

Yonkers.

15 The Amended Complaint can be found in the Record on Appeal filed in the New York Court of Appeals in the case at 136.

16 *CFE*, 86 N.Y.2d at 319.

17 8 N.Y.C.R.R. § 100.2(p)(6).

18 Jonathan Kozol, *The Shame of the Nation* (2005) at 12.

19 Unreported Opinion is set forth in the Record on Appeal, filed with the New York Court of Appeals, at 24-32.

20 *Id.* at 31-32.

21 *CFE v. State of New York*, 295 A.D.2d 1, 744 N.Y.S.2d 130 (1st Dept. 2002)

22 *CFE v. State of New York*, Unreported Decision at 26-28.

23 *Id.* at 30-31.

24 *CFE*, 100 N.Y.2d 893, 993 (2003).

25 *CFE*, 100 N.Y.2d at 911.

26 *CFE*, 100 N.Y.2d at 919.

27 *NYCLU v. State of New York*, 3 A.D.3d 811, 771 N.Y.S.2d 563 (3rd Dept. 2004).

28 *NYCLU*, 3 A.D.3d at 812-813.

29 *NYCLU*, 3 A.D.3d at 813.

30 *NYCLU*, 3 A.D.3d at 813-814.

31 *NYCLU v. State of New York*, 4 N.Y.3d 175 (2005).

32 *Id.* at 181.

33 *Id.* at 183-184.

34 David Tyack and Larry Cuban, *Tinkering Toward Utopia, A Century of Public School Reform* (1995) at 76-77.

35 Ira Glasser, "The Burden of Blame," a pamphlet issued by the New York Civil Liberties Union (1969).

36 Arthur M. Schlesinger, Jr., *The Cycles of American History* (1986).

13 [1]Beyond Educational Adequacy: Looking Backward and Forward Through the Lens of New Jersey

by Paul L. Tractenberg

Introduction

New Jersey's school funding and education reform litigation is larger than life. By any imaginable standard, it far exceeds the litigation in any other state.[2] Depending upon one's point of view, it either illustrates the extraordinary achievements of a remarkably committed and courageous judiciary,[3] or is the ultimate in misguided judicial zeal.[4] Because of the sheer size, seemingly endless duration, and great complexity of New Jersey's litigation, it is very tempting to marginalize it — to treat it like de Tocqueville's classic work *Democracy in America*,[5] often said to be the most quoted but least read book ever written.[6] In my judgment, however, that would be a huge mistake because New Jersey's litigation, and particularly *Abbott v. Burke*, the current case, provides an indispensable lesson plan.

Anyone interested in educational reform, school funding equalization, the education of poor, at-risk students, or the role of courts in both defining and assuring implementation of constitutional rights cannot ignore New Jersey's long and ambitious court-directed effort. The New Jersey story, whether one deems it to be inspirational or cautionary, should be required reading.

In this article, I present that story in a manageable and understandable format. I put it in a national historical, jurisprudential, and educational policy context. I emphasize that the main thrust thus far of New Jersey's long litigation — the road more traveled[7] — has focused on one word in a relatively brief state constitutional education clause.[8] That word is "thorough," and, as the litigation has proceeded, it has increasingly been given its plain dictionary meaning — complete, with attention to every detail — clearly distinguishing it from an "adequate" education.

But the education clause has other language that, surprisingly given the New Jersey litigation's length and comprehensiveness, has received only occasional, passing attention. That language — the road less traveled — is an "efficient system of free public schools."[9] In this article, I begin to sketch out a constitutional theory based on that language, designed to focus attention not so much on the inputs and outcomes of education, but on the process through which inputs produce outcomes.

The Background

What is now commonly called the educational adequacy movement began in the mid-to-late-1960s as the school funding reform movement. Its origin was the equal protection clause of the United States Constitution's fourteenth amendment.[10] To a substantial degree, it was an outgrowth of *Brown v. Board of Education*.[11]

Although *Brown* was widely considered to be a case about race and about breaking down de jure segregation of the schools, it was also from the start a case about equalizing the educational opportunities of black children. The cases preceding *Brown* systematically challenged separate schools for black students on the ground that they were educationally unequal in virtually every respect as well as racially separate. The cases implementing *Brown* increasingly focused on educational quality and equality issues, including school funding.

Beginning in the mid-1960s, when serious efforts to implement *Brown* were still in their infancy,[12] lawyers and educational policy scholars began to conceive of a Fourteenth Amendment challenge to the way most states funded their public schools. Largely because local property wealth figured prominently in the funding schemes of most states and because such wealth varied greatly among school districts, children living in property-poor districts — usually urban and rural communities — had much lower expenditures on their education than children living in wealthier, mainly suburban, districts.

Although there were, and still are, heated scholarly debates about the education production function — whether money matters in education[13] — large disparities in education spending traceable to large disparities in the property wealth of school districts seemed alien to the notion of equal educational opportunity to many.

Arthur Wise,[14] an education doctoral student at the University of Chicago, and Jack Coons,[15] a law professor at Northwestern and later at the University of California at Berkeley, are probably most widely credited with articulating federal equal protection theories for challenging those local property-based inequalities, but their work, published in 1968 to 1970, actually followed by several years the first article on the subject.[15]

At about the same time, the first modern school funding challenges were decided by two federal district courts.[17] Those cases relied heavily, if not exclusively, upon the equal protection clause and emerging judicial interpretations of it. Plaintiffs' advocates sought to persuade the courts either that school funding inequities fit comfortably within the emerging jurisprudence or that the courts should extend the doctrine to cover this newly identified form of inequality. Many early school finance reform theorists and litigators considered their efforts to be a logical, next step in the evolution of equal protection doctrine so dramatically highlighted by *Brown v. Board of Education*.

This reliance on federal equal protection doctrine did not launch the modern school finance reform litigation movement auspiciously, however. Both federal district courts dismissed plaintiffs' equal protection complaints, which they construed to be seeking rulings that students had a constitutional right to spending in response to their educational needs.[18] According to those courts, such a right presented no judicially manageable standards, and the cases therefore did not raise justiciable issues.[19] By construing plaintiffs' requests in that manner, the courts were able to rule that such substantively oriented claims were inconsistent with the more neutral approaches of other equal protection cases.[20]

Early school finance reform theorists and litigators were not significantly slowed by these initial defeats, however. Some characterized the more prominent of the two, *McInnis v. Shapiro*, as a "temporary setback," and a "predictable consequence of an effort to force the court to precipitous and decisive action upon a novel and complex issue for which neither it nor the parties were ready."[21]

As this statement by Coons, Clune, and Sugarman suggests, one way around the *McInnis* obstacle was to present the courts with a legal theory that was, or at least appeared to be, less novel and complex, and did not press the judiciary to take precipitous action. Another approach was to pursue the "novel and complex issue" in a different judicial forum — a state rather than federal court — and based on a different constitutional principle — a state constitution's education clause rather than the federal constitution's equal protection clause. *Serrano v. Priest*[22] in California and *Robinson v. Cahill*[23] in New Jersey exemplify these different responses.

Serrano was based on equal protection doctrine, initially federal and then state.[24] *Robinson* was based on a multiplicity of constitutional clauses, initially federal and state equal protection, and state education and tax uniformity, and then exclusively on the state education clause.

In *Serrano*, the California Supreme Court launched the school finance reform movement in earnest by ruling in 1970 on a motion to dismiss that, if the plaintiffs could prove their allegations, the state's school funding system would be unconstitutional. The theory was that, if property wealth were deemed relevant to the way schools were funded, it should be the wealth of the state as a whole and not of local school districts.

The initial remedial objective of at least some who argued on behalf of the plaintiffs was to equalize tax capacity, but to permit school funding to vary from district to district based on local tax effort. The court's remedy was different, however; it focused on equalizing school spending within a relatively narrow band.

The concept of educational adequacy, which apparently had been the undoing of the plaintiffs in the early federal cases, was eschewed by the plaintiffs and the California state courts in *Serrano*. Indeed, at one point in the litigation, a California court said of *Serrano*'s equal protection focus:

> What the *Serrano* court imposed as a California

> constitutional requirement is that there must be uniformity of treatment between the children of the various school districts in the State. ... If such uniformity of treatment were to result in all children being provided a low-quality educational program, or even a clearly *inadequate* educational program, the California Constitution would be satisfied. This court does not read the *Serrano* opinion as requiring that there is any constitutional mandate for the State to provide funds for each child in the State at some magic level to produce either an adequate-quality educational program or a high-quality educational program.[25]

By contrast, within two weeks of the U.S. Supreme Court's 1973 *Rodriguez* decision, the New Jersey Supreme Court firmly anchored its first decision in *Robinson* on the state's education clause.[26] Although the trial court had found violations of federal and state equal protection and state tax uniformity clauses, the New Jersey high court rejected those bases, each for a different reason, striking down the State's school funding system solely on the basis of the education clause.

As to federal equal protection, the court concluded that, despite some differences between the educational funding systems of New Jersey and Texas, "we do not believe the majority [in *Rodriguez*] would find a federal constitutional flaw in the case before us."[27]

As to state equal protection, the court chose not to decide the case on that basis because it saw no way to stop the decision's impact with education. Indeed, said the court, "[t]he equal protection proposition potentially implicates the basic tenet of local government that there be local authority with concomitant fiscal responsibility," and the case was neither tried nor argued on that broad issue.[28]

Finally, as to tax uniformity, the New Jersey Supreme Court simply disagreed with the trial court's construction. The plaintiffs had persuaded the trial court that taxes imposed locally for education, a state function, should be considered to be state taxes subject to the constitutional requirement of statewide uniformity in tax rates. The high court viewed it differently: "The short answer is that the tax clause was not intended to say that a state function may not be delegated to local government to be met by local taxation."[29]

That left the education clause, about which the trial judge had been ambivalent. He had ruled that, given the partial funding of the state's recently-adopted school finance law, some New Jersey pupils were not being afforded a "thorough" education. Moreover, he had ruled that some aspects of the law — minimum support aid to all districts regardless of their wealth and "save harmless" aid — clearly were unconstitutional. But, he also indicated that, if the law were fully funded, it would probably satisfy the clause. Thus, he chose not to invalidate the law in its entirety on the basis of the education clause, presumably because he assumed the state would proceed to fully fund it.[30]

In the course of this discussion, the trial judge construed the education clause very expansively: "The word 'thorough' in the Education Clause connotes in common meaning the concept of completeness and attention to detail. *It means more than simply adequate or minimal.*"[31]

In its *Robinson* decision, the New Jersey Supreme Court went both further and less far than the trial court regarding the education clause. As to the constitutionality of the funding statute, the court said, "[w]e see no basis for a finding that the 1970 Act, even if fully funded, would satisfy the constitutional obligation of the State."[32] This was based on a sequence of findings: that the State had never defined the constitutionally required education; that it had never required school districts "to raise moneys needed to achieve that unstated standard;"[33] and that the state aid program was not designed "to compensate for local failures to reach that level."[34] The bottom line, said the court, was that "our present [school funding] scheme is a patchy product reflecting provincial contests rather than a plan sensitive only to the constitutional mandate."[35]

The state high court stopped short of the trial court, however, in its definition of a "thorough" education. It seemed to quote approvingly from the 1895 *Landis* decision, which had referred to the constitutional education clause's purpose as creating a legislative duty to provide "each student with such instruction as is necessary to fit it for the *ordinary* duties of citizenship."[36] In the same passage from *Landis*, there was explicit reference to the permissibility of "tendering peculiar advantages" to some students so long as the "common rights of all" were secured.[37] In other words, so long as all students were assured an "ordinary" or adequate education, some students could be afforded greater educational opportunities.[38]

The New Jersey Supreme Court updated and expanded the *Landis* statement in two respects: by extending the "common rights of all" to include high school, and by reframing the constitutional guarantee "to embrace that educational opportunity which is needed in the contemporary setting to equip a child for his role as a citizen and as a competitor in the labor market."[39] Still, the court seemed to adhere to the *Landis* view that, if "thorough" education were provided to all students, perhaps even through state funding, the State could "authorize local government to go further and to tax to that further end, provided that such authorization does not become a device for diluting the State's mandated responsibility."[40]

That statement is entirely consistent with the concept of educational adequacy, but not with the trial court's view that "thorough" education meant a "complete" education, one beyond adequate or minimal. The meaning to be given New Jersey's education clause returned to prominence in the second phase of the state's ongoing school funding and educational reform litigation — the *Abbott v. Burke* phase.

The rest of the *Robinson* phase, from the New Jersey Supreme Court's April 1973 decision discussed above until its final decision in July 1976, focused on the arduous process of legislative adoption and funding of a new law — the Public School Education Act of 1975 (the "1975 Act").[41] Indeed, the entire *Robinson* litigation focused more on the intricacies of school funding formulae and their resource equalization effects across school district lines than on the educational dimensions of "thorough and efficient" education.

The court, in a sharply divided set of opinions, found the 1975 Act facially constitutional, but acknowledged there were problems with it that might require the court to consider the law as applied.[42] *Abbott* was filed five years later, on February 5, 1981, as that challenge.[43]

Ever since — for 27 years — the *Abbott* litigation has proceeded unabated. Not only the 1975 Act, but also two subsequent school funding laws — the Quality Education Act of 1990[44] and the Comprehensive Education Improvement and Financing Act of 1996[45] — have been found unconstitutional. A new school funding law, enacted at the 11th hour of a lame-duck legislative session ending in January 2008 — the School Funding Reform Act of 2008 ("SFRA")[46] — is already back in court on the State's motion to have the court rule that SFRA is constitutional and that, as a consequence, the remedial measures previously ordered by the court, except for facilities remedies, are no longer required.[47]

Any detailed or comprehensive consideration of this enormously long and complicated constitutional litigation is far beyond the scope of this article.[48] Instead, I will focus on the constitutional roads more traveled and less traveled in this case.

The Road More Traveled

As I have indicated, since the first New Jersey Supreme Court decision in *Robinson* in 1973, the exclusive constitutional focus has been on the state constitution's education clause.[49] And initially the main emphasis was on the school funding system's capacity to provide equality of educational opportunity to students in property-poorer school districts. Educational rights were the foundation of this inquiry — and the constitutional standard even emphasized student outcomes — but the main battle was over the extent to which school funding formulae adequately equalized the resources necessary to equalize the opportunity of students to secure a "thorough and efficient" education.

In the litigation's *Robinson* stage, the constitutional phrase was usually referred to as if it consisted of three hyphenated words irrevocably tied together and having a singular meaning. But that changed early in the *Abbott* stage when much greater emphasis was placed on the word "thorough" and, in short order, the constitutional requirement began to be expressed in terms of "thorough education."[50]

Interestingly, the word "education" does not appear in New Jersey's education clause, and the operative constitutional phrase is "a thorough and efficient system of free public schools."[51] Still, in *Abbott*, the New Jersey Supreme Court's road more traveled was the "thorough education" road, and the road much less traveled, or not taken at all, was the "efficient system of free public schools" road.

The transition from *Robinson* to *Abbott*, in terms of the meaning attributed to the state constitutional education standard, is also notable. In *Robinson*, the supreme court rejected the dictionary definition of "thorough"[52] — which the trial court had adopted. The interpretation given the constitutional phrase "thorough and efficient" throughout *Robinson* was the earliest incarnation of the "adequate education" movement.[53] What was required was an equal educational opportunity for all that "must be understood to embrace that educational opportunity which is needed in the contemporary setting to equip a child for his[54] role as a citizen and as a competitor in the labor market,"[55] but not the best possible education. If some districts, by dint of greater resources, greater educational commitment or a combination of both, wished to go beyond a "thorough and efficient" (read "adequate") education for their students, they were free to do so as long as it did not dilute the statewide standard. That, of course, presupposes there can be a meaningful absolute, as opposed to relative, standard for equalizing educational opportunity and attainment.

Although the New Jersey Supreme Court began its consideration of the 1975 Act's constitutionality in *Abbott* where the court had left off in *Robinson* regarding the meaning of a "thorough and efficient" education,[56] over the course of the litigation it steadily moved closer to, if it did not fully reach, the dictionary definition of "thorough" education and the view that it constitutes an excellent, if not the best possible, education.

Related to that evolution, in the court's first truly substantive opinion in *Abbott*, it described a shift that had taken place in *Robinson* from a primary focus on dollar disparities in the first supreme court decision in 1973 to a primary focus on substantive educational content in the fifth supreme court decision in 1976.[57] This focus on substantive educational content rather than dollar disparities, coupled with an even greater focus on equality of educational opportunities for disadvantaged children, were at the core of the New Jersey Supreme Court's *Abbott* jurisprudence.

While the focus on substantive educational content gave greater prominence to the State's role in defining the required level of education and assessing whether or not all students were actually receiving it, it did not eliminate the relevance of disparities in funding and expenditures per pupil.[58] Indeed, the court recognized that the factual record it had before it in *Abbott II* provided "a new potential gloss to the constitutional obligation" — that the State might have an obligation "to spend in excess of the norm in view of the presumed greater needs of [disadvantaged] students."[59] And the *Robinson* standard of ability in the contemporary setting to function as a citizen and competitor in the labor market was expressly elevated. Referring to it as a "new element of considerable relevance to this case," the court stressed that "poorer disadvantaged students must be given a chance to be able to compete with relatively advantaged students."[60] Later in the opinion, the court puts it more pointedly — whether "the Constitution indeed requires that poor children be able to compete with the rich."[61]

In this opinion, the court also begins its long and detailed inquiry into the details of education and educational opportunity. The parties' competing visions press the court to make judgments about whether substantive education is better evaluated based on disparities in pupil spending, curricular breadth, and staffing, the plaintiffs' position; or, management, community relations, parental interest, staff attention, and other factors not directly related to funding the State's position.[62]

The court well understood the controversial and far-reaching issues it was addressing:

> The central issue is here joined, including whether a thorough and efficient education requires that children with greater needs are entitled to greater resources. Whatever else the evidence shows, it is clear that the reverse is the fact: in New Jersey today, as we assume in the United States, the greater the students' needs, the less their education. And this raises yet another issue: to what extent does the requirement of thorough and efficient education impose on the schools the responsibility to account for and attempt to remedy the problems students bring with them to the schools, intractable problems, problems never dreamed of in the past as being within the schools' responsibility, problems created not by the schools but by society?[63]

These questions, and the court's answers in this opinion and throughout the long life of the *Abbott* litigation, clearly show that the New Jersey Supreme Court had moved far beyond relatively narrow issues of funding disparities or even "adequate education." The doctrinal view expressed in *Robinson* and even the court's first opinion in *Abbott* that, once all students in New Jersey received a "thorough and efficient" education, some districts, by dint of greater wealth or greater commitment, could do more educationally for their students had been supplanted. The court's clear, laser-like focus was on the State's responsibility to meet the needs of its most disadvantaged students in a manner that would enable them to compete with its most advantaged students.

In that regard, the court concluded that "in most poorer urban districts, the education needed to equip the students for their roles as citizens and workers exceeds that needed by students in more affluent districts," and that "the education provided depends to a significant extent on the money spent for it, and on what that money can buy — in quality and quantity — and the ability to innovate."[64]

The court's conclusion, thus, effectively inverts not only the historic pattern in New Jersey and most other states of spending less on disadvantaged students than on advantaged students, but also the governing constitutional principle in *Robinson* that so long as all students received an adequate education (albeit called "thorough and efficient") some districts could provide their students with more. Realistically, that was a constitutional license for wealthy districts to continue spending more than poor districts, a license that *Abbott II* rescinded.

The rest of the *Abbott* decisions[65] filled in the details or sought to ensure effective implementation of the remedies mandated. Stated succinctly, those remedies required the State, largely through state education aid, to provide students in the Abbott "special needs" districts with:

- Funding for their regular education at a level equal to the average per-pupil spending in the State's highest-wealth and most educationally successful districts ("parity funding");
- Supplemental funding for programs and services designed to meet the particularized educational needs of poor, disadvantaged students in the special needs districts, including full-day, high-quality early childhood education for all three- and four-year-olds;
- Renovation or replacement of all educationally-deficient or unsafe school buildings and facilities; and
- Standards-based educational reform under a system of state monitoring, assessment, and accountability.

The fiscal and educational consequences of *Abbott* have been nothing short of revolutionary. From 1997-1998, when the *Abbott* remedies began to be seriously implemented, to the present, the poor urban districts designated as "special needs" have leapfrogged over most of New Jersey's school districts in per-pupil spending to rival the State's highest-wealth and highest-spending districts.[66]

Although improvements in educational achievement have been uneven among the Abbott districts,[67] overall they have been impressive, especially in the lower grades where most of the initial emphasis was placed,[68] and in some districts and schools they have been spectacular.[69]

The challenge now is to maintain the enormous fiscal gains made and to sustain the momentum for educational improvement, extending it to all special-needs districts and schools. And the challenge is great in light of the State's continuing budget plight. Since education funding is by far the largest state budget line, constituting about one-third of the entire state budget, controlling or even reducing that funding is likely to be a top priority in the effort to reduce New Jersey's structural deficit.[70]

Many believe that to be precisely the purpose of the newly enacted School Funding Reform Act (SFRA).[71] By seeking to eliminate special-needs district status, parity funding for regular education, and needs-based supplemental funding with a special right of appeal — the core of the Abbott remedies — and to replace them all with a widely-attacked weighted "adequacy budget," the State has laid down the constitutional gauntlet. Indeed, the governor has indicated that the State would initiate a review in the New Jersey Supreme Court "shortly."[72]

Ultimately, the constitutional fight is likely to be over whether the Abbott remedies have led to sufficient educational progress to permit them to be eliminated or at least phased out. The great concern is that the result will be backsliding to the bad old days of unequal educational opportunity.

The battle lines are clearly drawn and the constitutional issues are relatively well-defined, even if complex. The ultimate decision will turn on how the court construes the "thorough" education requirement of the state constitution's education clause in the current situation.

The Road Less Traveled

At the risk of diverting energy, resources, and attention from the important work of preserving our hard-won gains on the road to a thorough education, I believe we must consider now taking the road less traveled — the road to an "efficient system of free public schools." Unlike Robert Frost, I believe we can and should take that second road.[73] Where will it lead us? In this paper, I will look down it as far as I can, but concede that I cannot clearly see the entire route and the ultimate destination.

Why, unlike Frost, have I found my way back to the "road not taken" after almost forty years on the other road? Perhaps it's because I have come to the realization that without successfully traveling the second road we cannot fully reach our destination on the first road. Perhaps it's because I have come to recognize that the constitutional framers who chose the phrase "thorough and efficient" may have understood that the two operative words, although they have different and separable meanings, function best in tandem, that ultimately thoroughness in education can't be fully realized without efficiency and that efficiency in service of a minimal education isn't worth striving for.

So what, then, did the framers mean by their choice of language — an "efficient system of free public schools"? Using the same approach we adopted in *Robinson* to define "thorough," let's start with the plain meaning of the words "efficient" and "system," and then place them in the context of the constitutional phrase.

Among the most common definitions of "efficient" are the following:

- "Acting directly to produce an effect";
- "Acting or producing effectively with a minimum of waste, expense or unnecessary effort";
- "Exhibiting a high ratio of output to input"; and
- "Able to accomplish a purpose; functioning effectively."[74]

Another way to consider the meaning is with reference to what renders a "system" *not* "efficient." The definitions above instruct us that that would occur if the system is wasteful, overly expensive, involves or requires unnecessary effort, has a low ratio of output to input, or is incapable of or ineffective in accomplishing a purpose.

In the constitutional provision, the adjective "efficient" modifies the noun "system," making the definition of the latter at least equally important. Like "efficient," "system" has a number of common definitions:

- "A group of interacting, interrelated or interdependent elements forming a complex whole";
- "A functionally related group of elements";
- "A social, economic or political organizational form";
- "A condition of harmonious, orderly interaction";
- "An organized and coordinated method";
- "An organized array of individual elements and parts forming

and working as a unit"; and

- "A usually large entity composed of interconnected parts."[75]

The dominant theme of these definitions is that a system is characterized by a functional relationship, organization, coordination, interconnection, and interdependence, not by its antonyms of disorder and disorganization. Given that, a threshold question is whether New Jersey's public schools constitute a "system" within the plain meaning of the state education clause.

The definitions of these individual terms — "efficient" and "system" — raise a broader issue as to how they fit within the key constitutional phrase — "a thorough and efficient system of free public schools."

Actually, construing the phrase backwards may be more productive of a useful interpretation. After all, the educational building blocks are the "free public schools." The purport of the constitutional phrase seems to be that those schools should constitute a "system," that the "system" should be "efficient," and that the result should be "thorough [education]."

Borrowing from a definition of "efficient," a question to be addressed is whether the input committed to the "system of free public schools" produces a high ratio of output, where the input is dollars spent and the output is student achievement in relation to the constitutional goal of enabling students, whatever disadvantages they bring to school, to function in the contemporary world as citizens and as workers.

Obviously, the input-output relationship has been at the heart of school funding litigation, both in terms of the plaintiffs' central claim that inadequate or unequal spending violates the constitutional rights of some students and the warring expert arguments about the education production function/cost-quality issue. In that litigation, the focus has been on the initial inputs — dollars — or the intermediate inputs — teachers, facilities, equipment, materials, and supplies — and their relationship to the outputs — student performance. Little or no attention has been paid to the questions raised here as to whether or not there is a "system of free public schools" and as to whether or not any such system is "efficient."

Ironically, in New Jersey's litigation, efficiency arguments were made by the State, but in a different manner and seeking a different end. A major state defense was that sufficient money to enable poor urban school districts to meet their students' constitutional rights was available, but that the districts were using it wastefully because of mismanagement and corruption.[76] It's not clear how, if at all, that argument relates to the State's constitutional obligation to operate an "efficient system of free public schools." Can an efficient statewide system exist if many of the largest school districts within it — serving almost twenty-five percent of New Jersey's students — are, by the State's own claim, operating inefficiently?[77] Indeed, can a public education structure that provides so much up-front autonomy to local school districts, in obeisance to home rule, satisfy the constitutional standard of a "system"?[78]

Before we travel too far down the road less traveled with "plain meaning" as our guide, however, we should consider other interpretative approaches to giving meaning to the constitutional phrase. The originalists undoubtedly would argue that in 1875, when New Jersey's education clause was added to the State's 1844 constitution, a statewide "system of free public schools" could not have looked anything like the current "plain meaning" of the term suggests and that, even if the constitutional framers had been utopian and expansive in their vision, they could not have had in mind anything remotely approximating a highly-structured, unified state system of free public schools.

Certainly, it is true that in 1875 public education was only just beginning to emerge from what had been a highly localized approach. Still, even then, educators were using the language of a state "system."[79] Moreover, the New Jersey Supreme Court made clear in its decisions in *Robinson* and *Abbott* that "thorough and efficient" education was an evolving concept, not limited to what had been the common view in 1875, 1895, or any earlier period.[80] There seems to be no reason why the court would not apply a similar approach to the "efficient system of free public schools" language in the same constitutional provision.

Plain meaning and original intent are not the only ways to construe constitutional provisions, however. Contemporaneous and subsequent interpretations by responsible public agencies — executive, legislative and judicial — are relevant and can be instructive. Moreover, New Jersey's constitutional language has exact or close parallels in other states, so the construction given to that language elsewhere can be of use in construing New Jersey's clause.

Aside from New Jersey, four other states use the "thorough and efficient system" language in their constitutions.[81] Much like New Jersey's highest court, states with similar constitutional language have acknowledged the fluid concept of a "thorough and efficient system." The Pennsylvania Supreme Court has stated that "because educational philosophy and needs change constantly, the words 'thorough and efficient' must not be narrowly construed."[82] In West Virginia, the supreme court recognized that "[t]he debates and cases often mention that ingredients of a thorough and efficient education system are changeable, and must adapt to conditions its beneficiaries need met."[83]

Although the states with "thorough and efficient system" clauses have tended to define them as embodying a unified concept, several have considered the separate meaning of individual words as a step in ascribing meaning to the entire clause. Using a dictionary definition of "efficient," the West Virginia Supreme Court found that the term meant "'...marked by ability to choose and use the most effective and least wasteful means of doing a task or accomplishing a purpose: competent . . . marked by qualities, characteristics, or equipment that facilitate the serving of a purpose or the performance of a task in the best possible manner; eminently satisfactory in use. ...'"[84] In a less direct approach, the Ohio Supreme Court chose to describe "efficiency" in terms of what it does not mean.[85]

While an exploration of state constitutions containing "thorough and efficient system" language provides some guidance, another fruitful approach is to examine states whose constitutions provide only for an "efficient system" of education.[86]

Kentucky's case law, especially *Rose v. Council for Better Education*,[87] is particularly helpful in illuminating how the concept of efficiency has been interpreted.[88] In *Rose*, the court explained that, under the Kentucky Constitution, "efficiency" was defined as "a system which required 'substantial uniformity, substantial equality of financial resources and substantial equal educational opportunity for all students.' Efficient was also interpreted to require that the educational system [ ] be adequate, uniform and unitary."[89]

Kentucky's highest court was guided by the ideals of its constitutional framers in giving meaning to the word "efficient." Included among those ideals were that: "[e]ducation must be provided to the children of the rich and poor alike," "[e]ducation of children should be supervised by the State," "[t]here must be a constant and continuing effort to make our schools more efficient," and "[a]ll schools and children stand upon one level in their entitlement to equal state support."[90]

The *Rose* court listed the following five elements of an "efficient" system, as determined by a group of experts in the field:

1. The system is the sole responsibility of the General Assembly.
2. The tax effort should be evenly spread.
3. The system must provide the necessary resources throughout the state — they must be uniform.
4. The system must provide an adequate education.
5. The system must be properly managed.[91]

Then the court specified its own listing of the nine "essential, and minimal, characteristics of an 'efficient' system . . ." of education:

1. The establishment, maintenance and funding of common schools in Kentucky is the sole responsibility of the General Assembly.
2. Common schools shall be free to all.
3. Common schools shall be available to all Kentucky children.
4. Common schools shall be substantially uniform throughout the state.
5. Common schools shall provide equal educational opportunities to all Kentucky children, regardless of place of residence or economic circumstances.
6. Common schools shall be monitored by the General Assembly to assure that they are operated with no waste, no duplication, no mismanagement, and with no political influence.
7. The premise for the existence of common schools is that all children in Kentucky have a constitutional right to an adequate

education.

8. The General Assembly shall provide funding which is sufficient to provide each child in Kentucky an adequate education.
9. An adequate education is one which has as its goal the development of the seven capacities recited previously.[92]

As indicated, the New Jersey Supreme Court tended in *Robinson* to treat the "thorough and efficient system" language as a unified concept speaking largely to fiscal resources and their relationship to educational outcomes, and in *Abbott* to focus increasingly on "thorough" education in both fiscal and programmatic respects. To the extent the New Jersey Supreme Court considered the process between educational inputs and outcomes, it was largely in terms of either rejecting periodic state assertions that all the problems were attributable not to inadequate or unequal funding, but to waste and mismanagement at the local level; or to requiring, with a notable lack of success, that the state identify particularized student needs in poor urban districts or determine which Abbott programs were working and which were not.[93]

There were some instances, though, in which the New Jersey courts did provide meaningful hints about the meaning that might be attributed to the "efficient system" language. The trial court opinion referred with approval to a statutory list of elements of a "thorough and efficient" education, the last three of which seem clearly to address "efficient system" notions — "[e]fficient administrative procedures," "[a]n adequate State program of research and development," and "[e]valuation and monitoring programs at State and local levels."[94]

In one of the most important decisions in the *Abbott* litigation, *Abbott IV*, the New Jersey Supreme Court provided some additional helpful insights, although not in the guise of construing the "efficient system" language of the state education clause. Rather, the court was considering the impact of the State's Core Curriculum Content Standards on the quality of education provided, when it said:

> The standards themselves do not ensure any substantive level of achievement. Real improvement still depends on the sufficiency of educational resources, successful teaching, effective supervision, efficient administration, and a variety of other academic, environmental, and societal factors needed to assure a sound education. Content standards, therefore, cannot answer the fundamental inquiry of whether the new statute assures the level of resources needed to provide a thorough and efficient education to children in the special needs districts.[95]

As this quote suggests, the "efficient system" language constitutes a bridge between sufficient resources and educational achievement — between the inputs and outcomes of public schooling. It literally can encompass everything that goes on in the educational process. In a subsequent article, I plan to elaborate on the legal, educational, and public policy aspects of satisfying the constitutional mandate of an "efficient system of free public schools." For now, let me sketch out in broad terms the possible dimensions of that mandate and the challenges involved in satisfying it.

To start, the notion of an efficient system of free public schools clearly implies obligations at both the state and local levels. It is beyond debate in New Jersey and virtually every other state that education is ultimately a state responsibility. Of course, it is within the State's authority to establish local and regional educational and administrative entities to carry out important functions, and all states, except possibly Hawaii, have done so. However, in many states, including New Jersey, these local and regional entities have no constitutional status. They can be altered or even eliminated by legislative or executive action. Their powers and duties can be adjusted as deemed appropriate.

Consistent with my idea of working backwards from smaller to larger to give meaning to the education clause, though, let me begin to consider the import of an efficient system of free public schools by focusing on the local level. A starting point is relevant state statutes and regulations that address educational efficiency and effectiveness.

In New Jersey, we have a substantial statutory and regulatory structure speaking to the constitutional requirements of educational thoroughness and efficiency. Actually, because of the frequency with which school funding statutes have been struck down as unconstitutional, we have a more elaborate and periodically updated structure than most states.

Starting in the mid-1970s, when New Jersey's school funding litigation began to have a major impact, a number of New Jersey statutes and implementing regulations have addressed the efficiency concept, at least in passing and as part of an ongoing effort to define the requirements of a thorough and efficient education.

The easiest way to trace the long, complex history of legislative responses is by perusing New Jersey's education code, Title 18A of the New Jersey Statutes Annotated, and especially the sequence of statutes that have appeared as Chapters 7A through 7F. They include the Public School Education Act of 1975 (1975 Act) (Chapter 7A),[96] enacted in response to the New Jersey Supreme Court's 1973 ruling in *Robinson*, which struck down the State School Incentive Equalization Aid Law of 1971;[97] the Quality Education Act of 1990

(QEA) (Chapter 7D),[98] enacted in response to *Abbott II*'s 1990 invalidation of the 1975 Act; the Comprehensive Education Improvement and Financing Act of 1996 (CEIFA) (Chapter 7F),[99] enacted in response to *Abbott III*'s 1994 invalidation of QEA; and the School Funding Reform Act of 2008 (SFRA) (also Chapter 7F),[100] belatedly enacted in response to *Abbott IV*'s 1997 partial invalidation of CEIFA.

Interspersed among those comprehensive school funding statutes, the legislature enacted three other chapters dealing with more specific, but related, subjects — the State Facilities Education Act of 1979 (Chapter 7B),[101] the High School Graduation Standards Act in the same year (Chapter 7C),[102] and the School Report Card & Efficiency Programs Act in 1995 (Chapter 7E).[103]

Many of those statutes have invoked the word or concept of efficiency, either in connection with the constitutional phrase "thorough and efficient" or as part of a different phrase — "efficiency standards." Yet, very little specific content is given to the word or phrase in the statutes and, to the extent they seem to contemplate or even require regulatory elaboration, seldom has this been done.

In fact, SFRA's legislative scheme seems the sketchiest of any in that regard. The Commissioner of Education is required to "develop and establish… efficiency standards which define the types of programs, services, activities, and materials necessary to achieve a thorough and efficient education,"[104] as he already was by prior law. However, the vehicle for him to do so is a report to be submitted to the legislature by the governor, not the commissioner, and the statutory description of that report addresses only school funding formula elements and not efficiency standards. SFRA also eliminated language in the prior law referring to a Commission on Business Efficiency in the Public Schools whose charge was to "develop advisory cost benchmarks for the efficient provision of non-instructional services by school districts. ..."[105]

There are, however, several relatively recent and more specialized New Jersey statutes that provide greater traction with respect to defining local educational efficiency. One is a statute enacted in 2007, which combines provisions designed to encourage savings among local governmental units,[106] through shared services and consolidation among others, with other provisions that substantially augment the powers and duties of county superintendents and re-designate them as executive county superintendents.[107]

The latter provisions virtually quintupled the number of functions assigned to the county superintendents, increasing them from five to twenty-four, with most of the new functions relating specifically to aspects of efficiency.

These include measures empowering the executive county superintendent, either on a voluntary or, with the approval of the commissioner of education, mandatory basis to: enhance "administrative and operational efficiencies and cost savings within [individual] school districts;"[108] consolidate administrative services among school districts or educational services commissions;[109] within one year, eliminate non-operating districts located in the county;[110] within three years, develop a regionalization or consolidation plan that would eliminate all districts not providing preschool or kindergarten through grade twelve programs; "[p]romote coordination and regionalization of pupil transportation services;"[112] "disapprove a portion of a school district's proposed budget if he determines that the district has not implemented all potential efficiencies in the administrative operations of the district or if he determines that the budget includes excessive non-instructional expenses;"[113] permit a district to seek additional funds from local voters only if it assures the executive county superintendent in writing that it is participating in shared services arrangements, has tried to do so, or that such arrangements would not produce cost savings;[114] and "[p]romote cooperative purchasing… of textbooks and other instructional materials."[115]

Additionally, there is a series of provisions regarding the executive county superintendent's powers and duties relative to the tracking, coordination and regionalization of special education services.[116]

Clearly, this statute delegates to the executive county superintendents extensive responsibilities relating to local and regional efficiency efforts. As gubernatorial appointees, they may have sufficient status to make a significant impact. Still, the jury is very much out. Filling the twenty-one positions has proven difficult,[117] and the resistance to many of the initiatives contemplated is likely to be formidable. Prior efforts to advance efficiency have been far less successful than hoped, and in several high visibility instances vocal public opposition caused the State to retreat from the fray entirely.

The other recent statute that takes an even more comprehensive approach to educational efficiency underscores the problem of successful implementation. The New Jersey Quality Single Accountability Continuum (NJQSAC) system[118] ambitiously seeks to bring together in a unified fashion all state and federal monitoring and accountability requirements applicable to the state's school districts.

Focusing on five key components of school district effectiveness — instruction and program, personnel, fiscal management, operations, and governance — NJQSAC involves an elaborate process under which local self-assessment and county and state verification are designed to determine each school district's effectiveness and local capacity based on a matrix of quality performance indicators comprising the District Performance Review.

School districts that perform above a specified level on each of the five components are deemed "high-performing" and largely left to their own devices. Districts that fall below the prescribed level in one or more of the five components have to prepare improvement plans on their own or in collaboration with the state education department. The State monitors plan implementation and may offer technical assistance as appropriate. If a district fails to develop or successfully implement an improvement plan, or "other emergent circumstances warrant," the State Education Department may, "intervene," partially or fully, in the educational or fiscal operations of that district. The stated purpose for such intervention is "to build local capacity to provide a thorough and efficient education."[119]

In substantial measure, NJQSAC seeks to address important aspects of local district efficiency regarding educational as well as administrative, personnel, fiscal, and governance matters. The problem is that the early stages of implementation have revealed many problems, with the process itself[120] and with the State Department of Education's capacity to carry it out.[121]

The problems already identified regarding NJQSAC point toward another critically important dimension of implementing the constitutional mandate of an "efficient system of free public schools" — the central role of the State. Not only must the State assure that local school districts operate efficiently, but the State itself must discharge its paramount constitutional responsibilities.

At one point in the development of my thinking about this article, I produced a list of all the conceivable "Elements of an 'Efficient System of Free Public Schools,'" culled from judicial opinions and other sources, in New Jersey and elsewhere. The list ran to twenty-two and most of the items related entirely or partially to the state's role and responsibilities in ensuring that New Jersey has an efficient system of public schools.

Prominently featured were a number of elements that may have special relevance to a constitutional challenge based on New Jersey's education clause. These include:

- A school district structure that maximizes economy and educational effectiveness
- Substantial uniformity among districts and possibly schools
- Efficient procedures at the state and local level that minimize waste, duplication, mismanagement, and political interference
- A comprehensive statewide data system, including a student database that permits the tracking of individual students' academic performance
- Effective monitoring, assessment, evaluation, technical assistance and, where necessary, intervention by the State
- Funding earmarked for educational programs that work
- An adequate state program of research and development
- An adequately staffed and organized state department of education[122]

In all these respects, serious and — in many cases, substantially documented — criticisms have been leveled at the State's operation of its public schools.[123]

Elaborating on all these dimensions is beyond the scope of this article, but will be the focus of future articles. Later in this article, however, in discussing a possible legal advocacy strategy, I will deal in some detail with one of the enumerated efficient system issues — the unusual number and size of school districts in New Jersey.

Getting to the Nitty-Gritty: What Should We Do with this Constitutional Theory?

Even if I've persuaded you that there's a promising new constitutional theory somewhere along the road less traveled, based on the constitutional language regarding an "efficient system of free public schools," the big question remains — what should be done with that theory?

Ought it to find a home in legal advocacy rather than theoretical scholarship? And if so, what should be challenged, by whom and in what kind of legal advocacy?

Let me admit something to you. I've been a law professor for almost forty years, but I've never had the patience to write in the realm of legal theory hoping that eventually it might influence someone to change the law or to use law to influence for the better the lives of people, let alone just to think differently about the law.[124] If there's a divide between theoretical and applied research and scholarship, I'm decisively on the applied side. Indeed, to be totally candid, I'm not even patient enough just to do applied research and leave it to others to do the applying. Fortunately, I'm a law professor and a lawyer so my lack of patience has a ready outlet in legislative and judicial advocacy.

Given that bent, my answer to the question of theoretical scholarship versus legal advocacy should be obvious. I plan to develop a legal advocacy strategy based on the introductory thinking reflected in this article. The details of that strategy will have to await a much more elaborate and fully researched follow-up article.

For now, though, let me sketch out some preliminary thoughts about such a legal advocacy venture. Although I understand, and to a degree accept, the argument that more of our time, energy, and talent should be devoted to community organizing and legislative lobbying, I remain unconvinced that such efforts alone can carry the day. Perhaps I am too mired in the world of yesterday where the goals we sought of equal educational opportunity for poor children of color were so clearly "minority" interests threatening to many in the "majority."

I recognize that we are a nation in transition; that soon we will be a majority minority country, and that in some states we have already reached that status. That should open up legislative possibilities, which previously have not existed. Still, old orders die hard and so, I believe, will this one. Moreover, it is not just a matter of race and ethnicity; it actually may be more a matter of social class and, if poor people remain in the minority, their plight and that of their children may not improve as much as we might like to believe with changes in the nation's dominant color scheme.

Therefore, I still believe that majoritarian governmental structures may continue to be more a part of the problem than the solution, and that legal advocacy in the courts will have to be a significant part of the ongoing effort. At least, my plan is to keep working in that direction. If I am proven to be too pessimistic about the powers of political persuasion and moral suasion, then the constitutional principles and litigation strategies I develop could become part of a community-based legislative strategy.

Indeed, one of the school funding reform movement's most important accomplishments across the country has been to elevate the issue of educational equity to the top of the public agenda in most states. That has been true not only in states where litigation has successfully overturned unequal school funding laws, but also in states where litigation has not been successful.[126] Developing a credible constitutional theory for advancing the right of students, parents, taxpayers and other citizens to an "efficient system of free public schools," therefore, is likely to have that agenda-setting effect whether or not litigation succeeds, or even whether or not a lawsuit actually is pursued in any given state.

That leaves the questions I raised earlier: what should be challenged, by whom, and in what specific advocacy format? The short answer to what should be challenged, as I have already suggested, is everything that significantly impedes the effort of a state such as New Jersey to create a meaningful system of free public schools capable of efficiently providing a thorough education to all its students, and especially to its poor and disadvantaged students.

However, the essence of effective legal strategy is to select carefully the best points of attack and to integrate them into a plan of action. That is exactly what was done in the run-up to *Brown v. Board of Education*. Although there was some effort to replicate that approach in school funding litigation, the fact that a thousand — or at least several dozen — flowers were permitted to bloom in a lot of different gardens led to a much less systematic approach, even at the federal level.

Many tried to persuade the plaintiffs' lawyer in *San Antonio v. Rodriguez* that his case might not be the best opening wedge to the United States Supreme Court on the issue, but that urging fell on deaf ears and history has recorded the result. I have little reason to believe that my urging, in this and follow-up articles, will be more effective in channeling litigation based on the "efficient system" language of state constitutions, but that isn't enough to dissuade me from trying.

Following the interpretive approach I applied earlier to the constitutional language, I'll confront the tactical issue backwards as well. Therefore, the first question to address is what attributes of an "efficient system of free public schools" might be challenged and what criteria should be used to arrive at an answer? One could decide to start small — seeking to formulate a series of modest, relatively uncontroversial and viable legal challenges, each focusing on manifest defects in the State's response to the constitutional requirement that it create an "efficient system of free public schools." The notion would be to use such efforts as sequential and cumulative building blocks in a grand design.

An alternate approach, to which I, with my admitted impatience, am drawn, is a high visibility, high-leverage and perhaps high-risk/high-gain strategy — a go-for-the-jugular approach. For me, New Jersey's most dramatic example of the lack of a meaningful and unified statewide "system of free public schools," and a major contributor to educational, administrative, and fiscal inefficiency, has been the State's crazy quilt of school districts. Despite wide recognition of the problem for decades,[127] New Jersey has shown little inclination, at least until recently, to deal with it. In the vernacular, it has been a political third rail.

Cases like *Robinson* and *Abbott* have succeeded in overcoming other New Jersey political third rails — *Robinson* the aversion to a state income tax and *Abbott* the unwillingness to fund disadvantaged students in poor school districts at a level as high as, or even higher than, advantaged students in wealthy districts. So, constitutional litigation may be the only way to overcome the longstanding reluctance to consider seriously the consolidation of New Jersey school districts.

And the need is apparent. The state is said to have significantly more school districts and other local governmental entities per square mile than any state in the nation.[128] Not coincidentally, it also has the highest local property taxes.[129] There appear to be between 603 and

617 school districts or other local educational agencies — and no one seems completely certain about the correct number.[130]

The sheer number of New Jersey's school districts is further complicated by the small size of many of them. Since statewide pupil enrollment in 2006-2007 was about 1.39 million,[131] that makes the mean enrollment per district about 2250, but, as is often the case, the average is misleading. Barely more than one-third of all the districts — 220 — operate K-12 programs. Excluding the twenty-three non-operating districts, almost half of the state's school districts have fewer than 1000 students and are too small to operate K-12 programs.

Thus, 284 school districts — about forty-seven percent of the total — operate K-6 or K-8 elementary programs. Their students, part way through their careers, have to shift their educational venues to other districts. Incessant problems are created because, in many of these transitional situations, the district of residence has little say over the other district's educational program. Often, there are fiscal, management, or political dislocations resulting from the transition. In educators' vernacular, curriculum articulation also is a persistent problem.

According to one well-known expert, the number of New Jersey school districts could be dramatically reduced — from well over 600 to about 240 — without a single child attending a different school simply by requiring all districts to provide K-12 education.[132] That could be achieved by consolidating districts, which already have educational interrelationships.

For example, if three elementary school districts (K-8) currently send their high school age students to a third district, either a 9-12 or K-12 district, the four districts could be consolidated into one. That would change administrative and fiscal structures, but not necessarily the number, staffing, or student enrollments of existing schools. It would ensure that all four communities have some meaningful voice in the operation of the consolidated district's schools and would enhance the prospects of effective curriculum articulation since a student's entire public education career, K-12, would be under the aegis and supervision of a single school district.

Such consolidation also would produce significant cost savings over time, despite some initial start-up costs.[133] Moreover, other important efficiencies are almost certain to result. There should be a significant reduction in the oversight, monitoring, technical assistance, and intervention responsibilities of an over-burdened State Education Department. Creating and implementing an effective statewide student database should be facilitated.

Of course, this simple, relatively easily described consolidation model is hardly the only, or best, way to approach the task. Other more complicated and far-reaching models could serve different and more ambitious state goals. For example, restructuring of the state's school districts could facilitate realization of New Jersey's longstanding constitutional obligation to achieve racial balance in the schools wherever that is feasible.[134] Consolidation also could be designed to equalize local district property tax capacity, thereby reducing the fiscal equalization obligations of the state.

Consolidating school districts is not an alien concept to the rest of the country, but it seems to be in New Jersey. During the past three-quarters of a century, the number of school districts in the United States has declined from over 100,000 to less than 15,000.[135] During the same period, the number of school districts in New Jersey *increased* by about fifteen percent. As these numbers suggest, New Jerseyans have a strong commitment to educational home rule.

The question my theory poses is whether New Jersey's current structure satisfies the constitutional requirement of an "efficient system of free public schools." There certainly is a growing body of evidence in New Jersey, legislative and executive, that K-12 districts are preferable. To the extent that the new law creating and empowering executive county superintendents recognizes and acts on that preference, however, the adoption of that law may complicate a state constitutional challenge. Were such a challenge brought, the state is likely to defend by asserting that it has recognized the problem, if belatedly, and taken steps to deal with it. Undoubtedly, the State would ask the court to stay its hand, at least until the executive county superintendents have had the statutory three years to devise their regionalization or consolidation plans, seek the commissioner's approval, and submit the approved plans to the voters. The entire process could take five years or more, and it is quite conceivable that, during its pendency, New Jersey courts would defer to the other branches.

Is there a point, nonetheless, in developing, and perhaps even pursuing, a credible constitutional case for restructuring the state's school districts? There may well be. It could hold the State's feet to the consolidation fire, prompting it to take the statutory provisions seriously. Beyond that, it could pave the way toward immediate resort to the courts if the statutory process fails to lead to district consolidation.

The potential for substantial delay regarding a district restructuring challenge may, however, counsel for another, even bolder strategy — to combine a number of the efficiency elements listed above in a single omnibus challenge. The number and variety of inefficiencies alleged could add cumulative weight to the constitutional challenge and broaden the base of support for it.

Clearly, if the sole or primary challenge were to district structure, support might come from those who favor consolidated districts because they might facilitate more equalized local funding bases; greater racial, ethnic, and socioeconomic diversity in the schools; greater administrative efficiency; somewhat reduced administrative costs; and enhanced educational effectiveness. These are all weighty values with significant constituencies supporting them. But, on the other side are the historic forces of home rule and localism in New Jersey, aided and abetted by those newly persuaded of the virtues of small districts and schools.[136] Despite the fact that the very term "home rule" seems antithetical to the idea of a unified statewide system, it is not at all clear how that battle, even with judicial intervention, would turn out.

By contrast, it is difficult to imagine strenuous and formal opposition to many of the other efficiency elements listed previously, such as an adequately staffed and organized state department of education; an adequate state program of research and development; effective monitoring, assessment, evaluation, technical assistance and, if need be, state intervention in local school districts; and a comprehensive statewide data system.

In either case, of course, those challenging the State would have the burden of establishing that an "efficient system of free public schools" was not being provided. Assuming that showing can be made, or even that a credible constitutional argument can be constructed, the remaining questions to be considered here are who might initiate the challenge and in what form.

From *Robinson* and *Abbott* we know that students and parents have enforceable constitutional rights under the state education clause. Presumably, that applies to the efficient system language as well as the thorough education language. The focus on "efficient system," though, might make the involvement of taxpayer and business organizations more likely. At some level, clearly the asserted absence of an "efficient system of public schools" has significant fiscal and tax implications. Although taxpayers failed in *Robinson* to establish a constitutional right to equal taxation for education, the claim in an efficient system case is substantially different and unlikely to face the kind of dismissal taxpayers experienced in *Robinson*.

A related question is whether an "efficient system" challenge should be folded into the ongoing school funding litigation or be pursued independently. The argument for incorporating it into cases such as *Abbott* is that it could serve to rebut the frequent charges that school funding reform advocates are just "throwing money" at the problem of inadequate education of poor, disadvantaged students.

From the earliest days, advocates have responded to such charges with variations on the theme of "adequate funding is necessary but not sufficient to cure the educational problems of poor children." Although that response is clearly true, it has not been effective in defusing the argument. Moreover, the advocates' insistence on, and the court's ordering of, meaningful program evaluation and accountability in the poor urban districts has usually been ignored both by the State and the public. Giving prominence in cases such as *Abbott* to a new "efficient system" challenge, especially if new and different kinds of advocates emerged to press that challenge, might more effectively convey the rebuttal to the "throwing money" argument.

On the other hand, in states such as New Jersey, the school funding litigation is of such long standing and is so deeply engrained that it might be extremely difficult to introduce a major new dimension, or to attract substantial public attention to it. That may argue for a separate, independent legal challenge brought by different parties representing different interests.[137]

Conclusion

In truth, this article may have barely scratched the surface of developing and articulating a new constitutional theory, and considering how it might be used to augment, perhaps even complete, the historic effort to promote equal educational opportunity for poor, disadvantaged students through state education clause litigation. It does, however, challenge us to consider taking the road not yet taken in the hope that it will lead us to a destination that we have been seeking for so long.

---

1 Board of Governors Distinguished Service Professor and Alfred C. Clapp Distinguished Public Service Professor of Law, Rutgers School of Law — Newark; founder and first executive director, Education Law Center, Inc.; lawyer for the urban student plaintiffs in *Abbott v. Burke*; and founding director, Rutgers-Newark Institute on Education Law and Policy. I thank Ava Majlesi, a 2007 graduate of Rutgers School of Law-Newark, for her invaluable research assistance and the Institute for Educational Equity and Opportunity for its financial and other support. Finally, a version of this article was presented at the February 2, 2008 symposium on Education as a Civil Right at Stanford Law School, and I appreciated the opportunity both to preview it and to receive helpful feedback.

2 The state's first school funding challenge, *Robinson v. Cahill*, 287 A.2d 187 (N.J. Super. Ct. Law Div. 1972), was filed in 1970. Except for a hiatus from late 1976 until early 1981, when *Abbott v. Burke*, 477 A.2d 1278 (N.J. Super. Ct. App. Div. 1984), was filed, the litigation has continued unabated to the present. During those almost four decades, the New Jersey Supreme Court has issued almost twenty-five opinions and orders, and lower courts and administrative agencies have issued close to another dozen. *See infra* notes 50, 56, & 65.

3 At the end of 1999, New Jersey judges and lawyers overwhelmingly voted *Abbott* the most important state court decision of the twentieth century. Rocco Cammarere, Brown *and* Abbott*: Leading Rulings this Century*, N.J. LAW., Dec. 27, 1999, at 5. *Brown v. Board of Education*, 347 U.S. 483 (1954), was also

overwhelmingly voted the most important federal court decision. *Id.*

4 City of Pawtucket v. Sundlun, 662 A.2d 40, 59 (R.I. 1995) ("We point out one additional caveat: the absence of justiciable standards could engage the court in a morass comparable to the decades-long struggle of the Supreme Court of New Jersey that has attempted to define what constitutes the 'thorough and efficient' education specified in that state's constitution.").

5 ALEXIS DE TOCQUEVILLE, DEMOCRACY IN AMERICA (1835).

6 *See, e.g.*, Robert N. Bellah, Individualism and Commitment in American Life (Feb. 20, 1986), *available at* http://www.robertbellah.com/lectures_4.htm.

7 The "road" metaphor comes from Robert Frost's classic poem, *The Road Not Taken*. ROBERT FROST, MOUNTAIN INTERVAL (1920).

8 N.J. CONST. art. VIII, § IV, ¶ 1.

9 *Id.*

10 U.S. CONST. amend. XIV, § 1.

11 347 U.S. 483 (1954).

12 *See, e.g.*, HAROLD W. HOROWITZ & KENNETH L. KARST, LAW, LAWYERS AND SOCIAL CHANGE 239 (1969).

13 Compare ERIC A. HANUSHEK, MAKING SCHOOLS WORK: IMPROVING PERFORMANCE AND CONTROLLING COSTS (1994) (stating that school spending has limited impact on educational performance), with Ronald F. Ferguson, *Paying for Public Education: New Evidence on How and Why Money Matters*, 28 HARV. J. ON LEGIS. 465, 485 (1991) (arguing that school spending significantly affects educational performance).

14 ARTHUR E. WISE, RICH SCHOOLS POOR SCHOOLS: THE PROMISE OF EQUAL EDUCATIONAL OPPORTUNITY (1968).

15 JOHN E. COONS ET AL., PRIVATE WEALTH AND PUBLIC EDUCATION (1970) (expanded version of John E. Coons et al., *Educational Opportunity: A Workable Test for State Financial Structures*, 57 CAL. L. REV. 305 (1969)).

16 *See, e.g.*, Harold W. Horowitz, *Unseparate but Unequal — The Emerging Fourteenth Amendment Issue in Public School Education*, 13 UCLA L. REV. 1147 (1966). During the same year, a major study was published cutting the other way with its conclusion that "students' family and other background characteristics were more important than school resources in determining student achievement." MAKING MONEY MATTER: FINANCING AMERICA'S SCHOOLS 71-72 (Helen F. Ladd & Janet S. Hansen eds., 1999) (referring to JAMES S. COLEMAN ET AL., EQUALITY OF EDUCATIONAL OPPORTUNITY (1966)). For other early articles advancing Equal Protection Clause theories, see Harold W. Horowitz & Diana L. Neitring, *Equal Protection Aspects of Inequalities in Public Education and Public Assistance Programs from Place to Place Within a State*, 15 UCLA L. REV. 787 (1968); David L. Kirp, *The Poor, the Schools and Equal Protection*, 38 HARV. EDUC. REV. 635 (1968).

17 Ironically, in an early New Jersey case, *Landis v. Ashworth*, 31 A. 1017 (N.J.

Sup. Ct. 1895), plaintiffs representing outlying districts had argued unsuccessfully that the state constitution's education clause was violated by an education funding system under which wealthier city districts were able to provide their students with superior education.

18 *See* Burruss v. Wilkerson, 310 F. Supp. 572 (W.D. Va. 1969), *aff'd* 397 U.S. 44 (1970); McInnis v. Shapiro, 293 F. Supp. 327 (N.D. Ill. 1968), *aff'd sub nom.* McInnis v. Ogilvie, 394 U.S. 322 (1969) (mem.). Actually, the first modern school finance case was filed in Michigan state court in February 1968, but never was prosecuted to judgment. Board of Educ. v. Michigan, General Civil No. 103342 (Mich. Cir. Ct., filed Feb. 2, 1968). Both the *Burruss* and *McInnis* plaintiffs contended that the statutes failed to consider the educational needs of students in different counties and cities. *See Burruss*, 310 F. Supp. at 573; *McInnis*, 293 F. Supp. at 329. Rejecting plaintiffs' argument, the *McInnis* court stated that "the Fourteenth Amendment does not require that public school expenditures be made only on the basis of pupils' educational needs . . . ." *McInnis*, 293 F. Supp. at 329. Similarly, the *Burruss* court noted that courts "have neither the knowledge, nor the means, nor the power to tailor the public moneys to fit the varying needs of . . . students throughout the State." *Burruss*, 310 F. Supp. at 574.

19 *See McInnis*, 293 F. Supp. at 329 and *Burruss*, 310 F. Supp. at 574.

20 *See* Brief for Stephen D. Sugarman et al. as Amici Curiae Supporting Appellants at 35-38, Serrano v. Priest, 487 P.2d 1241 (Cal. 1971) (L.A. No. 29,820); *see generally* John E. Coons et al., *Educational Opportunity: A Workable Constitutional Test for State Financial Structures*, 57 CAL. L. REV. 305 (1969) (arguing that the courts should take a neutral approach).

21 *See* JOHN E. COONS ET AL., *supra* note 15, at 312.

22 487 P.2d 1241 (Cal. 1971).

23 303 A.2d 273 (N.J. 1973), *aff'g in part and rev'g in part*, 287 A.2d 187 (N.J. Super. Ct. Law Div. 1972).

24 After the U.S. Supreme Court's 5-4 decision in *San Antonio Indep. Sch. Dist. v. Rodriguez*, 411 U.S. 1 (1973), upholding Texas' school funding system against a federal equal protection challenge, the California courts in *Serrano* shifted to the state Equal Protection Clause. *See Serrano v. Priest*, 557 P.2d 929, 950 n.41 (1976). The *Rodriguez* majority's decision was based on its conclusions that education was not a "fundamental right," 411 U.S. at 37; property-poor school districts did not constitute a "suspect class," *id.* at 28; and that Texas' interest in local control provided a "reasonable basis" for its admittedly unequal school funding system. *Id.* at 47.

25 *Serrano*, 557 P.2d at 943 n.28 (quoting Serrano v. Priest, No. C 938254 (Cal. Super. Ct., Apr. 10, 1974) (memorandum opinion regarding intended decision)).

26 *Robinson v. Cahill*, 303 A.2d 273, 294 (N.J. 1973). New Jersey's clause, like that of a number of other states, provides for the "maintenance and support of a thorough and efficient system of free public schools . . . ." N.J. CONST. art.

VIII, § 4, ¶ 1.

27 303 A.2d at 281.

28 *Id.* at 287.

29 *Id.* at 288.

30 *Robinson v. Cahill*, 287 A.2d 187, 210-11 (N.J. Super. Ct. Law Div. 1972).

31 *Id.* at 211 (emphasis added). Amici curiae had pressed for this expansive definition in their briefs. *See, e.g.*, Brief for Educ. Comm., NAACP, Newark Chapter & ACLU of N.J. as Amici Curiae Supporting Respondents at 23-25, *Robinson v. Cahill*, 287 A.2d 187 (N.J. Super. Ct. Law Div. 1972) (No. A-8618).

32 *Robinson*, *supra* note 26, at 297.

33 *Id.*

34 *Id.*

35 *Id.*

36 *Id.* at 295 (emphasis added).

37 *Id.*

38 *Id.* at 294-95 (quoting from *Landis*, *supra* note 17, at 1018).

39 *Id.* at 295.

40 *Id.* at 298.

41 N.J. Stat. Ann. § 18A:7A (West 1975).

42 *Robinson v. Cahill*, 355 A.2d 129 (N.J. 1976). The five and a half months between this January 30, 1976 decision and the court's July 9, 1976 order dissolving an injunction and ending the *Robinson* phase were tumultuous. The legislature's failure to fund its own new law prompted the court in May 1976, after considering many remedial responses, to enjoin expenditure of any funds on the public schools effective July 1, 1976. *Robinson v. Cahill*, 358 A.2d 457 (N.J. 1976). For a brief period in July, this led to the closing of public summer schools until the legislature adopted New Jersey's first state income tax to generate the necessary funds.

43 Education Law Center, *History of Abbott*, http://www.edlawcenter.org/ELCPublic/AbbottvBurke/AbbottHistory.htm (last visited ?).

44 N.J. Stat. Ann. § 18A:7D-1 to -37 (repealed 1996).

45 N.J. Stat. Ann. § 18A:7F-1 to -42 (West 1996).

46 B. A500/S4000, 212th Leg. (N.J. 2008) (as approved by Pub. L. 2007, c.260).

47 Notice of Motion for Review of the Constitutionality of the School Funding Reform Act of 2008 for Defendants, Abbott v. Burke, No. 42,170 (N.J. March 17, 2008). The Education Law Center, lawyer for over 300,000 Abbott district students, and at least some of the Abbott districts themselves, will oppose the State's motion. Additionally, the ranks of those in opposition may be augmented by representatives of some high-wealth districts and by advocacy

groups representing special education students, among others, who strongly opposed SFRA in legislative hearings.

48 The legal, public policy, and educational literature about *Abbott* is enormous. *See, e.g.*, EDUC. LAW CTR., THE ABBOTT DISTRICTS IN 2005-06: PROGRESS AND CHALLENGES (2006), *available at* http://www.edlawcenter.org/ELCPublic/Publications/PDF/AbbottIndicatorsReport_2005_06.pdf; INST. ON EDUC. LAW AND POLICY, SETTING THE STAGE FOR INFORMED, OBJECTIVE DELIBERATION ON PROPERTY TAX REFORM (2005), *available at* http://ielp.rutgers.edu/docs/taxreform_bg.pdf; CLAIRE PASSANTINO & SUSAN KENYON, ABBOTT IMPLEMENTATION RESOURCE GUIDE : STANDARDS BASED REFORM (2004), *available at* http://www.edlawcenter.org/ELCPublic/Publications/PDF/AIRG_StandardsBasedReform.pdf. At the end of 2007, an excellent book was published about the *Abbott* litigation by a seasoned education writer. DEBORAH YAFFE, OTHER PEOPLE'S CHILDREN: THE BATTLE FOR JUSTICE AND EQUALITY IN NEW JERSEY'S SCHOOLS (2007).

49 *See* Paul L. Tractenberg, *The Evolution & Implementation of Educational Rights Under the New Jersey Constitution of 1947*, 29 RUTGERS L.J. 827, 897 (1998). The plaintiffs did include state and federal equal protection claims in *Abbott*, but neither argument got far.

50 *See* Abbott v. Burke, 575 A.2d 359 (N.J. 1990) (*Abbott II*); Abbott v. Burke, 643 A.2d 575 (N.J. 1994) (*Abbott III*); Abbott v. Burke, 693 A.2d 417 (N.J. 1997) (*Abbott IV*); Abbott v. Burke, 710 A.2d 450 (N.J. 1998) (*Abbott V*).

51 N.J. CONST. art. VIII, § 4, ¶ 1.

52 Dictionary.com includes "complete" and "extremely attentive to accuracy and detail" as definitions of "thorough." Dictionary.com, http://dictionary.reference.com/browse/thorough (last visited ?).

53 Commentators often date the start of the education adequacy movement as 1989, the year in which the Kentucky Supreme Court decided *Rose v. Council for Better Education*, 790 S.W.2d 186 (Ky. 1989). *See, e.g.*, Paul A. Minorini & Stephen D. Sugarman, *Educational Adequacy and the Courts: The Promise and Problems of Moving to a New Paradigm in Equity and Adequacy*, *in* EDUCATION FINANCE: ISSUES AND PERSPECTIVES 175 (Rosemary A. Chalk, Janet S. Hansen & Helen F. Ladd eds., 1999). However, a decade and a half earlier, ***Robinson*** was an adequacy case at least as much as an equity case.

54 In the first *Abbott* case, the New Jersey Supreme Court added to that quote the bracketed words "or her," suggesting a significant alteration of sensibility between 1973 and 1985. Abbott v. Burke, 495 A.2d 376, 382 (N.J. 1985).

55 Robinson v. Cahill, 303 A.2d 273, 295 (N.J. 1973).

56 *See* Abbott v. Burke, 495 A.2d 376, 387-89 (N.J. 1985) (*Abbott I*). Although the court was only deciding a procedural issue — whether plaintiffs needed to exhaust administrative remedies — it addressed, without resolving, the constitutional issues as guidance to the administrative process to which it assigned the case.

57 *See* Abbott v. Burke, 575 A.2d 359, 369-70 (N.J. 1990) (*Abbott II*).

58 *Id.* at 371. The court's conclusion in that regard was buttressed by its finding that, "despite great effort, the [State's monitoring] procedure ultimately fails to measure the district's system against the accepted definition of a thorough and efficient education — one that equips students to fulfill their roles as citizens and competitors in the market." *Id.* at 374.

59 *Id.* at 371.

60 *Id.* at 372.

61 *Id.* at 375.

62 *Id.*

63 *Id.*

64 *Id.*

65 Abbott v. Burke, 643 A.2d 575 (N.J. 1994) (*Abbott III*) (holding New Jersey's Quality Education Act unconstitutional for failure to equalize school funding and assure that necessary supplemental programs will be implemented); Abbott v. Burke, 693 A.2d 417 (N.J. 1997) (*Abbott IV*) (declaring CEIFA unconstitutional and ordering parity funding for poor, urban schools); Abbott v. Burke, 710 A.2d 450 (N.J. 1998) (*Abbott V*) (delineating specific programs that must be available to children in urban schools, including preschool for all three- and four-year-old children); Abbott v. Burke, 710 A.2d 450 (N.J. 2000) (*Abbott VI*) (ruling that New Jersey failed to implement preschool programs according to the court's guidelines); Abbott v. Burke, 751 A.2d 1032 (N.J. 2000) (*Abbott VII*) (reaffirming a prior ruling that New Jersey must provide all necessary funding for the Abbott school construction program); Abbott v. Burke, 790 A.2d 842 (N.J. 2002) (*Abbott VIII*) (directing the State to make decisions regarding preschool plans and budgeting and clarifying necessary components of the preschool program); Abbott v. Burke, 798 A.2d 602 (N.J. 2002) (*Abbott IX*) (ordering a temporary hold on further implementation of *Abbott* remedies); Abbott v. Burke, 832 A.2d 891 (N.J. 2003) (*Abbott X*) (accepting a mediation agreement reached by the parties); Abbott v. Burke, 832 A.2d 906 (N.J. 2003) (*Abbott XI*) (granting the State's request to extend relaxation of *Abbott V* remedies); Abbott v. Burke, 852 A.2d 185 (N.J. 2004) (*Abbott XII*) (granting the State's request to further extend the relaxation of remedies); Abbott v. Burke, 862 A.2d 538 (N.J. 2004) (*Abbott XIII*) (ordering the parties to participate in further mediation); Abbott v. Burke, 889 A.2d 1063 (N.J. 2005) (*Abbott XIV*) (ordering the State to submit annual reports and construction plans); Abbott v. Burke, 901 A.2d 299 (N.J. 2006) (*Abbott XV*) (ordering Abbott districts to resubmit 2006-2007 budgets in accordance with the Governor's proposed budget); Abbott v. Burke, 2006 WL 1388958 (N.J. May 22, 2006) (*Abbott XVI*) (clarifying *Abbott XV*); Abbott v. Burke, 935 A.2d 1152 (N.J. 2007) (*Abbott XVII*) (denying plaintiffs' request for an order directing the State to comply with certain remedial requirements of *Abbott V*, *Abbot VII*, and *Abbot XIV*).

66 Ford Fessenden, *Abbott School Districts Among the Top Spenders*, N.Y. TIMES,

June 10, 2007, §14NJ, at 7 (stating that "[t]he [Abbott] districts spent more money per student than most rich districts in New Jersey in 2004-5 . . ."). For example, during the 2004-2005 school year the per-pupil expenditure for elementary schools in Newark, an Abbott district, was approximately $20,482, compared to $16,080 in Princeton, one of New Jersey's wealthiest districts. Education Intelligence Agency, *Current Spending Statistics of Public Elementary-Secondary School Systems for 2004-05, District Rankings for New Jersey*, http://www.eiaonline.com/districts/NewJersey.pdf. This has occurred notwithstanding persistent recalcitrance and delay by the State, necessitating frequent return trips to the New Jersey Supreme Court on motions "in aid of litigants' rights."

67 The Education Law Center notes that this is because "[p]opulation characteristics and educational practices vary — from school to school and from district to district — as do achievement and other student outcomes." EDUCATION LAW CENTER, THE ABBOTT DISTRICTS IN 2005-06: PROGRESS AND CHALLENGES 6 (2006), http://www.edlawcenter.org/ELCPublic/Publications/PDF/AbbottIndicatorsReport_2005_06.pdf.

68 According to the Education Law Center, "[t]he achievement gap between children in the Abbott and non-Abbott districts is closing at Grade 4." *Id.* at 4. For 2004-2005, "[t]he percentage of general education students in Abbott elementary schools scoring at least proficient on the language arts literacy test" was seventy-seven percent, marking a fourteen percent increase from sixty-three percent in 2000-2001. *Id. See, e.g.*, Erica Harbatkin, *Rich, Poor Districts Still Show Testing Gap*, COURIER NEWS, Mar. 11, 2008, *available at* http://www.c-n.com/apps/pbcs.dll/article?AID=/20080215/NEWS/802150337/-1/NEWS06 (discussing sharp improvements in fourth and eighth grade test results in Perth Amboy, an Abbott District).

69 While only fifty-one percent of Asbury Park's general education fourth grade students scored at least proficient in mathematics, ninety percent of West New York fourth graders, ninety-one percent of Garfield fourth graders, and ninety-three percent of Union City fourth graders scored at least proficient in mathematics. EDUCATION LAW CENTER, *supra* note 65, at 6. Only fifteen percent of Trenton general education eighth graders scored at least proficient. In comparison, eighty-one percent of Union City and eighty-five percent of West New York eighth graders scored at least proficient in math. *Id.*

70 PAUL TRACTENBERG, DON'T FORGET THE SCHOOLS: FISCAL, BUDGET AND POLICY CONSIDERATIONS FOR TAX REFORM (2006), http://ielp.rutgers.edu/docs/DFTS1_web.pdf; *see also* Jon Corzine, Governor of New Jersey, State of the State Address (Jan. 8, 2008), *available at* http://www.nj.gov/sos2008/speech.html.

71 N.J. STAT. ANN. § 18A:7F-43 (West 2008). A broad-based coalition of education advocacy organizations expressed strong concerns about both the purpose of the statute and the lame-duck process used to push it through the

legislature:

Recently, Governor Corzine expressed his intent to have a school funding formula passed by the end of 2007. This would mean pushing it through a "lame duck" session after the November elections. The session would run from approximately November 7 to December 31, with Thanksgiving, Christmas, and Hanukah all intervening. On the Assembly and Senate Education Committees — the committees most likely to consider a new funding law — eight out of 15 members will be lame ducks themselves, either retiring, losing a primary, or relinquishing their seats to run for another office. Unless the plan is to simply push through a formula without deliberation, analysis, or public consideration, the prospects for passage of a credible statewide school funding formula by the end of the year appear very slim.

Advocates, school finance experts, and the media are voicing serious concern about what might emerge if the process of developing a formula is rushed. Instead they are calling for a thorough and deliberate consideration of any proposals.

New Cost Studies Expected to Reframe Debate On Funding Formula, OUR CHILDREN/OUR SCHOOLS (Educ. Law Ctr., N.J.) Oct. 1, 2007, at 1, *available at* http://www.ourchildrenourschools.org/Newsletters/nlf_iss11_ar2_detail.htm.

72 *See* Letter from Anne Milgram, Attorney General of New Jersey, to the Supreme Court of New Jersey (Jan. 14, 2008) (on file with author).

73 In his poem, Frost says, "Oh, I kept the first for another day! Yet knowing how way leads to way, I doubted if I should ever come back." ROBERT FROST, *The Road Not Taken*, MOUNTAIN INTERVAL (1920).

74 The Free Dictionary, http://www.thefreedictionary.com/efficient (last visited Apr. 18, 2008).

75 Answers.com, http://www.answers.com/topic/system (last visited Apr. 18, 2008).

76 Abbott v. Burke, 575 A.2d 359, 406 (N.J. 1990).

77 The State's argument, which failed to win over a single justice of the New Jersey Supreme Court, was augmented by the claim that the State would address the inefficiencies on a district-by-district basis, thereby securing a thorough and efficient education for all students. *Id.* at 390-91.

78 It is too well-established to discuss that education in New Jersey and every other state is ultimately a state function. That doesn't preclude, however, substantial tensions in many states between state responsibility and local discretion. A good example in New Jersey is the establishment of the Core Curriculum Content Standards (CCCS), successfully presented to the court as the State's educational definition of thorough education. In its dealings with school districts, the State stressed that CCCS was *not* a state curriculum, but only suggested curricular guidelines. STATE OF N.J. DEP'T OF EDUC., ACADEMIC & PROFESSIONAL STANDARDS, CURRICULUM AND INSTRUCTION: CCCS (2004), *available at* http://education.state.nj.us/cccs/?_intro (stating that

"[t]he New Jersey Core Curriculum Content Standards are not meant to serve as a statewide curriculum guide. Local school districts must use the standards to develop and/or align curriculum to ensure that students achieve the expectations"). Of course, the fact that CCCS is the basis for the State's student testing program does tend to blur the distinction between a state curriculum and curricular guidelines.

79 *See* REPORT OF THE STATE BOARD OF EDUCATION AND THE STATE SUPERINTENDENT OF PUBLIC INSTRUCTION FOR THE SCHOOL YEAR ENDING AUGUST 31, 5-6 (1875) (reporting to the Legislature that "[t]he experience of the year has afforded renewed proof of the general efficiency of our system of public instruction, and the organized educational effort of the State has been rewarded by a gratifying measure of success"); *see generally* Harriet Lipman Sepinwall, The History of the 1875 "Thorough and Efficient" Amendment to the New Jersey Constitution in the Context of Nineteenth Century on Social Thought on Education: The Civil War to the Centennial (1986) (unpublished Ed.D. dissertation, Rutgers University) (on file with the Rutgers School of Law-Newark Law Library).

80 Robinson v. Cahill, 355 A.2d 129, 133 (N.J. 1976) ("[W]hat seems sufficient today may be proved inadequate tomorrow, and even more importantly that only in the light of experience can one ever come to know whether a particular program is achieving the desired end."); Abbott v. Burke, 575 A.2d 359, 367 (N.J. 1990) ("[W]hat a thorough and efficient education consists of is a continually changing concept.").

81 This includes Maryland, Ohio, Pennsylvania and West Virginia. Kindle Merrell, *Constitutional Language: State Obligations for Public School Funding*, STATENOTES (Educ. Comm'n of the States), Aug. 2002, http://www.ecs.org/clearinghouse/38/62/3862.pdf. Many other state education clauses use the words "thorough' or "efficient," but not both, either alone or more commonly in combination with other words such as "general" or "uniform." *See* Molly McUsic, *The Use of Education Clauses in Public School Finance Reform Litigation*, 28 HARV. J. ON LEGIS. 307 (1991); William E. Thro, Note, *To Render Them Safe: The Analysis of State Constitutional Provisions in Public School Finance Reform Litigation*, 75 VA. L. REV. 1639 (1989). In my more detailed follow-up article, I will investigate the meanings attributed to those other similar state constitutional formulations for their possible relevance to New Jersey's phraseology.

82 Danson v. Casey, 399 A.2d 360, 366 (Pa. 1979). *See* Teachers' Tenure Act Cases, 197 A. 344, 352 (Pa. 1938) ("[E]verything directly related to the maintenance of a 'thorough and efficient system of public schools,' must at all times be subject to future legislative control.").

83 Pauley v. Kelly, 255 S.E.2d 859, 876 (W. Va. 1979).

84 *Id.* at 874 (quoting WEBSTER'S THIRD NEW INTERNATIONAL DICTIONARY, UNABRIDGED (1976) (alterations in original)).

85 "An efficient system could not mean one in which part or any number of the

school districts of the state lacked teachers, buildings or equipment." Miller v. Korns, 140 N.E. 773, 776 (Ohio 1923).

86 This includes Illinois, Kentucky, and Texas. Kindle Merrell, *Constitutional Language: State Obligations for Public School Funding*, STATENOTES (Educ. Comm'n of the States), Aug. 2002, http://www.ecs.org/clearinghouse/38/62/3862.pdf.

87 790 S.W.2d 186 (Ky. 1989).

88 In *State Board for Elementary & Secondary Education v. Howard*, 834 S.W.2d 657, 664 (Ky. 1992), the Kentucky Supreme Court interpreted "efficiency" in its school system to mean that schools would be "operated with no waste, no duplication, no mismanagement and no political influence."

89 *Rose*, 790 S.W.2d at 191-92.

90 *Id.* at 206.

91 *Id.* at 211.

92 *Id.* at 212-13.

93 The court twice, and the legislature once, mandated that the state education department conduct a "particularized needs assessment." The department simply never did it, and, eventually, the court assigned the responsibility to the special needs districts themselves. *See* N.J. ADMIN. CODE. §§ 6A:24-5.1, :24-5.2 (2005). More recently, the department has failed to comply with the court's order, and its own regulations, regarding an evaluation of Abbott programs. *See* Press Release, Educ. Law Ctr., ELC Files Suit to Compel State to Evaluate Abbott and Set Progress Benchmarks (July 10, 2007), *available at* http://www.edlawcenter.org/ELCPublic/elcnews_070710_StateSuedToEvaluateAbbott.htm.

94 Robinson v. Cahill, 355 A.2d 129, 133 (N.J. 1976) (quoting N.J. STAT. ANN. § 18A:7A-5 (West 1995) (repealed 1996)).

95 693 A.2d 493, 428-29.

96 N.J. STAT. ANN. §§ 18A:7A-1 to -60 (West 2008).

97 1970 N.J. Sess. Law Serv. ch. 234 (West).

98 N.J. STAT. ANN. 18A:7D-1 to -37 (West 1995) (repealed 1996).

99 N.J. STAT. ANN. §§ 18A:7F-1 to -63 (West 2007).

100 *Id.* § 18A:7F-43.

101 *Id.* §§ 18A:7B-1 to -13.

102 *Id.* §§ 18A:7C-1 to -12.

103 The reference to "Efficiency Programs" is tantalizing, but ultimately disappointing. The four relevant statutory sections contained some broad language about "efficient operation of public institutions" and "efficient spending practices in school districts," but wound up dealing only with spending above the level of "budgeted per pupil administrative spending" in particular districts relative to the median budgeted per pupil administrative

spending in like districts, imposing penalties for "excessive" administrative spending and rewards for low administrative spending. In any event, those provisions were repealed within about a year after wealthy and high-spending suburban districts ratcheted up the political pressure. N.J. STAT. ANN. §§ 18A:7E-7 to -8 (West 1995) (repealed 1996).

104 N.J. STAT. ANN. § 18A:7F-46(a) (West 2007).

105 N.J. STAT. ANN. § 18A:7F-4(d) (West 2005). Actually, the Commission on Business Efficiency in the Public Schools was created by a statute that became effective on April 10, 1979 and remains in effect. Under that statute, the Commission's charge was "to develop and implement a 5-year plan to monitor the implementation of recommendations of the task force on business efficiency and to recommend to the Legislature such statutory changes as may become necessary to facilitate improvements in the business efficiency of the public schools." N.J. STAT. ANN. §§ 52:9T-2, -4 (West 2007).

106 N.J. STAT. ANN. §§ 18A:7-8 (West 2007).

107 N.J. STAT. ANN. § 18A:7-13 (West 2007). New Jersey has twenty-one counties and each now has an executive county superintendent. These statutory provisions suggest the difficulty of drawing a precise line between local and state-level efficiency matters. The executive county superintendents are based in the counties and have regional responsibilities, but they form part of the state system of educational administration. Many of their new functions address local district efficiency, but from a state or regional perspective.

108 N.J. STAT. ANN. § 18A:7-8(d) (West 2007).

109 *Id.* § 18A:7-8(e).

110 *Id.* § 18A:7-8(g). New Jersey has twenty-three "non-operating" districts. They literally operate no schools, but exist as separate districts, and eliminating them has proven to be politically volatile, if not suicidal. *See, e.g.*, Laura Mansnerus, *To Control Property Taxes, Cut Spending, McGreevey Tells Mayors*, N.Y. TIMES, January 22, 2004; Tara Petersen, *Helmetta Scoffs at Consolidation, Mayor: Governor Should Focus on Solving State's Education-Funding Woes*, SENTINEL, Jan. 22, 2004, *available at* http://ebs.gmnews.com/News/2004/0122/Front_Page/001.html.

111 N.J. STAT. ANN. § 18A:7-8(h) (West 2007). This is subject not only to the commissioner's approval, but also to a favorable vote by local voters. If the voters do not approve, the statute makes no provision for an override and, presumably, the consolidation plan is not implemented. Given the affinity of many New Jersey residents to home-rule and local control, that is a quite conceivable result in many counties.

112 *Id.* § 18A:7-8(i).

113 *Id.* § 18A:7-8(l).

114 *Id.* § 18A:7-8(m).

115 *Id.* § 18A:7-8(n).

116 *Id.* §§ 18A:7-8(o) to (v).

117 By October 2007, only ten executive county superintendents had been nominated. At that time, the search to fill the remaining positions was still "ongoing." *See* Press Release, Governor's Press Office, Governor to Nominate 10 Executive County Superintendents (Oct. 22, 2007), *available at* http://politickernj.com/governor-nominate-10-executive-county-superintendents-13052; Posting of Ray Pinney to NJSBA BoardBlog, http://www.njsba.org/blog/?p=42 (Jan. 29, 2008, 16:35 EST).

118 N.J. STAT. ANN. § 18A:7A-10 (West 2008); N.J. ADMIN. CODE § 6A:30-1.1 (2008). Showing disdain for trendy or catchy acronyms, the system is referred to as "kew-sack." At a joint presentation with former commissioner William Librera, I indicated that the statutory system probably should have been the Single Quality Accountability Continuum, but then it would have been called "ess-quack."

119 N.J. ADMIN. CODE § 6A:30-1.1 (2008). Under the prior statute, N.J. STAT. ANN. § 18A:7A-15 (West 1995) (repealed 1996), the nation's first to provide for state takeover, intervention used to be called state operation. For a critique of that law, largely focusing on its failure to address local capacity, see INST. ON EDUC. LAW & POLICY, DEVELOPING A PLAN FOR REESTABLISHING LOCAL CONTROL IN THE STATE-OPERATED SCHOOL DISTRICTS (2002), *available at* http://ielp.rutgers.edu/docs/developing_plan_full.pdf. Although NJQSAC is, to some extent, derived from IELP's recommendations, it departed from them in many important respects. New Jersey's three largest school districts — Newark, Jersey City, and Paterson — continue to be under state operation after many years (Jersey City since 1989, Paterson since 1991, and Newark since 1995).

120 INST. ON EDUC. LAW & POLICY, NEW JERSEY QUALITY SINGLE ACCOUNTABILITY CONTINUUM (QSAC): 2006 PILOT PROGRAM EVALUATION 10-29 (2006), *available at* http://ielp.rutgers.edu/docs/QSAC_report_final.pdf.

121 *Id.* at 42-43; *see* KPMG, NEW JERSEY DEPARTMENT OF EDUCATION PERFORMANCE AUDIT 6-8 (2007), *available at* http://www.nj.gov/education/genfo/audit/performance_audit_s1_s5.pdf. The report noted that staffing levels at the Department of Education were inadequate to implement QSAC; the process for implementation lacked formality; training and assistance were not provided; and the DOE was in a general state of confusion as to the interpretation of the QSAC legislation.

122 With the benefit of hindsight, the ten statutory elements of a thorough and efficient education listed in *Robinson* constituted a surprisingly good effort. Robinson v. Cahill, 355 A.2d 129, 132-33 (N.J. 1976); N.J. STAT. ANN. § 18A:7A-5 (West 1995) (repealed 1996).

123 *See, e.g.*, KPMG, *supra* note 119; PHILIP E. MACKEY, INST. ON EDUC. LAW & POLICY, USING NATIONAL BEST PRACTICES TO IMPROVE NEW JERSEY'S MANAGEMENT OF EDUCATION DATA (2002), http://ielp.rutgers.edu/docs/bestpractices.pdf.

124 I suppose that, if I were really inclined toward theory, I wouldn't even care about the real world effect of my theoretical insights. But, I've always lived in fear of being like the proverbial economist who blurted out, "well, it may work in practice, but it can't possibly work in theory."

125 *See, e.g.*, William A. Fischel et al., *The Courts and Public School Finance: Judge-Made Centralization and Economic Research*, Nov. 1, 2003, *available at* http://papers.ssrn.com/sol3/papers.cfm?abstract_id=589562 (stating that school finance litigation has a significant impact regardless of whether the litigation was successful or not).

126 Any of the myriad ways in which the State's public schools lack an organized structure, functional relationships, interdependency, harmonious and orderly interaction, and unity could be singled out for challenge, whether they relate to administrative, management, or educational functions.

127 *See generally* ALAN J. KARCHER, MULTIPLE MUNICIPAL MADNESS (1999). Karcher was a prominent New Jerseyan, having served as Speaker of the State Assembly, so his criticism of the State's governmental structure deserves to be given great weight.

128 Eli Hiller, *SOAPBOX; Saving New Jersey $10 Billion a Year*, N.Y. TIMES, Nov. 23, 2003, § 14NJ, at 15 (stating that "New Jersey, the most urbanized state in the nation, has 1,635 units of local government — counties, municipalities, school districts, local public authorities and special taxing districts. Per square mile, no other state has fractured itself into as many pieces.").

129 The Tax Foundation, *State and Local Property Tax Collections Per Household and Per Capita by State, Fiscal Year 2005*, Feb. 6, 2008, http://www.taxfoundation.org/taxdata/show/251.html.

130 At a recent legislative hearing, a legislator asked the commissioner of education how many school districts there were in New Jersey. After conferring with an aide, the commissioner said she wasn't certain, but would check and get back to the legislator. According to the N.J. Department of Education's website, there are 593 operating, and twenty-three non-operating, school districts, for a total of 616. N.J. Dep't of Educ., *New Jersey Public Schools Fact Sheet* (2006), http://www.state.nj.us/education/data/fact.htm. According to the New Jersey School Boards Association, for the 2005-2006 school year, there were 580 operating, and twenty-three non-operating, school districts, for a total of 603, but fourteen "other education units," for a grand total of 617. N.J. Sch. Bds. Ass'n, *New Jersey Public School Statistics*, http://www.njsba.org/PI/facts/bmr30-43.pdf.

131 N.J. Dep't of Educ., *New Jersey Public Schools Fact Sheet* (2006), http://www.state.nj.us/education/data/fact.htm.

132 Ernest C. Reock, Jr., *Possible Cost Savings if Proposed Consolidated K-12 School Districts Budgeted as Existing Unchanged K-12 School Districts* (Feb. 9, 2007), *available at* http://www.lwvnj.org/news/School_District_Cluster_Paper.pdf.

133 *See id.* ("If the proposed new consolidated districts were to provide educational services at the same statewide cost level as the existing K-12 districts, there

could be substantial savings."). The savings might not be as great as imagined, though. Professor Ernest Reock's paper on the savings to be realized from school district consolidation suggests that they are substantial, but not overwhelming. *See also* Ernest C. Reock, Jr., *The Cost Impact of School District Creation and Consolidation in New Jersey* (Ctr. for Gov't Servs., Rutgers, The State Univ. of N.J., Occasional Paper No. 3, March 1995); Ernest C. Reock, Jr., *A Plan for School District Consolidation in New Jersey* (Ctr. for Gov't Srvs., Rutgers, The State Univ. of N.J., Occasional Paper No. 4, July 1995).

134 New Jersey has the nation's strongest laws requiring racial balance in the public schools. It is one of two states with an explicit state constitutional provision barring segregation in the public schools. N.J. CONST. art. I, ¶ 5. Pursuant to decisions of the state supreme court, New Jersey has eliminated both the distinction between de jure and de facto segregation, *Booker v. Board of Education of Plainfield*, 212 A.2d 1, 6 (N.J. 1965); and the inhibiting effect of school district lines on racial balance remedies. Jenkins v. Morris Sch. Dist., 279 A.2d 619 (N.J. 1971). Nonetheless, New Jersey's record on the ground is abysmal. Its public schools have been consistently ranked as among the nation's most segregated. G. ORFIELD & C. M. LEE, HARVARD CIVIL RIGHTS PROJECT, BROWN AT FIFTY (2004). In 2004, the then Chief Justice of the New Jersey Supreme Court wrote in an opinion that "[w]e have paid lip service to the idea of diversity in our schools, but in the real world we have not succeeded." *In re* Petition for Authorization to Conduct a Referendum on the Withdrawal of N. Haledon Sch. Dist. from the Passaic County Manchester Reg'l High Sch. Dist., 854 A.2d 327, 338 (N.J. 2004). Ironically, the opinion was in a case seeking to de-regionalize school districts.

135 CHRIS PATTERSON, TEXAS PUBLIC POLICY FOUNDATION, SCHOOL DISTRICT CONSOLIDATION AND PUBLIC SCHOOL EFFICIENCY: WHAT DOES THE RESEARCH SAY? (2006), *available at* http://www.texaspolicy.com/pdf/2006-02-PP-consolidation-cp.pdf (citing Paul E. Peterson and John E. Chubb, *Consolidate Districts, Not Schools, in Reforming Education in Arkansas: Recommendations from the Koret Task Force* (2005)).

136 A number of major national foundations — headed by the largest of all, the Gates Foundation — have invested hundreds of millions of dollars in small schools, especially at the high school level. This reflects, or perhaps has caused, a swing of the education reform pendulum away from the view of the 1980s and early 1990s that to meet contemporary needs high schools had to be comprehensive and quite large — in the range of 1500 to 2000 pupils.

137 Filing a separate law suit might raise some procedural issues, however. The state defendants might move to consolidate such a new case with the ongoing school funding litigation since they arise from the same state constitutional provision, albeit with an emphasis on different words and concepts. Alternatively, the state defendants might seek to have the new action dismissed on the theory that the "efficient system" issues could have been raised in the ongoing litigation. These possibilities will be discussed in my future article, which will delve much more deeply into all aspects of a constitutional challenge focusing on efficiency.

14 Mississippi Education Stuck at the Bottom: A Good Case For A New Frontier In Adequacy Funding Litigation?

by John C. Brittain, Michelle L. Woolley and Michele Keegan

Introduction

This short article describes a process for a civil rights legal organization to investigate conditions of inadequate educational opportunities in the very poor deep southern state of Mississippi. With a history of more than a half-century in the pursuit for educational equity, lawyers, working in close cooperation with advocates for educational reform, have learned to follow best practices in developing what might become a major civil rights case. Following in the foot steps of Charles Hamilton Houston, the intellectual father of the *Brown v. Board of Education*[1] landmark decision, the investigation begins with an assessment of educational conditions. Houston said, "A lawyer is either a social engineer or a parasite to society."[2] While Mississippi ranks near the worst in every statistical category that measures education in grades K-12, the law must support any contemplated legal action with a gambler's handicap determined by lawyers' seven in ten chances of success.

While many other articles in the book describe school finance and education adequacy cases in court, this article explains the pre-litigation process of making a case in Mississippi. The sections that follow in the article trace the history of efforts to increase funding for education in Mississippi; describe the dire need for educational reform in the state; analyze the weaknesses in the Mississippi State Constitution's education clause and ways to interpret a stronger fundamental right to education; review adequacy funding suits in other states; and finally, describe the lessons learned in education adequacy cases. While an educational adequacy or equal financing suit may not be ripe now, advocates and lawyers have constructed a solid foundation upon which to build such a case in the future.

History of Investigating Adequacy of Education in Mississippi

In 2005, after years of research and discussion, a coalition of organizations came close to initiating litigation seeking to fully-fund the Mississippi Adequate Education Program (MAEP), given the state's refusal to provide the complete funding called for by the MAEP formula since the law took full effect in 1997. Just as Hurricane Katrina struck Mississippi causing catastrophic destruction on the Gulf Coast and disruption throughout the state, the storm also forced the coalition to postpone any contemplated legal action out of deference to the state's emergency recovery efforts.

By the time the state started on the road toward recovery after the storm, the legislature and governor finally authorized full funding of MAEP in the spring of 2007. This action, along with an increased commitment to full-funding in future years by elected officials, effectively negated much of the preliminary research and strategizing done prior to Katrina. These developments have given advocates further reason to pause in going forward with litigation.

Mississippi Education — Many Children Left Behind

Mississippi has the highest poverty rate in the country and ranks only above post-Hurricane Katrina Louisiana for lowest per capita income in the nation.[3] Not surprisingly, Mississippi has the second-highest proportion of low-income students in its public schools with seventy-five percent of students deemed low-income.[4] Mississippi has consistently ranked near the top of the rankings for child poverty since the Census Bureau began tracking such data[5]. According to a study by the Southern Education Foundation, much of the lack of economic mobility for Mississippi's residents can be directly attributed to the lower quality of education provided in the state.[6]

Close to 5000,000 students currently attend Mississippi's public K-12 schools, and more than two-thirds of those students qualify for free or reduced-price lunches.[7] Statistics show that these poor children perform drastically below their higher-income peers. On the most recent National Assessment of Educational Progress (NAEP) fourth grade reading assessments, low-income Mississippi students scored 25 points below their wealthier peers on average.[8] This achievement gap remains virtually the same when looking at eighth grade reading test results, and scores in mathematics reflect a similar gap.[9] Overall, the state has not made significant progress in increasing NAEP reading scores since 1998.[10]

A significant achievement gap also exists along racial lines. African-American students, who make-up more than half the students in Mississippi's public schools, lag behind white students by an average of 27 points in reading proficiency in fourth grade. The gap only narrows two points by eighth grade.[11] Math scores show that in fourth grade, African Americans score on average 22 points lower than their white peers, while for eighth grade students the gap grows to a 28 point difference.[12] While Mississippi's education gap between white and black students is narrower than a few other states, this statistic offers little comfort because both groups of students perform near the bottom nationally, whether compared by grade or subject area.[13]

Moreover, and no doubt related to the quality of education, only 59 out of 100 ninth grade students in Mississippi are expected to graduate from high school.[14] The dropout statistics are significantly higher for male African-American and Hispanic students, less than half of whom graduated from high school in 2003.[15] Those who do graduate from high school are not as well-prepared for post-secondary education as other students across the country. In 2005, while the national average for graduating seniors taking at least one Advanced Placement (AP) exam was 23 percent, only nine percent of Mississippi's graduating seniors did so.[16]

The "bottom-of-the-barrel" student performance levels in Mississippi correlates with public education funding — the state ranks 49th fin the country on per pupil expenditures. In 2003, the highest per pupil expenditure in the state was $6300 and the lowest per pupil expenditure was below $4600.[17] To give those numbers perspective, in the 1999 – 2000 school year, the highest expenditure in a Mississippi school district was still less than the lowest per pupil expenditures in 22 states.[18] A mere three percent of Mississippi's students attend school districts where the per pupil expenditure is at or above the national average.[19] While the state has made improvements in education funding in the last year — see the discussion of Mississippi Adequate Education Program funding below — it still has not caught-up with the rest of the country. In Governor Haley Barbour's January

21, 2008 "State of the State Address," he noted that federal, state, and local funds now amount to $8600 being spent on each pupil during the school year.[20] Yet many of the states Mississippi was trailing behind in the 1999-2000 school year were providing higher funding eight years ago than what Mississippi is providing now.[21]

Legal Research — Public Education in Mississippi

Constitutional Guarantees for Public Education

Although Mississippi's state constitution contains a provision guaranteeing free public schools, the text of the provision appears to grant to the legislature substantial, if not complete, discretion on how to fund and operate public schools. Article 8, Section 201 of Mississippi's state constitution provides that, "The Legislature shall, by general law, provide for the establishment, maintenance and support of free public schools upon such conditions and limitations as the Legislature may prescribe."[22] The wording of this provision is more deferential than in other states where constitutions assert that education should be "thorough and efficient" or "general, suitable, and efficient."[23] Even in such states where the education provisions provide more substantive standards, not all courts have recognized such provisions as a basis for challenging the adequacy of public education.[24] Alternatively, some advocates have used a combination of the education provision and state constitution equal protection clauses as the basis for education adequacy suits; however, this option is not available in Mississippi since its constitution does not include an equal protection clause. Viewed in this context, there is probably a more ideal legal basis for challenging the adequacy of education in the state.

There is a possibility that the constitution could be a legitimate basis for an adequacy suit based on a case in 1985 where the Supreme

Court of Mississippi characterized public education as a "fundamental right."[25] In its opinion the Court noted that the legislature declared "quality" public education to be a matter of public policy.[26] The legislature reasoned that public education ought to prepare each student to "take his or her place in society" and to make a contribution to the state.[27] If public education is a fundamental right, this may dilute the perception that the legislature has complete discretion to manage public education without review, as interference with a fundamental right is subject to strict scrutiny upon judicial review. Whether or not that characterization would be upheld in an adequacy suit is uncertain.[28]

Additionally, and of potential legal consequence, is that in 1960, after the Supreme Court's decision in *Brown v. Board of Education*, the education provision in Mississippi's state constitution was amended and became dramatically more deferential to the legislature.[29] Before this, the education provision was amended last in 1890 and provided that:

> It shall be the duty of the legislature to encourage by all suitable means, the promotion of intellectual, scientific, moral and agricultural improvement, by establishing a uniform system of free public schools, by taxation, or otherwise...[30]

The contrast between the 1890 and the current version of Article 8, Section 201 illustrates a deliberate change from language favorable to judicial review to language that is not very favorable to review, due to its emphasis on legislative discretion. The fact that the most recent version was enacted in response to *Brown v. Board of Education*, and initially granted the legislature the power to abolish public schools,[31] suggests the provision likely was adopted for racial discrimination purposes — in order to avoid desegregation. The text and evolution of the education provision in Mississippi's constitution may provide advocates with both challenges and unique opportunities to use it as a basis for challenging the adequacy of public education in Mississippi.

Mississippi's Costing-Out Study for Funding Public Education

One of the most controversial and time-consuming elements of adequacy cases is the "costing-out" phase. This phase determines what financial resources are needed in order to meet the constitutional and statutory educational standards. Typically, such studies occur when a court determines the state is not meeting its constitutional requirements for public education and then directs the legislature to calculate the cost of meeting its requirements. A unique aspect in Mississippi is that the legislature effectively calculated a costing out formula when it enacted the Mississippi Adequate Education Program in 1994.[32]

State courts and legislatures have used a variety of methodologies in conducting costing-out studies. In MAEP, the legislature defined adequate funding as what is necessary for school programs to meet at least Level III of the accreditation system established by the State Board of Education, and is funded through a combination of state funds and local school district funds capped at 27% of program cost.[33] Although MAEP was passed in 1994, the legislature did not institute the funding scheme until three years later, when the legislature overrode Governor Kirk Fordice's veto in a special one-day session on April 23, 1997.[34] While the passage of MAEP was met with widespread approval of varied interest and citizen groups, the law does not remedy all funding equity issues. For instance, the MAEP formula is based on the cost of educating a "regular" child; it does not address equalizing funding for students considered "at-risk" or that have special, vocational, or gifted education needs. Moreover, it also excludes funding for transportation, classroom supplies, and school facilities from the equalization formula.

The enthusiasm for what was hailed as a big breakthrough in public education in Mississippi quieted to a murmur of frustration with the inconsistent funding of MAEP. Full-funding of the law was scheduled to be phased-in over a six year period ending in 2003. With 2003 being an election year and with projections for increased state revenues, there was widespread funding support. The funding bill passed unanimously through the Senate and 115 to 4 in the House, and came within $11 million of the full funding calculated by the formula.[35] The following week Governor Musgrove signed the funding bill into law.[36] However, in 2004, reportedly with pressure from new Governor Haley Barbour, the legislature under-funded MAEP and pushed a greater share of the funding to local taxpayers by directing local districts to use their maintenance reserve funds to offset state revenue shortfalls.[37] The legislature did not fully fund MAEP again until 2007, again an election year.[38] In the 2007 gubernatorial elections both major candidates promised to fully fund MAEP, signifying the importance of education finance to voters in Mississippi.[39]

The consistency with which the legislature funds MAEP in the coming years may impact the methodologies and strategy of advocates in Mississippi seeking to ensure an adequate public education to all students. While a majority of state legislators, the governor, and lieutenant governor have expressed a desire to fully fund MAEP during the 2008 legislative session, concerns over a tighter state budget related to the national economic downturn may interfere with funding promises made on the campaign trail.[40]

A Review of Fiscal Adequacy Lawsuits

Advocates in Mississippi may benefit from looking at the procedural and substantive hurdles encountered by advocates involved in adequacy suits in other states. While dodging pitfalls encountered in other states, advocates in Mississippi can simultaneously take the lead in advocating the inclusion of diversity and racial integration as a necessary component of an adequate education, a component which has not been actively pursued by advocates in other states.

A. Catch 22 — Granting a Motion to Strike Based on a Lack of Evidence Before Evidence Could be Amassed and Presented

Although the legislature in Mississippi enacted MAEP purportedly to adequately fund public education in the state, the enactment itself does not absolve the judiciary of its duty to ensure that the legislative branch is fulfilling its constitutional obligations. Courts throughout the country have recognized the involvement of the judiciary in determining whether the standard of public education meets the constitutional requirements as proper and not as an intrusion into the rights and duties of other branches of government.[41]

Although most state courts have found a challenge to public education funding systems to be justiciable,[42] a handful of state courts found the question to be nonjusticiable and thus never reached the merits of the case.[43] Recently a trial court in Connecticut granted the defendant's motion to strike and declared the question of whether the state was meeting its constitutional requirements in providing an adequate education to be justiciable, but still highlighted justiciability concerns in ruling that the right to an adequate education does not exist as a matter of law. The court rationalized that judicial involvement would be an "intrusion… into the constitutional prerogatives" of other branches of government.[44] This ruling was ironic because state law instructs that a determination of the contours of the state constitution be based on an inquiry that requires a "broad, fact-intensive evidentiary record,"[45] and yet the court dismissed the case before such an evidentiary record could be produced. If the Connecticut Supreme Court affirms the ruling of the lower court, plaintiffs will essentially be compelled to bear a significant evidentiary burden in the pleadings in order to survive a motion to strike.

Ultimately, the Connecticut trial court made a determination on the contours of the constitutional principle on education during the pleadings stage. Anticipating the possibility that the courts in Mississippi may be tempted to make a similar, yet unusual ruling at the pleadings stage, advocates may strategically decide to pre-empt this procedural hurdle by including data and other supporting information in the complaint to support their interpretation of the contours of the constitution's education clause.

B. Substantive Hurdle — Articulating Qualitative Standards

As discussed previously, Mississippi's state constitution does have an education clause. Although the text of the clause does not articulate the standards for public education in Mississippi, that does not preclude a finding of minimum qualitative standards. In fact, the highest courts of 18 states have found a minimum qualitative standard in the state's education clause.[46] Further, all 18 states found that the right to education must not only contain minimum qualitative standards, but additionally that those standards serve particular purposes, such as for preparation for civic participation and employment.[47] Interestingly, no court has held that the right to education does not include a minimum qualitative standard.[48] Therefore, it would be unprecedented if

Mississippi's courts were to find that there are no qualitative standards for public education in its state.

C. Diversity and Integration as Components of an Adequate Education

A discussion to determine what constitutes an "adequate" education is not complete without considering the value of diversity and racial integration in public school classrooms. Although the days of state-mandated segregation are long gone, the fact is that public schools are re-segregating and there are an increasing number of intensely racially isolated schools. The *Civil Rights Project* at the University of California at Los Angeles found that public schools have been gradually re-segregating for two decades and are now experiencing accelerating isolation.[49] Mississippi ranked as one of the most segregated states for African-American students in 2005-06.[50]

Addressing racial integration and diversity in public schools has become more complicated since the Supreme Court's decision in *Parents Involved in Community Schools v. Seattle School District*.[51] Regrettably in *Parents Involved in Community Schools*, the Supreme Court narrowed the ability of communities to voluntarily use race-conscious school assignment plans. The Supreme Court held that using race in determining school assignment plans is permissible if there is *de jure* segregation, but not necessarily if the racial segregation is *de facto*, yet the impacts of segregation do not adhere to the boundaries of the Court's legal formalism. In light of the decision in *Parents Involved in Community Schools*, many advocates and commentators urged states to integrate schools by household income as a way to enhance diversity in schools, and possibly to serve as a proxy for racial integration. That logic is flawed because while race and income do overlap at times, often they do not. Relying solely on economic integration can result in the continued or increased segregation of schools.[52] Another common antidote put forth to combat the re-segregation of schools is choice assignment plans. Without discrediting the value of choice assignment plans, research shows that "uncontrolled or managed" choice assignment plans that do not consider race as a factor tend to result in greater segregation or more racially homogenous schools.[53]

We propose that like diversity itself, a multi-dimensional concept, advocates in Mississippi and other states consider adopting a multifactor approach to school assignment plans. These plans should take into consideration a variety of socioeconomic factors, the level of social capital students have access to, and race, which together are likely to result in more diverse and racially integrated schools.[54] Importantly, such multifactor assignment plans are likely to comport with Justice Kennedy's framework articulated in his concurrence in *Parents Involved in Community Schools* for using race in school assignment plans.[55]

The need for diverse and racially integrated schools is critical, as it imparts significant individual and societal benefits. These benefits are so significant that a majority of the justices on the Supreme Court have recognized diversity as a compelling state interest.[56] Studies have determined that integrated education fosters significant societal benefits,[57] including reducing racial prejudices, enhancing students' ability to interact well with others in a multiracial setting,[58] and increasing the likelihood that all students will attend desegregated colleges, live in desegregated neighborhoods, and work in a desegregated environment.[59] Some studies have also found that integrated schools result in increased academic achievement, especially for minority students.[60] A review by the Lawyers' Committee of the data for two states, New Jersey and Maryland, showed that increased funding from adequacy suits does not uniformly result in narrowing the racial achievement gap. Rather, these preliminary results show that student achievement was greater in schools that both received increased funding and were racially integrated than in schools that received increased funding but were racially isolated. That result suggests that racial integration may aid student achievement while simultaneously promoting important social and civic goals.

The Supreme Court acknowledged that public schools can impart these societal benefits when it declared that they "are an important socializing institution, imparting those shared values through which social order and stability are maintained."[61] In addition to general societal benefits, businesses have spoken out on the benefits of integrated schools. For instance, media and telecommunication companies filed a brief in support of the respondents in *Parents Involved in Community Schools* asserting that it is "vitally important" to their business "that there be a well-educated, diverse pool of potential employees who have not learned the racial biases that are fostered in segregated schools and who have instead learned the skills of valuing and communicating with people of different backgrounds and skin colors."[62] The brief likened the development of cross-cultural communication skills and tolerance to learning a new language, both being easier to learn when a person is young.[63]

Lessons Learned

An educational reform project to ensure a state fulfills its constitutional obligation to provide an adequate and suitable educational system is only as good as the support from educational advocates, beneficiaries of the reform, key legislative leaders, and the broader public. To garner the level of support, a legal organization must spend quality time building a consensus for a legislative, legal, and public advocacy strategy.

Prior to determining a strategy, litigators should reach out to organizations within the state with an interest in education, including government, grassroots, legal, business, and non-profit advocacy entities. These local experts can provide historical context — political, legal, and social — for educational disparities in the state. Knowing the root of the deficiencies and past efforts to correct them helps in determining what strategy is best to pursue in the present. Talking to a broad group of advocates can also help pinpoint what adequacy issues are most widespread or severe, and thus most need attention. Moreover, having a coalition that supports the litigation can mean having grassroots-based advocacy efforts that will appeal to the public's sense of justice, but it can also mean having a group of committed individuals who will pressure the governor and executive agencies to enforce any positive judgments. Finally, it is important not to just litigate a case but also to truly understand the community that litigation will impact. Legal and communication errors that can defeat a case before it has even begun can be made when attorneys do not do the necessary groundwork. Therefore, legal organizations and advocates for educational reform should continually assess the needs and strategic legal considerations within the state.

In line with assessing legal strategy, the Mississippi adequacy project recently took a very useful detour north to Connecticut to participate in filing an amicus brief concerning the role of the courts in defining the scope of the education clause in the state constitution. This experience in Connecticut enabled the Mississippi project to distinguish a weak from a strong education clause in state constitutions for purposes of commencing an educational adequacy lawsuit. While Mississippi's education clause in its constitution appears weak in defining an adequate education, the legislative history contains strong evidence that race motivated the change in the constitution in 1960 to avoid the command of *Brown v. Broad of Education* to dismantle, root and branch, the vestiges of the dual system of education based upon race. One could argue the old equity maximum that a party should not profit from its wrongdoing. In addition, a Mississippi State Supreme Court opinion offers a stronger interpretation of the Mississippi Constitution as ensuring a fundamental right to an education, which may include the concept of adequacy.

Thus, if the Mississippi coalition decides to take legal action, the Connecticut amici brief experience and research taught a valuable lesson to survive initial pleadings problems. The complaint should read like a sociological brief, with more data that would allow a judge to observe that inadequacy does in fact exist. This evidence would further support that there is a justiciable case and not a political question.

Another lesson learned was timing. Two events have altered the timing for possible litigation for adequacy of education in Mississippi. First, Hurricanes Katrina and Rita in 2005 postponed any legal action, and then the legislature and the governor fully funding MAEP in 2007. Both events required a period of time to evaluate the impact on the adequacy investigation before proceeding further. The educational advocates in Mississippi will wait until the 2008 State Legislature and governor complete the funding for MAEP to re-evaluate its direction and strategy.

Conclusion

None of the education advocates involved in plotting litigation strategy in Mississippi are ready to go forward with a lawsuit quite yet, but the work done over the course of the year by IFEEO Fellow Michelle Woolley and others will make a case ready to go when the timing is ripe.

Through support from the Institute for Educational Equity & Opportunity legal fellowship and research funding for this chapter, the foundation has been laid for an appropriate kind of educational reform effort in the near future. As the title of this article suggests, Mississippi is stuck at the bottom of educational indicators. Therefore, it is not a question of whether, but when and how, the next major educational reform initiative in the state will occur. Just as civil rights litigation and legislation killed Jim Crow segregation in the twentieth century, the same fundamental strategies combined with community-based support are essential to achieve adequacy in education for the schoolchildren in the State of Mississippi in this new millennium. A series of smaller suits paved the way for *Brown* to defeat the separate but equal doctrine with attacks on equal pay between black and white teachers and access to professional and graduate schools for African Americans. So too, the next educational reform movement in Mississippi may select discrete issues for litigation to further test the state constitutional right to a fundamental education before launching a full scale attack on the adequacy of the state's educational system.

For words of inspiration in what often appears as a bleak future at times for educational reform in Mississippi, we leave the reader with a quote by the veteran Congressman John Lewis from the Fifth Congressional District of Georgia in Atlanta and former Chairman of the Student Non-Violent Coordinating Committee (SNCC) during the Civil Rights Movement of the 1960s. He said:

> No matter what the present mood in Washington [or

> Mississippi] is like, no matter what the people who are setting policy today believe, or want us to believe, no matter what the sense of temporary hopelessness that many of us often feel, we cannot give up on the struggle we began and on the dream that brought us here. You cannot give up. We cannot give up. As a nation, as a people, I don't think we have any choice, but to reject this acquiescence, to reject defeat." [emphasis added in brackets][64]

Biographies

John C. Brittain is the Chief Counsel and Senior Deputy Directory of the Lawyers' Committee for Civil Rights Under Law. **Michelle L. Woolley** is the Institute for Educational Equity & Opportunity (IFEEO) Fellow (2007-2008) and Associate Counsel, Educational Opportunities Project at the Lawyers' Committee for Civil Rights. **Michele Keegan** provided invaluable research and writing assistance as a third year student at American University, Washington College of Law.

---

1 *Brown v. Board of Education of Topeka*, 347 U.S. 483 (1954).

2 Audio Tape: Charles H. Houston (Dec. 1949) (on file with author), quoted in GENNA RAE MCNEIL, GROUNDWORK: CHARLES HAMILTON HOUSTON AND THE STRUGGLE FOR CIVIL RIGHTS 84 (1983).

3 *See* SOUTHERN EDUCATION FOUNDATION, MILES TO GO MISSISSIPPI: REBUILDING EDUCATION: THE NEXT BIG CHALLENGE 5 (2006), *available at* http://www.sefatl.org/pdf/Ms%20MTG%20Report-Final%20Version.pdf.

4 *See* SOUTHERN EDUCATION FOUNDATION, A NEW MAJORITY: LOW INCOME STUDENTS IN THE SOUTH'S PUBLIC SCHOOLS 7-9 (2007), *available at* http://www.sefatl.org/pdf/A%20New%20Majority%20Report-Final.pdf.

5 *See id.* at 10.

6 *See* MILES TO GO MISSISSIPPI at 7.

7 *See* National Center for Education Statistics, The Nation's Report Card, http://nces.ed.gov/nationsreportcard/states/profile.asp (last vistited Feb. 4, 2008).

8 *See id.*

9 *See id.*

10 *See* SOUTHERN REGIONAL EDUCATION BOARD, GOALS FOR EDUCATION, CHALLENGE TO LEAD: MISSISSIPPI, 8 (2006), http://www.sreb.org/main/Goals/Publications/06Color_PDF/MS-color.pdf.

11 *See* NATIONAL CENTER FOR EDUCATION STATISTICS.

12 *See id.*

13 *See* SOUTHERN EDUCATION FOUNDATION, MILES TO GO MISSISSIPPI: REBUILDING EDUCATION: THE NEXT BIG CHALLENGE 9-10 (2006), *available at* http://www.sefatl.org/pdf/Ms%20MTG%20Report-Final%20Version.pdf.

14 *See id.* at 20.

15 *See* SOUTHERN REGIONAL EDUCATION BOARD at 17.

16 *See id.* at 20.

17 *See* MILES TO GO MISSISSIPPI at 11.

18 *See id.*

19 *See id.*

20 *See* Governor Haley Barbour, State of the State Address (January 21, 2008), *available at* http://www.allamericanpatriots.com/48741044_mississippi-governors-2008-state-state.

21 *See* MILES TO GO MISSISSIPPI at 11.

22 MISS. CONST. of 1890, art. VII, § 201 (last amended 1987).

23 *See e.g., Abbott v. Burke*, 575 A.2d 359, 368-69 (1990) (providing for a "thorough and efficient" system of public education); *Edgewood Indep. School Dist. v. Kirby*, 777 S.W.2d 391, 397 (guaranteeing an "efficient" public school system); *Lake View v. Huckabee*, 351 Ark. 31 (1979) ("the State shall ever maintain a general, suitable, and efficient system of public schools and shall adopt all suitable means to secure to the people the advantages and opportunities of education."); *Pauley v. Kelly*, 255 S.E.2d 859, 877 (providing for "thorough and efficient" education to "develop, as best the state of education expertise allows, the minds, bodies and social morality of its charges to prepare them for useful and happy occupations, recreation and citizenship, and does so economically").

24 *See e.g., Fair School Fin. Council of Oklahoma, Inc. v. State*, 746 P.2d 1135, 1149 (Okla. 1987) (holding the constitutional requirement to "establish and maintain" a public school system only guarantees "basic, adequate education according to [state] standards..."); *Olsen v. State ex rel. Johnson*, 554 P.2d 139, 148 (1976) (holding that the constitutional requirement of "uniform and

general system" of public education guarantees only minimum educational opportunities); *Thompson v. Engelking*, 537 P.2d 635, 647 (1975) (declaring that a "general, uniform and thorough system" of public education does not require equal educational opportunities).

25 In *Clinton v. Byrd*, 477 So. 2d 237, 240 (Miss. 1985) ("[T]he right to a minimally adequate public education created and entailed by the laws of this state is one we can only label fundamental.").

26 *Id.*

27 MISS. CODE ANN. § 37-1-2(n) (Supp.1984).

28 *Clinton* dealt with punishment in schools and not directly the right to education. *But see University of Mississippi Medical Center v. Hugnes*, 765 So.2d 528, 539 (Miss. Aug 24, 2000) ("This Court labeled as fundamental the right to a minimally adequate public education. This right, the Court noted, is created by the laws of this state, through which the state has accepted the responsibility of the provision of free public education."). The Court distinguished *Clinton* finding that the relevant statutes only guaranteed a free public education through high school and did not confer any right to graduate education. *Id.*

29 *See* Michael P. Mills & William Quin II, *Perspective: The Right to a 'Minimally Adequate Education' as Guaranteed by the Mississippi Constitution*, 61 ALB. L. REV. 1521, 1526-27 (1998); *Mississippi's Choice*, TIME, Jan. 3, 1955 (reporting that voters in Mississippi overwhelmingly supported a constitutional amendment to permit the legislature to abolish the public schools by a two-thirds vote as a way to get around desegregation orders). *See also* MISS. CONST. of 1890, art. VII, § 201 (amended 1960) (noting amendment to § 201 in 1960), http://www.sos.state.ms.us/ed_pubs/constitution/constitution.asp.

30 MISS. CONST. of 1890, art. VII, § 201, http://mshistory.k12.ms.us/index.php?s=extra&id=270. Prior to 1890, the education was before amended in 1868 and, like the 1890 version, referred to the legislature's duty, rather than discretion, in establishing and maintaining public education. MISS. CONST. of 1868, art. VII, § 1, http://mshistory.k12.ms.us/index.php?s=extra&id=269 ("As the stability of a republican form of government depends mainly upon the intelligence and virtue of the people, it shall be the duty of the Legislature to encourage, by all suitable means, the promotion of intellectual, scientific, moral, and agricultural improvement, by establishing a uniform system of free public schools, by taxation or otherwise, for all children between the ages of five and twenty-one years, and shall, as soon as practicable, establish schools of higher grade.").

31 *See* MISS. CONST. of 1890, art. VII, § 201 (last amended 1987) (indicating that § 213(b), which permitted the legislature to "abolish the public schools in this state" by a two-thirds vote, was repealed in 1987).

32 Law of Apr. 7, 1994, ch. 581, § 2, *amended by* 1997 Law, ch. 612, § 2 (codified as Miss. Code Ann. § 37-151-5 (2004)), *available at* http://www.mscode.com/free/statutes/37/151/index.htm.

33 Miss. Code § 37-151-5(a), 7(2)(a). The accreditation system is on a five-point

scale with Level V being the highest.

34 *See* HOUSE INFORMATION OFFICE, 1997 LEGISLATIVE SESS., HIGHLIGHTS OF 1997 LEGISLATIVE SESSION 1 (Apr. 1997), http://www.peer.state.ms.us/HiLites97.pdf.

35 *See* Julie Goodman, *Education Bill Sent to Governor*, THE CLARION-LEDGER, Feb. 1, 2003, at 1A.

36 *See id.*

37 *See* Sid Salter, *Education: Who Should Pay?*, THE CLARION-LEDGER, May 16, 2004, at 1G.

38 *See* Laura Hipp, *Gov. OKs $3.5B Education Bill*, HATTIESBURG AMERICAN, Apr, 18, 2007, at 1B. On March 30, 2007, the legislature fully-funded MAEP, and Governor Barbour signed it into law on April 17, 2007. *Id.*

39 *See id.*

40 *See* Associated Press, *Barbour Wants Tax Cuts This Year*, THE NATCHEZ DEMOCRAT, Jan, 22, 2008, at http://www.natchezdemocrat.com/news/2008/jan/22/barbour-wants-tax-cuts-year/.

41 *See* Brief of Plaintiff-Appellants at 32 n.15, Connecticut Coalition for Justice in Education Funding, et al v. Governor M. Jodi Rell, et al, S.C. 18032 (Conn. Dec. 21, 2007) [hereinafter Brief of Plaintiff-Appellants] (citing *Lake View Sch. Dist. No. 25 v. Huckabee*, 351 Ark. 31, 54 (2002) ("This court's refusal to review school funding under our state constitution would be a complete abrogation of our judicial responsibility and would work a severe disservice to the people of this state. We refuse to close our eyes or turn a deaf ear to claims of a dereliction of duty in the field of education."); *Idaho Schs. for Equal Educ. Opportunity v. Evans*, 123 Idaho 573, 583 (1993) ("[W]e decline to accept the respondents' argument that the other branches of government be allowed to interpret the constitution for us. That would be an abject abdication of our role in the American system of government."); Rose *v. Council for Better Educ., Inc.*, 790 S.W.2d 186, 209 (Ky. 1989) ("To avoid deciding the case because of 'legislative discretion,' 'legislative function,' etc., would be a denigration of our own constitutional duty. To allow the General Assembly . . . to decide whether its actions are constitutional is literally unthinkable."); *McDuffy v. Sec'y of the Executive Office of Educ.*, 415 Mass. 545, 611 (1993) ("[W]e have the duty . . . to adjudicate a claim that a law and the actions undertaken pursuant to that law conflict with [or fall short of] the requirements of the Constitution. 'This,' in the words of Mr. Chief Justice Marshall, 'is of the very essence of judicial duty.'") (quoting *Colo. v. Treasurer & Receiver Gen.*, 378 Mass. 550, 553 (1979)); *Columbia Falls Elem. Sch. Dist. No. 6 v. State*, 326 Mont. 304, 310 (2005) (rejecting *Baker v. Carr*-based political question argument and concluding that, "[a]s the final guardian and protector of the right to education, it is incumbent upon the court to assure that the system enacted by the Legislature enforces, protects and fulfills the right [to education]."); *Claremont Sch. Dist. v. Governor*, 138 N.H. 183, 192 (1993) (concluding that the constitutional right to adequate

education is justiciable and that "any citizen" has standing to "enforce the State's duty" to fulfill this right); *Abbott v. Burke*, 149 N.J. 145, 168 (1997) (holding that, while deference should be given to legislative content and performance standards, it is still the court's duty to ensure that these standards, "together with funding measures, comport[ ] with the constitutional guarantee of a thorough and efficient education for all New Jersey school children."); *Campaign for Fiscal Equity, Inc. v. State (CFE I)*, 86 N.Y.2d 307, 315 (1995) ("We conclude that a duty [to provide a sound, basic education] exists and that we are responsible for adjudicating the nature of that duty.") *Leandro v. State*, 346 N.C. 336, 345 (1997) (rejecting the "political question" argument and stating that "[w]hen a government action is challenged as unconstitutional, the courts have a duty to determine whether that action exceeds constitutional limits. . . Therefore, it is the duty of this Court to address plaintiff-parties' constitutional challenge to the state's public education system."); *DeRolph v. State*, 78 Ohio St.3d 193, 198 (1997) (holding school finance unconstitutional and stating, "[w]e will not dodge our responsibility by asserting that this case involves a nonjusticiable political question. . . and [ ] pass our responsibilities onto the lap of the General Assembly."); *Abbeville County Sch. Dist. v. State*, 335 S.C. 58, 67 (1999) (holding that because "[i]t is the duty of this Court to interpret and declare the meaning of the Constitution," the trial court should not have "us[ed] judicial restraint, separation of powers, and the political question doctrine as the bases for declining to decide the meaning of the education clause"); *Neeley v. West Orange-Cove Consol. Indep. Sch. Dist.*, 176 S.W.3d 746, 780-81 (finding that the judiciary was not precluded "from determining whether the Legislature has met its constitutional obligation to the people to provide for public education"); *Seattle Sch. Dist. No. 1 v. State*, 90 Wash. 2d 476, 502 (1978) (stating that a finding of nonjusticiability would be "illogical"); *Pauley v. Kelly*, 162 W.Va. 672, 690-91 (1979) (after reviewing decisions from other jurisdictions, noting the deference courts give to legislatively promulgated education policies but stating that "these jurisdictions have not hesitated to examine legislative performance of the [constitutional] mandate, and we think properly so, even as they recite that courts are not concerned with the wisdom or policy of the legislation"); *Vincent v. Voight*, 236 Wis. 2d 588, 599 (2000) (after noting that *Baker v. Carr* holds that "a court must decide on a case-by-case inquiry whether a so-called political issue is justiciable," concluding that "the [school finance] issues presented to us in this case are appropriate for decision by this court in the exercise of our constitutional role"); *Campbell County Sch. Dist. v. State*, 907 P.2d 1238, 1264 (Wyo. 1995) (rejecting the separation of powers argument and stating that "[a]lthough this Court has said the judiciary will not encroach into the legislative field of policy making, as the final authority on constitutional questions the judiciary has the constitutional duty to declare unconstitutional that which transgresses the state constitution.")).

42 *See* Brief of Plaintiff-Appellants, *supra* note 1 and accompanying text.

43 *See* Brief of Plaintiff-Appellants, *supra* note 1, at 17 n.8 (finding that the high court of only seven states found these cases nonjusticiable (citing *Ex parte*

James, 836 So. 2d 813 (Ala. 2002); *Coal. for Adequacy & Fairness in Sch. Funding, Inc. v. Chiles*, 680 So. 2d 400 (Fla. 1996); *Lewis v. Spagnolo*, 186 Ill.2d 198 (1999); *Neb. Coal. for Educ. Equity & Adequacy v. Heinman*, 273 Neb. 531 (2007); *Okla. Educ. Ass'n v. State ex rel. Okla. Legislature*, 158 P.3d 1058 (Okla. 2007); *Marrero v. Commonwealth*, 559 Pa. 14 (1999); *City of Pawtucket v. Sundlun*, 662 A.2d 40 (R.I. 1995)).

44 *Carroll-Hall. v. Rell*, 2007 Conn. Super. LEXIS 2478, at *39 (Conn. Super Sept. 17, 2007).

45 *See* Brief of Plaintiff-Appellants, *supra* note 1, at 5 (explaining that in *State v. Geisler*, 222 Conn. 672 (1992), the Court enumerated six factors to consider in determining the contours of the state constitution: (1) the text of the constitution; (2) prior holdings and dicta; (3) federal precedent; (4) sister state decisions; (5) historical information; and (6) economic and sociological considerations).

46 *See* Brief of Plaintiff-Appellants, *supra* note 1, at 17 n.8 (finding that the highest courts of eighteen states have found a minimum qualitative standard in their state's education clause citing *Lake View Sch. Dist. No. 25 v. Huckabee*, 351 Ark. 31 (2002); *McDaniel v. Thomas*, 248 Ga. 632 (1981); *Idaho Schs. for Equal Educ. Opportunity v. Evans*, 123 Idaho 573 (1993); *Montoy v. State*, 275 Kan. 145 (2003); *Rose v. Council for Better Educ., Inc.*, 790 S.W.2d 186 (Ky. 1989); *Hancock v. Comm'r of Educ.*, 443 Mass. 428 (2005); *Columbia Falls Elem. Sch. Dist. No. 6 v. State*, 326 Mont. 304 (2005); *Claremont Sch. Dist. v. Governor*, 138 N.H. 183 (1993); *Abbott v. Burke*, 149 N.J. 145 (1997); *Campaign for Fiscal Equity, Inc. v. State (CFE I)*, 86 N.Y.2d 307 (1995); *Leandro v. State*, 346 N.C. 336 (1997); *DeRolph v. State*, 78 Ohio St. 3d 193 (1997); *Abbeville County Sch. Dist. v. State*, 335 S.C. 58 (1999); *Neeley v. W. Orange-Cove Consol. Indep. Sch. Dist.*, 176 S.W.3d 746 (Tex. 2005); *Seattle Sch. Dist. No. 1 v. State*, 90 Wash.2d 476 (1978); *Pauley v. Kelly*, 162 W.Va. 672 (1979); *Vincent v. Voight*, 236 Wis.2d 588 (2000); *Campbell Sch. Dist. v. State*, 907 P.2d 1238 (Wyo. 1995)).

47 *See* Brief of Plaintiff-Appellants, *supra* note 1, at 20 (quoting *Campaign for Fiscal Equity v. State* (*CFE II*), 719 N.Y.S.2d 475, 486 (N.Y.S. 2001)).

48 *See* Brief of Plaintiff-Appellants, *supra* note 1, at 18.

49 *See* UCLA CIVIL RIGHTS PROJECT, HISTORIC REVERSALS, ACCELERATING RESEGREGATION, AND THE NEED FOR NEW INTEGRATION STRATEGIES 5-6 (2007), http://www.civilrightsproject.ucla.edu/research/deseg/reversals_reseg_need.pdf

50 *See id* at 30.

51 127 S.Ct. 2738 (2007).

52 *See* JOHN A. POWELL, KIRWAN INSTITUTE, K-12 DIVERSITY: STRATEGIES FOR DIVERSE & SUCCESSFUL SCHOOLS 2-3 (2007) [hereinafter POWELL], http://www.aasa.org/files/PDFs/K%2D12SchoolStrategiesUpdated.pdf.

53 *See* Brief of 553 Social Scientists as Amici Curiae in Support of Respondents at 41-45, Parents Involved in Comty. Sch. v. Seattle Sch. Dist., 127 S.Ct. 2738

(2007) (No. 05-908) [hereinafter 553 Social Scientists], *available at* http://www.civilrightsproject.ucla.edu/research/deseg/amicus_parents_v_seatle .pdf.

54 *See* POWELL, *supra* note 12, at 7-9.

55 *Parents Involved in Comty. Sch.*, 127 S.Ct. at 2797 (Kennedy, J., concurring) ("[A] district may consider it a compelling interest to achieve a diverse student population. Race may be one component of that diversity, but other demographic factors, plus special talents and needs, should also be considered.")

56 *See id.* ("A compelling interest exists in avoiding racial isolation, an interest that a school district, in its discretion and expertise, may choose to pursue. Likewise, a district may consider it a compelling interest to achieve a diverse student population."). He joins Justices Stephen Breyer, Ruth Bader Ginsburg, David Souter, and John Paul Stevens to comprise a majority on this key point.

57 *See* 553 Social Scientists, *supra* note 13, at 41-45.

Benefits of racially integrated classrooms include: cross-racial understanding; reduces racial prejudice and bias; improves critical thinking skills; modest positive effects on academic achievement of African American students, particularly for younger students; positive psychological impact on African American and Latino students through reduction of unfounded stereotypes of inferiority; improves life opportunities; increases minority high school graduation rates; provides greater access to social and professional networks; African Americans who attend integrated schools tend to have higher incomes than their peers who attended segregated schools; helps reduce residential segregation; and results in greater parental involvement in the schools. *Id. See also* Brief of the National Education Association, et al, as Amici Curiae in Support of Respondents, Parents Involved in Comty. Sch. v. Seattle Sch. Dist., 127 S.Ct. 2738 (2007) (No. 05-908) 2006 WL 2927085.

58 *See* Amy Stuart Wells, et al, Amicus Brief in Support of Respondents at 14-21, Parents Involved in Comty. Sch. v. Seattle Sch. Dist., 127 S.Ct. 2738 (2007) (No. 05-908).

59 *See* Robert Crain and Amy Stuart Wells, Perpetuation Theory and the Long-Term Effects of Schools

Desegregation, 531 REV. OF ED'L RESEARCH (Winter 1994); M. Dawkins and J.H. Braddock, The Continuing Significance of Desegregation: School Racial Composition and African American Inclusion in American Society, 53 J. NEGRO ED. 394 (1994).

60 *See* Rita E. Mahard & Robert L. Crain, *Research on Minority Achievement in Desegregated Schools*, *in* THE CONSEQUENCES OF SCHOOL DESEGREGATION 103, 107, 111, 113 (finding a positive link between desegregation and an increase in African American student achievement levels, generating gains on average of .3 of a grade year in student performance at the elementary/secondary school level, and gains on average of .57 of a grade year at the kindergarten level).

61 *See* Brief of Latino Organizations as Amici Curiae in Support of Respondents at 20, Parents Involved in Comty. Sch. v. Seattle Sch. Dist., 127 S.Ct. 2738 (2007) (No. 05-908) 2006 WL 2927070 (reminding that in *Plyler v. Doe*, 457 U.S. 202, 222 n.20 (1982), the Supreme Court held that public schools "are an important socializing institution, imparting those shared values through which social order and stability are maintained").

62 *See* Brief of Media & Telecommunication Companies as Amici Curiae in Support of Respondents at ii, Parents Involved in Comty. Sch. v. Seattle Sch. Dist., 127 S.Ct. 2738 (2007) (No. 05-908) 2006 WL 292065 [hereinafter Media & Telecommunication Companies].

63 *See* Media & Telecommunication, *supra* note 22, at iii.

64 JONATHON KOZAL, THE SHAME OF THE NATIONAL, THE RESTORATION OF APARTHEID SCHOOLING IN AMERICA, 316-317 (2005) quoted in JOHN LEWIS WITH MICHAEL D'ORSO, WALKING WITH THE WIND: MEMOIRS OF CONGRESSMAN LEWIS (1998).